NAMIB

The archaeology *of an* African desert

Abbé Henri Breuil SJ (1877–1961)
The father of Namib Desert archaeology

NAMIB

The archaeology *of an* African desert

John Kinahan

JAMES CURREY

Published in hardback in World excluding Southern Africa,
and as an ePDF worldwide, in 2022
by James Currey, an imprint of Boydell & Brewer Ltd
PO Box 9, Woodbridge, Suffolk IP12 3DF (GB) and
668 Mt Hope Avenue, Rochester NY 14620–2731 (US)
www.boydellandbrewer.com
www.jamescurrey.com

First published in Namibia by University of Namibia Press in 2020
Private Bag 13301, Windhoek, Namibia
www.unam.edu.na/unam-press

Published in Southern Africa exc. Namibia by Wits University Press in 2021
P.O. Wits, 2050, Johannesburg, South Africa
www.witspress.co.za

© John Kinahan 2020

All rights reserved. Except as permitted under current legislation
no part of this work may be photocopied, stored in a retrieval system,
published, performed in public, adapted, broadcast,
transmitted, recorded or reproduced in any form or by any means,
without the prior permission of the copyright owner

The right of John Kinahan to be identifed as the author of this work has been
asserted in accordance with sections 77 and 78 of the Copyright, Designs and
Patents Act 1988

This edition is published by arrangement with University of Namibia Press

ISBN   978-1-84701-288-3 (James Currey)
ISBN   978-99916-42-65-9 (University of Namibia Press)
ISBN   978-1-77614-760-1 (Wits University Press)

The publisher has no responsibility for the continued existence or accuracy
of URLs for external or third-party internet websites referred to in this book,
and does not guarantee that any content on such websites is, or will remain,
accurate or appropriate

A CIP catalogue record for this book is available from the British Library

This publication is printed on acid-free paper

Cover design: Handmade Communications
Illustrations: Author, unless otherwise stated

CONTENTS

Preface ix
Acknowledgements xiii
Notes to the Reader xv
List of Abbreviations xix
List of Figures and Tables xx

1. INTRODUCTION 1
2. FIRST FOOTSTEPS 39
3. TIME'S ARROW 81
4. MOUNTAIN REFUGE 127
5. ELEPHANTS AND RAIN 175
6. DESERT GARDEN 215
7. THE FAMILY HERD 259
8. THE BLACK SWAN 313
9. MEN IN HATS 351
10. THE DEATH OF MEMORY 385

Epilogue 429
Glossary 452
Bibliography 453
Index 505

Archaeological sites	(Chapter reference)
1. Serra Cafema	(2)
2. Ovizumburuku	(2)
3. Sebra	(2)
4. Rainman Shelter	(5)
5. Hungorob Ravine	(4, 7)
6. Ugab Mouth	(8)
7. Messum 1	(3)
8. Panner Gorge	(2)
9. ǂKhîsa-ǁgubus	(8)
10. Namib IV	(2)
11. Gorrasis	(3, 6)
12. Kubub	(3)
13. Elizabeth Bay	(3)
14. Apollo 11	(2, 3)
15. !Nabas	(9)

Place name synonyms

ǀUi-ǁaes	Twyfelfontein
Dâures	Brandberg
Otjikango Otjinene	Gross (Neu) Barmen
Otjomuise	Windhoek
(alt.) ǀAe ǁgams	Windhoek
!Gomen-ǁgams	Walvis Bay
Anixab	Sandwich Harbour
!Namiǂnūs	Angra Pequena/Lüderitzbucht

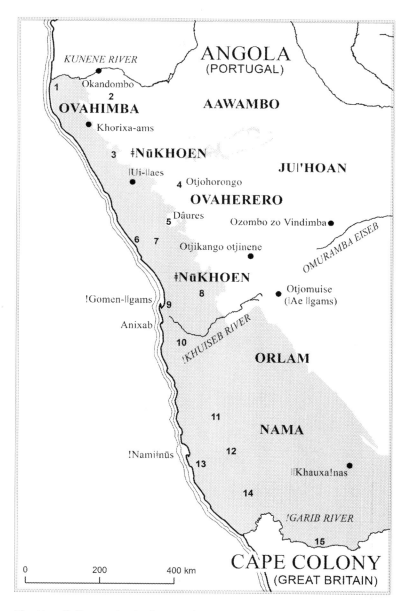

The Namib Desert in the late 18th century, on the eve of the colonial era, with places and peoples mentioned in the text, and principal archaeological sites numbered.

To those who went before,
Those I met along the way,
And for those still to come.

PREFACE

At its simplest, this is a story of human survival over the last one million years in one of the most hostile environments on Earth. The earliest evidence of human occupation in the Namib Desert is scanty but it speaks across the ages, of small hunter-gatherer bands venturing deep into this almost lunar landscape, in search of animal prey dependent on the same few sources of water. Over time, with occasional pulses of population expansion from better watered parts of the subcontinent, our distant ancestors left an extraordinarily rich body of evidence in the form of stone tools and the remains of the animals they hunted.

Complex systems of migration and intricate social networks developed here, under conditions that tried the limits of human endurance. Depictions of rain-making rituals appeared in remote rock art sites, and specialist shamans travelled over the landscape, officiating at secluded ceremonies dedicated to the initiation of young men and women into the roles and responsibilities of adulthood. Gradually, hunter-gatherer communities adopted pottery and livestock from farming communities on the margins of the desert and became successful pastoralists. Then, contact and trade with visiting seafarers in the last few centuries brought a floodtide of conquest, dispossession and genocide in the early colonial era.

To compose a nuanced account of these developments I have departed from the conventional approach of southern African archaeology in which human history is understood as a series of broad, clearly defined evolutionary steps, or stadia. Instead, I have adopted as a general framework the concept of the adaptive cycle, an approach based on a premise that is particularly appropriate to desert conditions. This is the notion of *resilience* in socio-ecological systems, combining an inherent flexibility and adaptive potential. In terms of the adaptive cycle, the archaeological sequence of the

Namib Desert is therefore a history of perpetual transition, of shifting and temporary states of balance.

Just as in nature, where there is no perfect adaptation, our own survival emerges from a series of ever-changing responses and solutions, with Man as the tireless *bricoleur*. The natural environment sets limits of permission and constraint for human adaptation, but it is not possible to simply infer from the conditions of Nature patterns in the evolution of human culture. We need to draw upon a very wide range of evidence other than that of ecology; as I will presently show, archaeology is in this sense a truly omnivorous discipline, employing concepts and techniques drawn from fields as diverse as neuropsychology and isotope chemistry to advance our understanding of the dusty fragments we find in our excavations.

Today, the Namib Desert has few indigenous inhabitants other than a small number of impoverished communities living on the margins of modern towns and mining settlements. What was once the domain of hunter-gatherers and the pasture lands of nomadic pastoralists is now one of the largest conservation areas in the world. In this book, we consider not only the archaeological record of ancient settlement on this landscape, and the relationship between its people and the environment, but also the historical process of their dispossession. Emptied of its people, the desert became a place of romance in the colonial mind; its delicate ecosystems exemplified purity and natural harmony, a veritable Eden, and its pellucid light an inspiration to landscape painters. Archaeology, ironically, has played its own small but significant part in this fanciful conceit.

Although I have drawn on the work of many previous archaeological studies, stretching over more than a century in this region, most of the material discussed here represents the results of the Namib Desert Archaeological Survey, a project that has documented more than 3,000 new archaeological sites between the Kunene and the Orange Rivers, an area of approximately 200,000 km^2. While much of this research has been published before, extensive further material and observations are presented here for the first time. In the course of protracted fieldwork, I have had the privileged opportunity to study and appreciate the subtleties of the desert and its archaeology.

To me, the Namib Desert represents an unparalleled library of the human past, its pages scattered and torn, as if blown by the wind into every dunefield, hillside and dry watercourse of this extraordinary landscape. Writing this book was supposed to be a pause from the proper occupation of the archaeologist, which is to dig. But the accumulated tumulus of old field notebooks, maps and drawings required another kind of excavation, just as painstaking, which brought to mind the words of the Irish poet Seamus Heaney: "Between my finger and my thumb, the squat pen rests. I'll dig with it."[1]

The archaeological record in the Namib Desert is extremely fragile. Much of it will disappear under the relentless impact of industry and modern development, effectively wiping away the physical memory of the landscape. If archaeologists cannot fulfil the urgent request of our historical ancestor Herodotus (ca 480 BC) to prevent the traces of human events from being erased by time, then we must at least endeavour to read, understand and communicate as best we can the traces we find. That is my purpose here, as I invite the reader to wander over the Namib and ponder the great depth of human experience its archaeology represents.

John Kinahan
Windhoek, September 2020

---

1 "Digging" from *Death of a Naturalist* by Seamus Heaney 1966 London: Faber & Faber.

ACKNOWLEDGEMENTS

I owe a very large debt of gratitude to my family for their patience, humour and support over years of nomadic life in the field. My wife, muse and companion, Jill, pursued her own archaeological career, and her research on the late pre-colonial period in the Namib Desert forms an important part of this book. I like to think that an infancy spent in excavation trenches gave our son, Tim, his unusually acute understanding of history, seen from the bottom up.

In writing this book I have benefited from the kindness of many scholars and friends who have exchanged ideas with me, given me access to unpublished material, provided the use of facilities and funding for analytical work, and helped me to attend research meetings that would have been otherwise out of reach. They include, in no particular order, Mike Smith, Peter Mitchell, Karim Sadr, Peter Ucko, Kapokoro Tjiramba, Paul Sinclair, Polly Wiessner, Erik Marsh, Sara Wurz, Jan du Plessis, Stefano Biagetti, Carla Lancellotti, Jekura Kavari, Wilfrid Haacke, Eliphas Eiseb, Werner Hillebrecht, Norman Green, Petrus le Roux, Christopher Bronk Ramsey, Siân Sullivan, Paul Lane, Karen Miller, Marion Bamford, Frances Chase, Peter Breunig, James Denbow, Peter Bruyns and Steven Dodsworth. I hope to be forgiven by those I have inadvertently neglected to thank.

I am greatly indebted to the originating publisher, the University of Namibia Press, for accepting the manuscript and steering it through the publication process. Jill Kinahan, Naitsikile Iizyenda and five very helpful reviewers added many improvements. When it began to look like this book might not come out, John Bernstein, whom I have never met, stepped into the breach and paid for its publication: a true example of generosity to a stranger in the desert.

Acknowledgement of permission to reproduce

Frontispiece: Henri Breuil photographed by Annelise Scherz, courtesy of National Archives of Namibia; Figure 1.5 from Gunderson & Holling (2002), reproduced by permission of Island Press, Washington, DC; Figure 2.9 photograph by Marcus Weiss; Figure 2.12 photograph by Riaan Rifkin; Figure 4.12 reproduced with permission of the late Harald Pager; Figure 6.1 reproduced with permission of Botanischen Staatssammlung München; Figure 8.5a reproduced by courtesy of the late Quentin Keynes; Figure 8.7 painting reproduced courtesy of Museum Africa, Johannesburg (MA 6336); Figure 9.13 American brig *Forrester*, January 1845 no. 508, Mystic Seaport Museum, Judy Beisler Photo no. 93-5-60, Mystic Seaport, Mystic, Connecticut; Figures 10.3, 10.4, 10.5, 10.10 reproduced by courtesy of National Archives of Namibia; Figure 10.8 courtesy of the Library, Parliament of South Africa, 18891 (66); Figure 10.13 courtesy of Orde Levinson. Figure 11.3 is reproduced with permission from Alamy/Gallo Images.

NOTES TO THE READER

Research permission and ethical standards

Archaeological excavations and surveys reported in this book were carried out under successive permits issued by the National Heritage Council of Namibia, and all materials resulting from the research are deposited at the National Museum of Namibia. Research presented here is in accordance with the World Archaeological Congress First Code of Ethics (Barquisimeto, Venezuela, 1990) and the Vermillion Accord on Human Remains (South Dakota, USA, 1989). Considering the particular sensitivity of human remains in modern Namibia, analyses and illustrations of human remains are included here on the basis of scientific merit and where this evidence provides unique insights into the human history of the Namib Desert.

Terminology, orthography and referencing

For the benefit of the lay reader, there are two basic conventions in the presentation of archaeological evidence: first is the use of the *site* as the geographical unit of analysis. The narrative developed here comprises a sequence of archaeological case studies based on systematic research focused on evidence from specific locations, with the field of view varying as required, from that of a small rock shelter to a mountain valley or drainage basin.

Second is that comparisons between particular sites are made on the basis of the archaeological *assemblage*, which is a body of material evidence such as of stone tools or food remains, of the same age or belonging to the same occupation event or phase. Where possible, and most especially in dealing with evidence from the last few centuries, these units of analysis are related to specific cultural groups or local communities.

To ensure continuity between the recent and the pre-colonial eras, I have wherever appropriate re-introduced indigenous place-names, especially with respect to sites of archaeological importance. Among others, the Khoekhoegowab name Dâures is used here rather than Brandberg, and |Ui-||aes rather than Twyfelfontein. Colonial names appear as synonyms at the first mention of the indigenous name in text, but not on the maps.

Namibian indigenous languages are generally phonetic in their modern orthography, but tonal Khoesan languages such as Khoekhoegowab incorporate a range of consonant sounds or clicks. The four click sounds used in Namibia are the dental (shown as |), alveolar (!), palatal (ǂ) and lateral (||). In the text, spelling is given in simplified form without the diacritical marks required for correct pronunciation.

Many of the names applied to southern African hunter-gatherer and nomadic pastoralist peoples have acquired pejorative meanings, especially generic terms such as Bushman or San. Archaeologists have vacillated in their terminology but increasingly adopt names used by the people themselves in a neutral and inclusive fashion. Where appropriate, and following current practice, I use self-identifying terms such as Jul'hoan when referring to the modern descendants of specific hunter-gatherer groups.

In colonial Namibia, historical ethnography was used to classify people in the interests of administrative convenience and simplicity. Some of these appellations became widely accepted. For example, 19th century accounts used the term Damara in reference to people who became properly known as Mbanderu and Ovaherero during the anti-colonial uprisings of the early 20th century. Damara then became the term applied to the ǂNūkhoen, whose name and language colonial administrators could neither pronounce nor understand.

To make the book more accessible to the general reader and to researchers in other specialities, I have limited direct reference to personal names in the main text, including only historical figures whose actions rather than writings were of singular importance. Literature citations are provided as abbreviated footnotes, with

NOTES TO THE READER xvii

full references listed in the Bibliography. The footnotes are also used to add commentary or clarification to points raised in the main text. A Glossary on page 452 explains technical terms which may be unfamiliar to the lay reader.

Archaeological age determination

Most age determinations used in this book are based on the ^{14}C, or radiocarbon method. For the reader without a background in archaeological dating, this technique entails the measurement of residual radiocarbon in an ancient organic material such as wood, charcoal or bone. Radiocarbon is created in the atmosphere by the interaction of cosmic rays and atmospheric nitrogen, and combines with oxygen to form radioactive carbon dioxide ($^{14}CO_2$), which is absorbed by plants through photosynthesis.

When the organism dies, ^{14}C is no longer absorbed but decays at a continuous and known rate. Analysis of the sample thus provides an age in radiocarbon years which is calibrated using known-age tree-ring series to produce a calendar age. Such age determinations have a varying margin of error and reliable dating usually requires multiple samples. Dating is generally limited to the last 50,000 years as older samples contain insufficient measurable radiocarbon.

Radiocarbon measurements for the last few centuries are notoriously unreliable due to the large scale consumption of fossil fuels since the advent of the Industrial Revolution, which increased the emission of CO_2 to the atmosphere. This source of error, known as the Suess effect, is one of several obstacles to precise dating. Radiocarbon dates from this period, the Anthropocene, are generally interpreted according to the archaeologist's discretion. I have excluded dates in several cases where either the archaeological context or the result was questionable.

In the text, key sets of radiocarbon dates are presented in diagrammatic form with age determinations calibrated using the ShCal 13 calibration curve, and with appropriate correction in the case of marine samples (following Bronk Ramsey 2016, OxCal 4.3.2). The radiocarbon calibration diagrams presented in the text show the full calibrated age range of the sample (thin horizontal line), with the calibrated median age (plus sign); the 1 Sigma 68% probability distribution (upper horizontal brackets), and the 2 Sigma 95% probability distribution (lower horizontal brackets). The diagrams, e.g. Figure 3.9, are accompanied by footnotes providing the uncalibrated radiocarbon age with laboratory sample numbers to allow for re-calibration against future revised calibration curves. Larger sets of radiocarbon data published elsewhere are referenced in the text.

Another dating method used here is Optically Stimulated Luminescence, or OSL, which is useful in desert conditions where organic remains are not available for radiocarbon dating. OSL dating measures the residual energy of electrons trapped within the atomic spacing of a mineral grain such as of quartz sand to calculate the period of time elapsed since the sand grain was last exposed to sunlight.

Radiocarbon and OSL dating are the most commonly applied methods to determine the *absolute* age of archaeological remains discussed here. Sometimes a *relative* age can be determined when an object is found above or below one that does have an absolute date. Relative dating can also be based on the occurrence and position of known-age objects such as coins or glass trade beads, and by using other evidence such as historical documentary sources to estimate the likely age of an object or site.

LIST OF ABBREVIATIONS

AD	Anno Domini (Gregorian calendar years since the birth of Jesus Christ)
AMS	Accelerator Mass Spectrometry (technique used to count carbon 14 atoms)
BP	Before Present (years before the introduction of radiocarbon dating in 1950 AD)
CAB	Congo Air Boundary (Indian Ocean and Congo Basin air convergence zone)
ENSO	El Niño Southern Oscillation (periodic sea surface temperature variation)
ESA	Earlier Stone Age (from approximately one million to 300,000 years ago)
ITCZ	Inter Tropical Convergence Zone (equatorial low pressure zone)
LGM	Last Glacial Maximum (most recent maximum extent of ice, ca. 22,000 years ago)
LSA	Later Stone Age (the last 20,000 years)
MIS	Marine Isotope Stage (oxygen isotope records of marine temperature changes)
MNI	Minimum Number of Individuals (number represented by skeletal parts)
MSA	Middle Stone Age (300,000 to 20,000 years ago)
PCA	Principal Components Analysis
UNESCO	United Nations Educational Scientific and Cultural Organization

LIST OF FIGURES AND TABLES

FIGURES

Frontispiece: Abbé Henri Breuil SJ (1877–1961) ii
1.1 Chowagas Mountain, southern Namib Desert 6
1.2 Abandoned 1952 Hudson sedan 8
1.3 Regional setting of the Namib Desert 17
1.4 A field camp near Tsaun Hill 27
1.5 Holling's adaptive cycle 32
2.1 Convective storm over the Namib Desert 45
2.2a Mid-Pleistocene archaeological site distribution 50
2.2b The Pleistocene lower !Khuiseb River 51
2.3 Evolution of the Kunene River 53
2.4 Mode 1 pebble tools from Serra Cafema 54
2.5 Mode 2 bifacial handaxes from Sebra 57
2.6 Mode 2 unifacial cleavers from Sebra 58
2.7 Dimensions of handaxes and cleavers from Sebra 59
2.8a The Late Pleistocene in the Namib Desert 65
2.8b Chert sites in the Namib Desert 66
2.9 View of Panner Gorge chert quarry 68
2.10a Plan of Panner Gorge chert quarry 69
2.10b Mode 3 assemblages, Panner Gorge 70
2.11 Mode 3 chert artefacts, Panner Gorge 71
2.12 Physical setting of Apollo 11 Cave 74
2.13 Refitted plaquette from Apollo 11 76
3.1 Mid-Holocene hunting camp, Namib Desert 82
3.2 Holocene palaeoclimate geoarchives 87

LIST OF FIGURES AND TABLES xxi

3.3 Mid-Holocene intrusion of the Angola Current 93
3.4 Holocene archaeological sites and radiocarbon dates 94
3.5 Summed probabilities for Holocene radiocarbon dates 95
3.6 Gorrasis Rock Shelter viewed from the north 97
3.7 Stratigraphic profiles from Gorrasis Rock Shelter................ 98
3.8 Ostrich gastroliths from Gorrasis Rock Shelter.................. 100
3.9 Occupation dates for Gorrasis Rock Shelter....................... 101
3.10 Occupation dates for Kubub Rock Shelter......................... 102
3.11 Plant remains from Kubub Rock Shelter 105
3.12 Mid-Holocene marine transgression and shell middens.... 108
3.13 Rock art sites and the escarpment watershed 111
3.14 Rock painting of trance dance, Dâures massif................... 116
3.15 Rock engravings of ostrich at |Ui-||aes............................. 119
3.16 Rock engraving of five-toed lion at |Ui-||aes 122
4.1 The Dâures massif from the south.................................... 129
4.2 Falls Rock Shelter in the upper Hungorob Ravine 138
4.3 Stratigraphic profiles from Falls Rock Shelter....................139
4.4 Occupation dates for Falls Rock Shelter and Snake Rock......140
4.5 Mode 5 stone artefacts from Falls Rock Shelter................. 142
4.6 Knotted plant fibre artefacts from Falls Rock Shelter........... 145
4.7 Common positions of leopard tooth marks 147
4.8 Radiocarbon dates for sheep *Ovis aries* remains................. 150
4.9 Strontium values for ostrich eggshell beads 154
4.10 Suspected sheep bone artefacts from Snake Rock 156
4.11 Suspected sheep bone splinters from Snake Rock 159
4.12 The so-called White Lady frieze, Tsisab Ravine................. 162
4.13 Shaman figure from Falls Rock Shelter 163
4.14 Falls Rock Shelter ritual vessel 166
4.15 Moth cocoons from Falls Rock Shelter............................. 168
5.1 Camelthorns in the southern Namib Desert..................... 180
5.2 Camelthorn growth dates and mortality dates.................. 183
5.3 Archaeological dates and regional climatic periods 186
5.4 Elephant in the rock art of the Namib Desert 189
5.5 Cross section of the Rainman Shelter, Otjohorongo 192
5.6 Rain animal frieze Rainman Shelter, Otjohorongo............ 194

xxii NAMIB

5.7 Elephant and human figures, Otjohorongo....................... 196
5.8 Cross-sections of vestibules at Otjohorongo and |Ui-||aes ... 198
5.9 The vestibule site at |Ui-||aes.. 199
5.10 The Dancing Kudu panel at |Ui-||aes................................ 203
5.11 Remains of woman's initiation seclusion shelter 204
5.12 Penis and //hūs board at men's initiation site, |Ui-||aes....... 207
5.13 Vestibule shelter with //hūs board, |Ui-||aes..................... 209
6.1 Habit and florescence of *Nicotiana africana* 221
6.2 Communal ambush hunting sites near Gorrasis 225
6.3 Layout of communal hunting site 226
6.4 Stone alignments at communal hunting sites..................... 229
6.5 Seed harvesting sites near Ganab 232
6.6 Example of a storage cairn at a seed harvesting site............ 236
6.7a Seed grinding site at Gorrasis viewed from the south 237
6.7b Grinding surfaces and rainwater ponds at Gorrasis........... 237
6.8 Photomicrographs of grinding surfaces at Gorrasis............ 238
6.9 Phytoliths from grinding surfaces at Gorrasis.................... 239
6.10 Diatoms from grinding surfaces at Gorrasis....................... 239
6.11 Posture for seed-grinding in the Namib Desert 240
6.12 Female kudu from a women's seed harvesting shelter........ 242
6.13 Namib Desert pottery attribute combinations 247
6.14 Radiocarbon dating of Namib Desert pottery 248
6.15 Example of 1st millennium AD pottery (Group A)............ 250
6.16 Example of 2nd millennium AD pottery (Group B) 251
6.17 Strontium values for pottery from the Namib Desert 253
7.1 Painting of Sanga cattle, Spitzkoppe 260
7.2 Ovahimba family, Okandombo.. 266
7.3 Livestock food resources and seasonality of rainfall............ 268
7.4 The impact of timber consumption on mopane woodland... 269
7.5 Schematic layout of an Ovahimba homestead or *onganda*.....271
7.6 Ovahimba grave (left), and sacrificial oxen (right) 274
7.7 Cattle loans (black dots) on the Kunene River 278
7.8 Rainfall and Ovahimba cattle numbers 1971–1996............ 280
7.9 Plan and section of Khorixa-ams cave site 282
7.10 Radiocarbon dates for Khorixa-ams................................. 283

LIST OF FIGURES AND TABLES   xxiii

7.11 Tooth ablation on mandible of young adult female 285
7.12 Peri-mortem trauma to crania from Khorixa-ams 287
7.13 Pastoral sites between the Huab and Ugab Rivers 289
7.14 Pastoral aggregation encampment, Hungorob Ravine 295
7.15 Pastoral transhumant pathway in the Hungorob Ravine ... 297
7.16 View to the south from the upper Hungorob Ravine.......... 298
7.17 Model of pastoral transhumance, Hungorob Ravine 300
7.18 Radiocarbon dates for Hungorob Ravine 301
7.19 Leather bag and contents, Falls Rock Shelter 303
7.20 Iron-tipped adze from Falls Rock Shelter cache 304
7.21 Granite roof spall palette, Falls Rock Shelter.................... 306
8.1   Wind erosion of a building at Elizabeth Bay...................... 316
8.2   Encampment of bones, Ugab River Mouth 319
8.3   Size and meat weight of *Donax serra*, Ugab River Mouth 320
8.4   Attrition and wind dispersal of a shell midden site 323
8.5a "Woman in Walwich Bay", T.B. Thompson, 1786.............. 326
8.5b Bone !nara melon knives from ǂKhîsa-ǁgubus................... 327
8.6   !Nara *Acanthosicyos horridus* melon, approximately 1 kg 327
8.7   "Topnaar Hottentots spearing fish", Thomas Baines, 1864 .. 330
8.8   Relative survival of selected sheep/goat skeletal elements..... 333
8.9   Pendant from sheep/goat 2nd phalange, !Khuiseb Delta...... 335
8.10 Seriation sequence for glass trade beads, !Khuiseb Delta 337
8.11 Imported 19th century ceramic bowls, !Khuiseb Delta........ 338
8.12 Radiocarbon dates for flood debris at Khaeros.................. 339
8.13 Human footprint in lagoon silt deposit, Walvis Bay........... 341
8.14 Lagoon silt surface with tracks, Walvis Bay 341
9.1a Location of !Nabas on Hendrik Wikar's map of 1779.......... 355
9.1b Layout of !Nabas... 355
9.2   "Kora-Khoikhoi preparing to remove", S. Daniell, 1805 357
9.3   Plan of ǁKhauxa!nas 358
9.4   Section of ǁKhauxa!nas perimeter wall 359
9.5   Elevation view of ǁKhauxa!nas perimeter wall 361
9.6   Access analysis of pastoral aggregation encampments 364
9.7   View of Otjikango Otjinene (Neu Barmen) in 1860 366
9.8   Plan of Otjikango Otjinene (Neu Barmen) in 1981 368

9.9 Congregants at Otjikango Otjinene, 1877–1890 369
9.10 Matchless Mine and indigenous copper-smelting sites 371
9.11 Radiocarbon dates for copper furnaces, ǀKhomas 372
9.12 Four examples of ǀKhomas copper smelting furnaces 374
9.13 Ships anchored at Ichabo Island in 1845 377
9.14 Fisheries and pastoral settlement, at Sandwich Harbour..... 379
10.1a Wells near Ozombu zo Vindimba, Omuramba Eiseb 392
10.1b Typical large well feature on the Omuramba Eiseb.......... 392
10.2 Gate sign of *Deutschesfarmgesellschaft* in central Namibia. 394
10.3a Contemporary view of Welwitsch Siding 400
10.3b Plan of Welwitsch Siding showing bottle dumps............. 400
10.4a Cranium and mandible from Welwitsch Siding burial..... 404
10.4b Railway transportation of prisoners 405
10.5a Female prisoners at work in Swakopmund 408
10.5b Building projects in Swakopmund 408
10.6 The Hohenzollern Building in Swakopmund, 1905........... 409
10.7 Swakopmund numbered metal pass tag........................... 411
10.8 Ovaherero scouts attached to General Botha's force........... 413
10.9 South African regimental insignia in the Namib Desert..... 415
10.10a Plan of General Botha's encampment at Husab 416
10.10b General Botha's breakfast table conference.................... 417
10.11a The approach to Riet, showing German positions........... 418
10.11b Plan of Botha's attack on Riet...................................... 418
10.12 Nazi ceremonial gathering site in the Namib Desert 423
10.13 Adolph Jentsch at work in the Namib Desert................. 426
11.1 Mineral exploration licence areas in the Namib Desert..... 445
11.2 The destruction of a Holocene rock art site..................... 447
11.3 A still image from *Mad Max – Fury Road* 450

TABLES

1.1 Modes of stone tool technology and their dating 19
1.2 Climate events and archaeological sequence 21
3.1 Terrestrial and marine geoarchives in the Namib Desert 90
3.2 Primary and secondary occupation sites in the Namib 107
3.3 Human and bird motifs in rock art 118
4.1 Faunal remains from Falls Rock Shelter and Snake Rock 144
4.2 Medium-sized bovid remains, Hungorob Ravine 149
4.3 Ritual preparation and performance, Falls Rock Shelter 172
5.1 Climatic variation in southern Africa 179
5.2 Radiocarbon dates for flood debris, lower !Khuiseb River ... 184
5.3 Illumination of vestibules 201
5.4 Principal features of initiation at |Ui-||aes 211
5.5 Areas of operation for ritual specialists 213
6.1 Nutritional analysis of plant foods from the Namib Desert .. 219
6.2 *Nicotiana tabacum* and *Nicotiana africana* 222
6.3 Late Holocene dating of Namib Desert hunting blinds 227
6.4 Distribution and density of seed digging sites 234
6.5 Dimensions of storage cairns and pottery vessels 235
6.6 Human stature and seed grinding surfaces at Gorrasis 240
6.7 Gender roles among late Holocene hunter-gatherers 243
6.8 Comparison of early and recent pottery groups 246
6.9 Ochre and haematite from necked pottery vessels 252

7.1 Dimensions of risk among Ovahimba pastoralists 277
7.2 Stature of individuals from burial sites, Namib Desert 286
7.3 Pasture and livestock carrying capacity, Hungorob Ravine .. 292
7.4 Colour and composition of cosmetic ochre 307
8.1 Metabolizable energy of shellfish, Ugab River 321
8.2 Slaughter age distribution of sheep/goat, ǂKhîsa-ǁgubus 332
8.3 Stable isotope data for human remains, ǂKhîsa-ǁgubus 334
9.1 Assay results for copper ore and archaeological slag 375
9.2 Assay results for experimental copper and slag 376
10.1 Burials at Swakopmund, 1904–1908 406
11.1 Namib Desert archaeological sequence 436

I

INTRODUCTION

"The desert could not be claimed or owned – it was a piece of cloth carried by winds, never held down by stones, and given a hundred shifting names..."
Michael Ondaatje, *The English Patient*

Seen through the eye of a satellite orbiting our planet, southern Africa has the light green tint of open savanna over most of its central and eastern extent. On the western side of the continent, as the gaze shifts towards the Atlantic coast, lies a pale landscape of dunes and gravel plains: the Namib Desert and the adjacent semi-arid interior. Here, modern humans and their ancestors adapted with increasing ingenuity to ecological opportunities and constraints that shifted back and forth over millennia in response to fluctuations in global climate. In a sense, the desert became a gigantic painted canvas of human history comprising many layers, more thickly applied in some parts than in others.

The landscape setting of the events and processes we examine in this book has changed remarkably little over the last one million years. In contrast to most of the more densely populated parts of the world, some altered beyond recognition, it might be said without too much exaggeration that in this region the Pleistocene environment is largely intact, at least for now. The diverse fauna, including large species such as elephant and giraffe and their progenitors, were with us throughout this time. If you look over this terrain today, the view is not very different from that which drew the eye of our most distant ancestors; there is the same heat, and the same desert wind, sometimes carrying the faintest rumour of rain.

Guillaume de L'isle, a late 17th century cartographer who made the first relatively accurate map of southern Africa, showed the interior filled with various kingdoms known to Europe at that time, including the fabled Mono-Emugi and Monomotapa, and the territory of the dreaded Jaga Casangi. But in the west, where there is little detail shown beyond the coastline of the Namib Desert, the area immediately south of the Kunene River bears the annotation: *Nation sauvage que l'on dit n'avoir pas seulem l'usage de la parole*.[2] It is possible to imagine that these people were indeed silent, as they gazed on the intruders from a safe distance before melting into the barren hills of Kaoko with their flocks. An earlier map had indicated this corner of Africa as *Cimbebas* which derives from the western Bantu term *otjivemba*, denoting a borderland.[3] Seen thus, the Namib Desert coastline was for colonial intents and purposes *terra nullius*, or no man's land,[4] a claim that is amply denied by a rich but until now little studied archaeological record. The map reproduced on page vii of this book indicates the region that came to be known as Namibia, as it existed on the eve of the colonial era.

---

2 Litt: "A savage nation that is said not to have the use of speech", annotation on *Carte du Congo et du pays des Cafres, par G. de L'isle de Academie Royale des Sciences, a Amsterdam Chez Jean Cóvens et Cornielle Mortier, Géographes.*
3 The name Cimbebas first appeared on Filippo Pigafetta's 1591 map, where it was applied to the region between Cape Negro and the Tropic of Capricorn. The Italian orthography in which the term is rendered as Cimbebasia lead to the erroneous view that it indicated "the land of the Tjimba". In 1879 the Prefecture Apostolic of Lower Cimbebasia was created in Rome with boundaries encompassing central and north-western Namibia (Kinahan, J.H.A. 1988a).
4 Berat (1990)

To understand the archaeological landscape of the Namib Desert it is necessary first to examine briefly the distinguishing physical characteristics of this region, before turning to the wider southern African context, and its human history. As we shall see in this chapter, there are some features here that have no close parallel elsewhere in the subcontinent and it will therefore come as no surprise that the archaeological record also differs, reflecting not only the environmental context but also cultural practices that are quite unique. At the same time, several key developments in pre-colonial southern Africa, such as early state formation and the rise of class-based society, did not occur in this desert region or on its immediate periphery. Evidence from the Namib Desert is important, however, in showing that the influence of these centres extended far beyond their immediate boundaries.

The desert and its margins

Although the Namib Desert is, as a biome, or ecological unit, confined to a strip approximately 200 km wide, between the Atlantic coast and the interior escarpment, the arid and hyper-arid parts of south-western Africa are far larger in extent. The margins of the desert have advanced and retreated repeatedly over time and in this book the desert is treated as a broad zone encompassing parts of two further adjacent biomes, the Nama Karoo and the Succulent Karoo,[5] and on occasion the further interior where this is relevant to the archaeology of the desert itself. The Namib Desert of today lies mainly within the boundaries of modern Namibia, where the present study is focused.[6]

---

5 Mendelsohn et al. (2002)
6 The modern state of Namibia covers an area of over 800,000 km², or three times the size of the United Kingdom. The capital, Windhoek, is located near the centre of the country, having been established there as a strategic stronghold several decades before the imposition of German colonial rule in 1884.

In all hot deserts,[7] climatic conditions are most easily characterized in terms of the quantity, timing and regularity of rainfall. The Namib Desert lies at the end of a regional gradient from moderately high summer rainfall in the north-east (500 mm^{yr-1}), to the extremely low, unreliable precipitation experienced in the desert itself (less than 100 mm^{yr-1}).[8] This rainfall regime is strongly associated with continental weather phenomena including the semi-annual movement into this region of the Congo Air Boundary (CAB), an appendage of the Inter Tropical Convergence Zone (ITCZ). Variation in the timing and intensity of rainfall is affected by El Niño Southern Oscillation (ENSO) events but the extreme aridity of the Namib Desert is also maintained by a near-permanent atmospheric high-pressure cell over the cold, northward flowing Benguela Current.[9] Such conditions of sustained or episodic aridity ensured that this was always a marginal environment for human settlement.[10] Indeed, early European travellers were appalled by the desolation of the Namib Desert, one nineteenth century missionary noting that "the eye rests, over a distance of many miles, on nothing other than signs of barrenness, no stream is there to quench the thirst, no root to still the gnawing hunger".[11]

Paradoxically, the desert contains a far more densely concentrated prehistoric record than the adjacent interior, and it has attracted the attention of archaeologists for more than a hundred years. Natural conditions favour archaeological preservation in the desert, while the general absence of vegetation improves the visibility of archaeological sites. The great scarcity of reliable water has also played a role in limiting the range and intensity of human occupation. Moreover, continuous wind erosion

---

7 Following the Köppen-Geiger climate classification system (cf. Sander & Becker 2002).
8 Mendelsohn et al. (2002)
9 Tyson (1986)
10 Spellman (2000)
11 Vigne (1991: 32) citing the unpublished 1823 account of James Archbell.

gradually deflates the surface, removing the accumulated sediment that would otherwise separate successive layers of occupation everywhere save within the rare shelter of rock overhangs. This has resulted in extensive scatters of stone artefact debris and other material representing millennia of human activity, lying on a common exposed surface.

The central highlands of Namibia, which have no perennial surface water, divide the drainage of the country towards the east and, via a rugged escarpment, to the Namib Desert and the Atlantic coast in the west. Dry for all but brief periods following torrential rainfall in the interior, these drainage courses support narrow swathes of riparian woodland which serve as linear oases in otherwise treeless or scrub-covered terrain. The western escarpment is the retreating edge of the ancient continental margin from which erosion has removed to the marine continental shelf a great mass of overburden, leaving the Namib Desert as an open, subdued landscape, relieved by scattered inselbergen of which the largest is the Dâures massif, or Brandberg, a feature much discussed in this book. North of the 23rd parallel, the Namib is a desert of gravel plains and exposed bedrock with minor dunefields, while to the south lies the southern Namib erg, a sand sea covering almost 35,000 km^2, tailing off south of the Orange River which was known as the !Garib, until Robert Jacob Gordon renamed it in 1779 after the Dutch monarch William V of Orange.

In northern Namibia, the margins of the arid zone are dominated by an extensive and largely treeless outwash plain of fine white sand deposited by seasonal floods known as *efundja*, of the Cuvelai drainage system. The sediments are moderately fertile, and the floodwaters can lie for many months in slowly shrinking pools or *iishana*, often containing large numbers of fish carried southwards by the floods. These relatively moist conditions reflect the higher rainfall regime of central Angola and Zambia, and give rise to the Kunene and Kavango rivers. In the north-east, the Zambezi feeds a complex network of channels such as the Kwando and Chobe which flow first

Figure 1.1: A view towards Chowagas Mountain (top right) in the southern Namib Desert, showing a typical combination of dunefields and inselberg features, with endoreic basin in the middle distance.

one way, with rising floods, and then the other, as the waters recede, presenting a rare example of regular reverse flow in an African river.

In contrast to the western escarpment, a gentler gradient leads the eastward drainage of the central highlands towards the Kalahari, the great basin at the heart of the southern African interior. The Kalahari is not a true desert in terms of rainfall, but an edaphic, or thirstland environment[12] characterized by a scarcity of surface water. Crustal warping and major geological fractures resulted in the formation of the vast inland delta of the Okavango in neighbouring Botswana, a feature that is matched by the similarly extensive endoreic Etosha Pan in northern Namibia. Circular pans in the semi-arid southern Kalahari are partly aeolian in origin, while wetlands further north formed on drainage lines known as *omiramba* between the parallel ridges of Tertiary dunes, are now covered by deciduous woodland.

There are folkloric explanations for features such as these. For example, the Jul'hoan maintain that their trickster deity Gllaua defecated by mistake on a puff adder: it bit his testicles which swelled to an enormous size and, as he ran about in agony, the valleys between the dunes were literally gouged into the Kalahari landscape by his inflamed gonads.[13] Archaeological evidence, even that relating to cognitive and ritual aspects of behaviour, provides very little direct insight into how people perceived and understood the environment in which they lived. Folklore therefore serves to remind us that human understanding and the often poetic responses of people to the world in which they lived cannot be inferred from environmental data alone.

In the early 1970s, I spent a year camped in a dry valley north of the Orange River, prospecting fruitlessly for copper and zinc among the barren, oven-hot hills. Few people lived along the lower reaches of the river then, but it drew a slow trickle of strange and restless characters, mostly quiet, secretive people who appeared

---

12 Deacon & Lancaster (1988)
13 The story of Gllaua's testicles is related by Suzman (2017)

Figure 1.2: Abandoned 1952 Hudson sedan on the route north from the Orange River to Uhabis.

to live on almost nothing. Down-and-outs, aspiring prophets and illicit diamond traders came and went against the backdrop of the wide, brown stream with its narrowly wooded banks, for centuries a frontier between ordered certainty to the south, and a loosely controlled world of anarchic possibilities to the north. From there the Namib Desert stretched across a bleak one and a half thousand kilometres into Angola, to the isolated bay once known as Moçâmedes, the most southerly slaving port on the west coast of Africa.[14]

Today, the Orange River forms the boundary between South Africa and the modern state of Namibia, and some of

14 Clarence-Smith (1979); Gustafsson (2005)

the historic contrasts between the two are still apparent, not least in the practice of archaeology. Systematic archaeological research began in Namibia with the arrival in the late 1940s of the Abbé Henri Breuil (see Frontispiece), pre-eminent scholar of Palaeolithic rock art. For a Jesuit, Breuil was unusually flamboyant, subscribing to a then fairly common idea that centres of cultural innovation, principally in the classical Mediterranean theatre, had a formative influence in other parts of the world, such as Africa. By claiming that the rock art of the Namib Desert confirmed this notion with evidence of an early Phoenician visit, Breuil inadvertently lent justification to the ideology of settler colonialism.

Breuil's reputation in this region was irretrievably damaged in a dispute with southern African scholars who ably demonstrated the indigenous authorship of the art.[15] Although this controversy presented a turning point for archaeology in Namibia, it did not take the direction one might expect, for Breuil's departure, rather than ushering in recognition of the extraordinarily dynamic and complex culture that had been denied the hunter-gatherer artists, had an almost opposite effect. The artists were simply relegated to a static ethnological category, becoming a people without history,[16] living fossils frozen in time. Precolonial peoples of Namibia, hunter-gatherers, pastoralists and farmers, came to

---

15 See Breuil (1955); Kinahan (1995a). The interpretation naïvely forwarded by Breuil, a prehistorian, was probably formulated by his assistant, Mary Boyle, a trained classicist (Straus 1992) but without any background in African archaeology. Because Breuil's place in the history of southern African archaeology is tainted by colonial sympathies evident from the discredited Mediterranean hypothesis (e.g. Le Quellec 2016), it is interesting to note that the only modern proponent of the rock art as evidence of a Phoenician expedition to the Namib Desert is an African scholar (Chami 2006).
16 In the sense of Wolf (1982). The intense debate resulting from revisionist criticism (e.g. Wilmsen 1989; Denbow 1984, 1986) of established views on Kalahari hunter-gatherer ethnography (see Barnard 1992a) had relatively little influence on archaeological thinking in southern Africa, an important exception being Mitchell et al. (2008).

inhabit, as it were, a hall of dusty glass cabinets, distinguished by neatly labelled items of material culture.

Early scholars like Breuil cast a very long shadow. In the present age of scientific archaeology it is well to remember that the history of our discipline is littered with discarded theories and assertions. In this, perhaps more than in other fields that rely on observation, the evidence is notoriously fragmented, and subject to the caprices of preservation. Archaeological knowledge is therefore unavoidably provisional and the firmest certainties may find themselves suddenly in question as new evidence and new insights emerge. It is as a hedge against criticism that archaeologists set particular store in precise documentation, for this discipline is inherently destructive: as we excavate we recover material evidence by destroying the very context that may hold the key to its meaning. Unfortunately, however, documentation has often become an end in itself, thereby creating an illusion of insight into the human past.

Breuil, when he handed over to Ernst-Rudolf Scherz the elaborately carved West African spear which he had carried everywhere in the desert (presumably to defend himself from snakes), declared to his successor: *'Je vous rends les armes'*.[17] And from that moment, archaeology in Namibia turned away from speculation to enter an era dominated by a form of antiquarianism from which it has yet to fully emerge. Namibian archaeology, most especially during the 75 years of South African occupation, became the research focus of German institutions practising a form of empiricism which avoided, in the supposed interests of scientific objectivity, almost all reference to the actual people of Namibia and their history.[18]

---

17 Kinahan (1995b: 83)

18 This anti-theoretical approach, sometimes referred to as the Kossina Syndrome (Härke 2000; Wolfram 2000), arose following the abuse of the discipline under the Third Reich during World War II, when archaeology was used to try and prove the racial superiority of the Germanic people. See also Kinahan (2000a).

INTRODUCTION   11

The main period of German archaeology in Namibia stretched from the late 1960s to the late 1980s and involved a research effort that has few equals in Africa, both in terms of its scale and high standards of survey and excavation. Most of this work, which continues intermittently, was carried out by archaeologists and their students attached to the Heinrich Barth Institute at the University of Köln, with the major emphasis placed on documentation of rock art and the development of a securely dated late Pleistocene and Holocene sequence. This research, devoted to inventorizing the pre-colonial archaeological record, extended over large parts of Namibia and grew to encompass a variety of related fields such as ethnology and linguistics.

Archaeology has a broader purpose than to compile lists, descriptions and measurements in the hope that understanding will emerge by itself from accumulated observations. Our aim, rather, is to write history by interrogating the scattered and fragmentary evidence we excavate, formulating, testing, and quite frequently rejecting, successive hypotheses. Against this background, the chapters that follow are an attempt to set out in search of a new direction in the archaeology of the Namib Desert, linking as far as possible the distant and most recent past within a common general explanatory framework. This cannot be done without conjecture, the risky business of archaeology. I fully expect that the picture presented here will change as new research advances with improved methods and more sophisticated analysis.

The following poem[19] provides a lyrical insight into the nature of this discipline, part manual labour, part monastic contemplation, punctuated by unexpected moments of revelation when all of a sudden the evidence makes sense…

---

19 Exerpt from *Desert Archaeology*, by Mark O'Connor, written in appreciation of the life and work of Mike Smith, Australian desert archaeologist. See https://quadrant.org.au/magazine/2014/09/desert-archaeology/

> Archaeology
> Is not one-day cricket but a decades-long test;
> Quick conceptions, then a long slow fostering
> Of evidence, like rearing and training a wicked child.
>
> A few weeks romance and dig,
> Then that long monogamy of writing-up.
> Layers fade as you rapidly read them
> Before rodents or floods get in,
> It's a corpse you dissect till it vanishes,
> Each layer of tissue scraped off
> Into sketches and words.
>
> Dissecting the site is surgery, with washed, dusty hands.
> Peeling back the skin, dissecting its rusted
> Anatomy—how the nerves connect, bones articulate.
> That first trench
> Is a manhole inserted intuitively into Time.
>
> (Mark O'Connor)

Now, some readers may be surprised that two chapters in this book are devoted to the early colonial era which, for many, falls outside the proper field of archaeology as *prehistory*. I hope, however, to demonstrate here the value of archaeological evidence both as an adjunct to the documentary record and as an alternative voice in the discussion of Namibian colonial history. By adding the archaeological evidence to the documentary record, I will show that the historical archives of colonial Namibia extend far beyond the confines of a climate-controlled repository building in the capital city, and that the archaeological record of the colonial experience *on the land itself* deserves equally assiduous study.

The value of archaeological evidence for our understanding of recent history is manifold. For example, much of the land seized from indigenous Namibian communities under colonial rule, was divided into farms, and these occupy what were once the locations of Ovaherero, ǂNūkhoen and other settlements, many with well attested traditional histories. The archaeological evidence found on these same sites provides a valuable independent record of occupation and cultural ownership, often in the form of family burial sites, or locations on the landscape known from folklore and oral history. The particular circumstances of the early colonial period in Namibia, involving the explicit intention to exterminate entire peoples, and by implication all memory of them, makes it all the more imperative to reconnect the archaeological past with these events.

While archaeology can illuminate the twilight zone between the remembered past and events well beyond the reach of memory and tradition, thus greatly extending the time depth of written history, antiquarianism privileges objects over context, and description over meaning, absorbing the archaeological past into a research agenda that often retards rather than advances understanding of the human past. The antiquarian approach appropriates *place* (as represented by the site), *time* (archaeological dating), and *identity* (the cultural affinity of objects), removing them from historical discourse and placing them in an arbitrarily defined field, that of *prehistory*. Antiquarian archaeology has thus artificially truncated Namibian history; in my view, there is a lineal and ideological continuity between the precepts of colonial rule and those of antiquarian archaeology which tends to obscure rather than explain the human past.

Archaeology in Namibia is not unique in being burdened by its own history. In the region, the predominance of South African archaeology has its own implications for the course of argument and discussion in the chapters to follow. Although it is by any standard highly advanced in both method and theory, as well as showing an extraordinarily diverse range of approaches to the archaeology of the region, South African archaeology has had its own distinctive historical *Leitmotif*, one in which archaeological classification was easily accommodated by a social ideology of racial and ethnic ordering.[20] Thus, in the

---

20 cf. Mitchell (2002); Robertshaw (1990); Trigger (1989)

treatment of the Holocene epoch, covering the last 12,000 years, and of central concern in this book, there is a persistent focus in South African archaeology on identity rather than process. The archaeology of this period is a catalogue of identities, forming geographically and chronologically bounded entities[21] which recall the *Kulturkreis* archaeology of the Vienna School once popular in Europe, surviving in southern Africa as the basic framework of a deep-time material culture ethnology, the natural extension of the colonial ethnographic record.

One example of this approach is found in the study of Holocene rock art which affords many important insights into hunter-gatherer religious life. The existing consensus that the art is essentially shamanic rests on a large body of mainly historical ethnography serving as an almost exegetical framework for the interpretation of the rock art. Although the Namib Desert rock art agrees with this view in broad terms, it departs from it with new evidence that contradicts the conventional interpretation in several key respects, among others by showing that shamanic practice was specialized rather than communal, and itinerant rather than community-based. This is significant because it identifies the shaman as both an individual and as an agent of change in hunter-gatherer society, playing a central, if not key role in the adoption of cultural values from other groups and the emergence of food production, principally pastoralism. The Namib Desert evidence thus introduces individual agency and historicity to a field that is generally marked by an ahistorical reliance on the authority of ethnographic sources.[22]

A second example is provided by the prevailing view of the introduction of domestic livestock and pastoralism which is similarly based on historical ethnographic sources, augmented by archaeological evidence. The generally accepted notion that pastoralism was introduced by an immigrant people has little direct historical support and despite their economic dominance

---

21 See Mazel (1987)
22 Lewis-Williams (1983, 1984)

on the early colonial South African landscape, pastoralists themselves seem to have left scant archaeological trace.[23] In contrast, evidence of pastoral settlement is abundant in the Namib Desert where it provides comprehensive support for a general model of settlement and land-use based on the social characteristics of pastoral economy and land management.[24] The Namib Desert evidence thus points to a far more complex history of pastoralism than South African research which has until now dominated discussion, often to the exclusion of alternative evidence and interpretation.

A third and final example is that of the relationship between indigenous communities and early European visitors and settlers. Again, the historical ethnography on which the predominantly South African perspective relies, favours the idea that indigenous hunter-gatherer and pastoralist society collapsed in the face of this onslaught, and all but disappeared.[25] The Namib Desert evidence which reflects the nature of early contact in far more detail than elsewhere in the subcontinent, shows instead an invigoration of indigenous society, leading to a protracted if ultimately futile anti-colonial resistance. This evidence provides insights into pre-colonial societies that shed new light on their historical experience, potentially allowing a continuity of understanding between the documented and archaeological past.[26]

Regional perspective

Our evolutionary ancestors emerged from the genus *Australopithecus* about two million years ago.[27] The survival of hominin fossil remains in Africa is mainly due to their preservation in volcanic ash deposits such as occur in the eastern and north-eastern Rift Valley regions, and in southern Africa as fossil material recovered

---

23 See Sadr (2013); Sadr & Fauvelle-Aymar (2008)
24 Kinahan (2019)
25 Elphick (1985); Penn (2005)
26 Kinahan (2014); Kinahan, J.H.A. (2000)
27 Soodyall (2006)

from dolomitic cave breccias.[28] These cave deposits came to be known as the Cradle of Mankind, but the hominins who lived there had a much wider distribution within the southern African region.[29] Later forms such as *Homo erectus*[30] were well adapted to the arid conditions of the interior, and their expansion which scholars refer to as "Out of Africa 1" represents the first wave of human colonization beyond the limits of the continent, one and a half million years ago.[31] There are relatively few instances where artefacts have been found with fossil remains in a directly dateable context. Relative dating of stone artefact assemblages therefore employs an inferred series of advances in the technological mastery of tool production, from the simple pebble tools of the early Pleistocene era, to the highly advanced microlithic tools of the last few thousand years.[32]

Stone artefacts are the most common and widespread evidence of human occupation and – especially for the earlier phases of the archaeological sequence – such relative dating provides an adjunct to the conventional three-stage schema of an Earlier, Middle and finally, Later Stone Age, overcoming some difficulties in the comparison of undated or poorly dated Pleistocene assemblages. These broad stadial divisions imply clearly recognizable shifts from one stage to the next in the archaeological evidence when

---

28 Although primarily known from South Africa, one important Miocene hominoid fossil *Otavipithecus namibiensis* comes from a similar geological context in Namibia (Conroy et al. 1992; see also Pickford & Senut 1999).
29 Scerri et al. (2018) have argued on the basis of chronological and morphological evidence that humankind evolved from multiple interlinked centres in Africa, rather than a single point of origin in southern Africa.
30 As more fossils are found it appears that the genus probably included several species other than *Homo erectus*, such as *H. rhodesiensis* in south-central Africa (Wadley 2015) and *H. ergaster* in eastern and north-eastern Africa (Phillipson 2005: 29). Important later middle Pleistocene hominin remains from southern Africa are reported by Berger et al. (2017).
31 Soodyall (2006)
32 For a detailed rationale of this approach, see Barham and Mitchell (2008: 15–17).

INTRODUCTION 17

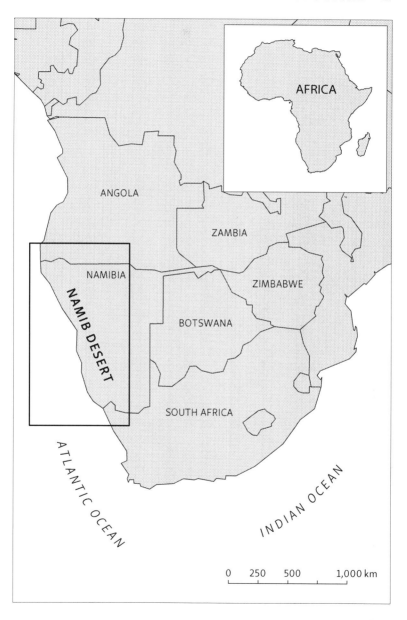

Figure 1.3: Regional setting of the Namib Desert.

in reality, stone tool assemblages are complex combinations of formal and informal tools that vary from one site to another, their characteristics being determined by many factors, including the properties of the raw materials available to their makers as well as a host of post-depositional processes affecting the survival of the evidence used in their description.

In southern Africa, archaeologists have employed a number of classificatory systems for the description of stone artefact assemblages and their assignation to specific chronostratigraphic entities comprising regional and supra-regional traditions and complexes.[33] For Holocene assemblages there exists a detailed descriptive scheme based on microlithic reduction sequences[34] which is broadly applied in this book. A more fine-scaled classification proposed for Namib Desert assemblages[35] I have found to be of limited utility and have therefore adopted the sequence of technological modes set out in Table 1.1,[36] with more detailed description of specific assemblages where this is warranted by the material under discussion.

Our understanding of the Pleistocene in southern Africa relies on a small number of key sites where securely dated evidence provides the building blocks for an integrated archaeological sequence. The Earlier Stone Age (ESA), commenced at least one and a half million years ago, with many sites showing that while the interior of the subcontinent was occupied during the early to mid-Pleistocene, the relatively cool and dry southern parts of the subcontinent were scarcely occupied until about one million years ago.[37] Although early humans were certainly not numerous,

---

33 See, for example, Barham and Mitchell (2008); Mitchell (2002)
34 Deacon (1984)
35 Richter (1991); see also Vogelsang and Eichhorn (2011); see also Ossendorf (2017) for a general review of stone artefact assemblage analysis in the Namib Desert.
36 The information in this table is after Clark (1969); Barham & Mitchell (2008); Phillipson (2005)
37 Klein et al. (1999)

Table 1.1: Modes of stone tool technology and their approximate dating

Mode	Description	Approximate dating and cultural affinity
Mode 1	Choppers and simple flakes struck off pebbles (pebble tools)	Early to mid-Pleistocene (Earlier Stone Age)
Mode 2	Bifacially worked tools (hand-axes and cleavers) produced from large flakes or cores	Mid-Pleistocene (Earlier Stone Age)
Mode 3	Flake tools produced from prepared cores	Mid- to late Pleistocene (Earlier to Middle Stone Age)
Mode 4	Thin blade flakes that may be retouched into various specialised tool forms	Late Pleistocene (Middle Stone Age)
Mode 5	Microlithic components of composite artefacts, often backed or otherwise retouched	Late Pleistocene to Holocene (Later Stone Age)

the evidence of stone tools shows that they were successful in establishing themselves in almost every possible natural habitat.[38] After about 300,000 years ago the broadly uniform character of ESA tool assemblages gave way to an increasing complexity and regional diversity of toolkits, ushering in a phase known as the Middle Stone Age (MSA), with the first appearance of *Homo sapiens*[39] and the rise of what is now termed "complex cognition".[40]

Several southern African MSA sites are firmly dated to more than one hundred thousand years ago and it is now evident that early *Homo sapiens* on the whole had a mental capacity similar

---

38 Gowlett (1996)
39 Wadley (2015)
40 Grine et al. (2017); Grün et al. (1996); Mounier & Lahr (2019); Schlebusch et al. (2017); see also Wadley (2015: 157)

to that of modern humans, as shown by evidence of an ability to plan and execute complex tasks, to experiment with the properties of raw materials, and to produce artefacts that seem to encode symbolic references. The important point to emerge from the early regional archaeology is that the species *Homo sapiens*, and the complex behaviours which developed during the late Pleistocene, first arose in southern Africa, leading to the second wave of human migration from this continent, also known as "Out of Africa 2".[41]

Global climatic events affected environmental conditions in southern Africa and had a profound influence on human adaptations during the Pleistocene epoch.[42] The framework for our understanding of the successive shifts in atmospheric temperature and moisture over the last 300,000 years is based on oxygen isotope data from deep sea cores. Table 1.2[43] shows the correlation of Marine Isotope Stages (MISs) with inferred climate changes and broad archaeological periods. Global climate changes are associated with variations in sea level, reducing and expanding the area of shoreline available to human foragers. In broad terms, higher sea levels were accompanied by higher temperatures and rainfall in the interior, improving conditions there for human survival. The converse obtained with lower sea levels in the Last Glacial Maximum (LGM), bringing drier conditions in the interior accompanied by a much larger area of exposed shoreline on the continental shelf,[44] which revealed a rich source of easily accessible food.

The human response to changing environmental conditions in the late Pleistocene laid the foundations for the diverse range of adaptations and sophisticated environmental knowledge that is apparent in the more recent Holocene evidence. Until recently, archaeologists relied mainly on detailed analysis of stone tool

---

41 Recent studies suggest that there were multiple pulses of migration from Africa during the late Pleistocene (Manica et al. 2007).
42 Burroughs (2005)
43 After Cohen & Gibbard (2019); see also Volman (1984); Wadley (2015)
44 Deacon & Lancaster (1988)

Table 1.2: Approximate start ages and Marine Isotope Stage correlation of climate events and archaeological chronostratigraphic units in southern Africa.

Years BP x 1000	MIS	World climate	Event and chronology
0	1	warm	Mid-Holocene Optimum
12		variable	Holocene
24	2	cold	Later Stone Age
59	3	variable	Last Glacial Maximum (LGM)
73	4	cool	End Middle Stone Age
75			**Upper Pleistocene**
84	5a	warm	Last Interglacial
93	5b	cold	*Homo sapiens* Out of Africa 2 migration
106	5c	warm	**Middle Pleistocene**
115	5d	cool	
130	5e	warm	Late Middle Stone Age
188	6	variable	Middle Stone Age
195	7	variable	**Lower Pleistocene**
291	8	cool	
730	19		
1,700			**Terminal Pliocene** Earlier Stone Age Early Homo Out of Africa 1 migration

assemblages to delineate Holocene populations.[45] Now this approach has been augmented by high resolution multi-proxy modelling combining evidence of environmental changes and human subsistence responses, showing that hunting and gathering strategies were highly productive and specialized.[46] The most

---

45 Deacon (1984)
46 Chase et al. (2018)

important feature of these strategies was their adaptive flexibility and this was crucial to the regional expansion of hunter-gatherer populations under the improved climatic conditions of the Holocene, commencing about 12,000 years ago.[47]

The later Holocene archaeological record shows that a sophisticated stone tool technology was in use throughout the subcontinent, with minor local variation to support an array of different hunting and gathering strategies suited to a wide range of environmental conditions. Overlying, as it were, this variation in subsistence strategies, was a remarkable regional uniformity in religious ideology,[48] evinced by a rich, well-preserved and regionally distributed body of rock art based on a common set of precepts and shamanic practices. Southern African rock art is primarily metaphorical rather than narrative in its content,[49] and was not well understood until the last few decades when, following a series of important theoretical advances, it has become fundamental to Later Stone Age (LSA) hunter-gatherer studies.[50] It remains, however, poorly integrated with the material archaeological record, due to difficulties of dating and persistent conceptual differences between the two fields. An emic model of LSA society that would accommodate the evidence of ritual and belief alongside that of subsistence and material culture remains to be developed.[51]

The LSA evidence is characterized by apparent shifts in the frequency of artefact assemblage items and in the type of plant and animal remains associated with them.[52] The major *a priori* change in the LSA subsistence landscape was the arrival, about 2,000 years ago, of domestic livestock and pottery, a combination that archaeologists at first accepted as a fundamental technological innovation brought by an immigrant pastoralist people, the ancestors

---

47 Mitchell (2002: 137–141)
48 Barnard (1992b)
49 Lewis-Williams (1981)
50 Davis (1990: 279–86)
51 See Kinahan (2018a)
52 Deacon (1984)

of the Khoe-speaking herders encountered by the first European settlers in southern Africa.[53] Newer interpretations suggest a more complex scenario in which these innovations were introduced and distributed in the arid western parts of the region through their acquisition by hunter-gatherers who adopted pastoralism via complex exchange networks, as well as by the movement of fully pastoral groups.[54] Problematically, archaeologists have been unable to consistently distinguish pastoralist from hunter-gatherer on the basis of the material evidence and some consensus has arisen that both came to exist within a common but variegated cultural identity, in which people shifted about in response to the vicissitudes of drought, disease and endemic raiding.[55]

During this same period, a series of movements into the subcontinent brought the first Bantu-speaking communities of mixed agriculturalists with livestock as well as domestic crops and a sophisticated tradition of metallurgy;[56] they also brought with them a complex array of languages and cultural traditions. The evidence is of successive migrations into southern Africa from the east, north and north-west, skirting the arid and semi-arid western parts of the region, including the Namib Desert, where rainfall was insufficient for cereal crops.[57] Early centralized class-based states emerged, with distant regional capitals linked to extended networks and the export of gold and ivory via Indian Ocean trade ports.[58] Similar polities emerged on the eastern edge of the Kalahari,[59] while others arose to the north of the Zambezi River. These developments laid the foundations of a diversified pre-colonial economy which endured in some parts of the region until the mid- to late 19th century.[60]

---

53 Guillemard (2020); Mitchell (2002)
54 Sadr & Fauvelle-Aymar (2008)
55 Sadr (2013)
56 Huffman (2006)
57 Phillipson (2005)
58 Sinclair, Pikirayi, Pwiti & Soper (1993)
59 Denbow (1983); Denbow & Wilmsen (1986)
60 Phillipson (2005)

The archaeological evidence makes it possible to trace the cultural antecedents of modern southern African communities,[61] and with the addition of further insights from genetic studies a more detailed picture of the population history of the region is becoming available.[62] Evolutionary diversification is evident from both the fossil record[63] and the more recent past, where genetic studies show that before about 2,000 years ago the region was exclusively inhabited by the ancestors of hunter-gatherer groups that merged with other populations,[64] giving rise to the genetic profile associated with pastoralists who occupied the arid and semi-arid southern and western parts of the region[65] prior to the arrival of Bantu-speaking farmers.[66] The assimilation and displacement of the original hunter-gatherer population intensified during the last 350 years with the arrival and spread of European and other colonists. While the genetic data provide a general framework for the human biological prehistory of southern Africa, casting new light on many questions of origins and of biological relationships, our understanding of human adaptation through inventiveness and social interaction is written primarily from archaeological evidence.[67] This will probably remain the case while genetic studies are focused on ethno-biological identity and migration, rather than questions emerging from current archaeological concerns with adaptation, subsistence, social organization and ideology.[68]

---

61 Blench (1993)
62 Dusseldorp et al. (2013); Schlebusch & Jakobsson (2018); see also Mitchell (2010)
63 Stringer (2006); Soodyall (2006)
64 Schlebusch et al. (2016)
65 Macholdt et al. (2014)
66 Li et al. (2014)
67 See Stoneking and Krause (2011), and also Eisenmann et al. (2018) for an important critique of assumed equivalence between archaeological and genetic data.
68 In Namibia, the legacy of German colonial race science (Stone 2001) cast human genetic studies in a negative light.

Against the background of the wider southern African archaeological record the Namib Desert is relatively under-studied. However, the archaeological sequence is known in broad outline and a number of detailed investigations have established informative links to the regional archaeology as well as identifying some critical differences, especially in the more recent record. Research has progressed in piecemeal fashion and there is as yet no unifying model which considers the archaeology of the Namib Desert as a whole. This evident lacuna represents an important opportunity to develop a conceptual framework that takes into account the particular conditions of human settlement in the desert and to propose an integrated model accommodating the available evidence, while also pointing to possible future research goals.[69]

The chapters to follow draw on earlier studies but, as indicated in the Preface, they are based mainly on the results of recent fieldwork by the Namib Desert Archaeological Survey. This project involved more than 250 local surveys carried out over the last twenty years, mainly on foot and covering most of the desert over an area of about 200,000 km^2 and its adjacent interior between the Kunene River at 17° south latitude, and the Orange River at 29° south latitude. The combined survey results comprise more than 3,000 previously unrecorded archaeological sites. The explicitly landscape-based approach of the survey seeks to integrate scattered surface occurrences with chronological evidence from excavations of selected sites where stratified occupation sequences are supported by a chronological framework of more than 700 radiocarbon dates. The interpretation of these results draws on conventional archaeological methods aided by a range of laboratory analytical techniques. Wherever appropriate, the interpretation offered here links the more recent archaeological

---

[69] The only regional-scale treatment of southern hemisphere desert archaeology is that of Smith (2013). Mitchell (2002) provides a detailed review of southern African desert archaeology in the context of the wider region, while Thomas and Shaw (1991) consider the archaeology as a component of the Kalahari environment.

evidence to the recorded history of the desert and its margins in order to assemble a narrative covering the *longue durée* from the first appearance of humanity in this region, to the colonial period.

The framework of research outlined below and elaborated in the chapters to follow is a suggested alternative to the general approach to Namib Desert archaeology that has prevailed until now. For the last fifty or more years, research has focused on the inferred cultural affinity of artefact assemblages and their technological characteristics. Research was characterized by an avowed empiricism in which interpretation of material evidence was explicitly deferred, on the assumption – widely rejected among archaeologists as a logical fallacy – that a reliable understanding of the human history of the desert would naturally emerge from more comprehensive data. Empiricist approaches to the archaeology of this region, having no explicit theoretical framework of general explanatory principles, cannot provide testable hypotheses with archaeologically observable consequences.

Desert archaeology

Tropical deserts are by definition severely water-limited environments with erratic rainfall and minimal biotic productivity.[70] True deserts such as the Namib, averaging less than 100 mm annual rainfall, have little or no surface water; their combination of high temperatures and evaporation rates generally results in a near-permanent water deficit.[71] Historically, this and other desert regions of the world were characterized by very low human population densities with few centres of permanent settlement and a high dependence on widely scattered and often ephemeral resources. While the southern hemisphere desert regions of South America and Australia were occupied at a relatively recent stage in human history, the Namib Desert has a far longer record, extending over the last one million years.[72]

---

70 Louw & Seely (1982)
71 McGinnies (1979); Meigs (1953); Noy-Meir (1973)
72 Smith & Hesse (2005)

INTRODUCTION 27

Figure 1.4: A field camp of the Namib Desert Archaeological Survey near Tsaun Hill. Tsaun refers to *sâun*, Khoekhoegowab for grass seed found as underground caches in the nests of Harvester ants, described in Chapter 6.

In the long term, all tropical deserts have experienced major variations in rainfall and temperature related to global climatic changes. These shifts have sometimes spurred population expansion into marginal environments and in some circumstances have led to the isolation of small, increasingly specialized populations. The archaeology of these desert regions reflects human tolerance of hyper-arid conditions and is therefore of great interest to our understanding of human responses to climatic uncertainty and the limits of human resilience.[73] Although these issues form the backdrop, and provide a general framework for many investigations, there has been relatively little development of formal approaches to the effects of desert conditions on patterns of human settlement in the past.

---

73 Fitzhugh et al. (2019)

The archaeology of human settlement in deserts is conventionally focused on major sites which fulfil the requirements for well-stratified occupation records as the basic framework of cultural sequence construction. It is in most circumstances difficult to relate such records to the wider landscape of occupation and resource use, with the result that some activities essential for the survival of desert communities may go unaccounted for, and the relationship between settlements and their broader environment is often poorly documented. The general practice of evaluating occupation evidence against its environmental context does alleviate this problem but may overlook cultural aspects of resource-use as well as the effects of small-scale variations in resource availability.

A problematic aspect of conventional archaeological approaches is the simple extrapolation from the remains of food consumed at the site to the availability of plant and animal species in the surrounding environment. Whether food resources are seasonal or perennial does not, however, account in ecological terms for the relationship between the resource and consumer, which is critical to an understanding of human ecology. This is especially important in desert environments where access to one resource such as plant foods may depend on the availability of another, water. In ecological terms, occupation of desert sites with reliable water is *density dependent*, being limited by the availability of sufficient food resources accessible in their vicinity. These are therefore primary resource sites, as opposed to secondary resource sites where occupation is *density independent*; at these sites water is in short supply, such as following local rain events, and occupation cannot be sustained long enough to fully exploit available food resources.[74]

Specialized desert communities may be able to mitigate these limitations to achieve a degree of food security. One strategy could be food storage; another could be intensive cooperative exploitation of food resources when scarcity of water limits the window of opportunity for their exploitation. Resource conservation strategies

---

74 Vandermeer & Goldberg (2013)

may also help to extend the availability of food at primary sites subject to density dependent limitations, such as by imposing social restrictions on access to water sources and by selective cropping of food plants. Such mitigating strategies are the essential means of risk alleviation in desert environments; they cannot be inferred simply from the availability or seasonal timing of natural resource occurrence, since they are fundamentally social and cultural practices, however stringent their ecological limitation might be.

A landscape-based approach has the advantage of integrating primary resource sites with evidence of dispersed occupation of secondary resource sites in the context of social relations affecting access to these resources. This includes evidence of networks which form the social web of interdependency between what might appear as isolated communities. The relationship between desert communities and the resources on which they depend rests on practical, or so-called traditional knowledge systems in which the interface between people and environment is ideologically conditioned; it is informed by social and cultural beliefs, not by formal scientific principles. Ideology cannot be inferred from the remains of food found at an archaeological site, although important insights into its role and functions are found in ritual practices and evidence such as from rock art.

Human settlement in deserts is commonly characterized as nomadic, implying an almost constant movement across the landscape in search of water, food and pasture for livestock. But in reality, movement and access to resources is highly regulated; it is constrained by social restrictions that are essential for the long-term sustainability of desert life. Access is negotiable in some circumstances and large displacements of population are inevitable consequences of climatic shifts which may so increase pressure on resources that some communities are obliged to move into less than optimal areas. Sudden expansion or movement of desert populations may result in violent conflict and the maintenance of strictly controlled boundaries. Among desert populations such divisions are overtly expressed through material culture, marriage patterns and symbolic behaviour.

Archaeological preservation and site formation processes directly affect the survival and visibility of evidence relating to land-use and social identity in these populations. Resource-rich localities serve as attractors and often have evidence of repeated occupation over long periods. Successive occupations can result in a palimpsest effect in which individual occupation events are difficult to separate. In the case of open-air sites, the layout and relative positioning of site components, determined by social behavioural factors, provides a critical framework of interpretation. Within these as well as stratified sites, some materials may remain in circulation for long periods, resulting in an heirloom effect which creates anomalous associations between objects of different ages and cultural contexts.

Because desert communities are highly mobile and therefore retain relatively limited amounts of cultural material, archaeological evidence of important innovations often depends on chance discovery of highly fragmentary remains. It is therefore important to consider that the circulation of new materials may have to achieve a certain critical threshold before it can survive natural attrition in visible concentrations. This process has implications for the dating of early evidence for pottery, metallurgy and even domestic livestock. The taphonomic processes affecting the depletion of scarce materials both organic and inorganic can be particularly acute under desert conditions, further reducing the archaeological visibility of the human presence.

Archaeological visibility is an important consideration in any attempt to reconstruct the movement of scarce items or materials through extended social networks. Prestige items are by definition relatively scarce and may therefore be distributed well beyond their point of origin. The decline in their occurrence with distance from source, a process resembling that of monotonic decrement, can have the result that important social links and evidence of artefact circulation depends on extremely scarce pieces of evidence. This may be further complicated when mobile communities serve as shifting points of dispersal in a circulation network that was continually adjusted in response to ecological and other influences.

The dynamic nature of human settlement in desert environments points to a high potential for change and social re-organization. This naturally raises the question as to the degree to which desert cultures arose as autochthonous developments in the form of specific and often highly specialized responses to particular environmental conditions and bearing identifiable traits which distinguish them from other cultures. Alternatively, the question may be asked as to whether desert cultures resulted from peripheral expansion from less arid areas, becoming more specialized over time. The archaeology of desert peoples probably reflects both processes. It is, however, a certainty that desert conditions impose severe adaptive pressures at different temporal and spatial scales; archaeological models need to accommodate these considerations.

Fragmentary evidence and the difficulty of accurate age measurement are impediments to any archaeological attempt to observe and understand change in ancient human society. Because change and a degree of stability are characteristic of all human societies, these over time appear to follow trajectories of growth, adaptation and transformation, with shifts in social organization and, sometimes, collapse. Proceeding from these basic premises, a number of scholars have proposed that such changes represent a universal quality of socio-ecological *resilience*. From this perspective, there are two essential, and constantly variable qualities of resilience: *connectedness*, or the degree of inherent flexibility which allows adaptive change, and *potential*, or the presence of options for future states. Connectedness and potential are sometimes combined in the superordinate term, *complexity*.[75]

---

75 Bradtmöller et al. (2017)

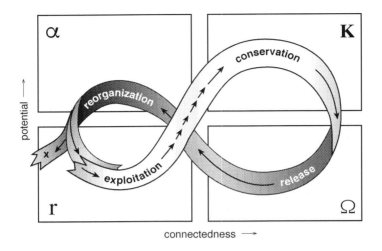

Figure 1.5: Holling's adaptive cycle. From *Panarchy* edited by Lance H. Gunderson and C.S. Holling. Copyright 2002 Island Press. Reproduced by permission of Island Press, Washington, DC.

A widely used metaphor of resilience in human systems is the adaptive cycle,[76] comprising four successive states, or domains: a growth or expansion r phase, an equilibrium or conservation K phase, a collapse or release Ω phase and a re-orientation α phase. This extends the conventional logistic curve $r \to K$ to include the collapse or alternatively, re-orientation phenomena that are known from diverse examples in ecological systems and in human history. The adaptive cycle is usually depicted as the Holling loop shown in Figure 1.5. To accommodate a range of data varying in scale and precision, the terms employed in resilience studies are unavoidably fluid and qualitative. While it is possible to measure some archaeological indicators of adaptive resilience, it is often difficult to combine quantitative data with equally critical evidence that is best understood in a qualitative sense. A lack of terminological precision and a tendency to oversimplification

---

76 See Fitzhugh et al. (2019) for a general discussion of human ecodynamics and the concepts discussed here.

are valid criticisms of resilience studies. Equally problematic is the challenge of identifying proxies, whether measurable or not, for change or stability in the evidence under study.[77]

Furthermore, the timespan occupied by any one domain in the adaptive cycle may, and generally does, vary, as does the speed of transition from one domain to the next, thus placing particular importance on archaeological dating and sequencing. The sequence of adaptive cycle domains may resemble a conventional archaeological cultural sequence but it differs in two important respects: one is that the data are used to identify the mechanism of transition, and not just to indicate the occurrence of change, as might be inferred by differences in the number and type of artefacts found in successive archaeological layers. The second is that the adaptive cycle approach attempts to consider all the evidence within a unitary framework based on the concept of resilience, while also employing cognate concepts to frame explicit hypotheses. Some of these can be evaluated on the basis of quantitative data such as the regional distribution of radiocarbon dates, while others depend on inferences about change such as in social organization and religious practices, based on circumstantial evidence. In some instances, however, the possible consequences of adaptive cycle changes can only be speculative proposals for future research.[78]

The approach adopted here broadly conforms to a prevailing trend in southern African archaeology to integrate evidence of subsistence patterns, technology, social organization and environment. It also has in common a foundation in general systems theory which some archaeologists have used to conceptualize a lineal sequence of punctuated equilibrial stages, or homeostatic plateaux, interrupted by responses to brief pulses of positive feedback, usually related to climatic shifts.[79] A lack of direct synchronicity between the archaeological and environmental

---

77 Gunderson & Holling (2002)
78 Fath et al. (2015)
79 Deacon (1976)

evidence suggests that delayed responses visible in archaeological assemblages reflect a degree of inertia that needs to be taken into account when attempting to specify the scale and rate of human adaptation to shifting environmental conditions.[80] It should be emphasized that the human behavioural response to climatic variation is broader and more complex than changes that seem to be reflected in the evidence of archaeological assemblages.

There is a widely held consensus that stable, and often regionally widespread patterns in the archaeological record support a stadial model of human history in this region, with relatively distinct and securely dated entities which allow for a gradual refinement of long-established assemblage groups characterized as archaeological complexes and so-called industries, or cultures.[81] The adaptive cycle approach is a refinement of this general view, sharing a number of key concepts such as the influence of feedback on system responses. In the adaptive cycle a socio-ecological system is subject to two principal types of feedback loop: a *response* loop reflecting the influence of other, intersecting adaptive cycles, and a *memory* loop in which the system draws on the internal history of its own previous responses through the adaptive cycle.

The interaction of feedback loops may help to explain delayed responses to environmental change, for example. The external influences on the system include climatic variation and the corresponding internal influence is represented by the range of responses to climatic variation in the history of the system. The most common proxies for these responses are found in subsistence practices, in demographic patterns, in social organization and in technological development or innovation. Integrating these sources of data may for example show a range of responses to climatic variation, from shifts in settlement patterns and demography, to an intensification of subsistence and the adoption of new subsistence practices.[82]

---

80 Mitchell (2002: 149) citing Parkington (1987) and Wobst (1990)
81 Mitchell (2002)
82 Bradtmöller et al. (2017), Freeman et al. (2017)

There are important differences between the adaptive cycle and the punctuated equilibrium model: one of the most critical of these is the linkage of socio-ecological systems with other, intersecting adaptive cycles. It is rarely the case that the adaptive cycle of a defined socio-ecological system exists in isolation, and in the African context as much as any other, differing trajectories of change and stability would have occurred in adjacent or intersecting cultural systems or entities. Multiple, intersecting adaptive cycles nested one within the other add to the complexity of the model when it is extended to take into account adjacent socio-ecological systems developing at different rates and on different scales.[83]

In the chapters to follow, we first consider the adaptive cycle evidenced by the archaeology of Pleistocene hunter-gatherer groups expanding over the landscape in the first visible presence of humankind in the Namib Desert. Improving preservation and archaeological visibility allows some elaboration of this model in the terminal Pleistocene and during the first millennia after the Last Glacial Maximum. With ever greater resolution of evidence, the nature of the adaptive cycle is explored in more detail for the Holocene archaeological record, allowing a nuanced view of hunter-gatherer responses to increasing aridification. During the last two thousand years, the adaptive cycle of desert hunter-gatherers intersected with that of food-producing groups on the same landscape as part of the general spread of farming and food production through the subcontinent. This interaction resulted in fundamental changes in hunter-gatherer society and the consequent rise of a nomadic pastoral economy. In the last few centuries, a further layer of complexity was introduced from an initially independent adaptive cycle represented by the expansion of European mercantile interests. Contact and, ultimately, economic encapsulation led to the collapse of some indigenous economies and the subjugation of others. We thus find in the archaeology of the Namib Desert a panarchy of nested adaptive cycles, local, regional and global.

---

83 Gunderson & Holling (2002)

The broadly chronological presentation of the Namib Desert archaeological sequence in this book is accompanied by a thematic approach which considers the evidence for particular ecological responses and their related cultural developments. Chapters 2 and 3 focus on hunter-gatherer responses to Pleistocene and early Holocene climatic and environmental changes in the desert. Chapter 4 is concerned with hunter-gatherer refugium settlement under increasingly arid late Holocene conditions, combining evidence of subsistence patterns with that of cultural adaptations such as regional exchange networks and the rise of specialized shamanism. In Chapter 5, more detailed evidence of ecological responses to recent Holocene climatic variation is combined with that of shamanic rain-making and the appearance of men's and women's initiation as part of the social transition towards food production. This theme is elaborated first in Chapter 6 which is concerned with evidence for systematic control and exploitation of wild food resources, and in Chapter 7 by the development of semi-nomadic pastoralism. Chapter 8 deals with the response of pastoralist communities to trading contact on the Namib coast during the late pre-colonial era. Indigenous responses to colonialism are discussed in Chapters 9 and 10, where archaeological evidence of this interaction is placed in the context of the written historical record.

Throughout, the book relates archaeological evidence from the Namib Desert and its semi-arid margins to the wider southern African setting. This serves to broaden and augment the regional picture, and to draw attention to a range of new insights that have important implications for southern African archaeology. Among these are evidence supporting a new perspective on the ecology of human adaptation to desert environments and of social strategies and responses that have not been recognized elsewhere. This new perspective necessarily involves several important departures from current southern African archaeological consensus. These arise from evidence for fundamental shifts in Holocene hunter-gatherer social organization in the context of sustained interaction, first with farming and livestock-owning societies which expanded into this region during the last few thousand years and then, as predominantly pastoral peoples, in relation to more recent colonial occupation.

The reader will notice that while the initial chapters combine archaeological with palaeoenvironmental evidence as a framework of interpretation, the emphasis gradually shifts towards more detailed discussion of social responses to climatic uncertainty. In the second half of the book these social responses become the central focus of discussion as I attempt to reconstruct the role of human cultural agency in relation to the desert environment. The final chapters take this process further by reflecting on the largely neglected archaeological record of the early colonial period.

Throughout, by integrating the ecological, climatic, archaeological and historical evidence, I attempt to demonstrate a chronological continuity of human response in the framework of the adaptive cycle model, where successive developments draw on the prior responses and the adaptive resilience of hunter-gatherer and pastoral society to explain changes in settlement and social organization. I may need to emphasize that this perspective does not suggest direct lineal continuity in a single cultural sequence, but of processes that were common to successive episodes of human occupation, some linked, others independent. These processes resulted in entirely new adaptations and practices, culminating during the late pre-colonial period in a combination of highly productive pastoral land-use and systematic control of wild plant resources, representing an effective and ecologically sustainable domestication of the Namib Desert landscape.

II

❧

FIRST FOOTSTEPS

The palm of our hand, as if from ancient memory, knows the perfection of shape, balance and purpose in a Pleistocene stone hand-axe. But beyond the purely sensual warmth it imparts – having lain forever baking on some desert valley floor – the tool is mute, or very nearly so. Perhaps it was not then as dry, and a brief time of rain and promise brought this loping, ever watchful early human, pressing deeper into the unknown. The hand-axe, we know, is a distillation of memory, of slowly refined dexterity, the tool a homunculus of the evolving mind. It tells us that someone passed this way, but little more than that.

The Pleistocene epoch is both the longest and the least well understood part of the Namibian archaeological sequence. It stretches from the first clear evidence of a hominin presence about one million years ago, to the end of the Last Glacial Maximum, about 12,000 years ago. This period is mainly represented by surface occurrences of stone artefacts, the age of which can only be estimated from the technique of their manufacture. Yet, this evidence helps us to understand the evolution of the archaeological landscape, and casts important light on human adaptations in response to the ebb and flow of climatic events.

In the Namib Desert, Pleistocene hominins were surely few in number, surviving where food and water were sufficient for their needs. Their range of movement was at first limited to the major drainage systems along which they were able to venture into the desert and exploit animal prey that was similarly tied to ephemeral water and grazing. Although the archaeological evidence is scanty and insecurely dated, the distribution of stone tool assemblages points to an expansion of hominin populations from more humid parts of the subcontinent, reaching in what were probably short pulses, those parts of the desert that were temporarily amenable to occupation. Then, there is an evident expansion in the range of mid-Pleistocene hominins in the desert, spreading out from the river valleys to the plains and mountains. In terms of the Holling adaptive cycle outlined in the previous chapter this growth, or expansion, was followed by a release, or Ω phase in the late Pleistocene with the occupation of sites on the inland escarpment which allowed some respite during dry periods associated with the Last Glacial Maximum commencing about 22,000 years ago. Chronological resolution of the Pleistocene sequence is relatively coarse, but it is likely that the occupation of the desert during this period was episodic and pulsed rather than continuous and that it was driven by major climatic variations. The onset of Holocene climatic amelioration about 12,000 years ago would have initiated a re-orientation, or α phase as hunter-gatherer groups began to take advantage of improved availability of food and water.

The growth, or r phase of the adaptive cycle earlier in the Pleistocene may have been accompanied by a slight population increase, but in the Namib Desert this is more clearly associated with an increase in both the geographical range of movement, and with this a greater diversity of resources that could be exploited. This would over time have led not only to an accumulating knowledge of alternative hunting and gathering opportunities, but through contact with other groups to the establishment of extended social networks. The evidence from the Namib Desert presented here shows that these two basic prerequisites of survival in an unpredictable and hyper-arid environment must have been in place almost one million years ago, if only in a rudimentary form.

In this chapter, we begin by considering in more detail the landscape characteristics described in Chapter 1. These are fundamental to an understanding of the physical processes that determine the survival and visibility of the Pleistocene evidence. Fluvial and aeolian forces contribute to the mass removal of sediments through episodic flooding in poorly defined drainage systems, and through wind erosion, the gradual deflation of unconsolidated sediments, resulting in lag deposits containing artefacts representative of long accumulation periods together on the same surface. Also important is the effect of both mobile and permanent dune cover, which generally predates the earliest archaeological evidence. Despite these limitations, there remain not only relict desert surfaces on which Pleistocene material has survived *in situ*, but a number of rock shelter sites with stratigraphically sealed occupation deposits.

The second part of this chapter deals mainly with evidence of stone tool assemblages representing a series of technological modes ranging from the simplest and earliest tool forms, to the complex reduction sequences that developed in the late Pleistocene. In some instances Pleistocene artefacts or assemblages may be linked either to tool-making traditions with known geographical distributions over the southern African region, or to characteristic tool production methods associated with well-defined moments in the sequence. The coarse resolution of the sequence based on such criteria nonetheless allows some understanding of surface artefacts as proxy evidence for the relative timing of geomorphological processes and provides some evidence of human behavioural developments during the Pleistocene.

More detailed evidence is available from the terminal Pleistocene, including the Last Glacial Maximum which peaked about 21,500 years ago and ended with the onset of warmer conditions at the start of the Holocene epoch approximately 12,000 years ago.[84] Although the evidence from the Namib Desert

---

84 Cohen & Gibbard (2019)

is limited to a small number of detailed studies, these provide valuable evidence showing the geographical extent of human settlement as well as faunal remains indicating the range of animals hunted during this period. The association with rock shelter sites at this time indicates a possible shift in behaviour, towards the use of fixed home-base sites located in complex ecotone situations which allowed a broader range of subsistence opportunities and provided relatively dependable water supplies under otherwise dry conditions. This period is also associated with the earliest examples of rock art in the Namib Desert, generally accepted as evidence for shamanic religious practice.

The Pleistocene desert

Reliable information on the Pleistocene climatic history of southern Africa is patchy and synthesis of regional patterns is therefore problematic. In the case of the Namib Desert, the present consensus is that hyper-arid conditions prevailed throughout the late Pleistocene, with changes in climate generally of low amplitude.[85] The same may be said of the Kalahari, in that the palaeoclimatic data indicate relatively slight changes over this period, a major difference being the local environmental effects of hydrological events in the Kalahari resulting from inflow of water via major river systems such as the Kavango, arising outside the region.[86]

 The poor resolution of the climatic history and the importance of local as opposed to regional phenomena, present difficulties for the regional interpretation of Pleistocene archaeological evidence. However, two events are of particular archaeological importance in this region. The Last Interglacial probably ameliorated climatic conditions in the Namib to a sufficient extent that human occupation was more widespread and sustained. And on the other hand, the extreme aridity of the Last Glacial

---

85 Ward et al. (1983); Lancaster (1984)
86 Thomas & Shaw (1991)

Maximum would have rendered much of the region inimical to human survival.

The Namib Desert is characterized by a complex array of drainage systems. Of these, only the far northern Kunene River, rising in the interior of Angola, and the Orange River in the south, which rises in the Lesotho highlands, are perennial under prevailing climatic conditions. In between are the catchments and lower reaches of numerous ephemeral river systems; those lying to the north of 23° SL occasionally debauch into the Atlantic,[87] while those further to the south terminate on the edge of the dune sea as large semi-seasonal pans. All the ephemeral rivers carry significant volumes of water after rainfall in the interior and often experience high energy flash-flooding events. Many of these drainage lines are fault-controlled and deeply incised, such that unusually heavy rainfall may exceed the capacity of the river course to discharge the volume of water it receives. This results in back-flooding and lateral inundation on either side of the river course, creating extensive impoundments and deposits of fine sediment in the lower reaches of the rivers. Ephemeral waterbodies such as these would have had an effect on the movement of both animals and early humans during the Pleistocene.

The Namibian central highlands have relatively few indications of Pleistocene occupation, partly due to the effects of sheet erosion on high angle slopes. Fluvial dynamics thus affect the survival and visibility of archaeological materials, and artefacts found in the drainage systems frequently show evidence of rounding and attrition. Rainfall events within the desert itself sometimes lead to deflection of flow from one drainage line to another, and the capture of drainage systems through watershed erosion. The continuous lowering of the desert surface within local catchments is evident from the exposure of inselberg features. The larger of these, such as the 650 km² Dâures massif, produce significant runoff from rainfall and maintain local drainage dynamics

---

87 Greenbaum et al. (2014)

with energy levels comparable to those emanating from the escarpment. Closer to the Atlantic coast, where large convective rainfall events (Fig. 2.1) are less common, extensive gravel plains form desert pavements which are resistant to erosive forces.[88] The same resistant characteristics are found in large expanses of exhumed and pedogenic calcrete and both types of surfaces, being relatively flat, often preserve *in situ* scatters of stone artefacts which are sometimes associated with evidence of quarrying for localized artefact raw materials.

Dune landscapes in the Namib Desert show a dominant northerly sand transport direction along the Atlantic coast, originating from the depositional fan deposits of the Orange River mouth. Ancient dune landscapes such as the southern Namib erg are highly stable in these major alignments, with marginal zones of mobile dunes which are also subject to the forces of opposing seasonal winds from the interior.[89] Although the sand sea effectively truncates several drainage systems, the !Khuiseb River valley remains open due to regular flooding events. Some truncated rivers also deliver small volumes of water at the coastline via percolation beneath overlying sand cover. A combination of decreasing energy in the lower reaches of desert drainage systems, and the effect of powerful long-shore drift driven by the Benguela Current, results in the northward deflection of some river mouths and the development of extensive delta deposits in a few cases. The scarcity of fresh water at the coast is an important factor limiting the distribution of past human settlement, while the occurrence of rich and complex ecosystems associated with delta and lagoon deposits served as a significant attraction throughout the history of human settlement on the Namib coast.[90]

The driving forces responsible for dune accumulation in the Kalahari are essentially the same as for the Namib: sand supply

---

88 Matmon et al. (2018); Van der Waterin & Dunai (2001)
89 Lancaster (1995)
90 Kinahan & Kinahan (2016)

Figure 2.1: A large convective storm over the central Namib Desert.

and wind velocity, although the result is a distinctly different landscape.[91] A series of palaeo-sandflow regimes have existed in the Kalahari and remnants of these remain visible today under dense vegetation, the dune alignment serving to indicate past circulation patterns.[92] Vegetation cover also exercises a strong influence on the mobility of aeolian sands,[93] and surface visibility of archaeological remains is poor in the wooded northern Kalahari region of Namibia, being mainly limited to gulley exposures, where artefacts sometimes rest on ferricrete surfaces overlain by more recent sand cover.[94]

Surface artefacts are found in the vicinity of certain terrain features: localized outcrops and inselberg features such as the Aha Hills in Namibia and the Tsodilo Hills in neighbouring Botswana, as well as smaller outcrops forming rapids in larger river systems such as the Kavango and Zambezi. Also of importance are pans, which occur in great profusion and variety throughout most of the Kalahari. Sometimes these are associated with artefact scatters which indicate their importance as temporary water sources and focal points for hunting in the Pleistocene. The age of pan features is difficult to determine, but the association of Pleistocene archaeological material may assist relative dating.[95]

A combination of the deflated gravel surfaces found in the Namib and the characteristic sand cover of the Kalahari is found in southern Namibia, where the sparse vegetation cover allows better archaeological visibility. This points to a strong association between Pleistocene occupation and localized resources – especially water – in the form of springs and ephemeral ponds. In contrast, the unconsolidated sands of northern central Namibia have poor archaeological visibility, and the near absence of archaeological material in exposed sections of erosion gullies

---

91 Lancaster (1995)
92 Thomas & Shaw (1991: 181); Lancaster (1981)
93 Deacon & Lancaster (1988)
94 Phillipson (1978)
95 Thomas & Shaw (1991)

and excavations for roadworks and sand-winning, suggests that the alluvial deposits in this region do not contain or conceal substantial artefact concentrations. However, some outcrop features flanking the drainage linking the Kunene River and the Etosha Pan basin do have extensive surface scatters of Pleistocene material.

The overall visibility of Pleistocene archaeological material in Namibia therefore reflects erosional deflation, resulting in extensive surface accumulations especially in the arid western and southern parts of the country, aided by the low density of vegetation. The converse applies in the eastern and northern parts of the country where Quaternary sand cover and relatively dense vegetation in some areas is associated with low archaeological visibility. Exceptions occur in both general situations, and these indicate that Pleistocene occupation was strongly influenced by local topographic features and the availability of water. The characteristics of mid- and late Pleistocene site distributions are examined in more detail below.

Pleistocene archaeology

The regional distribution of Mode 1 artefacts shows that Pleistocene hominins were able to survive under a wide range of conditions, including the arid and relatively resource-poor environments of south-western Africa. Mode 1 stone artefact production, involving opportunistic flaking of pebbles and other suitably sized rock fragments indicates a set of technological skills involving raw material selection and an understanding of lithic mechanical properties, to produce flakes which were efficient cutting tools suitable for butchery of large animal carcasses.[96] Because these flake tools have minimal or no retouch, their outward simplicity belies the technological expertise of their production.[97] Tool production

---

96 Toth (1985)
97 Barham & Mitchell (2008)

involved the removal of waste and of usable flakes, or *debitage*, for immediate use, as well as the more easily recognisable end products resulting from this process: hand-axes, cleavers and picks. A common and widespread technique involved a longitudinally split pebble, shaped by further removal of usable flakes from the outer surface to produce tools characteristic of Mode 1.

An elaboration of this technology in the form of bifacially worked artefacts is the identifying feature of Mode 2, associated with the production of bifacial Acheulean hand-axes. These are generally teardrop-shaped, bi-laterally symmetrical and lenticular in section, with a well-defined tip and dense, overlapping flake removal usually over the entire surface. This type of production exemplifies *façonnage*, or deliberate shaping according to an intentional design.[98] Mode 2 artefacts also show that raw materials were selected from particular outcrops and sometimes transported over considerable distances, unlike those of Mode 1. In broad terms, the contrast is between tools expediently made, used and discarded in Mode 1, and tools fashioned in Mode 2 according to a deliberate design repertoire, with the expectation of their use in potential future tasks.[99] There is, however, no clear or sudden break between the two technologies; informal pebble tools occur in Mode 2 and even later assemblages, as do the equally informal and ubiquitous *debitage* flakes that were employed for a wide range of tasks.

Evidence for the controlled use of fire by *Homo erectus* appears between 1.6 and 1.0 million years ago and is generally taken to indicate the start of important developments in the control of environment, in food preparation and in social organization.[100] In arid south-western Africa changes in stone tool technology, in subsistence and in social organization arising from these

---

98 Roche et al. (2003)
99 Wynn (1993); Jones (1994)
100 James (1989); see also Barham and Mitchell (2008: 141–4), Chazan (2017) and Wrangham (2017) for an extended discussion of the evidence.

developments would have led to more effective hunting of large game animals and greater mobility over the landscape. The evidence discussed below shows that Mode 1 tool assemblages are often, though not exclusively, confined to sites within easy reach of water, while Mode 2 artefacts show a more general distribution, a pattern that corresponds with the evidence from sites elsewhere in the region.[101] The association of Mode 1 with available water and other resources is exemplified by archaeological sites in the lower !Khuiseb River, in the lower Kunene River valley and on the Atlantic coast immediately north of the Orange River mouth (Fig. 2.2a).

Responses to extreme aridity

The lower !Khuiseb achieved its present course in the early Pleistocene, having been deflected approximately 30 km north by the advance of the southern Namib erg. The shift in the river course is associated with a new suite of deposits, commencing with the coarse Oswater gravels and followed by a succession of finer sediments, with the extended deposit of Awa-gamteb silts into the !Khuiseb Delta indicating frequent river flow both here and at other sites in the central and northern Namib Desert.[102] The former position of the river is marked by patchy exposures of the Khommabes Carbonate Member which occur as shallow basins or dolines[103] in the underlying Tertiary-age Tsondab sandstones (Figure 2.2b). These were sites of ephemeral ponding and seepages that persisted until the late Pleistocene, as evidenced by *Phragmites* reed root casts and various fossil gastropod species associated with standing water. Although the field evidence indicates that the Khommabes sediments could have been deposited during one or more humid intervals at any

---

101 Hay (1976)
102 Ward (1987: 5–31)
103 Marker (1982)

50 NAMIB

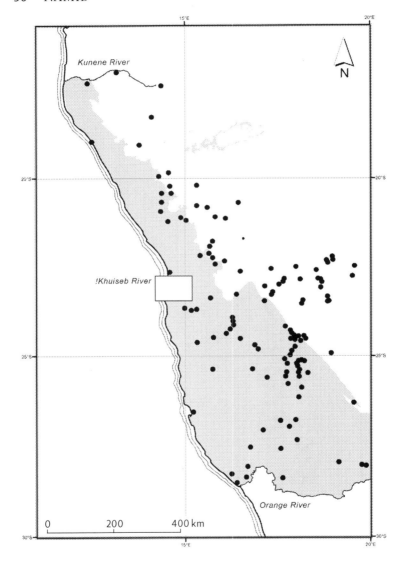

Figure 2.2a: Mid-Pleistocene archaeological site distribution in the Namib Desert. The white block indicates the lower !Khuiseb area shown in Figure 2.2b.

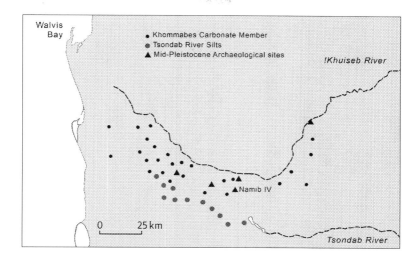

Figure 2.2b: Pleistocene sediments and associated archaeological sites in the lower !Khuiseb River

stage during the Pleistocene,[104] the archaeological evidence for mid-Pleistocene occupation is compelling.

A number of small Khommabes pan deposits have relatively dense concentrations of artefact material and fossil mammal remains which are lightly cemented into the surface. The site of Namib IV extends over 62,500 m^2, with an artefact assemblage dominated by heavy tools (75%), a core and core-chopper component (4.4%), unretouched flakes (16%), and a small number of retouched flakes (7.3%). Some of the latter are suspected to represent a subsequent occupation of the site and, indeed, the entire assemblage of stone artefacts and faunal remains probably represents a lag deposit combining successive occupation events on a common erosional surface. The heavy tools, mainly hand-axes, are typical of Mode 1, being made on pebbles; most show

---

104 Ward (1987: 37)

intensive use-damage and some have broken tips.[105] The flakes vary between 15 and 85 mm in length and about half are primary cortex-removal *debitage*, indicating that the large tools were made on the site, probably from pebbles procured nearby. The stone tools occur with the fossil remains of zebra-like equids, as well as rhinoceros and a range of medium-sized alcelaphine antelope. Most significant among the fossil remains, however, are those of the extinct elephant *Elephas recki,* which suggest a date of between 400,000 and 700,000 years.[106]

The evidence from Namib IV and a number of related sites in the same vicinity points to opportunistic hunting focused on ephemeral ponds and reedbeds. The sites do not provide detailed evidence of hunting and butchery techniques, but given the size of some prey, it is safe to assume that this involved planned and collaborative effort, possibly involving the use of fire. The heavy use-damage noted on the artefacts would be consistent with butchery of large animals, although some of the carcasses processed on the site could have been obtained by scavenging from predator kills. It is also significant that while the site assemblages include some bifaces, these typical Mode 2 artefacts tend to predominate at sites further afield, outside the major drainage lines.

Further evidence of the relationship between Mode 1 artefact assemblages and riverine environments is found in the lower Kunene River at Serra Cafema where extensive surface scatters are associated with cobble beds indicating a high energy flow regime. Until the late Pliocene the upper Kunene fed the Etosha palaeolake but was captured by headward erosion of a relatively minor desert valley and diverted to the west,[107] forming the perennial Kunene

---

105 Shackley (1980; 1985: 35–43)
106 Deacon & Lancaster (1988: 52); Owen-Smith (1992: 17) maintains a more recent extinction date of 35,000 years BP for the East African *Elephas* lineage.
107 The headwaters of the palaeo-Kunene probably extended as far as the present-day Epupa Falls (Fig. 2.3).

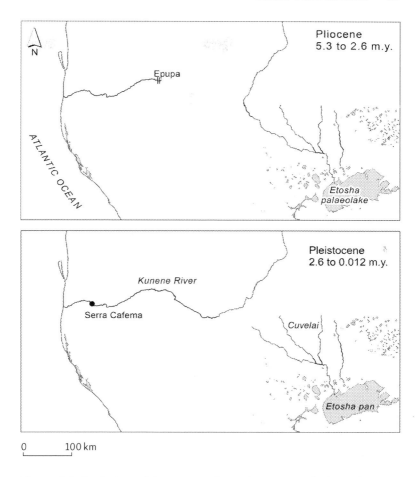

Figure 2.3: Evolution of the Kunene River drainage in the late Pliocene and early Pleistocene, and location of Serra Cafema.

drainage of today (Fig. 2.3).[108] There was probably reliable water in the vicinity of Serra Cafema throughout much of the Pleistocene and this would have provided an optimal combination of resources in an otherwise hyper-arid environment. It is also likely that the

---

108 Schneider (2004: 70); Buch (1996)

Figure 2.4: Mode 1 pebble tools from Serra Cafema on the lower Kunene River, obverse faces on right.

deeply incised valley of the lower Kunene would have presented advantageous conditions for the ambush hunting of large game. As in the case of Namib IV, the Serra Cafema artefacts appear to have been made from river cobbles in the immediate vicinity, where they were also discarded (Fig. 2.4).

There is comparable evidence of mid-Pleistocene occupation from the vicinity of the Orange River mouth, where Mode 1 assemblages, including hand-axes, cleavers and an array of unretouched flakes, are associated with a calcrete horizon which appears to form an ancient land surface capping an earlier beach level. The calcrete surface had large numbers of fossilized *Trigonephrus* gastropod shells, evidence of hyper-arid conditions similar to those of the present day.[109] It is therefore significant that the stone artefact evidence indicates that the main focus of activity was near the river mouth and up to a maximum of 30 km to the north, pointing to an association with water similar to that found in the lower !Khuiseb and Kunene Rivers. Further similarities are found in the assemblages themselves which are dominated by heavy tools (75%) and large quantities of *debitage*. Hand-axes from the Orange River sites were produced on locally procured quartzite and were generally crude and asymmetrical, with minimal trimming. Flakes ranged in size between 30 and 160 mm, with more than half (61.2%) bearing traces of cortex, indicating that these were expedient tools discarded where they were made.

Taken together, the evidence of Mode 1 sites in the Namib Desert indicates the spread of early hominins with an established stone artefact technology, probably combined with tried and tested strategies for hunting animals as large as elephant and rhinoceros, possibly with the aid of purposely set fires in habitats such as dense reedbeds. The likely presence of large predators would certainly have added the possibility of scavenging as a source of food for early hominins. The available evidence is that Mode 1 occupation focused on sites near large waterbodies, such as the ephemeral ponds in the lower !Khuiseb and Kunene, the mouth of the perennial Orange River, as well as the Atlantic shore to the north of it. The location of Mode 1 sites near water had the advantage that the water would have attracted a range of animals suitable for hunting by the techniques available at the time. If this association with water in an otherwise dry environment was integral to the survival of early hominins such as *Homo erectus*, then the concentration of mid-Pleistocene sites in the Namib Desert might be more than an accident of preservation and desert geomorphology; it could point to the optimal combination of

---

109 Corvinus (1983: 11); Pickford & Senut (1999)

resources required by mid-Pleistocene hominins exploiting a narrow ecological niche.

Mode 2 hand-axes found in the desert up to 30 km away from riverine environments suggest a more widespread use of the later Pleistocene landscape, possibly involving opportunistic and planned ambush hunting.[110] Mode 2 assemblages comprising bifacial hand-axes, cleavers and other tools are in almost every instance isolated finds and the fact that the artefacts are generally not of locally procured raw material further illustrates the mobility of Mode 2 hunters. An unusual concentration of Mode 2 artefacts at the site of Sebra exemplifies the characteristics of such assemblages and their landscape setting. The site, an open surface scatter covering almost 10,000 m^2, lies in an open valley approximately 100 km east of the present margin of the Namib Desert, between extensively outcropping Mokolian granites of the Huab Complex. The site does not appear to be stratified.

The Sebra valley-fill is of decomposed granite re-cemented as a coarse gritstone with thin interleaving calcrete layers indicating the former presence of shallow groundwater. The artefact assemblage consists predominantly of fine-grained quartzites with some meta-sedimentary rocks, none of which occur in the same vicinity. Most of the assemblage comprises utilized large core flakes but it includes 27 bifacial Acheulean hand-axes (see Fig. 2.5 for examples) and 13 mainly unifacial cleavers (see Fig. 2.6 for examples). There is a striking absence of small flaking debris and cortex removal fragments, suggesting that the artefacts were manufactured elsewhere. The presence of 12 medium-sized polyhedrals and three unifacial points showing Mode 3 prepared platform flaking indicates a subsequent occupation of the site.[111]

The Sebra hand-axes range between 88 and 258 mm in length, with a mean of 149 mm, and at their widest range between 54 and 91 mm, with a mean of 83 mm. All but one are bifacial and all but

---

110 Lieberman et al. (2009)
111 cf. Klein (2000)

Figure 2.5: Mode 2 bifacial Acheulean hand-axes from Sebra.

two are made on fine to medium-coarse quartzite. The remaining two were of fine-grained silcrete. Most of the hand-axes are entire and show a relatively uniform teardrop shape, most with convergent tips, all cortex having been removed. In all but one example there are no traces of the original flake blank and the entire surface of the artefact is covered by secondary flaking scars. Only two show a small degree of end-retouch; the assemblage includes two hand-axe tips cleanly broken at about one quarter of the original tool length. The combination of deep alternating flake scars and sinuous

Figure 2.6: Mode 2 Acheulean unifacial cleavers from Sebra.

working edges indicates the use of hard hammer reduction typical of early Mode 2 biface production.[112] The cleavers are uniformly ovate and range between 90 and 164 mm in length, with a mean of 132 mm, and at their widest range between 63 and 108 mm, with a mean of 85 mm. Half the cleavers are unifacial and some retain up to 50% cortex. Most are made on the same quartzite as the hand-axes but the cleavers also include examples of hydrothermal vein quartz and metasedimentary rocks.

Measurements of the Sebra hand-axes and cleavers summarized in Figure 2.7 show that most of the hand-axes are marginally

---

112 Barham & Mitchell (2008: 190)

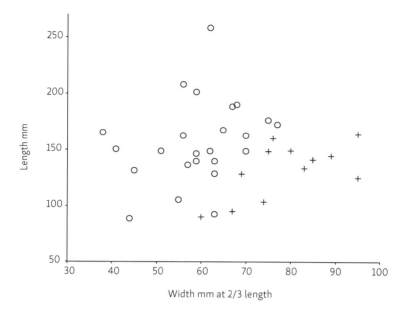

Figure 2.7: Dimensions of Mode 2 hand-axes (circles) and cleavers (crosses) at Sebra.

longer and that the cleavers are generally wider relative to their length. The size of the assemblage and the relatively uniform state of weathering shown by these artefacts and the utilized core flakes with which they are associated is suggestive. It is probable that they were accumulated through a series of visits to an isolated water source in the course of movements over a wider area which included suitable raw material outcrops up to 20 km distant, as well as other water sources. On this basis, it is estimated that the Sebra assemblage formed part of a foraging area of about 1,200 km^2 in extent.[113] Sebra differs from Mode 1 kill and butchery sites such as Namib IV, and points to a more wide-ranging occupation

---

113 This compares with the foraging areas of historical hunter-gatherer groups in similar conditions (e.g. Kelly 1983).

pattern associated with Mode 2 assemblages, which shows less dependence on riparian woodland and localized marshland environments with relatively high densities of prey species.

It is arguable that Mode 2 artefact distributions indicate a refinement of ambush hunting strategies by small groups within socially bounded territories. In this context, the formalization of artefact design evident at sites such as Sebra shows a marked contrast between informal flaking products with some indications of edge damage, and the typically symmetric form of the Mode 2 Acheulean hand-axe. The character of the Sebra assemblage shows that while many tasks would have been adequately performed using expedient flakes, time and effort was invested in hand-axe production according to what is commonly considered to have been a "mental template".[114]

There is some debate as to the possibly symbolic purpose of bifacial Acheulean hand-axes and although they show a high degree of consistency in design, it is not clear whether in the southern African context this was the result of trimming on flake blanks that already showed a natural and fortuitous balance.[115] Nonetheless, the widespread appearance of these relatively standardized tools marks a clear shift in both technology and landscape occupation patterns which also represents a social threshold in the mid- to late Pleistocene archaeological sequence in the Namib Desert and the subcontinent as a whole.[116]

Mid-Pleistocene occupation of the Namib Desert was apparently a response to climatic amelioration resulting in a pulsed, episodic western range extension of southern African hominins. Within the Namib, ephemeral west-flowing drainage systems served as linear oases, with low-gradient terminal reaches that supported areas of marshland, suitable habitat for a concentration of animal species in an otherwise hyper-arid

---

114 Soressi & Dibble (2003)
115 McNabb et al. (2004)
116 Mitchell (2002)

environment. The terminal reaches of the river valleys also brought hominin groups within range of highly nutritious and easily procured marine resources.

There is no direct evidence of hominin exploitation of marine resources on the Namib coast, but the near-coastal desert environment controlled by the cold, northward-flowing Benguela Current has a significantly higher concentration of mid-Pleistocene sites than either the tropical coast of northern Angola, or the temperate coast of the southern Cape in South Africa.[117] This occurrence of mid-Pleistocene sites may, therefore, indicate that a combination of marine and terrestrial resources supported early human populations in the Namib Desert. Detailed investigation of this possibility would however be hindered by the dynamic and highly changeable geomorphology of the coastline.[118]

It is also important to consider that hominin expansion into the Namib Desert, focusing on local resource anomalies, may not have been reversible by means of a slow contraction in the western range of a population centred in the subcontinental interior. The available evidence of mainly surface archaeological material in the Namib suggests the presence of small, localized groups. If isolated by an aridification of the upper drainage of the river systems on which they depended, these groups would probably not have survived as biologically viable populations. Occupation of the Namib during the mid-Pleistocene therefore suggests two possible scenarios: short-lived movement into the desert on a semi-seasonal expeditionary basis, or sustained expansion into the desert followed by isolation and, possibly, local extinction. Of these, the second is most likely given the distance (up to 500 km) from the interior, which would with the rapid onset of an aridity cycle quickly become as hostile to human occupation as the desert itself.

---

117 Ervedosa (1980); Barham & Mitchell (2008); Mitchell (2002)
118 Kinahan & Kinahan (2016)

Evidence from the late Pleistocene

An extended period of climatic instability set in about 450,000 years ago, characterized by successive, extended cycles of cold and warm extremes,[119] resulting in the extinction of several large mammal species including *Elephas recki*. These conditions also affected both *Homo erectus* and the descendent precursor of modern humans, *Homo helmei*, and are thought to have caused a steep numerical decline in hominin populations, with regional isolation and possible local extinction.[120] It is, however, important to note that climatic variation, and the appearance of *Homo helmei* do not neatly correlate. The transition from Mode 2 to Mode 3 was part of a fundamental shift in stone artefact technology, which saw a widespread disappearance of bifacial hand-axes between 240,000 and 280,000 years ago.[121] In this transition period *Homo sapiens* gradually emerged[122] as the evolutionary successor to *Homo heidelbergensis*, and the human presence became increasingly apparent on the late Pleistocene landscape of southern Africa.

Long cave sequences at several southern African late Pleistocene sites show significant advances in stone tool technology during this period, especially the development of composite tools in which vegetable adhesives were crucial to the mounting of retouched flakes in wooden or bone hafts,[123] and spears, which gave the advantage of greatly improved penetration and hunting

---

119 Jouzel et al. (2007)
120 Jorde et al. (2000); Ingman et al. (2000), cited in Barham & Mitchell (2008: 203)
121 Barham & Mitchell (2008: 221)
122 McBrearty (2003)
123 Barham (2013) has described the emergence of tool hafting as humankind's first "industrial revolution" by greatly increasing the utility of stone tools. However, Wadley et al. (2019) caution that some early southern African examples of organic residues resembling hafting adhesives on stone artefacts may have resulted from accidental exposure to smouldering plant material in cooking hearths.

efficiency.[124] Mode 3 tool production involved the intensive use of prepared cores, employing the Levallois technique to produce relatively standardized trapezoidal-section flakes, struck from the core and retouched by direct pressure using a fabricator of bone or wood.[125] Flakes could be broken into short sections and retouched as components to a variety of hafted tool forms, although both blade and point flakes were undoubtedly also used in the hand without retouch or mounting.[126]

Bone points thought to represent the earliest use of bow and arrow technology first appear approximately 60,000 years ago in southern Africa.[127] The development of the bow and arrow conferred significant advantages in hunting and implies an important behavioural shift from the largely communal practice of ambush hunting in the earlier Pleistocene with spears, probably using men, women and children as beaters to help drive animal prey to a point at which they could be attacked. Projectile technology enabled hunting by stealth, where the hunter might operate alone or with only a few companions.[128] We might surmise that it is at this stage that the social and economic phenomenon of the highly mobile men's hunting party emerged, along with its counterpart: exclusively female parties focusing on gathering plant foods. In the context of this rapidly evolving technology and subsistence behaviour, evidence of important cognitive advances first appears in the form of shell ornaments, the use of pigments and symbolic engravings on some artefacts.[129]

An exceptionally well-resolved component of the late Pleistocene archaeological sequence is the Last Interglacial (Marine Isotope Stage 5e), from 127,000 to 116,000 years ago, associated with a peak

---

124 Barham & Mitchell (2008: 220); Dusseldorp (2010); Lombard (2005b)
125 Eren & Lycett (2012)
126 Wurz (2002)
127 Blackwell et al. (2018); Lombard (2011), Lombard & Haidle (2012)
128 Wadley (2014)
129 Henshilwood et al. (2002); d'Errico et al. (2001, 2005)

sea-level rise of up to 8 m 125,000 years ago.[130] The southern African interior experienced warm conditions and relatively high rainfall, and in keeping with the longitudinal response of environments to climatic change in this region, the arid and semi-arid western desert biomes would have narrowed appreciably,[131] extending the range of early human populations into otherwise hostile desert and dry savanna environments. Thus, the distribution of late Pleistocene archaeological sites is found to cover large parts of the Namib Desert and the adjacent interior (Fig. 2.8a). Artefact assemblages from these sites represent a series of relatively distinct moments in the late Pleistocene sequence, marked by differences in the relative abundance of tool types and *debitage*, associated with a small number of radiometric dates from ten principal sites in south-western Namibia, of which three have revealed a stratigraphic succession from Mode 3 to Mode 4 assemblages.[132]

An undated Mode 3 assemblage from the base of the sequence at Apollo 11[133] and two further sites contain few formal tools among high numbers of standardized blade flakes, and a small number of points. Tool manufacture appears to have been carried out at the sites themselves and is accompanied by high densities of flaking debris with evidence of faceted striking platforms. The assemblage is based on raw materials found in the near vicinity of the sites, mainly quartzites. Faunal remains associated with the assemblage include the extinct Cape horse *Equus capensis* and a possible quagga *Equus* cf. *quagga*, together with a range of antelope and other species, although the most numerous prey items were rock hyrax *Procavia capensis,* a species that is still

---

130 Deacon & Wurz (2001)
131 Barham & Mitchell (2008: 202–5); Mitchell (2008)
132 Vogelsang (1998: 227) proposes a series of four Middle Stone Age "Complexes" which are here re-assigned to the modal sequence of Clark (1969) used in this book.
133 The locality of the site was traditionally known as Goachanas. Wendt (1972: 20) named the site Apollo 11 on 24th July 1969 in commemoration of the successful return of the first Moon-landing mission.

FIRST FOOTSTEPS 65

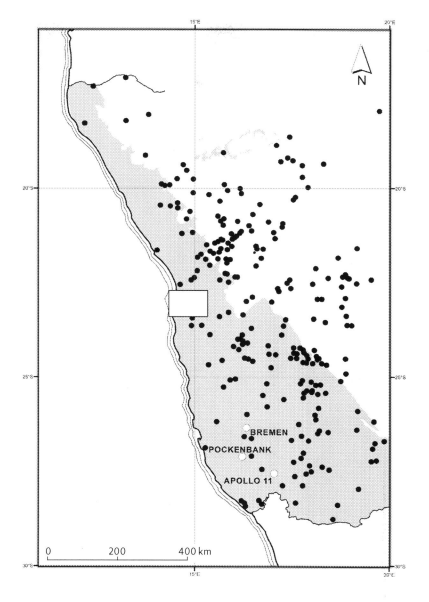

Figure 2.8a: Undifferentiated distribution of late Pleistocene archaeological sites, showing the position of important dated sites in the southern Namib Desert (white circles).

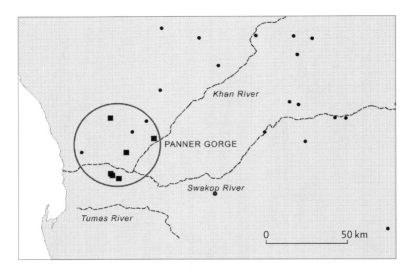

Figure 2.8b: Chert workshops and quarry sites including Panner Gorge (black squares, circled) in relation to other late Pleistocene sites (black dots) in the central Namib Desert.

abundant in the vicinity of the Apollo 11 site today.[134] A developed form of the Mode 3 assemblage from these sites is estimated to have an age of at least 49,000 years[135] and is characterized by increased flake retouch and the production of both formal points and artefacts based on blade flakes. The assemblage also contains the first evidence for the use of mastic as a mounting adhesive for composite tools.[136]

The dating of Mode 3 assemblages is highly variable, as are the artefact characteristics of the assemblages themselves.

---

134 Thackeray (1979) and Cruz-Uribe and Klein (1983), cited in Vogelsang (1998: 242)

135 Vogelsang (1998: 227); however, Lombard and Högberg (2018) consider that these assemblages refer to the Still Bay phase at the site and would therefore date to approximately 70,000 years ago; see also Vogelsang et al. (2010).

136 But see Footnote 123.

Where Mode 3 assemblages do occur in stratigraphic succession, there is little clear-cut separation and the assemblages tend to grade into each other; Mode 2 bifaces are relatively common in assemblages dominated by Mode 3 artefacts. This raises some difficulties for an understanding of technological change based largely on formal tool types, since these commonly represent less than 5% of the retouched assemblage and the comparison of assemblages may therefore rest on numerically inadequate samples.[137] These problems are most acute in surface assemblages, which – though they predominate among late Pleistocene sites in the Namib Desert and arid interior – offer no means of direct dating and may represent extended periods of accumulation.[138] However, late Pleistocene surface sites in this region can provide important insights into general occupation patterns as well as the use of resources, particularly water and lithic raw materials (Fig. 2.8b).[139]

An example is Panner Gorge (Fig. 2.9), largest of six documented chert workshop and quarry sites in the central Namib.[140] The site, covering an area of 22,000 m^2, centres on a massive vein of fine-grained to cryptocrystalline chert exposed by erosion of uraniferous leucogranites of the Rössing Formation; numerous artefacts were found to have a visible encrustation of uranium oxide on the lower surface if this had been in contact with the weathered granite.[141] The dense chert talus accumulation on the slopes beneath the outcrop averages 13.7kg/m^2, of which 21%

---

137 Barham & Mitchell (2008: 233)
138 Vogelsang (1998: 171-226); Ossendorf (2017) points out that sealed stratigraphic contexts in the Namib Desert are not free from problems of assemblage integrity commonly found on surface sites.
139 Nicoll (2010)
140 Kinahan & Kinahan (2009)
141 Preliminary x-ray spectroscopy carried out by the Colorado School of Mines found uranium at approximately 100 ppm on surfaces of chert artefacts from the site. The presence of high background radiation levels on the site excluded the application of OSL dating to determine the age of the weathered sediment beneath the artefact lag.

Figure 2.9: Panner Gorge chert quarry site viewed from the south.

is flaking and core debris. The site plan shown in Figure 2.10a shows the massive outcropping chert and the downslope extent (dashed line) of chert talus in relation to sample quadrats QD 1-3 and other localized artefact scatters (grey squares). Figure 2.10b shows the surface density of artefact distribution on one 10 x 10 m sample quadrat (QD 1).

A detailed analysis of three 100 m² quadrats yielded a total of 272 cores, mainly flattened polyhedrals with a mean thickness to diameter ratio of 0.58. Evidence of multiple quarrying and artefact manufacture episodes is evident from the presence of at least fifty small Mode 2 bifaces; these have a mean length of 79.0 mm and a mean length to maximum width ratio of 0.71. Mode 3 denticulate points and blades (see Fig. 2.11 for examples) were also present, including more than 45 blade flakes with lateral retouch and use damage, and 27 blades with terminal scraper retouch. Unretouched blade flakes, of which 116 were found, showed a high degree of uniformity, with a mean length

FIRST FOOTSTEPS 69

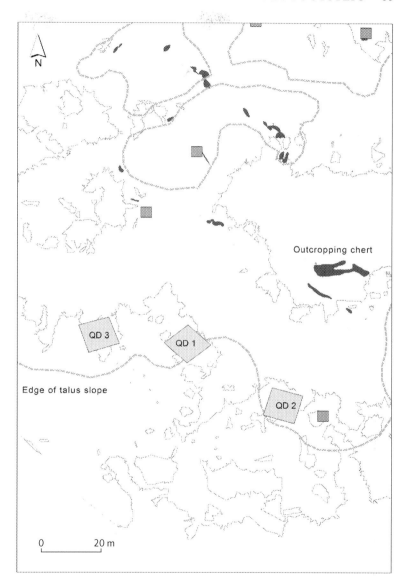

Figure 2.10a: Late Pleistocene quarry site at Panner Gorge, showing massive outcropping chert and the downslope extent (dashed line) of chert talus in relation to sample quadrats QD 1-3 and other localized artefact scatters (grey squares).

70 NAMIB

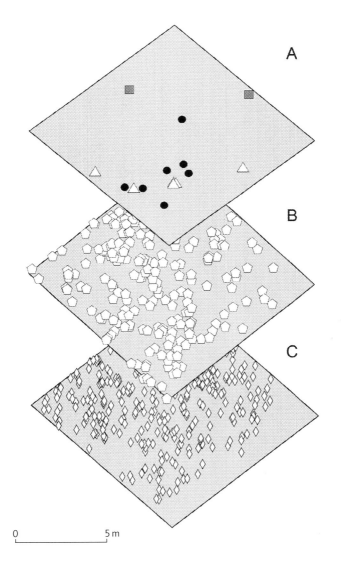

Figure 2.10b: Mode 3 artefact assemblage components from Panner Gorge quarry site (QD1). A: hammerstones (grey squares), bifaces (black circles), points (triangles); B: cores; C: utilized flakes.

FIRST FOOTSTEPS 71

Figure 2.11: Mode 3 chert assemblage from Panner Gorge.

and thickness of 56.9 mm and 10.5 mm, respectively.[142] Among the artefacts made on blades and points were several examples of pressure-flaking retouch typical of Mode 4.

The Panner Gorge site served as an important source of high quality raw material over an extended period during the late Pleistocene, and although episodes of erosion occurred, the artefact scatters show a degree of apparent integrity: bifaces, for example, are clustered and spatially associated with hammerstones that were probably involved in their production, and the distribution of retouched blades and points is demonstrably non-random. Very dense scatters forming stable and enduring pavement layers can provide useful clues to Pleistocene behaviour. At Panner Gorge, the site slope has a gradient of 1:10, yet the distribution of cores, which are rounded and therefore more likely to roll than other artefacts, shows no correlation between roundedness and position: instead of migrating to the foot of the slope, the cores are locked in place by the dense chert debris, irrespective of shape.

At another chert workshop site in the same area, flaking debris, together with the parent core and hammerstone were documented *in situ*,[143] integral to a relic erosion surface of late Pliocene age.[144] Thus, the particular setting and characteristics of surface sites may occasionally help to preserve ancient evidence of human activity in the form of working areas that are difficult to observe in the stratified late Pleistocene occupation deposits that have been studied in this region. The selective use of chert, which in the central Namib Desert is only available from a small number of localized sources, adds a further dimension to the relationship between artefact manufacture and raw materials in the late Pleistocene. Whereas the expedient use of mainly river cobbles at Mode 1 sites is succeeded by the movement of finished Mode 2

---

[142] It is conceivable that the Mode 3 assemblage at Panner Gorge is of similar age to the Still Bay phase dating to approximately 70,000 years ago at Apollo 11; see Lombard and Högberg (2018) and Vogelsang et al. (2010).
[143] Kinahan (2010b)
[144] Van der Waterin & Dunai (2001)

artefacts from raw material sources to the sites at which they were used, Mode 3 chert artefacts were manufactured both at quarry sites and from unprocessed raw material taken to encampment sites. The use of chert from known sources on this landscape also suggests that Mode 3 assemblages were implicated in foraging activities covering a minimum extent of about 4,000 km².

In the period between 25,500 and somewhat beyond 40,000 years ago, the southern Namib sites are associated with the appearance of a distinct tool assemblage comprising backed segments and small numbers of blade flakes, preferentially made on fine-grained siliceous raw materials. These are characteristic of the Howiesonspoort Industry, a regionally widespread component of the late Pleistocene in southern Africa, which was previously considered to represent the transition between Mode 3 and Mode 4–5 tool technologies.[145] At Apollo 11 (Fig. 2.12), the Howiesonspoort assemblage is distinguishable from assemblages with characteristic pressure flaking assigned to the Still Bay Industry,[146] in keeping with a general hypothesis that these represent evidence of technological diffusion from areas of innovation elsewhere in the southern African region.[147] In the southern Namib, as at several other southern African sites,[148] these assemblages are superseded by a continuation of Mode 3 in the form of a relatively unstandardized blade assemblage, with abundant *debitage*, mainly in hydrothermal vein quartz, marking the transition to Mode 4 and 5 assemblages of the terminal Pleistocene and early Holocene.[149]

The upper horizons of the Apollo 11 archaeological deposit have relatively poor stratigraphic definition and the excavation there was conducted on the basis of arbitrarily defined spits of between 5 and 20 cm, later combined or separated on the basis

---

145 Lombard (2005a); Guérin et al. (2013); McCall & Thomas (2012); Schmidt et al. (2016)
146 Vogelsang et al. (2010)
147 Wadley (2015); Bousman & Brink (2018)
148 Barham & Mitchell (2008); Lombard & Högberg (2018)
149 Chase (2010)

Figure 2.12: Physical setting of Apollo 11; the site is in the middle distance overlooking the streambed from the base of the cliff on the left.

of radiometric dating.[150] The surface layer of the site dates to within the last millennium and overlies a 0.75 m deep occupation accumulation of mid-Holocene to recent date, associated with a diverse microlithic assemblage comprising convex scrapers and scraper-like artefacts, as well as crescents, terminally-retouched tools, borers and *outils écaillés* typical of Mode 5 in the Namib and elsewhere in southern Africa.[151]

Directly beneath the Holocene component of the deposit, a further occupation layer between 0.3 and 0.6 m thick yielded

---

150 Wendt (1972: 6–7)
151 Deacon (1984); Mitchell (2002)

relatively few stone artefacts, but well preserved organic remains, as well as ostrich eggshell beads, fragments of marine shell and pigments. These deposits at the interface of the terminal Pleistocene and Holocene occupation of the site, initially dated to between 10,000 and 14,350 years ago,[152] were associated with seven rock fragments, or plaquettes, four bearing discernible paintings in black, white and various shades of ochre pigment, and representing the earliest dated figurative rock art in Africa.[153] Subsequent research found that the archaeological context of the painted plaquettes was older than previously believed and an inferred revised dating of approximately 30,000 years is now generally accepted.[154]

Among the paintings from Apollo 11 are a supposed feline figure (Fig. 2.13), and possible depictions of a zebra *Equus zebra*, a black rhinoceros *Diceros bicornis*, and a springbuck *Antidorcas marsupialis*, in each instance a single animal figure on a plaquette, in size no larger than the human hand. The plaquettes are not spalls from the roof of the cave and so represent portable pieces, or *art mobilier*. The subject matter of the paintings is uncertain, but not because they are crude and therefore indecipherable; instead, their execution appears deliberately non-naturalistic and seems to combine elements of different species, and to exaggerate the features of others. This is most noticeable in the figure described initially as human,[155] having plainly visible feet and well-defined calves. The same figure was later recognized as a composite of a feline predator, or *raubtier* (Gr.), apparently with antelope horns, when re-fitted with a second fragment of the same plaquette.[156] This combination of animal and human

---

[152] Wendt (1972: 21) explains that the painted plaquettes were not found in direct association with the samples used to date the excavation spit from which they were recovered. It is also important to note that the paintings, while they do contain microscopic amounts of carbon, have not been directly dated.
[153] Wendt (1975, 1976)
[154] Jacobs et al. (2008); Vogelsang et al. (2010); Rifkin et al. (2015)
[155] Wendt (1972: 21 and Plate 11c)
[156] Wendt (1974)

Figure 2.13: Refitted plaquette from Apollo 11 showing possible feline combined with human figure; charcoal pigment on quartzitic schist, length 12 cm. Based on image supplied by R. Rifkin, of the original housed in the National Museum of Namibia, Windhoek.

characteristics is the basis of an argument that the Apollo 11 paintings represent an early manifestation of the shamanic rock art tradition that predominated among southern African Holocene hunter-gatherers.[157]

The occupation of Apollo 11 during the Last Glacial Maximum is not an isolated phenomenon: a further seven sites with evidence of occupation between 22,000 and 10,000 years ago have been investigated along the eastern edges of the Namib Desert, as far

---

157 Lewis-Williams (1984); see also Rifkin et al. (2015).

north as the vicinity of the Kunene River valley.[158] Several of these rock shelter sites are in environmental locations with dependable water supplies and varied resources, including animal species with resident rather than seasonally migratory populations. At sites with evidence of sustained occupation such as Apollo 11, these species would have included klipspringer *Oreotragus oreotragus*, steenbuck *Raphiceros campestris*, rock hyrax *Procavia capensis* and hare, both *Lepus* sp. and *Pronolagus* sp., among other animals present at the time of earlier Pleistocene occupation.[159] At the site of Oruwanje these species were also available, along with small antelope and leopard tortoise *Geochelone pardalis*.[160] These and other sites in optimal locations such as at the Tsodilo Hills in the north-eastern Kalahari, may have served as refugia under conditions of low rainfall and reduced resources during the Last Glacial Maximum.

Considering the Namib Desert Pleistocene record as a whole, it appears that initial hominin occupation was to a large extent tethered to water resources and depended on hunting strategies that were able to maximize the dependence of large game on the availability of water in an otherwise hyper-arid environment. The combination of factors, including the evidence of large game, suggests that mid-Pleistocene hunters with Mode 1 technology employed ambush techniques, probably assisted by fire. The wider landscape distribution of Mode 2 artefacts does not necessarily suggest a different hunting strategy, although it does indicate greater mobility. Mode 3 technology involved a more diverse toolkit including hafted spears, suggesting that ambush hunting continued to be the dominant strategy, but the association with rock shelter occupation could indicate a shift in social organization, ultimately towards ritual practice and stable groups by the Last Glacial Maximum.

---

158 Albrecht et al. (2001); Breunig (2003); Freundlich et al. (1980); Vogelsang & Eichhorn (2011); Vogel & Visser (1981)
159 Vogelsang (1998: 242–4, Table 21)
160 Albrecht et al. (2001: 13–5, Table 3)

Pleistocene hominin populations appear to have expanded into the Namib Desert and the adjacent interior in a series of irregular pulses, the relatively sparse evidence of Mode 1 and 2 artefact scatters suggesting that these were probably widely spaced and of short duration. There is insufficient chronological evidence to estimate the likely timing of these events, although the relatively high density of Mode 3 surface scatters – even allowing for their younger age and higher visibility – may indicate a more sophisticated adaptation to desert conditions and a consequently higher tolerance to climatic instability. There does appear to be a more systematic use of the landscape in the late Pleistocene and large, dense artefact scatters could indicate more intensive occupation. If occupation was fundamentally determined by climatic conditions it would follow that events such as the Last Interglacial were opportunities for more sustained and widespread occupation, interrupted by periods of hyper-aridity.

The coarse scale of mid- to late Pleistocene dating and site distribution in relation to broad climatic variation is insufficient to reveal detailed patterns of landscape use beyond a reliance on specific localities with available water and some evident preferences for certain sources of lithic raw material. The evidence is not as yet sufficient to reconstruct movements in response to short-term variations in resource availability or the degree of social cohesion this might have entailed. It is therefore not possible to know from the available evidence whether early hunter-gatherer groups maintained particular territories and controlled access to limited resources of food and water within these. However, the nature of the desert environment would have required flexible and opportunistic strategies of survival and it is reasonable to expect that this included some form of social network which permitted sustained occupation of suitable sites as refugia during extended dry periods.

Pulses of occupation in the late Pleistocene are believed to have links to large subcontinental demographic responses, as indicated by systematic comparison of well dated artefact assemblages.[161] More sustained occupation during the Last Glacial Maximum at Apollo 11 in particular, suggests a shift towards the use of refugium sites with reliable water and other resources within a relatively small area. The ability to survive within the ecotone of contiguous and overlapping biota on the edge of the Namib Desert is in itself evidence of an increasingly advanced understanding of environmental conditions, including most importantly the consequences of inter-annual variation in temperature and rainfall.

Refugia may have been geographically isolated but hunter-gatherer groups living at these sites would have needed to move elsewhere if their resources of food were exhausted. At the same time, viable refugium sites would have been relatively uncommon and it is therefore likely that periods of climatic adversity saw intensified social interaction, both in the form of increased competition and in cooperation between local groups. Certainly, climatic instability in the late Pleistocene suggests a continuously shifting balance between human ingenuity and the biological thresholds of tolerance for extreme aridity, a theme to be pursued in the next chapter.

---

161 Jacobs et al. (2008); Schmidt et al. (2016)

III

TIME'S ARROW

If there is a threshold of tolerance for climatic adversity, such as the extreme aridity that gripped southern Africa at the end of the Pleistocene, humankind has always evaded its worst consequences. This is because over time, our ceaseless experimentation and curiosity nurtured the one resource that never failed: memory, or accumulated, shared and refined human experience. The lack of certainty in the world could be met with imagination and invention, one innovation leading to another, all drawing from the well of history. In this way, the arrow we loosed from the bow embodied an intuitive physics of prediction, and our religious beliefs the metaphysics of causation.

Archaeological evidence for the expansion of southern African hunter-gatherer populations at the beginning of the Holocene includes large numbers of rock shelter sites with stratified occupation deposits which have yielded both stone tool assemblages and well-preserved organic materials. Bone, wooden and leather artefacts form part of an increasing range of material culture items accompanied by food remains reflecting the diversity of plant and animal resources on which hunter-gatherers depended. Many of the sites are also associated with rock art, providing a body of further evidence for a florescence of complex ritual practices during the last ten millennia.

Early Holocene hunter-gatherers in some parts of the subcontinent responded to climatic variation by adopting patterns of movement to maximize exploitation of seasonally available resources (Fig. 3.1). Conditions in the Namib Desert were less predictable and required more opportunistic responses to episodic and shifting patterns of rainfall. Hunter-gatherer groups were able to penetrate remote parts of the desert to exploit short-lived concentrations of migratory antelope and a limited range of wild plants. During the first half of the Holocene hunting techniques became more specialized and the use of inland escarpment locations during dry periods intensified with the appearance of major rock art sites indicating an increasing reliance on ritual sanctions in the maintenance of community relations.

Figure 3.1: Mid-Holocene hunting camp in the Namib Desert with anchor stones of a shelter oriented away from the prevailing south-westerly wind.

Relatively moist conditions during the early Holocene probably enabled a growth, or *r* phase in the adaptive cycle leading to an equilibrial, or *K* phase as expansion was curtailed by the onset of mid-Holocene aridification. Increasing aridity in the mid-Holocene is associated with the use of primary resource sites as aggregation[162] centres on the eastern escarpment of the desert. It is likely that a rapid onset of aridity in the desert would have placed considerable stress on hunter-gatherer groups and that equilibrial dynamics tipped eventually towards a release or Ω phase in the adaptive cycle. The sustainability of the *K* phase would be strongly influenced by stability or otherwise of climatic conditions and the adaptability of hunter-gatherer social and technological organization.

A dynamic equilibrium between early Holocene hunter-gatherers and the desert environment depended on access to highly variable food and water resources. This imposed a number of fundamental conditions, most importantly mobility, social access and the need for a detailed knowledge of the desert terrain. Thus, Namib hunter-gatherers would have moved back and forth through a socially ordered landscape of shifting resource opportunities. During the early Holocene, hunting technology grew in sophistication and in its specialized focus on particular animal species. Timing of animal movements and the availability of plant foods introduced a measure of regularity. Social and ritual sanctions were also necessary to maintain an equilibrium that was not entirely ecological in nature,[163] for in these circumstances human interaction with the desert environment was mediated by a complex ideology based on supernatural causality and egalitarian values of cooperation and sharing.

---

162 Aggregation and dispersal as settlement components in the archaeological record of southern Africa (see Wadley 1987, 1992) represent the specifically social approximation of the ecological alternation between primary and secondary resource sites subject to density dependent and density independent consumer and resource dynamics as discussed in this book.
163 cf. Fath et al. (2015)

This chapter considers the adaptive response of hunter-gatherers to climatic amelioration following the Last Glacial Maximum. Their α phase re-organization and r phase expansion through the Namib Desert established a pattern of occupation tied to shifting availability of food and water. Favourable conditions persisted until the end of the mid-Holocene Optimum, a period of higher rainfall in the desert ending approximately 6,000 years ago. Thereafter, increasing aridity and climatic instability set in over much of the southern African interior, and in large parts of the Namib Desert this prompted a major shift in population distribution, the first in a series of fundamental adaptive changes during the last 6,000 years. In the first part of this chapter we review the Holocene palaeoclimatic record which incorporates a wide range of geoarchives from sediment series, sea-level data, pollen records and evidence of temperature variation from oxygen isotope data. These records indicate the geographical extent of climatic amelioration and of subsequent aridity in the Namib Desert.

The second part of this chapter discusses the archaeological evidence of early Holocene hunter-gatherers in the Namib Desert, characterized by Mode 5[164] microlithic stone tool assemblages including projectile points and barbs such as would be used in composite arrows, as well as a range of larger backed microliths, borers and scrapers. The assemblages are associated with the remains of diverse animal species ranging from medium and large antelope to smaller species such as hyrax and hare that were probably caught using snares. The distribution and dating of early Holocene archaeological sites in the Namib Desert suggests an occupation strategy with two alternate states: one based on localities with reliable water and food resources, and another based on remote ephemeral water sources that were accessible for short periods following rainfall events.

In the mountainous eastern escarpment of the desert the Namib and Succulent Karoo form an overlapping ecotone

---

[164] See Chapter 1, Table 1.1

environment associated with weak but generally reliable springs. These localities served as primary sites that could sustain occupation during prolonged dry periods. Because food resources rather than water limited the duration of residence, occupation was in ecological terms *density dependent*. Secondary sites allowed dispersal to remote parts of the desert when, following occasional rainfall events, ephemeral food resources became available. Occupation of these sites was *density independent* because rainwater ponds were widely scattered and short-lived, and hunter-gatherer groups would be unable to remain long enough to exhaust the available food resources. This alternating consumer and resource relationship first appeared during the early Holocene and provides a general framework for the human ecology of the Namib Desert.[165]

Although the distribution of early Holocene sites in southern Africa is associated with an abundance of rock art, detailed links between the rock art and archaeological occupation are difficult to establish. In the Namib Desert rock art is widespread but relatively scarce at early Holocene sites, suggesting that this component of ritual life among hunter-gatherer communities was as yet not well developed. The third part of this chapter presents a general overview of the existing consensus on the interpretation of the rock art as an introduction to more detailed discussion of rock art in Chapters 4 and 5 where the evidence from the Namib Desert reveals a series of fundamental shifts in ritual practice that were essential to the development of new social practices and more sophisticated adaptations to environmental uncertainty.

The Holocene desert

Episodic weakening of the high-pressure cell along the Atlantic coast by equatorial Benguela Southern Oscillation (BSO) events[166] allows convective storm systems associated with the movement

---

165 Kinahan (2005); Illius & O'Connor (1999)
166 Nicholson & Entekhabi (1986)

of the Congo Air Boundary to penetrate the Namib Desert occasionally from the north and north-east, bringing scattered rainfall, mainly in the central and northern parts of the desert. Although the southern Namib lies on the margins of the winter rainfall zone, it is also affected by these events,[167] receiving rainfall in both summer and winter.[168] Increased rainfall, in terms of both quantity and distribution would have had a marked effect on the desert ecosystem.[169] It is thought that humid phases when they occurred in the past, were a consequence of sustained variation in these conditions,[170] bringing increased rainfall over the whole extent of the Namib.

Palaeoenvironmental geoarchives providing climate proxy evidence for the Namib Desert during the Holocene are summarized in Table 3.1 and the distribution of the sites from which these data are derived is shown in Figure 3.2. Terrestrial and marine geoarchives provide evidence of warm/moist conditions between approximately 8,000 and 5,000 years ago, and predominantly cool/dry conditions thereafter. Detailed comparison of these studies does not yield a precise delineation of optimal conditions during the mid-Holocene, due to factors affecting the precision of dating[171] and differences in terrestrial and marine environmental response times.[172] However, the available data show both a broadly synchronous Holocene environmental signal, and a general trend towards late Holocene aridification in both rainfall indicators and the ecosystem responses that would have affected human resources.

Pollen evidence shows an increase in desert grass taxa between 6,300 and 4,800 years ago, suggestive of episodic desert responses

---

167 Lancaster (1996: 218); Lee-Thorp et al. (2001)
168 Mendelsohn et al. (2002)
169 Noy-Meir (1973); Seely & Louw (1980)
170 Eitel (2005)
171 Jull et al. (2013); Wright (2017)
172 e.g. Cowling et al. (1997); Goudie (1996); Pickett et al. (1989)

TIME'S ARROW 87

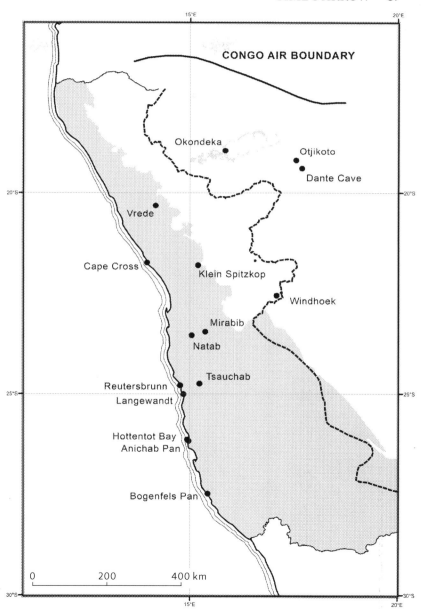

Figure 3.2: The distribution of Holocene palaeoclimate geoarchives referred to in Table 3.1. The dashed line indicates the watershed for westward-flowing drainage into the Namib Desert.

to rainfall,[173] and is generally corroborated by other research in the Namib environment. For example, evidence from hyrax middens indicates maximum Holocene humidity 8,200 years ago, and identifies two markedly arid events thereafter.[174] A series of silt accumulations in the lower !Khuiseb valley date to between 8,300 and 4,300 years ago,[175] suggesting episodic flooding of the river as a result of rainfall along the interior watershed, and not necessarily in the desert itself. This is corroborated by indications of flooding in the Tsauchab River 7,000 years ago[176] which provide further evidence of moist conditions in the early Holocene. Improved conditions between 7,000 and 6,000 years ago are also evidenced by changed ratios of rodent prey species in owl pellets at Mirabib.[177]

The effect of higher rainfall is apparent in the adjacent interior, beyond the desert margins, with an expansion of dry woodland vegetation between 6,300 and 4,800 years ago.[178] This is matched by pollen evidence from karst cave systems at Otjikoto in north-eastern Namibia indicating relatively moist conditions between 7,000 and 6,000 years ago, followed by dry conditions after 3,500. Pollen representing flora associated with springs at Windhoek in the central highlands of the country points to increased artesian flow between 7,000 and 6,000 years ago, and the onset of dry conditions after 3,500 years ago.[179] Data from strandlines of the endoreic Etosha basin in northern Namibia are in general agreement with these results and show a series of four discrete pulses of moist conditions, with the first between 7,000 and 5,000 years ago.[180] Speleothem

---

173 Gil-Romera et al. (2006)
174 Chase et al. (2009)
175 Vogel (1989)
176 Brook et al. (2006)
177 Brain & Brain (1977)
178 Shi et al. (2000: 76)
179 Scott et al. (1991)
180 Brook et al. (2007)

data from northern Namibia indicate a gradual aridification in the last 4,600 years.[181]

Holocene fluctuations in temperature and humidity are relatively small in comparison with those of the Late Pleistocene.[182] Nonetheless, fluctuations observed in marine data generally agree with changes in the terrestrial record and offer some confirmation of the link between conditions associated with the Benguela Current and rainfall patterns over the Namib Desert and interior. For example, a rapid deposition of offshore clays between 6,000 and 5,000 years ago[183] suggests increased fluvial activity in the interior drainage systems of the Namib Desert. Evidence of lower sea surface temperatures is associated with dry conditions during the same period,[184] while higher sea surface temperatures are associated with increased rainfall in this region.[185]

Direct dating and measurement of Holocene sea-level changes on the Namib coast is available from a small number of sites. At Bogenfels Pan, a mid-Holocene highstand of 3 m above present mean sea-level (amsl) occurred between 7,300 and 6,500 years ago, followed by further eustatic fluctuations around a mean of approximately 1 m amsl, becoming static at present sea-level by 4,200 years ago.[186] Comparative measurements at Anichab (Hottentot Bay) indicate a highstand at between 7,000 and 6,300 years ago, and a return to present sea-level by 5,300 years ago.[187] Other measurements at Hottentot Bay indicate a highstand of 2.1 m amsl at 6,300 years ago and a return to present sea-level by 5,600 years ago.[188] At both Bogenfels and Hottentot Bay, the mid-Holocene marine transgression is associated with evidence of

---

181 Sletten et al. (2013)
182 Deacon & Lancaster (1988: 157)
183 Gingele (1996)
184 Kirst et al. (1999)
185 Nicholson & Entekhabi (1986)
186 Compton (2006)
187 Compton (2007)
188 Kinahan & Kinahan (2009); see radiocarbon dates in Figure 3.12.

short-lived colonization by tropical shellfish species presumed to be associated with a southward penetration by the warm Angola Current at this time.[189]

Table 3.1: Terrestrial and marine geoarchives for the last 10,000 years in the Namib Desert, with inferred warm/moist and cool/dry climatic conditions.

Geoarchive	Locality (see Fig. 3.2)	Source	WARM/ MOIST	COOL/ DRY
TERRESTRIAL	Otjikoto	pollen	7,000–6,000	3,500
	Windhoek	pollen	7,000–6,000	3,500
	Vrede	pollen	6,300–4,800	n.d.
	Okondeka	lake-shore	7,000–5,000	n.d.
	!Khuiseb River	river silt	8,300–4,300	n.d.
	Tsauchab	river silt	7,000	n.d.
	Dante Cave	speleothem	n.d.	4,600
	Mirabib	owl pellets	7,000–6,000	n.d.
	Spitzkoppe	hyraceum	8,200	4,800–2,700
MARINE	offshore	phytoplankton	n.d.	4,000
	Bogenfels	beach level	7,300–6,500	4,200
	Hottentot Bay	beach level	6,300	5,600
	Anichab	beach level	7,000–6,300	5,300
	offshore	sediments	6,000–5,000	n.d.
	offshore	sediments	7,000	4,500
	Cape Cross	shell	n.d.	4,800
	Langewandt	shell	7,600	n.d.
	Reutersbrunn	shell	6,700	n.d.

Inferred dating in years before present

---

189 Compton (2006, 2007)

Among the shellfish associated with high beach levels at Bogenfels and Hottentot Bay, the mollusc *Lutraria lutraria*, and the bivalve *Solan capensis*, do not occur on the Namib coast under normal Benguela Current conditions.[190] Similarly, fragments of oyster (probably *Saccostrea* spp.), which also do not occur under present conditions, were dated to 7,600 years ago at Langewandt, and 6,700 years ago at Reutersbrunn,[191] both associated with relic beach deposits. At Cape Cross, *Dosinia hepatica* beds are dated to 4,800 years ago;[192] their presence in a normally hyper-saline lagoon deposit suggests that rainfall over the desert may have reached the lagoon through flash floods which would have lowered its salinity to within the limits of tolerance for this species.[193] The array of shellfish species associated with mid-Holocene sea-level fluctuations therefore indicates warmer ocean conditions as well as tropical rainfall events in the Namib Desert and the interior.

In summary, relatively moist conditions prevailed over the Namib Desert and surrounding region in the early to mid-Holocene, with peak humidity at about 8,000 years ago.[194] Indications of higher than present rainfall levels are shown by a range of geoarchives over the ensuing two millennia.[195] This climatic amelioration coincides with a mid-Holocene sea-level highstand between 6,000 and 8,000 years ago.[196] The return to present sea-levels after 5,000 years ago coincides with widespread evidence of increasing aridity in the Namib Desert and interior.[197] This evidence points to anomalously high ocean temperatures, resembling a Benguela Niño Event,[198] leading to a weakening of

---

190 Branch & Branch (1981)
191 Vogel & Visser (1981)
192 Kinahan (2015)
193 cf. Branch & Branch (1981)
194 Chase et al. (2009)
195 Deacon & Lancaster (1988)
196 cf. Compton (2006)
197 e.g. Scott et al. (1991)
198 Kirst et al. (1999); Shannon et al. (1986); West et al. (2004)

the Angola-Benguela Front (normally located at approximately 16° south latitude) in the mid-Holocene.

The southward extension of the Angola Current as far as 25° south latitude[199] reduced the influence of the Benguela Current, allowing the westward penetration into the Namib Desert of summer rainfall events associated with the ICTZ.[200] Consequently, while conditions in the Namib Desert may have remained relatively dry, the desert itself narrowed appreciably with the westward advance of the 200 mm mean annual rainfall isohyet.[201] In considering the effects of higher than normal rainfall in a water-limited, hyper-arid environment, it is important to note that this would have been accompanied by a lower coefficient of variation in rainfall and a higher level of biotic productivity,[202] with the potential to improve conditions for human survival.[203]

Shifts in circulation patterns associated with the mid-Holocene Optimum and with late Holocene aridification are presented in Figure 3.3 which shows a marked westward advance of the 200 mm and 400 mm rainfall isohyets.[204] The subsequent weakening of the Angola Current resulted in the restoration of the Benguela high pressure regime and the north-eastward retreat of the 200 mm and 400 mm isohyets. The relationship between this climatic variation and the dating and distribution of Holocene archaeological sites is considered below.

Human mobility in the Holocene

The Namib Desert contains a large number of Holocene archaeological sites, although their distribution is patchy and many are surface scatters or isolated rock art sites which remain undated. Relatively few stratified occupation deposits have been investigated, thus limiting the possibilities for a chronologically

---

199 Kirst et al. (1999); Stuut (2001)
200 Tyson (1986)
201 Eitel (2005: Fig 4.2)
202 cf. Louw & Seely (1982); Noy-Meir (1973)
203 Gluckman et al. (2005)
204 Following Eitel (2005)

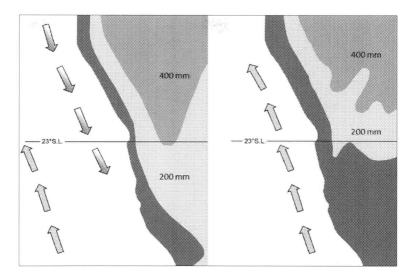

Figure 3.3: Mid-Holocene (left) southward intrusion of the Angola Current (shaded grey arrows) to approximately 25° south latitude, with Benguela Current (solid grey arrows) displaced to the west. Late Holocene (right) with Benguela Current in normal alignment and showing variation in the 400 mm and 200 mm isohyets. Map information from Kirst et al. (1999); Mendelsohn et al. (2002) and Eitel (2005)

controlled reconstruction of the Holocene sequence. A tentative sequence based on excavation results that are available does, however, allow an evaluation of the archaeological record. Figure 3.4 presents a simplified distribution of Holocene archaeological sites and radiocarbon dates over the geographical extent of the Namib Desert.

A set of 250 archaeological radiocarbon dates from the Namib Desert forms the basis of the Holocene sequence presented here. The conventional and calibrated radiocarbon values, with 2 Sigma ranges (95.4% probability) and calculated median ages, are published elsewhere.[205] Of the dates, 189 (75%) are from

---

205 See Kinahan (2018b)

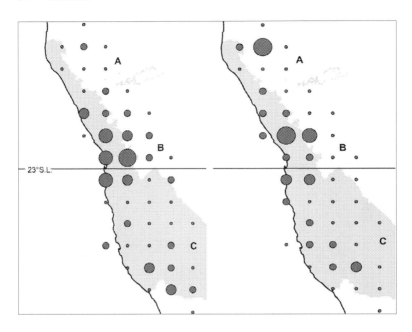

Figure 3.4: The distribution by degree square of archaeological sites (left) and Holocene radiocarbon dates (right), showing the relative concentration of sites in the northern (A), central (B) and southern (C) Namib Desert, and the relative numbers of radiocarbon dates from the same areas. The maps are based on data from the Namib Desert Archaeological Survey (n sites = 3,194), and a cumulative record of Holocene radiocarbon dates (Kinahan 2018b). The map symbols represent Jenks natural break values for numbers of archaeological sites: 21, 59, 176, 343, 904; and for numbers of radiocarbon dates 2, 7, 12, 51, 84.

24 stratified rock shelter contexts, with some sites having up to 30 radiocarbon dates. The remaining dates are from open sites (including shell middens), burials and surface finds. The samples were predominantly charcoal, with some dates based on unburnt plant material, bone, bat guano, and, in a few cases, ostrich eggshell. Most are legacy dates based on conventional

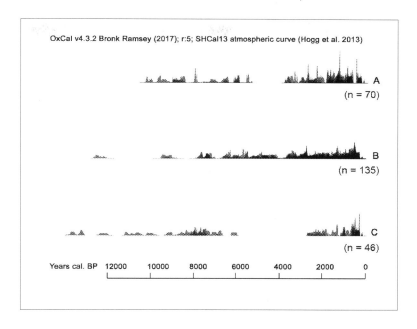

Figure 3.5: Summed probabilities for calibrated Holocene terrestrial archaeological radiocarbon dates from the northern (A), central (B) and southern (C) Namib Desert.

radiocarbon rather than AMS analysis. The combined probability distributions of the dates are presented as three zones in Figure 3.5, northern (A), central (B) and southern (C) Namib Desert.[206] The main focus of research in the northern zone (A) is a series of rock shelters situated on the outer margins of the desert, with evidence of occupation over almost the whole span of the Holocene sequence, initially as a series of discrete pulses, followed by a hiatus between 3,800 and 5,300 years ago.[207] In the central zone (B), Holocene occupation is initially sporadic,

---

[206] Williams (2012) has drawn attention to analytical weaknesses in the method of summed probability distributions.
[207] Vogelsang & Eichhorn (2011)

with strong clustering around granitic inselbergs after the onset of late Holocene aridification from 5,000 years ago.[208] The dating evidence indicates a relative continuity of occupation at these sites, in contrast to the pattern in the southern zone (C), where mid-Holocene occupation is associated with isolated sites in a highly dispersed distribution which is interrupted by the onset of late Holocene aridification.[209] There is a strong radiocarbon signal in all three areas during the last three millennia.[210]

Periodic dry episodes during the early Holocene would have restricted access to some desert sites, just as occasional rainfall in remote parts of the desert may have allowed brief incursions into areas that were otherwise unoccupied. Opportunistic response to short-term variation in desert conditions was therefore the most likely pattern of hunter-gatherer subsistence, although it might not be easily detected in the radiocarbon record that is presently available. The pattern of occupation and abandonment, while it is consonant with the climatic record at the millennial scale, is presently insufficient for more detailed correlation. Possible exceptions are small peaks in the archaeological radiocarbon record which clearly correspond with the generalized climate record, such as humid pulses at 7,000 and 8,000 years ago,[211] and dry periods of varying length that have been shown to correspond with the northern (A) archaeological record.[212]

Focusing now on changes in the Holocene occupation of the southern Namib (C) with the onset of increasing aridity in the last 5,000 years, we turn first to the evidence from the Gorrasis-Awasib basin, near the eastern fringe of the sand sea. This local drainage system extends over approximately 1,000 km^2 and contains a dispersed distribution of archaeological sites representing late

---

208 e.g. Kinahan (2001a); Richter (1991); Sandelowsky (1977)
209 Wendt (1972)
210 See Kinahan (2018b)
211 Brook et al. (2006); Vogel (1989)
212 Vogelsang & Eichhorn (2011: 201)

Figure 3.6: Gorrasis Rock Shelter viewed from the north.

Pleistocene to recent occupation. The sites include extensive stone artefact scatters, a number of rock shelters, burial cairns and complex arrangements of stone hunting blinds, as well as other features. Rock art, however, is scarce. Near the centre of the distribution is a prominent outcrop of syenite core boulders exposed by the erosion of the gravel plains on the edges of the basin.[213]

Located on the northern side of this outcrop, Gorrasis Rock Shelter (Fig. 3.6) has a floor area of about 25 m², and excavation revealed a 0.45 m deep archaeological deposit resting on bedrock weathered by hydrolysis, indicating an episode of high soil moisture conditions prior to the occupation of the site during the mid-Holocene. The initial occupation layers, Units 1 and 2, containing large roof spall debris, included a well-defined hearth feature associated with small quantities of stone artefact debris, fragmented antelope bone and human remains comprising an infant that seemed to have been interred within the hearth itself, possibly on the eve of the site's abandonment about 6,600 years ago. Following a long occupation hiatus, the site was briefly

---

213 Kinahan & Kinahan (2006)

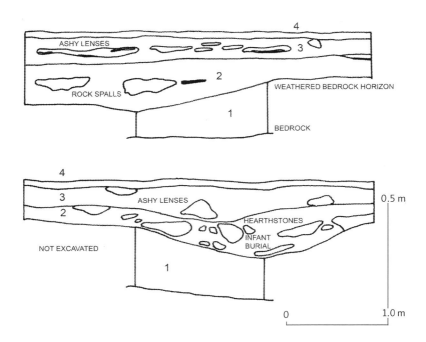

Figure 3.7: Stratigraphic profiles from Gorrasis Rock Shelter with units referred to in the text.

reoccupied during the last one thousand years, as represented by Units 3 and 4 (Fig. 3.7).

The rock shelter deposit comprising these two distinct occupation phases had significant concentrations of stone artefact debris (raw counts n=2,273 pieces), dominated by hydrothermal vein quartz (60%), with chert (24%), crystalline quartz (13%) and other raw materials including quartzite (3%). Formal microlithic type tools characteristic of Mode 5 comprised only 1.5% of flaked stone. The tools were mainly backed pieces, including segments (18) and points (6), with lesser numbers of other tools such as scrapers (8), and a single awl. The segments had a mean length[214] of 14.6 mm (range 10.3 – 28.9 mm) and the points had a mean length of 16.6 mm (range 11.3 – 21.0 mm). Scraper working edges had a mean width across the chord of 13.1 mm (range 9.4 – 17.4 mm). In broad terms, accepting that formal tools may have been employed for various purposes,[215] the Gorrasis assemblage is apparently dominated by hunting projectile components[216] (73%), represented by segments and points. Smaller numbers of scrapers (24%) which could have been used in hide working[217] suggest that while some other activities were undertaken, the site served primarily as a hunting camp.

Faunal remains from the site comprised small and medium-sized bovids (size classes I and II[218]) most likely representing klipspringer *Oreotragus oreotragus* and springbuck *Antidorcas marsupialis*. The deposit also contained fragmentary remains of mountain zebra *Equus zebra hartmannae*. Although the deposit contained abundant ostrich *Struthio camelus* eggshell fragments, including a number of beads, no ostrich bone was recovered. However, the deposit yielded 34 suspected gastroliths, small stones probably ingested by ostrich as an aid to digestion. The stones, with a mean diameter of 9.2 mm (range 6.1 – 16.6 mm) fall within the preferential size range of 8 – 20 mm found in the gizzard of ostriches[219] (Fig. 3.8). This suggests that ostrich were actively targeted on the gravel plains surrounding the site.

Other food remains include seeds of both tsamma *Citrillus lanatus* and !nara *Acanthosicyos horridus* melons. The latter species does not occur in the vicinity of the site and the seeds show that

---

214 Measurements following Deacon (1984: 405, 408)
215 See Binneman (1982) and Williamson (1997) for discussion of functional interpretation of Holocene microlithic tools.
216 cf. Deacon (1984); microwear analysis of larger backed microliths indicates that these were also used as cutting implements and that not all were projectile components (Wadley & Binneman 1995).
217 Binneman (1982)
218 cf. Brain & Brain (1977)
219 Wings (2004: 58)

Figure 3.8: Suspected ostrich gastroliths from Gorrasis Rock Shelter.

foraging expeditions from the Gorrasis Rock Shelter extended as far as 50 km to the west where !nara grow on the edge of the dune sea. A fragment of marine shell indicates that hunter-gatherers at Gorrasis also had links to the Atlantic coast 100 km away, while a single copper bead shows that during its more recent occupation, the site formed part of extensive exchange networks in the interior. The presence of chert and crystalline quartz in the stone artefact assemblage points to more localized sourcing of raw materials, possibly obtained en route to the site following rainfall in the desert.

Radiocarbon dates from Gorrasis Rock Shelter are presented in Figure 3.9 [220] which shows that the initial occupation of the site between 7,000 and 6,600 years ago was followed by an extended hiatus until the last one thousand years. The initial occupation

---

[220] Uncalibrated radiocarbon dates: 7,150±50 (Beta-207919); 6,720±70 (Beta-207918); 6,630±60 (Beta-213466); 660±50 (Beta-213465); 310±40 (Beta-207920); 200±50 (Beta-207921).

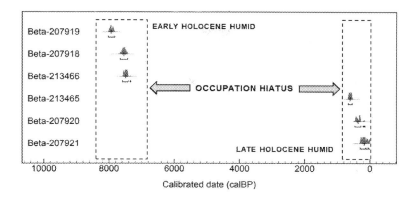

Figure 3.9: Calibrated radiocarbon dates for the occupation of Gorrasis Rock Shelter (see explanation in Notes to the Reader: Archaeological age determination, p. xvii).

coincides with the climatic amelioration of the mid-Holocene Optimum defined on the basis of palaeoenvironmental evidence presented in the first part of this chapter, and the subsequent occupation hiatus indicates the abandonment of the Gorrasis area under conditions of late Holocene aridification. The more recent re-occupation of the site (to be discussed in Chapter 5) indicates a response to improved rainfall shown in the regional palaeoclimatic record. On the basis of this evidence, it seems that the occupation of Gorrasis Rock Shelter serves as a record of hunter-gatherer responses to climatic shifts in the southern Namib.[221] Short-term, opportunistic use of Gorrasis Rock Shelter provides an example of secondary site occupation when remote desert areas could be exploited following isolated rainfall events. Movement to sites such as Gorrasis would have taken place from primary sites along the eastern escarpment of the Namib at least 100 km away.

---

221 Kinahan (2016a, 2018b); Kinahan & Kinahan (2006)

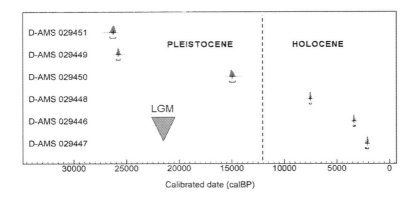

Figure 3.10: Calibrated radiocarbon dates for the occupation of Kubub Rock Shelter.

An example of a primary site with a record of prolonged occupation is Kubub Rock Shelter, located on the escarpment overlooking the plains of the southern Namib Desert. The site, which has a floor area of about 48 m² overlooks rugged outcropping gneissic granites where rainwater collects in crevices and hollows, emerging as small but persistent seepages and springs. The back wall of the site is dominated by a large monochrome red-brown ochre elephant and, painted with the same pigment, a broad spiral motif approximately 0.8 m in diameter, with two bold parallel stripes extending almost 15 m along the length of the rock shelter. Excavation at Kubub revealed a well-stratified deposit more than one metre in depth, yielding abundant stone artefact debris, an array of formal stone tools, and well preserved faunal and plant food remains.

Provisional dating of the Kubub sequence indicates three main phases of occupation: the first immediately prior to the onset of the Last Glacial Maximum about 25,000 years ago, followed by a second phase corresponding to the terminal Pleistocene and early Holocene between 15,000 and 8,000 years ago, and a final third phase of occupation during the late

Holocene between 3,500 and 2,000 years ago (Fig. 3.10).[222] The site has some surficial evidence of occupation during the last one thousand years, including the immediately pre-colonial period. As with the Gorrasis site, Kubub Rock Shelter yielded considerable quantities of stone artefact debris (raw counts n=1,220 pieces), with the most abundant being hydrothermal vein quartz (37%) and chert (33%). Crystalline quartz was present (23%), as was a fine-grained quartzite (6%), the latter mainly associated with the earliest occupation phase. Formal Mode 5 microliths comprised 4% of the total quantity of flaked stone, and among these tools, scrapers (43) were predominant throughout the sequence, with small numbers of segments (9) and a single borer. Scraper working edges had a mean width of 19.6 mm (range 12.9 – 29.1 mm) and segments had a mean length of 16.6 mm (range 9.8 – 22.8 mm). Although marginally larger on average than the same tool classes at Gorrasis, the scrapers and segments recovered at Kubub did not vary appreciably in their dimensions over the occupation sequence.

The relative difference in tool assemblage composition between Gorrasis and Kubub is significant, however, as the ratio of segments to scrapers at roughly 4:1 and 1:4, respectively, points to a difference in emphasis most likely reflecting the predominant tool-using activities at the two sites. While Gorrasis appears to have been primarily a hunting camp where, among other activities, projectile points were made or repaired, the occupation of Kubub was more likely associated with manufacture and repair of various artefacts, probably including carrying bags and clothing such as karosses. Food remains at Kubub comprised small and medium-sized bovids (size classes I and II) including klipspringer *Oreotragus oreotragus* and springbuck *Antidorcas*

---

222 Uncalibrated radiocarbon dates: 22,104±103 (D-AMS 029451); 21,501±99 (D-AMS 029449); 12,652±54 (D-AMS 029450); 6,692±57 (D-AMS 029448); 3,200±35 (D-AMS 029446); 2,163±36 (D-AMS 029447).

marsupialis. The deposit also yielded remains of mountain zebra *Equus zebra hartmannae* and small animals including hyrax *Procavia capensis*. A notable difference between Kubub and Gorrasis was the presence of tortoise, probably *Homopus areolatus*, endemic to the winter rainfall Succulent Karoo biome in southern Namibia. The range of hunted species at the two sites appears to be broadly the same, reflecting both availability and probable specialization in hunting technique focused on these particular animals. Larger prey such as oryx *Oryx gazella* may have been butchered in the field, and represented only by large non-diagnostic bone fragments at the site.

An informative contrast between the two sites is evident in well-preserved corm jackets of the iris *Lapeirousia rivularis*, a species that does not occur in the desert biome west of the escarpment. The edible corms, or food storage organs of this species are mainly available in winter and their presence thus points to the occupation of Kubub during this season. The tsamma *Citrillus lanatus* and !nara *Acanthosicyos horridus* melons represented at Gorrasis are mainly available in mid- to late summer, although the fruit of both species can be stored and transported, thus increasing the period and geographic range of its usefulness.[223] Plant remains thus support the general environmental framework in which desert sites were used following summer rains and then abandoned for escarpment sites during the winter (Fig. 3.11).

The dating of the mid-Holocene occupation and abandonment of Gorrasis Rock Shelter broadly corroborates a postulated hiatus between 5,100 and 2,300 years ago in the southern Namib.[224] Evidence of occupation events during this apparent hiatus is an important indicator of human responses to climatic shifts during the mid- to late Holocene, although other evidence is not entirely consistent with this view. For example, Rosh Pinah Rock Shelter

---

223 Fox & Norwood Young (1982)
224 Sievers (1984); Vogel & Visser (1981); Vogelsang (1998)

Figure 3.11: Food plant remains from Kubub Rock Shelter, with corm jackets of *Lapeirousia rivularis* (left), seed coats of *Citrillus lanatus* (centre) and *Acanthosicyos horridus* (right).

was occupied between 9,700 and 8,900 years ago,[225] but apparently not at the height of the mid-Holocene Optimum. On the other hand, after periodic occupation in the late Pleistocene and early Holocene, Pockenbank Rock Shelter was abandoned about 6,900 years ago, more or less at the same time as Gorrasis, but reoccupied between 3,100 and 3,300 years ago.[226] The sequence at Kubub confirms the widespread occupation pulse in the mid-Holocene while at the same time indicating the importance during the late Holocene arid period, of primary sites in escarpment ecotone environments with dependable water.

There is limited archaeological evidence as yet from elsewhere in the Namib Desert to support the argument that occupation of remote secondary sites is associated with microlithic assemblages related mainly to hunting rather than maintenance activities associated with primary sites. The site of Messum 1 Rock Shelter lies between the Dâures massif and the Atlantic coast

---

225 Sievers (1984)
226 Freundlich et al. (1980); Vogel & Visser (1981)

in a remote and generally waterless location similar to that of Gorrasis Rock Shelter and this site also yielded microlithic assemblages dominated by backed artefacts.[227] Further north, assemblages from the sites of Ovizorumbuku Rock Shelter and Omungunda Rock Shelter were similarly dominated by projectile components.[228] These assemblages appear to be in contrast to Etemba 14 Rock Shelter, Austerlitz Rock Shelter and Fackelträger Rock Shelter[229] which are located in mountain or escarpment environments and might therefore have served as primary sites. The general characteristics of primary and secondary sites as evidenced by the examples discussed here are set out in Table 3.2 as a provisional model.

Because the southern Namib lies marginally within the winter rainfall zone, it is possible that the weakening of the ENSO-driven summer rainfall regime was partly compensated by the occurrence of more regular winter rainfall events in this region. It appears that the decline in reliability of desert resource bases also led to a new emphasis on coastal sites. South of the Orange River there is evidence of markedly intensified exploitation of coastal shellfish between 3,300 and 2,000 years ago,[230] and it is therefore significant that the accumulation of very large shell middens commences on the southern Namib coast at Elizabeth Bay 3,300 years ago and continued until about 1,100 years ago. The mid-Holocene sea-level rise which accompanied the southward intrusion of the warm Angola Current would have diminished the abundant shellfish fauna associated with normally cold-water conditions on the Atlantic coast, but when the Benguela marine ecosystem was restored to normal about 3,000 years ago, coastal sites such as Elizabeth Bay became important settlement foci when arid conditions set in during the late Holocene. The dating of the Elizabeth Bay sites and the mid-Holocene marine transgression

---

227 Richter (1984, 1991); Wendt (1972)
228 Vogelsang & Eichhorn (2011)
229 Wendt (1972)
230 Jerardino et al. (2013); Jerardino & Navarro (2018)

Table 3.2: Environmental and archaeological comparison of primary and secondary occupation sites in the Namib Desert

	Primary sites	Secondary sites
Environment	Escarpment/ecotone	Plains/desert
	Perennial springs	Rainwater ponds
	Localized fauna	Migratory fauna
Archaeology	Large rock shelters	Small rock shelters
	Maintenance tools	Projectile parts
	Abundant rock art	Little rock art
Occupation	Extended Aggregation	Restricted Dispersal
	Density dependent	Density independent

that preceded the establishment of the shell middens is presented in Figure 3.12.[231]

Clearly, conditions in the late Holocene appear to have exceeded the threshold of human tolerance in the southern Namib Desert, in terms of absolute requirements for food and water, and in the resilience of the desert resource base itself. Sustained periods of very low rainfall, or none at all, would have led to a decline in water resources, pasture and antelope populations. During the last one thousand years, re-occupation of Gorrasis Rock Shelter coincided with climatic amelioration in the form of successive years of higher than normal rainfall which ensured the establishment and survival of camelthorn trees in the Awasib-Gorrasis basin.[232] From this evidence, discussed in more detail in Chapter 5, it may

---

[231] Dates from Compton (2006, 2007) and Kinahan & Kinahan (2016). Uncalibrated radiocarbon dates: 3,653±27(D-AMS 028237); 2,811±25 (D-AMS 028236); 2,281±29 (D-AMS 028238); 1,909±28 (D-AMS 028239); 1,200±50 (Pta-9276); 7,640±80 (Pta-1287); 7,013±82 (Pta-9275); 6,750±80 (Pta-1235); 6,710±60 (Pta-9268); 6,310±45 (GrA-24384); 6,220±60 (Pta-9282); 5,600±80 (Pta-9097); 5,340±60 (Pta-419).
[232] Kinahan (2016a)

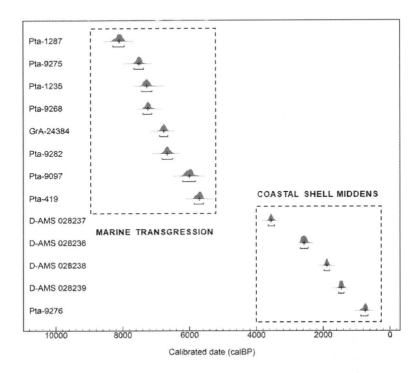

Figure 3.12: Calibrated radiocarbon dating of the mid-Holocene marine transgression and the subsequent occupation of shell midden sites on the southern coast of the Namib Desert.

be inferred that a similar degree of amelioration was essential for the establishment of pasture and the antelope on which hunter-gatherers depended in order to re-occupy desert landscapes.

The archaeological record reflects short-term, opportunistic occupation in the southern Namib Desert, without the possibility of prolonged residence even under the most favourable conditions. It appears that hunter-gatherers had to retreat from the desert towards the escarpment (and possibly to the Atlantic coast, as indicated by the evidence of shell middens at Elizabeth Bay) in response to variation in the availability of resources. Under normal conditions, resources essential for such occupation are more reliable in the escarpment zone and could have sustained occupation during the dry months of the year. Significantly, this is where the greatest concentration of rock art sites is to be found. Next, we review the evidence of the rock art as a reflection of those aspects of hunter-gatherer life that are not apparent in the excavated remains of mid-Holocene occupation.

We have seen that as a consequence of highly variable rainfall, desert water sources were short lived and unreliable, and it follows that primary resource sites became focal points of occupation under dry conditions. Primary resource sites are mainly located along the escarpment and would have supported aggregations of otherwise dispersed groups during times of diminishing food and water supplies. Such circumstances would have led to heightened social tensions and consequently to intensified ritual healing which provided the means to maintain and restore social harmony.[233] It is therefore conceivable that primary sites with relatively high concentrations of rock art represent places of temporary aggregation in landscapes where wide-ranging mobility was only possible following brief spells of rainfall which might replenish water supplies at secondary sites.[234]

Rock art in the Namib Desert

Chapter 2 showed that complex rock art existed in the Namib Desert during the late Pleistocene. The art discovered during excavations at the Apollo 11 site[235] is paralleled by evidence from elsewhere in southern Africa that rock art formed part of the cultural repertoire of hunter-gatherers on the eve of the

---

233 Lee (1972, 1979)
234 This inference overcomes criticisms of landscape and environment in southern African rock art studies (Smith & Blundell 2004) because it is based on the generally accepted framework of shamanic ritual and its social context (cf. Lewis-Williams 1982).
235 Other rare examples of stratigraphically controlled and dated rock art in southern Africa are reported by Breunig (1985) and Jerardino and Swanepoel (1999).

Holocene.[236] Most rock art in this region is probably Holocene in age and this points to a significant regional increase during this period in the importance of ritual practices associated with it. However, there are persistent obstacles to reliable dating of the art,[237] and this, together with an apparent continuity in subject-matter and style of execution,[238] limits the degree to which it can be attributed to defined archaeological phases of occupation.

In southern Africa, painted rock art is most abundant in the southern and eastern escarpment zones, while rock engravings predominate in the interior. In the Namib Desert and its eastern margins, rock art is also concentrated along the escarpment (Fig. 3.13) but the distribution of painted and engraved rock art overlaps significantly, with both genres sometimes found on the same sites. While painted rock art is generally confined to rock shelter sites where it is often associated with stratified archaeological deposits and other evidence of sustained or repeated occupation, engravings generally occur on open sites, usually among outcrops or isolated boulders. A common characteristic though, is that painted and engraved rock art tend to occur within reach of reliable water, the most essential requirement for hunter-gatherer occupation in this hyper-arid region, most especially during periods of low rainfall.

Namib Desert rock art conforms to the same regional hunter-gatherer ideological and religious system as that of the wider subcontinent.[239] This regional affinity locates both painted and engraved rock art within a common set of precepts. Supernatural causality is the most central of these, together with the belief that certain individuals, acting as healers, were able to gain supernatural powers from particular animals while in a state

---

236 Mitchell (2002: 192 ff)
237 For a discussion of attempts to date southern African rock art, see Bonneau et al. (2011, 2012, 2017), Conard et al. (1988), Mazel (2003, 2009), and Mazel and Watchman (1997).
238 Lewis-Williams (1984); Lewis-Williams & Dowson (1989)
239 Kinahan (2001a)

TIME'S ARROW 111

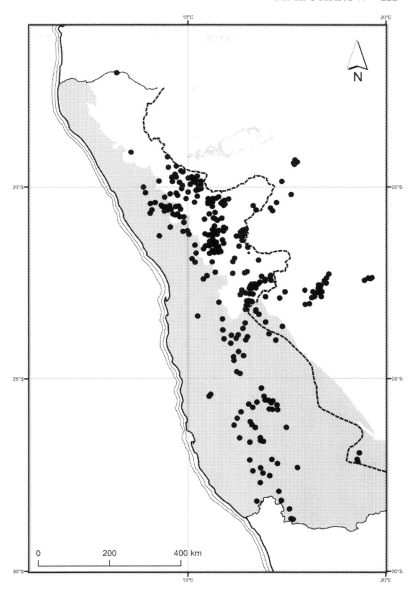

Figure 3.13: Distribution of rock art sites showing high concentration west of the escarpment zone (dashed line). Many sites include both paintings and engravings.

of altered consciousness, and use these powers to heal social divisions as well as other sources of discord or misfortune within their community. Supernatural powers were also invoked for purposes such as to ensure successful hunting and to make rain. Beyond these most basic principles, set out in more detail below, the rock art of the Namib Desert exhibits a number of important differences which cast new light on the critical role of ritual practice in processes of social transition both in the desert and, by implication, in the southern African region as a whole.

The regional distribution of rock art clearly relates to hunter-gatherer settlement and subsistence, but the art is not a compendium of huntable game, nor is it a simple reflection of the fauna occurring in the vicinity of the sites. Furthermore, while the depiction of various animals in the rock art shows an intimate naturalistic apprehension, this is rooted in a relationship with the animal world that goes beyond appearance, behaviour and food. Based on these general principles an established consensus has arisen among rock art scholars that the art is essentially shamanic, and it is generally agreed that the content and meaning of the art are metaphorical, encoding specific social values attached to the supernatural qualities of a relatively narrow range of species. Thus, historical and recent ethnographic studies identify certain key species, including eland, giraffe and kudu, for example, as repositories of supernatural potency made accessible through the agency of shamans[240] who could include both men and women.[241]

---

240 While there is criticism of shamanistic explanations in the broader field of rock art research (e.g. Bahn 2001, 2010; Bednarik 1990; McCall 2007; Quinlan 2000), in southern African rock art studies this approach is considered theoretically sound and has strong empirical support from hunter-gatherer ethnography (Lewis-Williams & Dowson 1990; Lewis-Williams & Pearce 2012, 2015). Ambiguities in the evidence continue to sustain vigorous debate among southern African scholars (e.g. Skotnes 1996; Solomon 1998, 2013; Wessels 2010; Lewis-Williams 2003; Lewis-Williams & Pearce 2012, 2015).

241 Lewis-Williams (1981, 1982)

It is generally agreed that the most important and central practice in the ritual life of southern African hunter-gatherers was the trance dance,[242] a communal event that is widely depicted in the rock art and shows close correspondences with trance rituals described in numerous eye-witness accounts by anthropologists who have documented its remarkably consistent features.[243] The trance dance usually takes place at night around a central fire with an inner circle of women seated close together, clapping and singing accompaniment for an outer circle of dancing men.[244] The combination of rhythmic sound and movement, of hyperventilation, intense concentration and trained imagination, helps the shaman to enter a state of trance in which he interacts with supernatural forces and beings that are not visible to other participants in the ritual.

Clearly, trance experience informs the rock art, and while it may be true that not every painting directly represents a trance experience,[245] the art as a whole is articulated through rituals centring on the trance dance.[246] The shaman achieves a state of trance in three broad stages recognizable as a progression of mental imagery.[247] The first of these is an involuntary disturbance of vision accompanied by entoptic hallucinations. With training, this disorienting experience leads to a second stage of altered consciousness in which hallucinations are construed as iconic visions drawn from culturally conditioned reality such as familiar or significant animal species, their behaviour and distinguishing features. In the third stage, the shaman experiences a disassociation from the real world and assumes, for example, the form and identity of certain animal species, thus migrating from one realm of existence to another, that of the supernatural, gaining the ritual potency he requires to carry out his work as healer and sorcerer.

---

242 Lewis-Williams & Pearce (2012)
243 Barnard (1992b); Guenther (1999)
244 Marshall (1999); Biesele (1993)
245 Lewis-Williams & Pearce (2012)
246 Barnard (1979, 1992b); Guenther (1975, 1999)
247 Lewis-Williams & Dowson (1988)

Physical symptoms of altered consciousness including nasal haemorrhage and collapse while performing the trance dance, are also accompanied by sensations such as of flying or changes in the length and proportions of the limbs. These are commonly depicted in the rock art, together with conventionalized dance postures which include men dancing while supporting themselves with sticks,[248] or with arms back, slumped forward, and sometimes shown either prone or being helped to remain upright while applying ritually potent body perspiration to participants in the trance dance.[249] These features of the trance dance appear in the rock art (Fig. 3.14) with accompanying groups of women, seated with hands and fingers extended as in clapping.

The size of groups participating in the trance dance varies both in the rock art and in ethnographically documented performances. As communal events these could involve up to a hundred or more people, some travelling over considerable distances to attend.[250] As we shall see in the following chapters, specialized shamanism in the Namib Desert differed from this general pattern; shamans began to operate in isolation, as itinerant practitioners who moved about the landscape officiating in different contexts such as rainmaking and initiation rituals. The evidence suggests that there were probably not many such specialists, and that their work was carried out at designated ritual sites rather than in the context of large communal gatherings, as is generally assumed by most rock art scholars in southern Africa.[251] From the evidence of Namib Desert rock art it appears that the services performed by shamans among both hunter-gatherer and pastoralist communities established an important link between the two, and served as a vector for the transmission of cultural practices that became common to both. Chapters 4 and 5 address these issues in detail.

---

248 Jolly (2006)
249 Lewis-Williams (1981)
250 Guenther (1975, 1999), Lewis-Williams & Pearce (2012)
251 Lewis-Williams & Pearce (2012)

There is considerable variation in the style and complexity of the rock art found across the southern African region and this can conceal its basic conceptual unity. That the art is ideologically conditioned rather than simply documentary is, however, immediately apparent both from a common bias towards ritually important species, and by the general absence from the art of those species the remains of which are most commonly found among the faunal evidence of hunting activities indicated by evidence from excavations at the same sites. Moreover, ritually important animal species in the rock art often exhibit human features, and vice-versa, sometimes adopting postures that closely parallel those of ritual participants in states of trance. It follows that the culturally mediated selection of subject-matter and the combination of human and animal traits is a caution against simple comparison based on the relative frequency of animal species in the art, and that following the concept of shamanic agency, animals in the art are in fact people.

Although rock art in the southern African region does show wide diversity in the relative numerical importance of different animal species from one area to another, such differences do not contradict the ideological nature of the art. For example, eland are of central importance in the eastern escarpment of the Drakensberg, but uncommon in Zimbabwe and Namibia; the same applies to mountain rhebuck which are wholly absent in the latter two areas. Giraffe are common in Namibia and Zimbabwe but not in the rock art of the Cape or Drakensberg. These and many other disparities have encouraged an empiricist view that the meaning of the rock art must emerge from local inventories rather than being derived from a general overarching interpretative framework such as I have outlined here.[252]

Apparent differences in the relative frequency of animal subjects in painted as opposed to engraved rock art might be taken to indicate separate cultural or religious systems, but the usefulness

---

252 e.g. Lenssen-Erz (1998); Richter (2002)

Figure 3.14: Monochrome red brown painting of human figures in various conventionalized attitudes of the trance dance, including lines of dancing men, some supported by dancing sticks, others with arms

TIME'S ARROW 117

back or prone. The figure at lower right appears to show streaming perspiration, a prelude to ritual healing. The frieze is approximately 1.8 m in length, Hungorob Ravine, Dâures massif.

of species inventories as a basis of comparison is limited, as the following example illustrates. A survey of the Hungorob Ravine in the central Namib yielded a total of 613 identifiable figurative images, all painted, while a survey of the major rock engravings site of |Ui-||aes, located further to the north, yielded a total of 554 identifiable figurative images.[253] Both site concentrations are discussed in detail in the next and succeeding chapters. The simplified comparison of rock art motifs from the Hungorob and |Ui-||aes in Table 3.3 shows that human figures constitute the majority of painted images while forming an insignificant proportion of engravings.

A further contrast is found in the proportion of ungulates, where all antelope and related species combined represent less than a quarter of the proportion of human figures in the paintings but more than half of those among the engravings. Several ungulates are common to both, such as oryx and giraffe, as are some species not included in the analysis, for example, elephant and rhinoceros. Ostrich form a minor but revealing component of both the painted and engraved rock art in Table 3.3. While not all birds depicted in the rock art at these sites can be identified with certainty as ostrich (some appear to be bustards), the significant fact is that all are non-passerines: this is the class of birds that stride rather than hop; their gait resembles that of humans, and in the rock art, ostrich are

Table 3.3: Comparison of human and non-passerine bird rock paintings in the Hungorob Ravine and rock engravings at |Ui-||aes.

MOTIF Site	PAINTED Hungorob % (n)	ENGRAVED |Ui-||aes % (n)
Human	98 (496)	9 (60)
Non-passerine bird	2 (6)	90 (541)

253 Kinahan (2001a, 2010a)

TIME'S ARROW 119

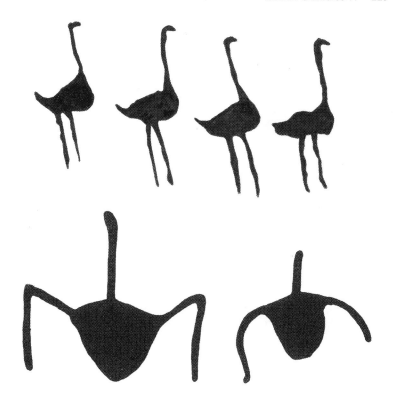

Figure 3.15: Rock engravings of ostrich at |Ui-||aes, as metaphorical representations of dancers moving in file at the onset of trance, and as trance dancers experiencing sensations of weightlessness and physical exertion.

therefore metaphorical humans.[254] The proportion of human and bird motifs is almost exactly the reverse in the Hungorob paintings and the |Ui-||aes engravings. The human figures in the |Ui-||aes engravings include 58 footprints, while there are as many as 338 identifiable bird spoor, an element that is largely absent from the painted rock art of the Namib Desert.

---

254 See Hollmann (2001); Lewis-Williams (2000)

The upper row of birds in Figure 3.15 shows four ostrich proceeding in single file, facing in the same direction, as they appear in a rock engraving at ǀUi-ǁaes. All four have tails raised and the legs taper to a point. These two features may appear quite mundane but are in fact characteristic of trance experience: the raised tail is common in rock art animal motifs and in animals on the point of death. The onset of trance is known also as the "little death", and is accompanied by sensations of rising or weightlessness, brought about through dancing in file as shown here, and by hyperventilation which is suggested by the inflated chest of the ostrich.[255] In the second row, the ostrich are shown end-on; the legs are entirely absent and the wings (or the arms of the dancer) are angled downward as they are when the ostrich is overheated and breathless after sustained exertion, like the arms of the human dance participant. Ostrich thus portray, via slight artistic modifications of their natural attributes and habits, specific aspects of trance experience and these show that animal subjects are in fact metaphorical representations depicting human experience of the supernatural.

An example of complete transformation from human to animal in the context of trance experience at ǀUi-ǁaes is shown by the engraving of a lion reproduced in Figure 3.16. The backline and general shape of the lion are unmistakeable, but closer examination shows that the paws have five rather than four toes, thus revealing its human rather than feline identity. Moreover, the tail ends in a paw with toes; this otherwise puzzling feature exemplifies the phenomenon of polymelia, in which the shaman in trance sometimes experiences the sensation of having extra limbs or digits as well as other unnatural physical attributes.[256]

In this chapter we have seen that Holocene hunter-gatherer occupation of the Namib Desert combined the high mobility of small groups with the possibility, or necessity, of aggregation at sites with reliable water during dry periods. This pattern suggests

---

[255] Lewis-Williams (1983)
[256] Lewis-Williams & Dowson (1989); Guenther (2020)

without necessarily demonstrating that extended social networks existed through which groups could gain access to resources and maintain a degree of social cohesion during times when limited options were available. Although the rock art of the Holocene period is difficult to integrate with the controlled dating of stratigraphic sequences in the area, two reasonable inferences can be made. One is that most of the rock art belongs to the same broad period of Holocene occupation by virtue of its evident concentration at Holocene sites, and the other is that when areas such as the southern Namib were abandoned in the face of increasing aridity, the rock art sites also would have been abandoned at the same time.

Rock art represents a crucial component of the early to mid-Holocene occupation sequence and indicates the increasing importance of the escarpment ecotone environment during this period. The close association of the rock art sites with this part of the overall site distribution shows that ritual activity was an integral part of hunter-gatherer life, and that it was particularly important when groups were concentrated on primary resource sites along the escarpment. An apparent link between rock art as representative of ritual activity, and the environmental imperative for social aggregation at suitable sites during dry periods corroborates the established view that ritual was primarily communal in nature.[257]

In the next chapter we discuss unique evidence from both the rock art and the related archaeological remains in the Namib Desert, showing a trajectory of change towards more specialized ritual practice. It is appropriate at the close of this introduction to the rock art to consider briefly a question that has received insufficient attention in the southern African rock art literature: that of the purpose of making rock art. Conventionally, scholars believe that while the meaning of rock art imagery can be understood chiefly through careful study of historical and contemporary ethnography, the motivation of the artist would reflect an individual state of mind which cannot be inferred from

---

257 Lewis-Williams & Pearce (2012)

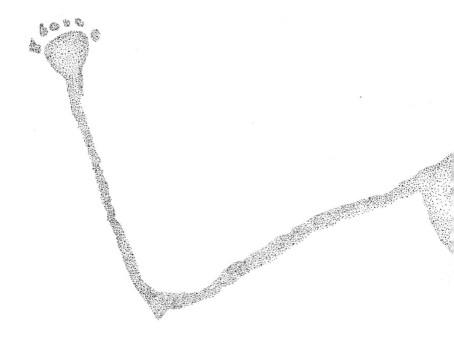

Figure 3.16: Rock engraving from |Ui-||aes showing five-toed lion with paw at end of the tail.

TIME'S ARROW 123

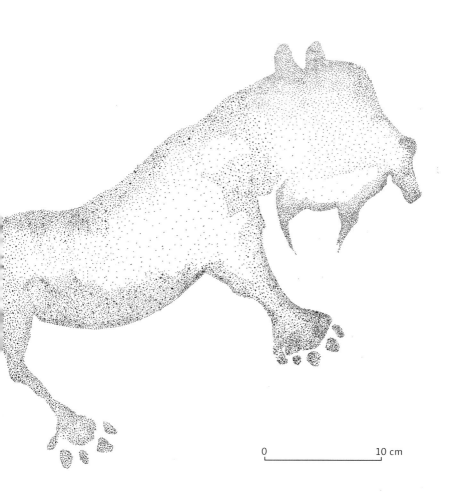

the paintings or engravings.[258] The artist, it has been claimed, depicted his experience of the supernatural, after the event, as it were, in a state of Wordsworthian tranquility.[259]

As we turn in the next chapter to the evidence of specialist shamanism, we arrive perforce at a different point of view, namely, that the rock art formed a fundamental and necessary part of the process of ritual activity. Thus, the rock art of rain-making was executed as part of the process of rain-making, not afterwards as a record of the event. It is possible that only in certain specific circumstances such as this is it possible to discern the motive of the artist. An argument that rock art depicting rain is no more than a shamanic recollection is difficult to sustain in the face of ethnographic evidence that rain-making formed an essential component of the relationship between hunter-gatherers and other communities of pastoralists and farmers who engaged shamans for the explicit purpose of making rain. Although necessarily speculative, more general discussion of the motivation for the making of rock art images is important for the general argument pursued in this book.

In Chapter 4, I introduce the notion of agency in rock art and shamanic ritual and develop a new conceptual model for the understanding of ritual performance both in the rock art and in the material paraphernalia of ritual practice. This model I develop further in Chapter 5 which deals with ritual performance in the context of rain-making and rituals of initiation, all of which form the basis of important panarchic intersections between hunter-gatherer and food producing economies. Agency in this context is purposive, leading towards a particular and desired outcome in which the shaman is not simply the performer of a pre-existing and essentially static ritual catechism, but an inventive manipulator, a *bricoleur*, occupying the ill-defined terrain between ideology, or belief, and concrete reality. Negotiating the boundary between the

---

258 Lewis-Williams (1982)
259 Lewis-Williams (1995)

sacred and the profane is universally the work of the priest or ritual practitioner, and there is no reason to suppose that the work of the Holocene shaman was different. In this view, it is not the art that is powerful, *but the act of making it*, and moreover, making the art is a purposeful act with a specific motivation. Without this shift of perspective away from the conventional approach to rock art studies, it is not possible to understand the rock art of the Namib Desert and its place in the archaeological sequence.

The work of the shaman and artist in the later Holocene represents an important development beyond that of communal healing and the maintenance of social harmony as shown by the rock art found at aggregation sites strung out along the desert escarpment. This social function undoubtedly persisted as an essential of social life but the far more complex rock art to be considered in the next chapter reveals the shaman as one engaged with metaphysical forces that cannot be directly observed.[260] The rock art is therefore not merely the reflection of a ritualized interaction between people and the supernatural; it is the material evidence, fortuitously preserved, of a sustained tradition among people in the Namib Desert, of cognitive engagement with the world in which they lived. In this sense, the shaman is operating at the very outer limits of knowledge at the time, using and refining a culturally conditioned set of precepts to make sense of a changing world.

In the next and subsequent chapter we proceed from the basic understanding of the rock art as part of a wider regional cognitive system encompassing both the painted and engraved genres as intrinsic elements of shamanistic ritual practice, to explore in greater detail some specific examples from the Namib Desert that cast important new light on the archaeological sequence. The examples we address in Chapter 4 show that changes towards a more elaborate painted rock art relate to the first of two fundamental transitions in Namib Desert hunter-gatherer

---

260 Kinahan (1995a)

society by showing evidence for the rise of specialist shamanism in the context of communal ritual, and of specific individual practitioners and the adoption of domestic livestock. The rise of specialized shamanism is associated with the transition from the equilibrial K phase under increasing environmental and social stress, to a release Ω phase and re-organization α phase associated with a number of fundamental shifts in hunter-gatherer social organization, including the adoption of domestic livestock and pottery. This line of interpretation is pursued further in Chapter 5 with evidence for the appearance of specialist shamans who operated not only outside the communal setting, but on an itinerant basis, as rainmakers for neighbouring pastoral communities. This interaction introduced to hunter-gatherer society not only technological innovations such as livestock and pottery, but a range of novel social practices and values to be discussed in the chapters to come.

IV

MOUNTAIN REFUGE

It is not just an accident of archaeological preservation that makes our hunter-gatherer forbears appear with the passage of time to become increasingly well equipped, efficient and successful. Complexity, whether in a material form as the technology of hunting, or the less obvious but immanent knowledge that underlies it, is the basis of human resilience and therefore apt to increase. When the archaeological evidence is as abundant and varied as we find it in the Holocene, it becomes possible to see the connectedness of widely dispersed communities and their potential for adaptive change.

Hunter-gatherers throughout much of southern Africa were faced with widespread aridity in the wake of the generally warm humid conditions that prevailed in the early Holocene. This change constrained settlement in some parts of the interior,[261] but led to marked intensification in others, with increasing use of seasonally abundant resources such as marula *Sclerocarya birrea* fruit[262] in woodland biomes, and geophytes including *Watsonia* spp., and *Hypoxis argentea*, especially in temperate montane

---

261 Deacon (1974)
262 Walker (1995)

environments.[263] Falling lake levels in the northern Kalahari lead to greater dependence on fish,[264] as part of a regional emphasis on the exploitation of smaller, r-selected and relatively localized food sources, including in some areas, tortoise and small antelope such as steenbuck *Raphiceros campestris*.[265] Improved marine ecosystem productivity resulted in greater reliance on coastal sites, and the accumulation of large shell midden deposits along the Atlantic littoral.[266] These developments reflect an increased specialization of hunter-gatherer subsistence, which also brought fundamental changes in social networks, landscape relations, and ritual activity.

In the second half of the Holocene there is evidence in many parts of the subcontinent for the rise of elaborate exchange networks,[267] suggesting increased interdependency between local groups. These relationships helped to mitigate the risks to survival in uncertain environments. There is evidence for more structured gender roles[268] and a possible increase in the status of women as a result of heightened reliance on gathered food,[269] as well as complex ritual activity apparent from a profusion of shamanic rock art[270]. While the archaeology of the late Holocene is generally taken to represent the apex of hunter-gatherer technological, social and cognitive development in the late pre-colonial period, the evidence from the Namib Desert instead shows that this was a point of transition rather than climax. Hunter-gatherers responded to increasing aridity in the late Holocene by moving to mountain refugia such as the Dâures massif (Fig. 4.1), where intensified hunting focused on a narrow range of species, and extended social networks helped to offset shortages in food and water.

---

263 Barham (1989) cited in Mitchell (2002); Carter et al. (1988); Deacon (1984)
264 Robbins et al. (2000)
265 Mitchell (2002: 179)
266 Jerardino (1996)
267 Mitchell (2003); Stewart et al. (2020); Wadley (1984)
268 Wadley (1984)
269 Mazel (1989)
270 Lewis-Williams (1984)

Figure 4.1: The Dâures massif approached from the gravel plains to the south.

Alternating occupation of primary and secondary sites was evidently well established among hunter-gatherer groups in the Namib Desert during the early Holocene. Reliance on primary sites as centres of aggregation under dry conditions is associated with relatively high concentrations of rock art which reflect ritual activity as a means to maintain social harmony in the face of dwindling resources as equilibrial K phase dynamics were brought under increasing strain. This pattern of intensification as a response to increasing aridity in the late Holocene is associated with dependence on ecological refugia, where sustained occupation of the desert involved increasingly narrow and specialized subsistence strategies. Greatly elevated levels of ritual activity led to a remarkable elaboration of rock art and spurred important developments in shamanic practice with the initiation of a release or Ω phase in which the shaman played a central role in the re-organization or α phase of the hunter-gatherer transition to pastoralism. The evidence presented here favours the view that the most important and influential agent of interaction between hunter-gatherer and pastoralist was the specialist shaman, establishing in the course of a re-organization α phase, 'new domains of influence, opening an entirely new set of adaptive pathways'.[271] Importantly, the evidence discussed in this chapter shows that refugium occupation did not lead to the isolation of hunter-gatherer groups and that wider social networks continued to provide an important element of adaptive behaviour, in the adjustment to the vicissitudes of unpredictable rainfall and the availability of food resources.

Thus, while hunter-gatherer intensification might soon exhaust the technological potential represented by a relatively static tool assemblage and subsistence opportunities, social responses such as the elaboration of exchange networks could ensure greater resilience and adaptive potential. Ritual practice, which is specifically concerned with mediating ideology and real-world phenomena can provide an even more critical reflection of hunter-gatherer responses. We pursue this theme here, using evidence that indicates the rise of specialist shamanism apparently commencing with the move to refugium sites. Refugium occupation thus represents an advanced point in the equilibrial K phase of the adaptive cycle, with narrowing options and increasing risk of isolation and famine.

As the driest region of southern Africa, it follows that climatic limitations on human occupation would be particularly severe in the Namib Desert. Mitigating responses involving high mobility would also have required extended social networks similar to those found in less arid parts of the subcontinent. The presence of shamanic rock art shows that hunter-gatherer occupation of the Namib, in common with hunter-gatherer groups throughout the subcontinent, included the same basic ideological values in which intimate social networks ensured access to as wide as possible a range of resource alternatives. Significant concentrations of rock art in the Dâures massif and other desert inselbergen associated with late Holocene occupation[272] provide detailed insights into

---

271 Gunderson & Holling (2002)
272 Parkington & Hall (1987); Wadley (1979)

adaptive responses, allowing clear links to be drawn between settlement and subsistence behaviour as well as ritual practices.

From this evidence we see that rather than a merely sporadic[273] use of such mountain environments, occupation of the Dâures massif in particular represents a critical phase of intensification and transformation of Namib Desert hunter-gatherer society. The unusual concentration of food and water at the Dâures massif made it an attractive focus of settlement under conditions of increasing aridity during the late Holocene. It is remarkable that there is little evidence of occupation in the early Holocene when conditions were more consistently moist. As we shall see in this chapter, archaeological preservation on the mountain is exceptionally good, such that evidence of earlier occupation certainly would have survived. A likely explanation for the shift towards a late Holocene occupation of the mountain is that the surrounding desert no longer offered a reliable resource base for an economy oriented towards hunting plains antelope. Moving into the mountain refugium entailed a fundamental shift from K- to r-selected prey species, from plains antelope towards dependence on small animals such as rock hyrax. Significantly, however, the rock art of refugium occupation in the Dâures massif retained a major focus on the symbolic importance of antelope and other fauna of the plains and the major river drainage environments of the desert.

We begin here with an overview of the Dâures massif and the general distribution of rock art and archaeological sites in relation to water resources on the mountain, before turning to the results of excavations at two major sites, Falls Rock Shelter and Snake Rock. Evidence from these sites reflects on the narrow ecological niche hunter-gatherers occupied in this environment, while also demonstrating the wider social networks on which their survival depended. Unique evidence of shamanic paraphernalia and an elaboration of both technique and content in the rock art adds a crucial dimension to this interpretation. Here, we also

---

273 Mitchell (2002: 187)

see that social networks extending beyond the Dâures eventually brought the first domestic sheep to this area through the agency of specialist shamans who initiated contact with pastoralist communities about two thousand years ago.

An island in the desert

In 1980 my wife and I made our way up the Hungorob Ravine, staggering under a month's supply of food and the most basic excavation tools. We were not to know, as we began our four-year field project, that our timing could hardly have been worse: this was the start of the most severe drought in recent times. The climb to Falls Rock Shelter, repeated dozens of times through the project, took about ten hours each way. Searching for water became a daily task and we dug more and more holes in likely-looking spots; open water was very scarce and usually stagnant. As conditions worsened, a deep silence fell: hyrax disappeared and their alarm cry was no longer heard; baboons left in search of easier pickings, and we were no longer plagued by bees. A single leopard held its ground for months, becoming bolder as water diminished and our tattered containers hoisted in the branches of a tree, were all that remained. Then, one April afternoon in 1984, the heavens opened. It rained for days on end and within a few short weeks, the mountain became a paradise.

Approached from the desert plains, the Dâures massif presents a domed profile of high boulder-strewn slopes which glow like dull embers in the light of late afternoon, illustrating the colloquial etymology of its name, which translates from Khoekhoegowab as 'burning mountain'.[274] Geologically, the mountain is a relatively

---

274 The approximation "Dourissa" first appeared on British hydrographic charts in 1878 and was later translated to Brandberg on German colonial-era topographic maps (J.H.A. Kinahan 1990: 126). The indigenous name Dâures, retaining the conventional female suffix (following Haacke and Eiseb, in litt.), has been reintroduced (Kinahan 2000b) although there remains some confusion in the use of Khoekhoegowab orthography with some writers appending the male suffix, thus Dâure*b* (e.g. Breunig et al. 2019; Lenssen-Erz 2004: 255).

young feature of post-Karoo age, consisting of several intrusive granite masses, emplaced in the mouth of an ancient volcanic pipe.[275] It covers nearly 650 km² and has an elevation of 2,573 m.a.s.l., dominating the surrounding terrain which on average lies at about 650 m.a.s.l. In summer, the top of the mountain is often covered in cloud, and localized orographic rainfall supports a higher density and diversity of vegetation[276] than the plains of the central Namib which receive an average precipitation of only 100 mm per annum.[277] In this sense, the Dâures massif is effectively an ecological island in the desert.[278]

Our experience showed most vividly that the mountain refugium probably could not have sustained even small groups of hunter-gatherers for more than a few years of unbroken drought. While rock hyrax and plant foods steadily diminished without rain, the surrounding desert was suddenly and immediately without game, and whatever water did remain was so brackish as to be undrinkable. Hyrax numbers, under the island-like conditions imposed by the mountain, are limited by browse which in turn requires rainfall to survive. Plains antelope, in contrast, move away *en masse* when grazing is exhausted. While the Dâures massif could bridge the gaps between irregular rains, human survival imposed one unnegotiable requirement, the possibility of access to alternative resources, a principle already demonstrated in the evidence of early Holocene settlement discussed in Chapter 3.

Large parts of the mountain flanks are dominated by unbroken granite sheets, and even though the smallest precipitation will produce a remarkably high runoff, only the heaviest of downpours will cause streams of water to leave the mountain by way of the thirteen major ravine systems that drain in radial fashion from the

---

275 Diehl (1990); Hodgson (1972); Miller (2000)
276 Moisel (1982); Nordenstam (1974). Olszewski (2000) has derived a general climatological profile from the available data which unfortunately lacks continuous rainfall records for the mountain.
277 Mendelsohn et al. (2002)
278 Olszewski (2000)

summit area. Water is trapped in pools or within the sheet joints of the granite, seeping out through tiny fissures hidden among the rocks. Such springs, often no larger than a hand basin, may last three years or more without replenishment by rain. Where dykes of intrusive rock block the course of tributary streams, larger amounts of water accumulate, safe from evaporation just beneath the sand.[279]

Due to its relative inaccessibility, the mountain supports a limited range of mammal fauna, with hyrax, rock hare and klipspringer as its principal herbivores, along with their main predator, the leopard. The mountain oases are beyond the reach of larger fauna. In the lower parts of the ravines there are some fickle springs, and to reach these, zebra and plains antelope traverse vast distances, as do flocks of desert sandgrouse which fly in from their feeding grounds each evening to drink. The evident fact that people could not have depended simultaneously on water in the higher parts of the mountain and the resources of the desert plains has supported a general view that the Dâures massif was an entity by itself.[280] The first Europeans to reach the mountain,[281] found small encampments of nomadic pastoralists at the foot of the Hungorob Ravine,[282] which drains towards the south-west and forms the main focus of discussion in this chapter. The last inhabitants of the ravine left in the 1930s, when nomadism was outlawed as vagrancy.[283]

The Hungorob Ravine

Palaeoclimatic evidence presented in Chapter 3 showed a number of correspondences with the radiocarbon record for human settlement

---

279 Kinahan (2000b)
280 Burfeindt (1970); Pager (1980)
281 An account by Messem (1855) is unverified, but that of Gürich (1891) refers to the Hungorob by name.
282 Drawing on Nienaber and Raper (1980), Pager (1993: 25) suggests that the name refers to a route, or pathway into the mountain.
283 Köhler (1959)

in the Namib Desert. Our attention here focuses on the apparent contrast between the occupation of the central Namib and that of the northern and southern parts of the desert during the late Holocene. Whereas the increasing aridity of the Namib in the last 6,000 years probably resulted in a depopulation of the northern and southern areas, the evidence from the central Namib indicates a degree of continuity over this period. This continuity of occupation is reflected in the archaeology of the Dâures massif as well as other inselbergen that served as refugia until the onset of relatively higher rainfall conditions during the last two thousand years.

The intensity of occupation in the Dâures massif is apparent from a concentration of rock art that is far greater than in any other part of the Namib Desert. Detailed surveys have documented approximately one thousand rock art sites, mainly concentrated in the upper parts of the mountain, with densities of up to three sites per square kilometre.[284] Archaeological evidence from systematic excavations indicates that intensive hunter-gatherer occupation began here about 4,500 years ago.[285] This dating is broadly consistent with palaeoenvironmental evidence for the commencement of the marked aridity phase between 4,600 and 4,800 years ago,[286] discussed in Chapter 3 which also drew attention to circumstantial evidence of flash flooding events on the Namib coast nearly 100 km to the west of the Dâures massif about 4,800 years ago.[287] The available evidence thus points to intensified human occupation of the Dâures massif and other refugia under conditions of increasing aridity, broken by episodic desert rainfall events such as may have led to the brief occupation of Messum 1, a remote desert site discussed in the previous chapter.[288]

---

[284] Pager (1980, 1993)
[285] Limited evidence of mid-Holocene occupation at the eastern foot of the massif has been reported by Vogel and Visser (1981).
[286] Chase et al. (2009); Sletten et al. (2013)
[287] Kinahan (2015)
[288] Richter (1984)

The most detailed archaeological and rock art studies of the Dâures massif have been carried out in the 15 km course of the Hungorob Ravine[289] where 44 rock art sites yielded a total of 815 paintings, with 75% of these identifiable to species or higher taxon. Less than 20% of the paintings were of animal subjects, the majority showing human figures singly or in groups of up to 26 individuals.[290] A notable characteristic of the Hungorob rock art is the uneven distribution of paintings, a small minority of sites having both a high abundance of rock art, as well as a high diversity of subject matter. Of the sites in the Hungorob with more than 50 paintings, Falls Rock Shelter and Snake Rock show higher than average diversity (H=5/> as opposed to H=<2.5).[291] These two sites are situated only 1.5 km apart in the upper ravine and occupy a local drainage area with numerous natural rock basins and small seepages. When other surface water supplies diminished after the brief summer rains as a result of rapid evaporation, this area would have become a natural focus of residence, supported by a range of food resources, including a variety of edible plants and small game.

Among the human figures recorded in the Hungorob rock art,[292] the great majority are monochrome red to reddish brown in colour, with men and women in roughly equal proportions and many examples of what appear to be communal dances. There are multiple instances of such figures adopting conventionalised postures associated with ritual trance as described in Chapter 3: these include gestures and attitudes of dance such as hand-clapping, bending forward, nasal haemorrhage and hands held to the face, while several depict physical experiences associated with states of altered consciousness, including attenuation of

---

289 Pager (1993); Kinahan (2001a); Breunig (2003)
290 Numerical discrepancies between the site documentation of Pager (1993) and Kinahan (2001a) are due to differences in survey coverage and the identification criteria used for subject matter.
291 Based on a calculated Shannon H Index, cf. Magurran (1988)
292 Pager (1993)

limbs, polymelia and the appearance of human figures with antelope heads or legs[293] as described in the previous chapter (see Figure 3.14).

Formed by the horizontal parting of a sheet joint in the granite, Falls Rock Shelter is relatively shallow, having a floor area of 120 m² consisting mainly of exposed bedrock (Fig. 4.2). A waterfall cascades over the shelter after rain and a small but persistent seepage emerges immediately below the site, providing water for many months after larger and more exposed rainwater pools have dried up. Conditions for the preservation of archaeological deposits are less favourable at Snake Rock. The site is formed by a single boulder of monumental proportions, supported by several smaller rocks. From the north it is possible to see at a distance of nearly half a kilometre the giant painted snake from which the site is named. Beneath the shelter of the rocks the floor covers about 66 m². Rainwater runoff is able to flow through from the back of the shelter and part of the deposit has been washed out onto the talus slope.[294]

The archaeological deposit at Falls Rock Shelter comprised a series of sandy silt layers with admixtures of decomposed granite, ash, charred plant material and animal dung. Three phases of occupation were apparent from the stratigraphy shown in Figure 4.3. The first phase (A) comprised Units 1 to 4; the second phase (B) comprised Units 5 to 9, and the final occupation phase (C) was represented by Unit 10. The first phase began about 4,500 years ago; pottery appeared during the second phase accompanied by

---

[293] Pager (1993), citing Lewis-Williams (1981); Lewis-Williams and Dowson (1989); Yates et al. (1985). The detailed evidence of trance-related postures is overlooked by Lenssen-Erz (1998) both in a catalogue of postures and material culture items in the rock art, and in the statement that "Not one... picture...unambiguously matches the model of a trance dance" (1998: 24). However, this is not borne out by the rock art documentation of Pager (1989, 1993, 1995, 2000, 2006) which is replete with examples of trance performance imagery.

[294] Detailed descriptions of Falls Rock Shelter and Snake Rock are presented in Kinahan (2001a).

Figure 4.2: Falls Rock Shelter in the upper Hungorob Ravine, viewed from the west.

the first evidence of domestic sheep, about 2,000 years ago, and the site was evidently abandoned in the last 500 years after being used as a livestock fold during the final phase of occupation. The Snake Rock deposit is comparable, showing a first phase (A) of occupation comprising Units 3 to 5 dated to about 4,500 years ago, and a second occupation phase (B) represented by Units 9 to 11 dated to about 2,000 years ago (Fig. 4.4).[295] At both sites, the initial occupation deposit rested on a layer of hydrolized granite indicating the presence of warm, moist conditions prior to the late Holocene aridification noted in Chapter 3.[296]

---

295 Uncalibrated radiocarbon dates in years BP: 143±25 (D-AMS 030826); 730±70 (Wits-1100); 1,880±50 (Pta-2927); 2,040±50 (Pta-2930); 2,100±50 (Pta-2929); 3,370±60 (Pta-3121); 4,200±30 (Beta-462931); 4,380±60 (Pta-3122); 1,640±70 (Wits-1249); 1,840±50 (Pta-2886); 2,590±60 (Pta-2926); 4,510±70 (Pta-2917).

296 Similar indications of hydrolysis resulting from elevated moisture conditions in the mid-Holocene were observed at Gorrasis and described in Chapter 3.

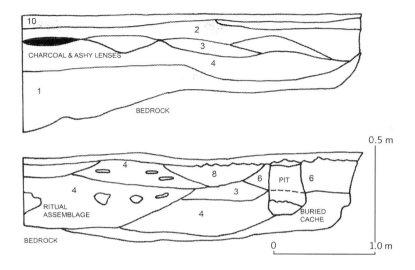

Figure 4.3: Stratigraphic profiles from Falls Rock Shelter, with units referred to in the text and indicating the ritual assemblage described in this chapter as well as the cache of metal beads, cowrie shells and other items described in Chapter 7.

Lithic assemblages from Falls Rock Shelter and Snake Rock were relatively large, totalling 15,076 and 2,149 pieces, respectively. Raw material usage in the Falls Rock Shelter assemblage was dominated by locally derived basalt (32.5%), with hydrothermal vein quartz (28.7%) and crystalline quartz (24.3%) also found in high numbers throughout the occupation record. Chert (5.6%) contributed a relatively small fraction of total raw materials, although it was the most intensively used, together with crystalline quartz which also had markedly low abundance of waste in relation to formal artefact numbers. As is typical of Mode 5 assemblages, only a small component consisted of formal tools, with a total of 157 from Falls Rock Shelter and 54 from Snake Rock. At Falls Rock Shelter, scrapers predominated (64) over segments (37) throughout the occupation sequence, with only small numbers of points and awls (17).

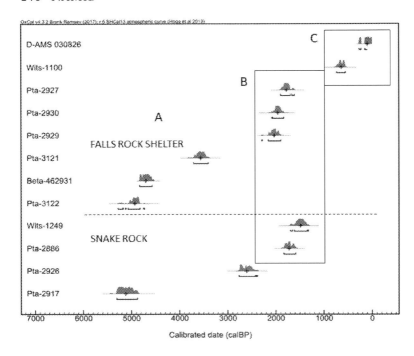

Figure 4.4: Calibrated radiocarbon dates for occupation phases A, B and C at Falls Rock Shelter and Snake Rock (see explanation in Notes to the Reader: Archaeological age determination, p. xvii).

When compared to the assemblages from Gorrasis and Kubub described in Chapter 3, a slight difference of emphasis is apparent. At Gorrasis, the overall assemblage was dominated by segments, with a ratio of 4:1 over scrapers, suggesting that the site was primarily used as a hunting camp, while at Kubub segments occurred less frequently, with a ratio of 1:4 over scrapers, suggesting that activities such as hide-working were important there. Gorrasis was occupied for brief periods when water and game were available, while Kubub appears to have served as a dry season refuge. The lithic assemblages from Falls Rock Shelter include both tool types, with scrapers and segments in an overall ratio of approximately 2:1. At Snake Rock the ratio is 3:1. In the case of the Hungorob sites there appears to be an overall emphasis on scrapers, suggesting a similarity to Kubub in the emphasis on activities which probably included hide-working, although the number of segments is relatively high, suggesting that hunting or the maintenance of hunting equipment was important. Thus, the Gorrasis and Kubub assemblages may represent polar extremes of opportunistic hunting as opposed to dry season residence, while the Hungorob assemblages represent a more balanced combination which might be characteristic of refugium occupation.

The relatively small formal tool assemblages from the Hungorob sites do not reveal any marked shifts in assemblage composition through the occupation sequence. However, it is possible to obtain a measure of the resemblance between the assemblages by an analysis of tool attribute combinations. This approach increases the number of variables, by scoring each tool for a number of common attributes, providing scores high enough to permit statistical comparison. To carry out this analysis, the sample of formal tools was sub-divided on the basis of retouch technique, thus tools with scraper retouch were separated from tools with backed retouch as characterizes segments, forming two mutually exclusive groups. Attribute scores were obtained for tools in the two groups according to one of three or four states offered by each of eight attributes of raw material, various size measurement classes, and attributes of retouch extent, angle and condition. The attribute scores were analysed to determine the degree of homogeneity within the assemblages as a whole, according to both retouch technique and occupation phase.[297]

The results of the attribute analysis are shown in the accompanying homogeneity dendrograms (Fig. 4.5). Overall, the similarity of stone tools in the initial occupation (A) and the occupation with the first appearance of pottery (B) at Falls Rock Shelter suggests that pottery was introduced to an existing technological assemblage which remained initially unchanged

---

297 Following Beavon and Hall (1972). The attribute analysis is described in detail in Kinahan (1984a).

142 NAMIB

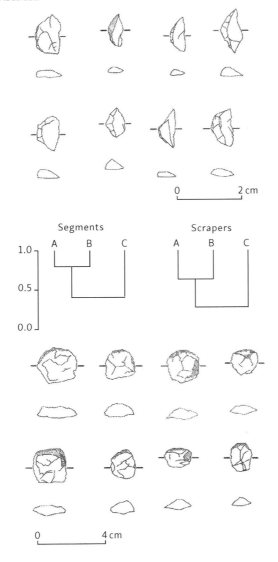

Figure 4.5: Mode 5 stone artefacts from Falls Rock Shelter, with examples of segments above and scrapers below (note difference in scale). The diagram at centre shows the similarity between assemblages from the three occupation phases A, B and C on the basis of attribute combinations among segments and scrapers.

by this innovation, and that marked differences only became apparent with established livestock-keeping in the final phase (C) of occupation.[298] The evidence from the two sites indicates permutations of a common and limited set of attributes. The evidence of the stone tool assemblages is therefore of a single evolving technological tradition rather than a series of different and successive traditions. The implications of this will be addressed in the rest of this chapter from the point of view of other sets of evidence including faunal remains, ritual objects and other miscellaneous finds from the two sites.

Faunal remains at Falls Rock Shelter and Snake Rock were dominated by hyrax *Procavia capensis*, rock hare *Pronolagus randensis*, and klipspringer *Oreotragus oreotragus*. These three species are represented in approximately the same proportion as their local abundance, thus reflecting their availability rather than cultural preference. Hyrax make up between 61% and 74% of individuals throughout the occupation sequence at both sites[299] (Table 4.1). Slow moving and gregarious, hyrax display effective anti-predator behaviour,[300] and where populations of hyrax face little grazing competition, such as in the Dâures massif, it is possible for the species to reach a biomass comparable to that of plains antelope.[301] Hyrax therefore present an important food source where few other species are available. Indeed, the age profile of hyrax remains as represented by dental eruption patterns indicated that both young and adult individuals were taken. This suggests that during occupation of the sites use of this resource was apparently sustainable. In comparison, the rock hare,

---

298 This evidence concurs with the observation of Miller and Sawchuk (2019) that the diameter of Holocene ostrich eggshell beads remained relatively uniform until in the last two millennia, and coincident with the introduction of pottery and livestock, assemblages began to include small numbers of beads with markedly greater diameters.
299 A detailed analysis of the faunal assemblages is presented in Kinahan (2001a)
300 Estes (1991: 251)
301 Hoeck (1982)

like all African hares[302] is solitary and mainly nocturnal; being difficult to run down on rocky ground, it is therefore possible that fibre cordage recovered from the sites was used to construct snares (Fig. 4.6). Klipspringer, on the other hand, are wary and difficult to approach on the mountainsides; they could have been hunted with bow and arrow although the species makes habitual use of communal latrine sites and could have been snared when visiting these.

Table 4.1: Species list and phase occurrence of principal faunal remains from Falls Rock Shelter and Snake Rock.

Site	Falls Rock Shelter			Snake Rock	
Phase Taxon MNI* (%)	A	B	C	A	B
LEPRORIDAE					
Pronolagus	9 (15)	19 (20)	3 (12)	6 (19)	12 (29)
PROCAVIIDAE					
Procavia	39 (66)	60 (63)	18 (69)	23 (74)	25 (61)
BOVIDAE					
Medium bovid					
cf *Ovis*	2 (3)	3 (3)	1 (4)	0 (0)	1 (2)
Oreotragus	9 (15)	14 (15)	4 (15)	2 (7)	3 (7)
Total	59	96	26	31	41

*Minimum Number of Individuals

Excavations at Big Elephant Shelter located 130 km south-east of Falls Rock Shelter yielded a comparable range of species, although there the faunal analysis suggested that hyrax in particular might represent the prey of leopards,[303] a possibility that could cast doubt on the faunal remains from the Hungorob

---

302 Smithers (1986)
303 Wadley (1979)

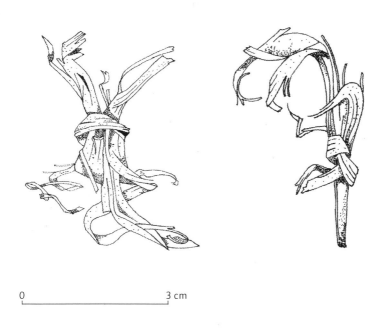

Figure 4.6: Knotted plant fibre from Falls Rock Shelter.

sites as evidence of human diet and refugium ecology. Additional evidence to address this question was therefore derived from two sources: an analysis of leopard scats collected in the vicinity of Falls Rock Shelter, and a series of experiments in which captive leopards were fed domestic rabbits to recover comparative scats and uneaten food remains showing indications of damage caused by leopard teeth. Analysis of scats from both sources yielded few identifiable skeletal parts; most bone ingested and passed as scats was so finely splintered that it contained very few identifiable elements. Overall, the remains suggested that breakage patterns and the relative survival of skeletal elements was determined by the physical properties of the bones, an observation that could explain compositional similarities in the experimental and archaeological assemblages.[304]

Other evidence of damage does allow reliable distinction between predator and human diet in this instance. Hyrax from archaeological contexts appear to have been roasted whole and consequently the bones show clean breaks, as opposed to the ragged breaks made by predators on fresh bone. Leopard, it was found in the course of experimental feeding of captive animals, also leave easily recognizable tooth marks on the cranium and on the pelvic bones of small prey, such as shown in Figure 4.7. Such marks are mainly visible on bones that were not fully ingested but found among regurgitated remains. Using these criteria, comparison of the experimental data and the archaeological evidence confirms that hyrax from Falls Rock Shelter are, with a small number of possible exceptions, human rather than predator food.

Dependence on the three principal prey species found in the upper Hungorob illustrates both the isolation of the sites from the food resources of the desert plains, as well as the relative sustainability of refugium occupation. Other species were scarce and appeared to have had little importance in the diet. However, bone splinters with cortical thickness exceeding 4 mm and therefore presumably derived from plains antelope and larger species were found among the faunal remains. Many of these had been worked into spatulas, scrapers, awls and link-shafts for composite arrows. Clearly, heavier bone than could be provided by the various mountain species formed a valuable raw material. The faunal assemblages also yielded a small number of bones from medium-sized bovids and of these the identifiable

---

304 A total of 25 individual domestic rabbits *Oryctolagus cuniculus* were fed to three different captive leopards; scats and uneaten remains were collected after each feeding, cleaned, analysed as to representation of skeletal elements and examined for indications of surface damage. Chi^2 values exceeded 16.92 for the frequency of ten selected skeletal elements from the Falls Rock Shelter and Big Elephant Shelter hyrax assemblages, and from the experimental domestic rabbit assemblages, suggesting that assemblage frequencies were not governed by chance association.

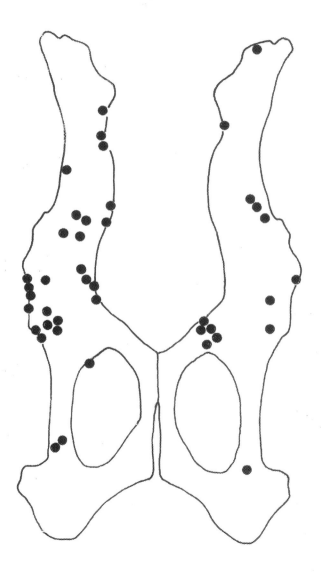

Figure 4.7: Common positions of leopard tooth marks on the pelvic girdle of small mammal prey items.

specimens were primarily associated with the pottery (B phase) occupation at the two sites. These bones include the earliest evidence of domestic sheep in the Namib Desert, identified on the basis of morphology, comparative measurements from sheep *Ovis aries*, and the only other similar-sized wild antelope in this general area, klipspringer *Oreotragus oreotragus* and springbuck *Antidorcas marsupialis*.[305]

The stratigraphic distribution of the medium-sized bovid remains from Falls Rock Shelter and Snake Rock is presented in Table 4.2. The dating of units associated with sheep remains at Falls Rock Shelter and Snake Rock is set out in Figure 4.8.[306] Diagnostic medium-sized bovid remains include a proximal femural epiphysis from Unit 10 at Falls Rock Shelter which has a maximum diameter of 19.4 mm, compared to 19.3 mm for a modern comparative sheep specimen from the same part of Namibia. This diameter is substantially greater than that of the klipspringer at 15.5 mm and substantially less than that of the springbuck at 22 mm and that of impala *Aepyceros melampus* at 23 mm. These measurement differences do not reflect natural variation within the different taxa, but they strongly suggest that the specimen in question is from a sheep. Similar comparative observations can be made on a number of other skeletal parts, with greater or less certainty of identification, as discussed below.

For example, medium-sized bovid metapodial bones occur at both Falls Rock Shelter and Snake Rock; two distal metatarsal epiphyses from Unit 6 at Falls Rock Shelter have a maximum diameter (measured across the articulation) of 14.4 mm and 15 mm respectively. The comparative measurements are 12.7 mm for klipspringer and 18.3 mm for springbuck. The same measurement for the comparative sheep specimen is 15 mm, suggesting that the archaeological specimens are from sheep.[307] A distal metatarsal

---

305 Kinahan (2016b)
306 Uncalibrated radiocarbon dates: 1,880±50 (Pta-2927); 2,040±50 (Pta-2930); 2,100±50 (Pta-2929); 1,640±70 (Wits-1249); 1,840±50 (Pta-2886).
307 Measurements of specimens are indicative rather than diagnostic.

epiphysis from Unit 10 at Snake Rock is marginally larger than the comparative klipspringer and its identification is therefore uncertain. A calcaneus upper (posterior) half from Unit 6 at Falls Rock Shelter closely resembles the same element from the comparative sheep, both in size and general morphology, but the specimen is incomplete and cannot provide comparative measurements. The carpal and tarsal bones from Units 6 and 9 at Falls Rock Shelter are ambiguous; however, first phalanges from Units 6 and 8 at Falls Rock Shelter included four specimens with a mid-shaft minimum diameter of 7.7 mm, similar to that of the klipspringer at 7.2 mm and are therefore unlikely to be from sheep. In contrast, the specimen from Unit 10 at Snake Rock has a mid-shaft minimum diameter of 9.4 mm and a length of 38.3 mm, which closely compares with that of sheep at 10 mm and 37.7 mm, respectively.[308] The same measurements on klipspringer are 7.5 mm and 35 mm and on springbuck 10 mm and 46.8 mm, respectively.

Table 4.2: Stratigraphic distribution of medium-sized bovid remains from Falls Rock Shelter and Snake Rock post-dating 2,100 BP.

Skeletal part	Falls Rock Shelter				Snake Rock
Unit	6	8	9	10	10
Femur				1	
Metapodial	2			2	1
Calcaneus	1				
Carpals			1		
Tarsals	1				
Phalange 1	2	2			1
MNI	1	1	1	1	1

---

308 cf. Zeder & Lapham (2010)

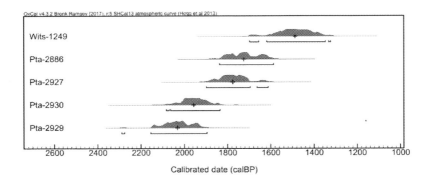

Figure 4.8: Radiocarbon dating of stratigraphic units associated with sheep *Ovis aries* at Falls Rock Shelter and Snake Rock.

In terms of diagnostic skeletal elements, therefore, sheep are represented at Falls Rock Shelter by six limb extremity bones in Unit 6, two in Unit 8, one in Unit 9, and three in Unit 10. The concentration of bones in Unit 6 (Table 4.2) is considered to represent an acquisition of sheep at approximately 2,000 BP. Sheep are represented at Snake Rock by two diagnostic elements in Unit 10, associated with a younger date which, however, also falls within the early first millennium AD.

Pottery at Falls Rock Shelter is associated with the B and C occupation phases, and with the B occupation phase at Snake Rock. Early pottery in the Hungorob is represented by an array of thin-walled and finely burnished body sherds, rim sherds bearing a variety of punctate and incised decoration, and, from Falls Rock Shelter, a small, globular pot, entirely without decoration. The pot was most probably made from coarse clays found in the immediate area and had been extensively repaired with patches of vegetable gum. It could be that pottery was initially introduced from multiple sources, in some cases reaching the site as isolated sherds rather than whole pots. This question is addressed in more detail in Chapter 6 which examines the link between pottery and the technology of food production in the Namib Desert. Seen from the evidence found in the Hungorob excavations, pottery, and domestic sheep were acquired most likely via exchange relationships with pastoralist groups entering the region about 2,000 years ago, although they were not necessarily received together or from the same source.

Dry conditions, especially at Falls Rock Shelter, have ensured exceptional preservation of organic remains, providing evidence that supports a number of new insights into late Holocene human behaviour. Much of the preserved organic material at this site was associated with a series of grass-lined bedding hollows positioned around a central hearth area. Two important finds, an assemblage of ritual paraphernalia dating to the initial occupation of the site, and a cache of metal beads, cowrie shells and other objects dating from the final occupation phase, had been deliberately buried in the deposit below the bedding hollows. The ritual assemblage is discussed in the second part of this chapter and the cache of beads and other materials in Chapter 7.

Among the array of finds were large numbers of ostrich eggshell beads, including 1,329 from Falls Rock Shelter. Ostrich do not occur on the Dâures massif itself and the beads, as well as eggshell for their manufacture, would have been brought from the desert plains, or obtained as finished beads from even further afield. Unfinished beads and grooved stones that could have been used to smooth them show that beads were manufactured at Falls Rock Shelter. Apart from sheep and pottery introduced from elsewhere, there is little obvious evidence to reflect on the possible existence of the wider social networks posited in Chapter 3 as essential to hunter-gatherer survival in the desert. A single exception is an ochre-smeared marine limpet shell *Patella granularis*, indicating contact with the Atlantic coast nearly 100 km to the west. However, strontium isotope analysis of the Falls Rock Shelter ostrich eggshell beads provides new evidence for the existence of spatially diversified exchange networks throughout the occupation sequence at the Hungorob sites.

Isotopic tracers, particularly strontium, have proven useful as indicators of movement by human groups in the archaeological record.[309] Strontium in bedrock moves into soil and groundwater systems and thus into the food chain, without fractionation by biological processes. Consequently, the strontium isotope composition of materials such as bone reflect the nutrient and moisture pathway of organisms which in turn reflect the strontium isotope composition of the local geology.[310] Ostrich eggshell beads have been implicated in exchange networks both among hunter-gatherer communities in southern Africa and between hunter-gatherers and adjacent pastoralist and farming communities.[311] The strontium isotope composition of ostrich eggshell beads may therefore be expected to reflect the isotopic signature of their area of origin. It is assumed that even if their origin is not known, relative differences of isotopic composition should provide an indication of the relative diversity of bead sources represented within bead assemblages, seen against the background isotopic signature of the site locality.[312]

To test the expectation that diversity in isotopic ratios $^{87}Sr/^{86}Sr$ in ostrich eggshell beads would exceed that of their archaeological locality and indicate diversity of source areas represented in assemblages, three groups of beads were analysed from the A, B and C occupation phases, respectively, at Falls Rock Shelter. To characterize the local background isotopic signature, ten samples of hyrax bone were analysed from the same assemblages.[313] The overall distribution of strontium values for the Falls Rock Shelter ostrich eggshell beads is presented in Figure 4.9. The background samples from hyrax foraging in the

---

309 Ericson (1989); Sealy (1989); Sealy et al. (1991).
310 Blum et al. (2000); Faure (1986); Price et al. (2002: 118)
311 e.g. Cashdan (1985); Jolly (1996); Mitchell (1996); Wiessner (1982, 2009)
312 Stewart et al. (2020)
313 Analyses were performed by P. le Roux in the MC-ICP-MS facility, Department of Geological Sciences, University of Cape Town, using NIST SRM987 as reference standard.

vicinity of the site have an extremely narrow range. In contrast, the A, B and C occupation phase beads show much greater ranges, confirming that they represent an array of isotopic signatures from outside the site locality. Strontium values for a 150 km sampling transect, also shown in Figure 4.9, indicate the range of diversity from the sub-regional setting of the Dâures massif. When the site was first occupied in the A phase, its occupants evidently participated in a diverse (yet spatially undefined) social network. Although the site was a refugium, it was not socially isolated. The distribution of values in the B phase is marginally greater, and the increased diversity of strontium values during this phase is consistent with evidence of a more diversified social network, which brought sheep and pottery to the site. In these terms, the social network appears to contract slightly during the C phase when the site was integrated within a pastoral economy, and bead exchange may have played a secondary role in social network maintenance.

Evidence presented so far in this chapter corroborates the general pattern of late Holocene hunter-gatherer responses to climatic aridification observed elsewhere in southern Africa, involving an intensified use of local resources and the adoption of more specialized subsistence practices. This is demonstrated by the use of the Dâures massif as a refugium where occupation could be sustained by a combination of reliable water and sustainable exploitation of small game species. The Dâures massif was one among several island-like situations presented by inselbergen in the Namib Desert and on its interior margins which also saw intensified occupation during this period.[314] The arguments presented in Chapter 3 for the existence of alternating aggregation and dispersal of hunter-gatherer communities rested on ecological considerations and the assumption that such movements would be structured by extensive social networks. This is supported in the present chapter by the results of strontium isotope analyses

---

314 Well studied examples include the Spitzkoppen (Kinahan 1990) and Erongo mountains (Wadley 1979).

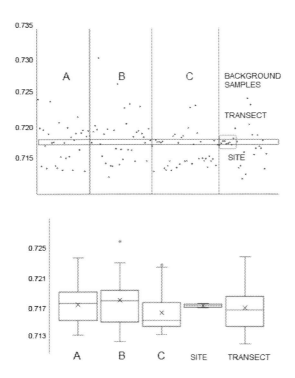

Figure 4.9: Distribution of $^{87}Sr/^{86}Sr$ values for ostrich eggshell beads from the A, B and C occupation phases at Falls Rock Shelter, with background values for hyrax bone from the site and from a 150 km transect through the sub-regional setting of the Dâures massif. Box-and-whisker plots indicate the range, mode, median and quartiles for the same data.

of ostrich eggshell beads which show that hunter-gatherers in the Hungorob formed part of extended social networks.

Stone tool assemblages from the Hungorob sites indicate a balanced emphasis on hunting and activities such as hide-working, and show a range of tasks previously separated by opportunistic hunting alternating with dry season aggregation; also, the basic toolkit remained the same throughout the sequence of occupation, suggesting a locally adapted technology that did not change with the introduction of pottery and sheep. These latter innovations probably reached the Hungorob via networks which the strontium evidence suggests may have expanded significantly at this time. The quantity of early pottery available from the Hungorob is small, but it is stylistically diverse, suggesting that multiple sources could have been involved, thus potentially corroborating the strontium analysis of ostrich eggshell beads from Falls Rock Shelter. Furthermore, although the technology of potting was evidently adopted, the significance of sheep remains as a food source appears to have been small, at least in the period before the rock shelter sites were abandoned for open encampments. More detailed analysis of pottery from the Hungorob and elsewhere in the Namib Desert is presented in Chapter 6 which also includes the application of strontium isotope analysis to the question of diverse origins for early pottery.

Sheep remains are difficult to identify with certainty, and although there are a number of reported instances from the Namib Desert, these are of generally questionable validity.[315]

---

315 Possible early first millennium AD sheep remains have been reported from four sites in Namibia. Sandelowsky et al. (1979) assigned a date of 1,550±40 BP to a sample of hair identified as sheep at Mirabib Shelter; Smith and Jacobson (1995) reported sheep bone from a context associated with a date of 1,790±80 BP at Geduld; Pleurdeau et al. (2012) reported sheep teeth dated to 2,270±40 BP at Leopard Cave, but the identification has been rejected on genetic grounds (Le Meillour 2017); and Albrecht et al. (2001) reported sheep bone from a context dated to 1,306±36 BP at Oruwanje. Difficulties with dating, stratigraphic control and identification of these finds is discussed in Kinahan (2016b).

Figure 4.10: Assemblage of suspected sheep bone splinters from Snake Rock, with polished tips and perforated for stringing.

The presence of sheep and possibly cattle is firmly established in the area immediately south of the Orange River in the early first millennium AD, although some identifications and dating have been disputed.[316] The absence of similar-sized bovids from the Dâures massif and the small range of similar-sized species from

---

316 See Webley (1992a,b, 2007); Dewar & Marsh (2018)

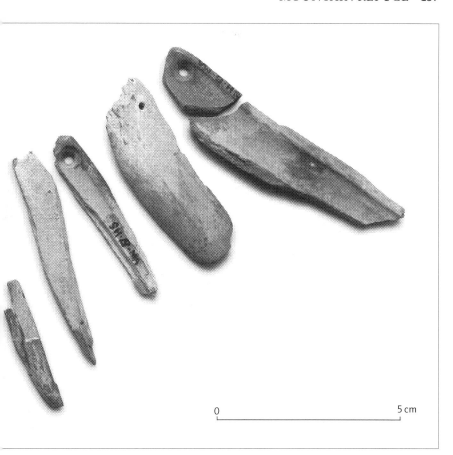

the surrounding area narrows the range of possibilities and allows greater confidence of identification based on the morphology and comparative measurement of skeletal elements.[317] Medium-sized bovid remains from these sites were highly fragmented, mainly

---

317 Identification of medium-sized bovid remains discussed here is based on comparative morphology and measurement of adult, fully fused skeletal elements from archaeological contexts, and reference material comprising specimens from single, unsexed adult individuals. The remains are dated by context only, due to the limited amount of available material, and no genetic confirmation is available for the specimens (cf. Horsburgh & Rhines 2010; Muigai & Hanotte 2013).

through butchery but also through the apparent modification of some bones for use as ritual objects. There is evidence for the use of small stock metapodial bones as personal ornaments among recent Namib Desert nomadic pastoralists (see Chapters 7 & 8). It is therefore significant that in the B occupation phase at Snake Rock fourteen slivers of suspected sheep bone were found buried in a stone-lined pit (Fig. 4.10).

The bone slivers show extensive modification including surface polish and end-perforations measuring approximately 2 mm in diameter on eight fragments, suggesting that they would have been strung together. The bone fragments are not diagnostic but their shape allows some to be matched with the diaphysis or shaft portions of specific skeletal elements. For example, satisfactory matches were made with the shaft of a sheep tibia (right side, posterior surface), and the posterior surface of a sheep radius (right side) near the mid-point of the shaft (Fig. 4.11). This indicates an element of ritual intensification associated with the introduction of pottery and sheep. In the next part of this chapter we consider the rock art in more detail, as part of a body of evidence for a fundamental transformation in hunter-gatherer society. The evidence includes material remains referring directly to shamanic ritual practice.

Rise of the shaman

The abundance of rock art in the Dâures massif, as illustrated by the evidence from the Hungorob, presents a marked contrast to the surrounding desert plains, where occupation is only feasible after rain for periods as short as a few weeks, by small groups.[318] The great concentration of rock art sites in the Dâures massif is not only evidence of more extended residence; it also points to intensive ritual activity coinciding with aggregated occupation during the driest months of the year.[319] Thus, while the occurrence and distribution of rock art agrees with ecological

---

318 e.g. Richter (1984); Sievers (1984); Kinahan & Kinahan (2003, 2006).
319 Kinahan (2001), citing Lee (1972) and Guenther (1999).

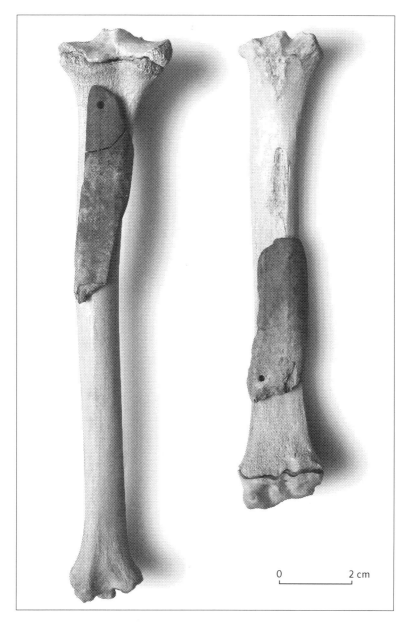

Figure 4.11: Suspected sheep bone splinters from Snake Rock matched to comparative sheep tibia (left) and radius (right).

conditions indicating that the Dâures massif was a refugium for desert communities, it also opens the possibility that the rock art and the material archaeological record would reflect aspects of hunter-gatherer social and ritual life, and not only the details of technology and subsistence behaviour.

Prominent in the rock art of the Dâures massif but far less numerous than the monochrome paintings described in the previous section, are detailed bichrome and polychrome human figures found mainly among the larger rock art sites in the Hungorob and elsewhere on the mountain.[320] These are frequently superimposed on the monochromes and are predominantly of men rather than women, all highly individualised in appearance. Such figures are well represented at both Falls Rock Shelter and Snake Rock. It is notable that in general they are not shown in the setting of the ritual dance characteristic of the monochrome figures. A further clearly distinguishing feature of these figures is the depiction of specialist ritual accoutrements, most commonly flywhisks, held in one or both hands and of dancing rattles shown around the ankles and sometimes the wrists. These figures sometimes also have what appear to be animal skin cloaks, or karosses, elaborate headdresses and various straps around the knees, elbows, belly and chest, again items suggestive of ritual attire.[321]

While most objects depicted in the rock art, such as bows, arrows, quivers, clubs and other recognisable items of material culture are clearly utilitarian,[322] elaborate ritual paraphernalia

---

[320] Lenssen-Erz states that the Hungorob polychromes are no more than[?] 'a small spot check' (2004: 133) and therefore not representative of the Dâures rock art. In fact, images similar to those on which my interpretation is based (Kinahan 2001a) are widely distributed over the mountain (e.g. Pager 1989: 153, 204, 247, 289, 309, 1995: 87, 201, 227, 259, 1998: 49, 336, 385, 398, 2000: 102, 159, 299, 330, 2006: 63, 92, 120, 133, 191, 240, 281, 309, 314, 372, 410) and thus provide general confirmation of the Hungorob records.

[321] Kinahan (2001a)

[322] cf. Eastwood (2006); Jolly (2006)

including headgear, flywhisks, dancing rattles and cloak-like garments are also widely featured in the more complex ritual art of southern Africa.[323] Until now, however, no definite archaeological evidence of such equipment has been found; indeed it is held that the practices shown in the rock art involved 'little manipulation of physical ritual objects...it is rather concepts that are being manipulated'[324] and that the shaman as depicted was a figure belonging more to the imagination than to the material world and — by implication — the archaeological record. Here, we consider evidence in the form of ritual paraphernalia excavated at Falls Rock Shelter and dated to the first occupation of the site approximately 4,500 years ago. The assemblage of ritual equipment provides a unique insight into shamanic practice and a material link, lacking until now, with the rock art of this region. We begin with the rock art itself, before examining the ritual assemblage.[325]

The most well-known example of the complex bichrome and polychrome rock art of the Dâures massif is found at the Maack Shelter in the Tsisab Ravine, about 14 km north-east of the Hungorob sites. The site is commonly referred to in terms of one particular figure: the so-called "White Lady", once proposed — but quickly dismissed — as evidence of an ancient Mediterranean connection with the rock art of the Namib Desert.[326] The central figures of the frieze (Fig. 4.12) illustrate the general characteristics of the bichrome and polychrome men described above. The figure on the left is the eponymous White Lady, whose male sex is clearly shown by an ornamented penis. This embellishment, together with the bow and arrow, serves as a common secondary sexual convention in both the monochromes and these more elaborate paintings. Visible in both figures are various individualised body decorations, including a sort of cummerbund, and headdresses

---

323 e.g. Lewis-Williams (1983); Lewis Williams & Dowson (1989).
324 Lewis-Williams (1981: 82).
325 The ritual assemblage is described in full elsewhere (Kinahan 2018a).
326 Kinahan (1995a); see discussion in Chapter 1.

Figure 4.12: The so-called White Lady frieze at the Maack Shelter, Tsisab Ravine, reproduced with permission of the late Harald Pager. The "White Lady" (left) is approximately 25 cm high. Note the presence of dancing rattles on the ankles of both figures, and various other decorative items including headdresses, knee-straps and a cummerbund worn above the ornamented penis.

with elaborate protrusions, possibly including feathers. Dancing rattles are shown on the ankles of the figure on the left and on the wrists and ankles of the figure on the right. The figure on the right holds two spatulate objects resembling large feathers, while that on the left has similar-shaped objects protruding from

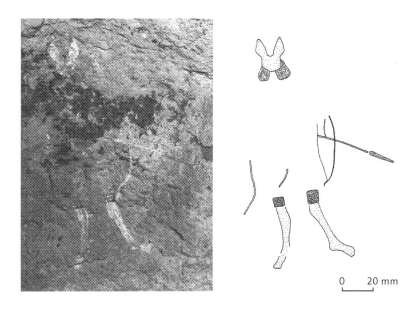

Figure 4.13: Shaman figure from Falls Rock Shelter showing antelope-eared headdress, flywhisk and knee straps. Note that the figure, approximately 13 cm in height, is in frontal view with the legs painted *genu valgum* to resemble an antelope.

bands around the upper arm. A feature unique to this frieze is the cup-shaped object, possibly a small vessel, held in front and at face level by the figure on the left. Both figures also have short strokes on various parts of the body, including the chest, belly and thighs.

In Figure 4.13, a painting from the south-western wall of Falls Rock Shelter is shown to comprise an isolated bichrome human figure painted, unusually, in frontal view. Clearly male, as indicated by a bow with a nocked arrow, the figure represents a shaman carrying a flywhisk and wearing decorated knee-straps. The legs are white below the knee, with slight *genu valgum* ("knock-knee"), the feet angled so that they resemble the hocks of an antelope. This is combined with a white antelope-eared cap with dark pendant cheek flaps. Thus, the figure is not only wearing antelope-like ornamentation or clothing but also has some physical attributes of the antelope itself, showing that it is therefore a metaphorical image rather than a realistic representation of a shaman figure disguised as an antelope. Elsewhere in the Hungorob, there are other examples of antelope shown in frontal view,[327] a perspective that renders them bipedal, and therefore human-like. In this instance, both the flywhisk and the knee-straps are conventionalised items associated with shamanic ritual, as is the eared headgear.[328] As items of equipment or clothing these might represent artefacts that were used as ritual paraphernalia and could therefore be expected to form part of the material assemblage of the site. However, ritual equipment or fragments of it would be recognizable only if utilitarian purpose could be excluded, such as if it were found in a context that supported its ritual association. This condition is met by the assemblage of items I will now describe from Falls Rock Shelter.

The ritual assemblage comprised a cup-like vessel made from the skull of a Cape hunting dog *Lycaon pictus*; a number of cocoons, probably of a saturniid, or emperor, moth (*Lasiocampidae* gen. et sp. indet.), suspected ostrich *Struthio camelus* feathers, and a fragment of finely stitched leather. The absence of ash, bone and other occupation debris from the context of the find suggests deliberate burial in an otherwise sterile layer. Supporting this interpretation is the fact that the items in the assemblage were found together rather than dispersed. The stratigraphic context of the ritual assemblage is the basal unit of the deposit, consisting of a layer of coarse weathered granite resting directly on bedrock. This unit belongs to the initial or A occupation phase of the site, dating to between 4,300 and 3,300 years ago. Confirmation of this association was obtained from a small sample of charred mastic-like compound adhering to

---

327 Pager (1993: 248–249)
328 Lewis-Williams (1981)

the base of the Cape hunting dog cranium which was dated to 4,200 years cal. BP (see Fig. 4.14). [329]

The cranial portion of the hunting dog skull was extensively modified by the removal of some parts, cutmarks, abrasion scars and surface polish, together with the application of vegetable resin both within and on the outside of the cranium. In contrast to the frontal and lateral parts, the posterior of the cranium, including the delicate ridge of the occipital crest, is largely intact (Fig. 4.14). This is noteworthy because the removal of the head from a fresh carcass usually causes severe damage especially to the occipital. In fact, the relative intactness of these parts indicates that the skull was probably obtained from a partly decomposed and disarticulated specimen, rather than from an animal brought down by hunters. To fashion the vessel, most of the frontal portion of the skull was cut away, leaving the parietal, squamosal, pterygoid and supra-occipital parts largely intact. The jugal arch was removed entirely on both sides, as was the sagittal crest, which appears to have been sawn and ground away at the base. The bullae and condyles were also removed. To seal the vessel, the foramen magnum was plugged with vegetable resin containing a dense admixture of fine charcoal, sand, bone fragments, grass and feathers, suggesting that the work was done in a living site rather than at some other location.

Although it is possible that the vessel was used as a storage container for aromatic herbs or similar medicinal preparations, the polished wear along the severed edge forming the rim of the vessel and over the base of the sagittal crest suggests otherwise. The fact that the rim of the vessel on the ventral surface of the skull is considerably lower than the extensively polished rim on the dorsal surface reduces its capacity as a container. Moreover, the form of the vessel and the indications of use-wear, together with the evidence of burial, and its association with other suspected ritual paraphernalia, point to its use in

---

329 The dating of the ritual assemblage is discussed in detail elsewhere (Kinahan 2018a).

Figure 4.14: Falls Rock Shelter ritual vessel made from the cranium of a Cape hunting dog *Lycaon pictus*.

a scooping or scraping action. We examine this possibility in more detail below.

Moth cocoons, such as those recovered with the hunting dog cranium, are relatively tough and fibrous when fresh. In the natural state, cocoons of this kind are found attached to the lower branches of shrubs and trees. They would have been available in the area near the site, but never within the shelter itself, and must therefore have been gathered and brought in. Moth cocoons become brittle and delicate with time and would not survive intact and together among rock shelter surface debris, which argues in favour of their deliberate burial with the cranium vessel. Significantly, two of the cocoons have visible puncture marks near the base (Fig. 4.15) consistent with piercing on ethnographic examples of moth cocoon dancing rattles. The cocoons at Falls Rock Shelter would thus have formed part of a string of dancing rattles, an artefact believed to possess ritual potency and used solely for ritual purposes among modern San.[330]

The feathers were found in direct association with the cranium vessel and the cocoons. Obtained from the body or underwing area of a large bird, probably an ostrich,[331] the feathers are pale and downy at the base and light brown in colour, with faint banding towards the mid-section and tip. These features, consistent with a juvenile ostrich or adult female, are also found in the plumage of other large species in this area, such as bustards. The natural colour of the feathers is obscured by a light reddish-brown staining derived from the basal deposit in the site or, more likely, from the haematite ochre found in the occupation deposit at the site. Last among the items associated with this assemblage was a fragment of stitched leather that probably formed part of a bag. The fragment consists of two pieces of thin leather joined by closely spaced stitches of finely twirled sinew. The seam joining the pieces of leather ends with a slender knotted thong.

---

330 Lewis-Williams & Dowson (1989: 44)
331 Hollmann (2001) and Lewis-Williams (2000) discuss the ritual importance of ostrich and their plumage.

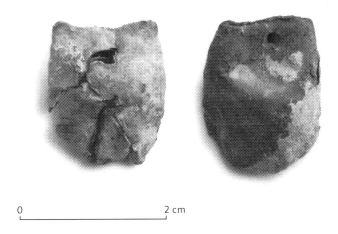

Figure 4.15: Moth cocoons associated with the ritual vessel at Falls Rock Shelter. Both are pierced to be strung as dancing rattles.

The items from this assemblage reflect on aspects of shamanic ritual practice that are not apparent in the rock art, yielding insights that are new to the study of rock art both in the Namib Desert and the wider region, as the following brief discussion will show. First, the hunting dog *Lycaon pictus* is a predator of the semi-desert plains and the skull would therefore have been taken up the mountain to Falls Rock Shelter rather than being obtained near the site itself. Furthermore, its use is probably not coincidental, for the animal possesses some remarkable traits: it is the most social of the African carnivores, to the extent that the survival of the young, as with hunter-gatherers, is entirely dependent on co-operative hunting and food-sharing in the pack.[332] Another human-like trait is an exclusive reliance on

---

332 Estes (1991: 410–8)

diurnal hunting, making the species almost a paragon among hunters. Also, aggression among members of the pack is unusual and the sociability of the hunting dog is commonly expressed in mutual grooming and a preference for close physical contact when at rest. There are a further two unusual traits that Holocene hunter-gatherers in the Namib are certain to have noticed: one is the fact that, like humans, each individual hunting dog is unique in its colouration and appearance. Another is the animal's powerful body odour, which might have recalled the perspiration of shamans in ritual performance.

Apart from an intriguing parallel with the cup-shaped object resembling a small vessel held by the so-called White Lady (Fig. 4.12), rock art offers few clues as to the identity or function of the skull vessel. However, the two central figures in that frieze have short strokes on various parts of the body, including the chest, belly and thighs, and I have suggested elsewhere[333] that these strokes may represent the ritually potent perspiration that the shaman would have applied to the bodies of people attending a healing ceremony or trance dance.[334] The form and surface wear on the vessel indicate that it may have served as a scoop, rather than as a storage container, and to function as such it would have been held upside down with the higher dorsal rim facing forward. Used in this way, the vessel would acquire its smooth glossy polish on the dorsal rim and the outside surface below. Surface polish over the rounded outside of the vessel could be the result of contact with a soft and pliable surface, such as the hand or another part of the human body. It is therefore conceivable that the vessel was used to collect and distribute ritually potent perspiration from the body of the shaman.

The vessel would have been an object imbued with ritual significance and potency, making it likely that this and the other objects associated with it, the dancing rattles and feathers, were deliberately buried to place them out of reach, and also

---

333 Kinahan (2001a)
334 Garlake (1990); Kinahan (2001a); Ouzman (2001)

out of sight. For this reason, the fragment of stitched leather found with the vessel and other objects is of particular interest. The fragment appears to be part of a bag, as indicated by the knotted thong at one end, and its association suggests that it is the remains of a container for the objects found buried together. This is significant, for while leather bags were common utilitarian items, they also served a metaphorical purpose, such that the ritual objects placed in the bag entered the skin and thus became part of the animal from which the bag was made.[335] In the ritual context, the objects would emerge from concealment in the bag, being taken out by the shaman to be used as powerful aids to performance in healing and related ceremonial activity.[336] Several of the bichrome and polychrome painted figures from Snake Rock carry items such as fly whisks and bows; they wear what seem to be long cloaks of animal hide, or karosses, and have animal heads. These along with the figures in the White Lady frieze, are all men, highly individualized in appearance, and probably represent the specialist shamans whose ritual work made use of artefacts such as I have just described.

The concealment of the ritual assemblage in the bag and the shaman entering the skin of the antelope in the form of a kaross prior to ritual performance both represent a stage of latency, or occultation, in which the shaman disappears from view. This is followed by his emergence for the purpose of ritual performance. A two-stage process, of ritual preparation involving concealment or occultation, and ritual performance involving revelation or manifestation, is consistent with shamanic art and ritual practice in southern Africa[337] although it has not been explicitly recognized as the basis of ritual performance depicted in the rock art, due to the absence until now, of evidence such as we have discussed here. With this evidence, a link is established via the

---

335 Lewis-Williams & Dowson (1989: 117)
336 cf. Dowson (1994); Eastwood (2008); Russell & Lander (2015)
337 Lewis-Williams (1983); Lewis-Williams & Pearce (2004); Eastwood & Eastwood (2006); Forsmann & Gutteridge (2012)

ritual assemblage from Falls Rock Shelter to ritual performance and rock art as part of a common tradition.

Parallels between this process and the lifecycle of the emperor moth were probably apparent to the hunter-gatherers of the Dâures massif and may explain why they were used for ritual purposes here and elsewhere in southern Africa. The cocoons used as dancing rattles represent the pupal (hidden) stage preceding the emergence, or eclosure of the adult moth.[338] In ritual practice, the cocoons are associated with the preparation or enclosure of the shaman and his emergence for ritual performance when he wears the cocoon rattles.[339] It is important to note that the most clearly depicted moths in the Dâures rock art show on their wings the characteristic eye-spot, or ocellus, of the emperor moth.[340] It is therefore possible to argue that these paintings also refer to the two-stage process of ritual behaviour described here, with the moth representing the emergent shaman. There is also, of course, a striking resemblance in the trailing wings of the emergent moths shown in the paintings, to the trailing cloak-like kaross worn by the shaman. The simplified model in Table 4.3 shows a series of links between the rock art depiction of the shaman, the life cycle of the emperor moth and the ritual objects recovered from the excavation of Falls Rock Shelter.

In this chapter we have seen that late Holocene hunter-gatherers readily adapted to increasing aridity by establishing themselves at refugium sites with reliable water and food resources. As occurred elsewhere in southern Africa, Namib Desert communities increasingly depended on localized populations of small game in a pattern of intensified subsistence that was largely sustainable. This strategy clearly required the maintenance of extended social networks as evidenced by the strontium isotope ratios

---

338 cf. Borror et al. (2004).
339 Paintings identified as moths among the rock art of the Dâures massif have been interpreted as evidence of a widely held Khoesan mythology by Hollmann (2007).
340 Documented by Pager (2000); Hollmann (2007: 93, Figures 10 and 11).

Table 4.3: The structural dimensions of ritual preparation and performance in the context of rock art and the ritual assemblage from Falls Rock Shelter, showing the common role of occultation or concealment in preparation for ritual performance.

Ritual context SHAMAN	Preparation OCCULTATION	Performance REVELATION
Rock art	Enclosure (skin of animal metaphor)	Shaman in action (ritual paraphernalia)
Ritual assemblage	Concealment (in leather bag and buried)	Exposure (used in ritual context)
Lifecycle of moth	Pupal stage (cocoon)	Eclosure (emergence and flight)

of ostrich eggshell beads. It was through these networks that hunter-gatherers acquired pottery and sheep as these innovations spread through the region in the last two millennia. The adoption of pastoralism is not so much a technological shift as a social phenomenon, involving the development of social relations of property in livestock. It is not surprising therefore to find that in the Hungorob the evidence of stone tools and other related artefacts is relatively insensitive to this change.[341]

Social networks based on gift exchange are generally associated with the customs of Kalahari hunter-gatherers among whom the practice is known as *hxaro*.[342] Strontium isotope analyses have shown that the exchange of ostrich eggshell beads by hunter-gatherer groups is of great antiquity in southern Africa.[343] The strontium isotope evidence presented in this chapter shows that ostrich eggshell bead exchange persisted after the adoption of pastoralism, indicating that the adaptive value of this practice was

---

341 Kinahan (1996a), citing Ingold (1980)
342 Wiessner (1982); Mitchell (2003)
343 Stewart et al. (2020)

not limited to hunter-gatherer social organization. The concept of *hxaro,* being specific to hunter-gatherer social organization is therefore insufficient to explain the existence of ostrich eggshell bead exchange networks under a fundamentally changed social organization. Indeed, an ecological basis for the maintenance of extended exchange networks is apparent in the need for socially negotiated mobility across the desert landscape, as demonstrated by evidence discussed in this and the previous chapter.

In this chapter we have seen that ritual practice, involving concepts of occultation and transformative shamanic states, played an important role in the integration of pottery and sheep into hunter-gatherer society, for example, through the possible use of sheep bones as ritual objects. The evidence here has revealed in considerable detail aspects of shamanic ritual performance that are crucial to an understanding of the further evidence of shamanic practice in the next chapter, where we examine the process by which the shaman effected fundamental shifts in the social values and behaviour of hunter-gatherer communities in transition towards the adoption of food production and livestock-keeping.

The rock art of the Dâures massif shows a sophistication and complexity that is unparalleled elsewhere in the Namib Desert, suggesting that the intensification of shamanic practice at these sites identifies the mountain refugium as an important and possibly unique centre of innovation and social transition. Indeed, ethnographic evidence from the Kalahari shows that the shaman, acting as mediator between hunter-gatherers and livestock-owning groups, could establish a nascent form of pastoralism, effecting a gradual broadening of the subsistence base towards a complex mix of hunting and gathering with livestock farming, thus confirming the hypothetical expectation that the release (Ω) phase would establish "new domains of influence, opening an entirely new set of adaptive pathways".[344] This evidence suggests a model in which shamans performing

---

[344] Gunderson & Holling (2002)

ritual functions for neighbouring pastoralists were able to amass considerable wealth in livestock, becoming, as described in recent ethnographic studies of hunter-gatherer shamans in the Kalahari, highly influential individuals, and nuclear growth points of pastoralism.[345] The next chapter considers this phenomenon in greater detail by exploring some of the consequences of complex shamanic practice in the changing social landscape of the Namib Desert during the last two millennia.

---

345 Ikeya (1993); Guenther (1975); Kinahan (2001: 46); Wiessner (1982). Criticisms of this view are answered in Kinahan (1996).

V

ELEPHANTS AND RAIN

Comparison of archaeological and palaeoclimatic evidence is useful and illuminating, but it evades the question of cosmology, of how people understood the world in which they lived. It may seem paradoxical that hunter-gatherers, as adept and practical survivors, also subscribed to notions of supernatural causality, but such precepts refer to a framework of higher-order explanations, rather than everyday reality. The natural and the supernatural do not necessarily refer to separate, parallel bodies of knowledge. Instead, the glimpses of hunter-gatherer cosmology which rock art and related evidence afford, point to an ideology in which visions and dreams are as valid a reflection of the world as observed reality.[346] It is within this milieu that the shaman is able to intervene in the workings of nature by moving back and forth between the concrete world and the supernatural, mediating contradictions of experience and perception.

The previous chapter laid out such a polyphase structure of shamanic ritual performance and supernatural experience, with an occultation, or hidden phase, preceding revelation, the phase of ritual action. Now, following an extended discussion of

---

346 cf. Craffert (2011)

palaeoclimatic evidence relating to shifting patterns of rainfall in the Namib Desert in the first part of this chapter, we address the ritual mediation of nature to make rain, in the second part of the chapter, where the polyphase nature of ritual activity explored in the previous chapter is extended to the performance setting of rain-making. Then, in the last part of the chapter, we explore two further examples of the same phenomenon in the context of specialized ritual initiation sites. The development of specialized ritual performance is linked to interaction with pastoral communities during the last two millennia, and rituals of initiation in particular show an increasing degree of panarchial integration between hunter-gatherer and pastoral economies in the Namib Desert.

The onset of the Holocene brought relatively stable climatic conditions to most of southern Africa, with higher rainfall in the more tropical eastern parts of the subcontinent and a more predictable rainfall regime in the semi-arid interior.[347] Human responses to Holocene climatic amelioration and more regular availability of food resources included a degree of seasonal or quasi-seasonal mobility, with increasing archaeological evidence of scheduled resource exploitation.[348] In the Western Cape, it at first appeared that hunter-gatherer movement between the interior and the coast mimicked seasonal abundance of plant food, mainly geophytes, in the montane interior, alternating with dependence on marine resources such as shellfish and fur seals.[349] The archaeological evidence of food remains supported this inferred pattern of mobility, but the evidence of stable isotopes from human skeletal remains suggested a more complex scenario including a degree of relative separation between inland and coastal communities.[350]

Although the seasonality hypothesis provides a plausible framework for human mobility in the past and presents a

---

347 Deacon & Lancaster (1988)
348 Mitchell (2002)
349 Parkington (1972)
350 Sealy & Van der Merwe (1986)

number of parallels with ethnographic descriptions of hunter-gatherer resource exploitation,[351] it does not specify the ecological relationship between hunter-gatherers and their subsistence base.[352] Seasonality can take into account the availability of food resources and the scheduling of their exploitation, but it does not address the degree to which particular environmental niches or food sources placed ecological limits on human consumption. In hyper-arid environments, such limitations may be particularly stringent, as for example when abundant food in one area is inaccessible due to a lack of water, or when water supplies are adequate but outlast available food supplies. This dynamic relationship between consumer and resource is fundamental to an ecological understanding of past human settlement.[353]

In Chapter 3 we saw that early Holocene human movement in the Namib Desert was characterized by a response to climatic variation which involved the use of remote areas, or secondary sites, with short-lived resource abundance followed by retreat to an escarpment ecotone, and primary sites that could support longer residence when conditions were dry. Chapter 4 showed that increasing aridification in the late Holocene led to occupation of refuge sites in the Dâures massif, an apparent intensification of the pattern developed during the preceding millennia. In ecological terms refugia such as the Dâures massif and the ecotone sites occupied earlier impose a high degree of density dependence in that residence is limited by available food. Rainfall events which allow more wide-ranging movement provide for a measure of density independence in which hunter-gatherer subsistence is temporarily uncoupled from the equilibrial relationship with the availability of food and is instead limited by water. Detailed examination of this alternating dynamic requires a finer scale of chronological control than is available for most of the Namib Desert Holocene archaeological record.

---

351 Parkington (2001)
352 Vandermeer & Goldberg (2013)
353 Illius & O'Connor (1999)

The late Holocene desert

Exploring the ecology of human occupation in the desert, we first compare the radiocarbon record from an array of archaeological sites with a proxy climate record based on dating of camelthorn *Vachellia (Acacia) erioloba* tree germination and mortality. The proxy record allows patterns in the dating of archaeological occupation to be compared and matched with an independent environmental response to climatic variation, represented by the germination and death of desert camelthorns. From this evidence it becomes apparent that human mobility did not simply mirror cycles of relatively wet and dry conditions as suggested by the more coarse-grained early Holocene climatic record. The comparison of archaeological and proxy climate evidence shows a more nuanced pattern based on the alternating use of primary and secondary resource sites. This approach demonstrates the value of a consumer and resource perspective as an alternative to the seasonality hypothesis.[354]

Climatic variation associated with the Medieval Warm Epoch between 1000 and 1300 AD, and the Little Ice Age, extending to about 1800 AD, had a marked influence[355] on agricultural settlement in the eastern parts of the subcontinent. The rise of wealthy centralized polities coincided with above average rainfall, and periods of drought had severe economic consequences.[356] In the drier western parts of the subcontinent, most particularly in the Namib Desert, these effects are less apparent because hunter-gatherer and pastoral communities coped with variation in rainfall by adopting highly mobile settlement and subsistence practices.[357] Furthermore, evidence of increasingly specialized desert subsistence strategies points to a high degree of tolerance for climatic variation.[358]

---

354 Kinahan (2016a); see Parkington (2001) for a detailed discussion of seasonality in the archaeology of southern African hunter-gatherers.
355 Tyson et al. (2000)
356 Huffman (1996)
357 Barnard (1992b)
358 Kinahan (2005)

The regional climate record for the last millennium in southern Africa is based mainly on analyses of aragonite stalagmites in South Africa,[359] which reflect a general cooling trend over this period. At fine resolution, the record indicates a series of wet pulses punctuated by abrupt commencement of drought conditions extending over several decades.[360] Five broad periods of alternating wet and dry conditions based on these data are set out in Table 5.1, with adjustments[361] on the basis of independent archaeological data relating to precolonial farming settlement in the eastern interior.[362] Thus, period I represents the warm and relatively wet Medieval Warm Epoch, while periods II to V represent alternating warm/wet and cool/dry conditions during the Little Ice Age in southern Africa.

Table 5.1 Climatic variation over the last one thousand years in southern Africa

Period AD	I	II	III	IV	V
Climate	Warm/wet	Cool/dry	Warm/wet	Cool/dry	Warm/wet
Palaeoclimatic	900–1300	1300–1500	1500–1675	1675–1780	1790–1810
Archaeological	900–1290	1290–1425	1425–1675	1675–1780	1790–1810

Until now, understanding of rainfall variation in the Namib Desert over the last millennium has relied almost entirely on this regional pattern, augmented by a small number of local records including flooding events in major drainage systems such as the !Khuiseb River. Evidence from radiocarbon-dated specimens of desert camelthorn trees offers a proxy record of recent climatic

---

359 Holmgren et al. (2003); Lee-Thorp et al. (2001)
360 Tyson & Lindesay (1992), amended by Tyson et al. (2000)
361 Huffman (1996, 2010)
362 Huffman (1996)

Figure 5.1: Camelthorns *Vachellia (Acacia) erioloba* in the southern Namib Desert, showing wide spacing of trees, with mature specimen and dead fallen tree.

variation. Isolated or thinly scattered camelthorn trees are an iconic feature of the Namib Desert landscape, sometimes occurring where little or no other woody vegetation survives (Fig. 5.1). Mature specimens tend to predominate, and there is often apparent size-cohortism in which local populations are characterized by old dead trees and a striking absence of young or intermediate aged trees. The structure of camelthorn populations therefore suggests episodic rather than continuous recruitment such as is characteristic of savanna woodland under more regular rainfall conditions. Desert camelthorns require successive years of favourable rainfall to survive early growth,[363] and although drought tolerant, mature trees are vulnerable under conditions of prolonged water deprivation.[364]

Radiocarbon dating of camelthorn trees was carried out on 38 samples from three Namib Desert localities: the Awasib

---

363 cf. Seymour & Milton (2003)
364 Woodborne (2004)

Gorrasis area, the Sossus Tsondab area and the Khan River.[365] Heartwood samples were selected as representing the assumed age of the established tree and in the case of dead trees, the youngest available material was also sampled to determine the age of mortality. Selection of oldest heartwood from a standing tree is based on subjective assessment, as is selection of the youngest tissue where sampling depends on the availability of outer growth rings from the trunk of the tree. In view of the fact that no more precise method is available to determine ages of germination and mortality, the camelthorn tree dates are treated as indicative, rather than corresponding to narrowly defined climatic events.

The oldest living trees, all from the Khan River, ranged between 900 and 600 years, which is significantly older than previous estimates of less than 300 years for the longevity of camelthorn trees in the Kalahari Desert.[366] Eight dead trees in the Khan River and Sossus Tsondab sample areas, each with paired heartwood and outer-ring samples, indicate an average lifespan of 310 years; of these the greatest and least values were 730 and 90 years, respectively. The oldest heartwood sample, dated to 1,630 years, was recovered from a dead stump in the Khan River. When sampled, the Sossus Tsondab specimens were still standing, although dead for five or more centuries, indicating extremely slow decay under desert conditions. This is confirmed by well-preserved dead trees in the Khan River and Awasib Gorrasis areas, which suggests that the groups of trees sampled in the three areas approximate the accumulated establishment and mortality of camelthorn trees over the last 1,000 years.

The calibrated radiocarbon results for the three sample areas are summarized in Figure 5.2, where values[367] are expressed as percentages of the total number of dates, germination dates being represented by positive values and mortality dates as negative percentage values for graphical convenience. Establishment of

---

365 Kinahan (2016a); Vogel (2003)
366 Steenkamp et al. (2008)
367 in 50-year age bins

trees in the Medieval Warm Epoch occurs in all three sample areas with a narrowly defined peak in the mid-1100s AD. Not all dates correspond with the pattern of variation in the regional sequence (Table 5.1), and camelthorn establishment episodes between 1200 AD and the late 1500s AD appear, therefore, on present evidence to be isolated Namib Desert phenomena, followed by an hiatus in the establishment of new trees, lasting until the mid-1700s AD. Two further episodes of mortality occur between the 1300s AD and 1400s AD, followed by a sustained period of mortality in the early 1600s AD.

Seen against the background of the regional sequence, these dates indicate a series of both episodic and sustained periods of climatic variation. For example, the early part of the Medieval Warm Epoch is elsewhere associated with generally moist conditions, whereas the Namib evidence points to more isolated rainfall events. A further comparison is in the extended series of tree establishment dates in the later part of the Medieval Warm Epoch, punctuated by two marked episodes of mortality, in the late 1300s AD and late 1400s AD, and followed in the Little Ice Age by a further three such episodes. These events match periods of severe drought in the eastern interior of the subcontinent, suggesting that while sustained dry conditions recorded elsewhere in the region are reflected in the mortality of Namib camelthorns, periods of higher than normal rainfall are not as clearly correlated.

Flooding of major desert river courses following heavy rain in the interior of Namibia leaves silt deposits with buried debris suitable for dating. Corroborating evidence in the form of radiocarbon dates for flooding events in the lower !Khuiseb River is presented in Table 5.2. Flood debris from the lower !Khuiseb is dated to mid-1100 AD,[368] and corresponds with establishment dates for camelthorns in the same period (Fig. 5.2). A date for flood debris and silt in the !Khuiseb during the 1400s AD[369] also matches establishment dates for camelthorns.

---

368 Vogel & Visser (1981)
369 Kinahan (2016a)

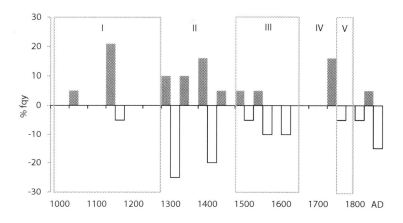

Figure 5.2: Percentage distribution of camelthorn establishment dates (solid) and mortality dates (hollow) in relation to alternating regional climatic warm/wet periods (I, III, V) and cool/dry periods (II, IV) (see Table 5.1)

Flooding events in the mid-1600s AD and the early 1800s AD do not match available establishment dates for camelthorn trees. It is possible, therefore, that these refer to rainfall events in the interior that did not extend to the Namib Desert itself, resulting only in downstream flooding in the desert reaches of the rivercourses.[370]

The !Khuiseb dates are associated with well-preserved tracks of elephant *Loxodonta africana* and other large animals which may have followed flooding of the !Khuiseb River into the desert while water and forage were available.[371] Further evidence of climatic variation was recovered from owl pellets at Mirabib in the central Namib Desert, where a decline in the frequency of the large-eared mouse *Malacothrix typica*, corresponds to the general cooling trend of the last 1,000 years.[372] This is accompanied by an

---

370 Kinahan (2016a); Kinahan et al. (1991); Vogel & Visser (1981)
371 Kinahan et al. (1991)
372 Brain & Brain (1977); cf. Holmgren et al. (2003)

Table 5.2: Calibrated radiocarbon dates for flood debris in the lower !Khuiseb River

Material and source	Age range cal. AD	Median cal. AD	Climate (cf. Table 5.1)
Wood debris	1044–1214	1148	I (warm/wet)
Charcoal in silt	1439–1626	1495	III (warm/wet)
Wood debris	1506–1798	1642	III–IV (variable)
Grass debris	1509–1799	1654	III–IV (variable)
Grass debris	1668–1895	1800	V (warm/wet)
Grass debris	1671–1949	1816	V (warm/wet)
Wood debris	1670–1949	1831	post-V (variable)
Wood debris	1672–1779	1835	post-V (variable)
Tree bark	1674–1949	1847	post-V (variable)
Debris in silt	1689–1949	1855	post-V (variable)

apparent increase in the hairy footed gerbil *Gerbillurus vallinus* in the mid-1500s AD as a response to rainfall in the desert. This evidence generally agrees with the regional climatic record, as well as the camelthorn establishment dates and the !Khuiseb River flooding event record.[373]

Taken as a whole, the camelthorn and related data discussed here suggest a loose teleconnection between climatic events in the Namib Desert and in the eastern interior of the subcontinent, with more direct correlation of dry than wet periods reflecting the intensity of El Niño events.[374] Data for the establishment of trees are as would be expected under highly episodic and variable

---

[373] Other evidence of rodent population response includes remains of *Parotomys brantsii* from the early 17th century AD occupation of Skorpion Cave in the southern Namibia desert, indicating an amelioration event (Kinahan & Kinahan 2003) coincident with Period III in the regional climate record summarized in Table 5.1.

[374] cf. Huffman (2010)

rainfall in a hyper-arid environment, making allowance for imprecision introduced by sample selection. The data indicate that climatic variation affecting the establishment and mortality of camelthorns is equally evident in the summer and winter rainfall zones. This confirms that rainfall in the Namib as a whole was determined by quasi-seasonal equatorial Southern Oscillation events, usually penetrating the desert from the north and east.[375] The influence of summer rainfall events declines further south, and winter rainfall conditions predominate south of the Orange River.[376]

Late Holocene climatic conditions in the Namib Desert show extremes of variation at the centennial scale, with periods of regular rainfall allowing the local establishment of camelthorn trees and accompanied by an overall increase in biotic productivity. These periods were followed by episodes of sustained aridity resulting in the mortality of camelthorn trees under conditions of very low biotic productivity. The pattern of aggregated and dispersed occupation established during the late Pleistocene and described in Chapter 3, and the use of refugia in the late Holocene described in Chapter 4, both show that human settlement under these conditions depended on primary resource sites or areas with reliable water, such as the Dâures and other desert inselbergen, alternating with opportunistic use of secondary resource sites where water was only available following episodic local rainfall. Evidence from archaeological sites over the whole extent of the Namib Desert during the last one thousand years summarized below, points to the widespread use of this strategy.[377]

Figure 5.3 presents a summary of radiocarbon dates for human occupation during the last one thousand years, differentiating between occupation of primary and secondary resource areas. The data show that under warm and moist conditions in period I (Table 5.1), representing the Medieval Warm Epoch, occupation

---

375 cf. Nicholson & Entekhabi (1986)
376 Chase & Meadows (2007)
377 Kinahan (2016a, 2018b)

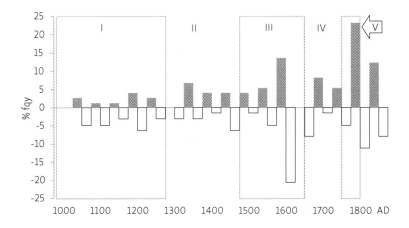

Figure 5.3: Percentage distribution of archaeological occupation dates for primary resource sites (solid) and secondary resource sites (hollow) in relation to alternating regional climatic warm/wet periods (I, III, V) and cool/dry periods (II, IV).

alternated between primary and secondary resource sites. However, most of the occupation dates from this period are associated with secondary resource sites (64%), indicating extensive mobility as a consequence of higher rainfall allowing a greater foraging range over the desert landscape. The shift to cool and dry conditions in period II at the start of the Little Ice Age is associated with a greater reliance on primary resource sites (58%). Increased access to secondary resource sites (56%) is evident under a return to warm and moist conditions in period III. Occupation reverts to primary resource sites (71%) under cool and dry conditions in period IV, with greater access to secondary resource sites (64%) evident under a return to warm and moist conditions at the end of the Little Ice Age in period V.

In ecological terms, the pattern of occupation alternating between aggregation at primary resource sites and dispersal to secondary resource sites is a response to density-dependent dynamics in a moisture-limited environment.[378] However, prolonged residence at primary resource sites risked depletion of food and therefore required access to alternative sites in the event of sustained dry conditions. Access to alternative sites was probably ensured through social networks such as were maintained, among other means, by the exchange of ostrich eggshell beads, and by means of various social sanctions. The evidence from strontium analyses of beads from the primary resource site of Falls Rock Shelter presented in Chapter 4 shows that refugium sites formed part of a larger social as well as ecological resource base as would be a requirement for survival in a hyper-arid environment.

How the rain was made

Large herbivores, including elephant *Loxodonta africana*, are important as agents of seed dispersal for desert camelthorn trees.[379] Seeds germinate successfully in animal dung, and elephant dung in particular provides both nutrient and moisture requirements for young seedlings,[380] although survival of seedlings under arid conditions is enhanced when above average rainfall occurs over several years.[381] Historically, elephant and other large herbivores were resident in all of the ephemeral river systems of the Namib,[382] but in the last two centuries their range contracted significantly as a result of the ivory trade and pressure of human settlement.[383] It is likely that in the past elephant played a role in the establishment of camelthorn populations during periods of higher than normal rainfall, and the absence of these animals from much of the Namib may therefore help to explain the relatively senescent tree population in the desert. A relationship

---

378 DeAngelis & Waterhouse (1987)
379 Seymour & Milton (2003)
380 Dudley (1999)
381 Wilson & Witkowski (1998)
382 e.g. Andersson (1861); De Villiers & Kok (1984); Kinahan et al. (1991)
383 Joubert & Mostert (1975)

between elephant and rainfall would have been quite obvious to the human inhabitants of the Namib Desert.

The survival of older living camelthorn specimens in the southern Namib may be partly attributable to a northward retreat of elephant during the last one thousand years under conditions of increasing aridity. Elephant, as well as being effective agents of seed dispersal, are also highly destructive of mature camelthorns when removing large branches to consume seed pods. Elephant thus affect tree cover by removing old trees and promoting the growth of new seedlings. However, it is likely that as mega-herbivores requiring large volumes of browse,[384] elephant distribution has fluctuated repeatedly in this region. The species was probably absent from the southern Namib at the height of the Last Glacial Maximum but returned to the area under the relatively moist conditions prevailing in the early Holocene. They may have retreated again in response to aridification in the late Holocene, returning with the short-lived amelioration of the Medieval Warm Epoch when they served as an agent in the establishment of the oldest dated specimens of camelthorn discussed here. The expansion and contraction of elephant distribution during the late Holocene appears to parallel that of human settlement, and it is therefore interesting to note the preponderance of elephant in the rock art of the northern parts of the Namib Desert and adjacent interior (Fig. 5.4). While elephant in the rock art may not be exclusively associated with it, there is compelling evidence that they were an important element in shamanic rain-making rituals, as we shall see below.

In view of its crucial importance to human survival in arid parts of southern Africa, it is not surprising that there should be an abundance of folkloric references to rainfall.[385] Commonly, ethnographic accounts describe the rain in metaphorical terms, as

---

384 Owen-Smith (1987)
385 Schmidt (1979); Prins (1990); Jolly (1996)

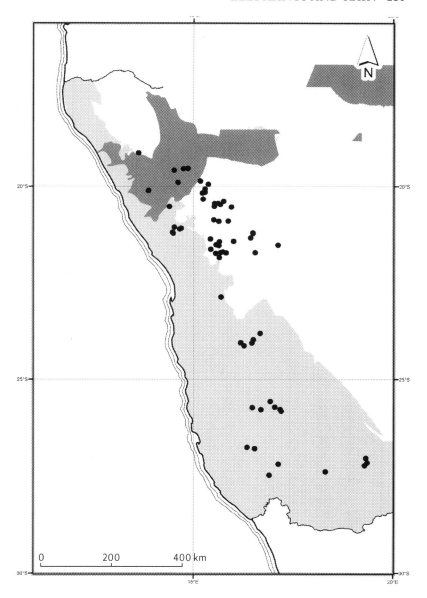

Figure 5.4: The distribution of elephant in the rock art of the Namib Desert and adjacent interior (black circles), shown in relation to the current distribution of elephant *Loxodonta africana* (dark grey). Map data from Scherz (1970) and De Villiers and Kok (1984).

an animal rather than a force of nature. The |Xam[386] of the northern Cape referred to dark rain clouds as the rain animal's body and to the columns of falling rain as its legs, likening as to walking its movement across the landscape.[387] Violent downpours were the male rain, or the blood of the rain animal, as opposed to the soft, soaking, female rain which represented its milk. To another group, the Kalahari Jul'hoan, these different kinds of rain left easily recognizable spoor in the sand.[388] Among southern African hunter-gatherer shamans, some were particularly acknowledged as rain-makers, and agriculturalists and pastoralists alike sought their skills.[389]

Ritual intensification during sustained dry periods in the late Holocene is evident in the rock art of the Hungorob Ravine, described in Chapter 4. The paintings include some clearly recognizable depictions of rain, showing that rain-making was an important ritual activity. One example, an elaborate frieze which combines streaming rain and a single bichrome shaman figure resembling those at Snake Rock, is located in a cramped and secluded shelter, difficult of access and apparently hidden from view, suggesting specialized and individual rather than generalized and communal ritual activity. There are further sites with paintings of rain in the Hungorob Ravine and more elsewhere on the Dâures massif, many of these being relatively secluded.[390] The importance of the Dâures massif as a primary resource site and as a centre of shamanic ritual practice is amply demonstrated by the high density of rock art sites, by the presence of more complex imagery than is found elsewhere in the Namib Desert, and by evidence of interaction with pastoral

---

[386] The lXam were an historical San group living in the drylands south of the Orange River (Hollmann 2004).
[387] Bleek (1933); Lewis-Williams (1981)
[388] Thomas (1988)
[389] Jolly (1996)
[390] Kinahan (1999: 345); Pager (1989: 153, 168, 171, 262; 1993: 82, 172; 1995: 50-1, 87, 157, 182, 267; 1998: 296; 2006: 410).

communities, including the absorption of sheep bone into the ritual assemblage, as described in Chapter 4.

One likely site of interaction with pastoral communities is Otjohorongo,[391] a prominent granite inselberg about 100 km north-east of the Dâures massif, on the edge of the mopane *Colophospermum mopane* woodland biome traditionally favoured by Ovaherero pastoralists.[392] Located near the top of the inselberg is a large overhang with a painted frieze approximately 30 m in length and including imagery related to rain-making. The site has very little floor space under shelter, and much of this is either in deep shade or permanent semi-darkness, conditions which are generally eschewed in the selection of residential rock-shelter sites (Fig. 5.5). Radiocarbon dates for a scaffold of poles at the back of the shelter indicate that it was last occupied in the early 1600s AD,[393] coinciding with a period of camelthorn mortality due to increased aridity in the Namib (see Fig. 5.2), and presumably a time of heightened rain-making activity. A socketed iron point for a small spear is consistent with this dating.

There are approximately 150 identifiable human and animal figures painted at the site, mainly in the daylight zone but also in the darker recesses of the shelter. The main part of the frieze depicts columns of rain and lightning issuing from the belly of an elephant (Fig. 5.6). Between the solid columns of the legs, rain is shown falling between bolts of lightning. These lines of rain resemble the way in which isolated downpours seem to end before reaching the ground, with a slight curve to one side or the other indicating the force of the wind. The painting thus shows the observable features of a typical convective rainstorm but conflates them with the image of the elephant in the form of a rain animal, accompanied by human figures in attitudes of

---

391 Historical sources on Ovaherero occupation are discussed by Köhler (1959) and Werner (1980).
392 Kinahan (2001b); Vogelsang & Eichhorn (2011)
393 Kinahan (1999: 348); uncalibrated radiocarbon dates for the site are 350±50 (Pta-5471) and 290±50 (Beta-69776).

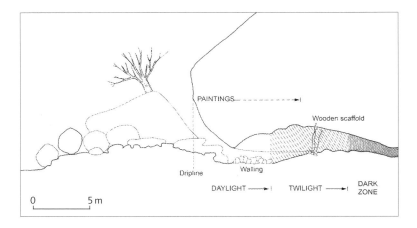

Figure 5.5: Cross section of the Rainman Shelter, Otjohorongo, showing the concealed entrance and dark interior.

ritual dance, some figures having fringed knee straps like those described from Falls Rock Shelter in Chapter 4.

At the western end of the Rainman Shelter is a small frieze that casts further light on the connection between elephant and rain, adding to this combination the physical setting of the granite inselberg itself. At first glance, the frieze appears to depict a hunt in which three elephants are confronted by armed men (Fig. 5.7). However, one of the men is shown without legs and another is painted with a hollow torso, both suggesting conventionalized symptoms of altered consciousness.[394] The portrayal of the elephant hunt is also clearly unrealistic, as shown by the fact that while one of the men holds onto the trunk of an elephant another is shown holding its legs. The depiction of the elephants themselves is equally unrealistic; all three are shown with hollow areas in their bodies and hump-like masses on their backs which may well refer to the expanding mass of rain clouds in a convective storm forming about the granite inselberg. Significantly, the hunters appear to be coaxing the three elephants towards an area

394 cf. Lewis-Williams (1981)

of the rock surface that is covered with a run of white calcareous precipitate from rainwater that occasionally courses down the back of the shelter.

The rock art at this site thus explicitly links rainfall, elephant and granitic features such as the Otjohorongo inselberg, brought together through the mediating actions of the shaman. The paintings, arguably, were executed in order to effect this association as a form of mimesis, in what might be seen as a "dialogue with nature",[395] as a practical attempt to make rain, carried out at a special purpose site. Underlining a more specific link between rain-making and pastoral communities is the apparent absence of residential rock shelter sites in this locality. Like other painted sites with similar subject matter in the Dâures massif, the Rainman Shelter is effectively concealed, in this case by dense vegetation and large fallen boulders. As the place of occultation and locus of the first phase of ritual performance, the setting and configuration of the site is evidently as important as the rock art imagery it contains.

We now turn to two further examples where the physical nature of the site itself sheds important light not only on its ritual purpose, but, moving beyond that, to the question as to how rituals were actually performed. The evidence of a specialized shamanic rain-making site without associated hunter-gatherer occupation at Otjohorongo suggests that the work of the shaman was carried out at a significant remove from the hunter-gatherer community. This geographical separation is indicative of the onset of a re-organization α phase in which shamanic activity is concentrated outside the mundane sphere of hunter-gatherer social life. The evidence presented in the next section confirms this by pointing to the rise of specialized ritual sites that were dedicated not just to the service of pastoralist needs, but to the transformation of hunter-gatherer society itself.

---

395 cf. Taussig (1993); Lévi-Strauss (1966: 19)

Places of performance

An unusual feature of the Rainman Shelter described above is a female kudu in white pigment, placed in a part of the site that is in permanent semi-darkness, so that the image can be viewed only by crawling backwards into a narrow crevice, or vestibule. The painting and its unusual position add a further dimension to the rock art at the site depicting the process of rain-making. The kudu painting shows that solitary preparation, while in a state of occultation such as is evidenced by the ritual paraphernalia described from Falls Rock Shelter in Chapter 4, occurred here in the context of rain-making. As with the use of ritual paraphernalia, this evidence of preparatory seclusion points to a performative

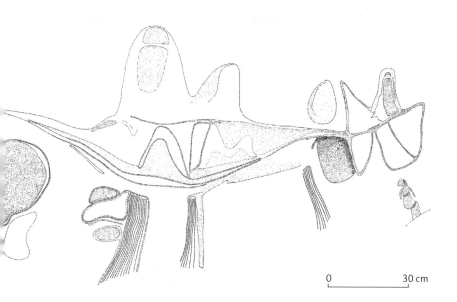

Figure 5.6: Rain animal and human figures at the Rainman Shelter, Otjohorongo.

aspect of shamanic ritual not previously noticed in southern African rock art.[396]

There is a parallel example of rock art in seclusion at the site of |Ui-||aes,[397] situated about 120 km north-west of Otjohorongo. Approached from the north, |Ui-||aes lies in an open valley flanked by cliffs of reddish-coloured sandstone, the remains of

---

396 Kinahan (2017a); but see Witelson (2019)
397 Also known as Twyfelfontein (Kinahan 2010a).

196 NAMIB

Figure 5.7: Elephant and human figures at the Rainman Shelter, Otjohorongo.

Jurassic era sand dunes which lie on mostly impermeable shales. Underground water flows between the shale and sandstone beds and emerges as a small spring beneath the cliffs, where a dense concentration of rock art shows that the site was used intensively over several millennia. Excavations at two painted rock shelters indicated that occupation here, as at the Dâures massif, commenced with the most recent aridification of the Namib Desert in the late Holocene.[398] Most of the rock art consists of engravings on scattered boulders at the foot of the cliffs, and there are in excess of 2,000 engravings concentrated in an area of little over 50 ha, depicting the same range of animal species as the painted rock art of the region.[399]

At |Ui-||aes, a hollow beneath a large sandstone boulder forms a vestibule with almost the same dimensions as that found at Otjohorongo. Both contain single paintings of female kudu in a position where reflected natural light hardly penetrates. Simplified cross-sections of the two vestibules are shown in Figure 5.8, which illustrates the cramped space and the position that would have to be adopted to execute or to view the paintings overhead (see also Fig. 5.9). In both instances there are some rock art images outside the vestibule entrance, but only one painting within. A comparison of light conditions in the two vestibules is presented in Table 5.3 which shows that ambient light levels under normal daylight conditions are between 150 and 250 times greater than lighting within the vestibule at both sites, and that the level of illumination in both vestibules is similar.[400] Looking outward from the vestibule cavities has the effect of producing light disturbance on the periphery of the vision when the gaze is shifted from the normally bright

---

398 Wendt (1972)
399 Kinahan (2010a); see also Breunig et al. (2019) for results of a wider area survey in the vicinity of |Ui-||aes.
400 Light measurements were carried out using a hand-held Extech® digital light meter with a minimum resolution of 0.1 Lux (0.00092 foot candles/fC), and fitted with a sensor calibrated to a standard incandescent lamp at a colour temperature of 2,856 K. Illumination was measured at the painting itself and immediately outside the vestibule.

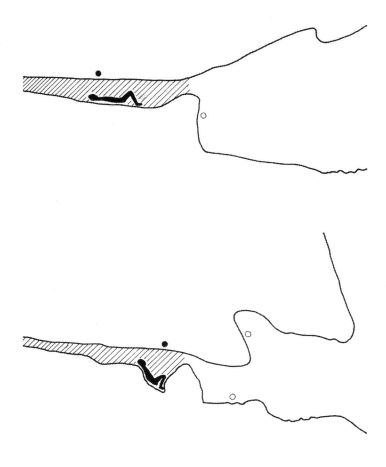

Figure 5.8: Simplified cross-sections of the vestibules at Otjohorongo (above) and IUi-IIaes (below) showing the area of darkness (hatched), as well as positions of paintings in daylight (open circles) and in darkness (black circles).

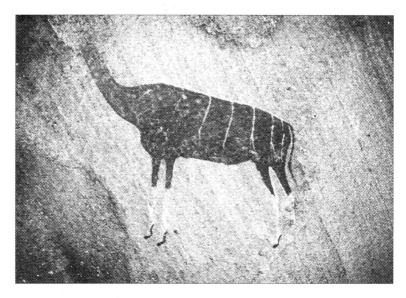

Figure 5.9: Entrance to vestibule site and female kudu painting at lUi-llaes

exterior to the dark interior and the painted ceiling. This, together with the confined space, the consistently cool temperature within the vestibules and the paintings themselves, could have helped to induce a state of altered consciousness by excluding distracting stimuli in preparation for ritual activity.

The ǀUi-ǁaes valley environment contains little evidence of prolonged residence in the form of artefact and other occupation debris during the late Holocene[401] when compared to other localities rich in rock art, such as the Dâures massif. It appears that while the site was initially one of many primary resource sites essential for hunter-gatherer survival in this area, its function changed during the last one thousand years, becoming a special-purpose ritual ceremonial centre rather than a focus of occupation when water and food were in short supply. The rock art in this valley includes motifs such as cattle, which cannot on present evidence significantly pre-date the last one and a half thousand years.[402] Of particular importance is the fact that the site contains two discrete locations that were evidently reserved for the performance of men's and women's initiation rites which were probably carried out by specialist shamans. Evidence from both sites points to their use in the last one thousand years.

In the ethnography of southern African hunter-gatherers there is a conventional division of labour by gender, with hunting as the principal domain of men, and gathering as that of women.[403] Although the roles of men and women were traditionally articulated and reinforced through rites of initiation,[404] this practice has left little archaeological trace, and it is therefore not known when and under what circumstances initiation rites were established or

---

401 Significant concentrations of artefact debris are associated with two mid-Holocene painted sites at ǀUi-ǁaes described by Wendt (1972), but not with the far more abundant groups of rock engravings at the same site (Kinahan 2010a).
402 See Orton et al. 2013
403 Winterhalder (2001: 26)
404 Barnard (1992b)

Table 5.3: Comparative illumination of the vestibules at the Rainman Shelter and |Ui-||aes, showing relative darkness of interior.

Site	Outside AMBIENT LIGHT	Inside REFLECTED LIGHT
Otjohorongo	2.75 kLux (255.48 fC)	0.011 kLux (1.02 fC)
|Ui-||aes	2.49 kLux (231.33 fC)	0.017 kLux (1.58 fC)

indeed how they might have evolved over time. At |Ui-||aes we see that initiation, being a ritualized transformation, is necessarily carried out following the same shamanic trope already outlined, of occultation, the hidden phase, followed by ritual performance and emergence in a new state, that of adulthood.

Approximately 400 m north of the secluded vestibule site at |Ui-||aes described above is an elevated plateau with several major concentrations of rock engravings, including one group centred on the iconic rock engraving known as the Dancing Kudu (Fig. 5.10).[405] The engraving is executed in the highly unusual technique of flat polishing, as opposed to the more common method of percussion. Kudu are scarce in the rock art of the Namib Desert: the 815 identifiable painted motifs spread over 44 sites in the Hungorob Ravine included only fourteen kudu.[406] At the site of |Ui-||aes, there are only seven kudu among 2,075 identified motifs.[407] The scarcity of the kudu in the rock art, however, belies the ethnographically attested role of the species in women's initiation,[408] where the female serves as metaphor and paragon of idealized qualities of women, in its gentle, sociable and sexually submissive nature, caring for its young until they are almost fully grown.[409]

---

405 Kinahan (2017b)
406 Kinahan (2001a: 20)
407 Kinahan (2010a)
408 Eastwood (2006)
409 Estes (1991: 169)

The Dancing Kudu engraving graphically illustrates the female kudu in the context of mating behaviour. For example, when courting, the animal lowers her neck and stretches forward,[410] thus hollowing the back and raising the hindquarters, as depicted in this engraving. Particularly noteworthy here is the heavily distended belly of the Dancing Kudu, showing that the animal in the engraving is both sexually receptive and simultaneously at an advanced stage of pregnancy, thus exhibiting a liminal combination of entering adulthood (oestrus) and being fully adult (pregnant). Women's initiation takes place during first menstruation, according to ethnographic records, when the young woman is secluded in a small hut and instructed by older female relatives on how to conduct herself in society.[411] This part of the initiation process appears to be represented at the Dancing Kudu by six repetitive motifs, each comprising a single arcuate line surrounded by a circle of closely spaced cupules (Fig. 5.10).

These particular motifs probably represent the seclusion shelters of initiates (the arcuate line), each surrounded by a procession of dancing women (the encircling cupules) participating in the ritual of her transition to adulthood.[412] There is further compelling evidence of the initiation ritual at this site, in the form of four stone circles which appear to be the remains of small huts or shelters (see Fig. 5.11). The circles have a mean diameter of 2.1 m (n = 5) and, significantly, no associated occupation debris, such as artefact waste, bone fragments, pottery or hearth ash, usually characteristic of a small encampment. Rather than facing inward as in an encampment, the openings of these circles face towards the Dancing Kudu panel, and thus appear to be component parts of an integrated performance space. The possible representations of seclusion shelters in the Dancing Kudu panel also have a common orientation. Taken together, the evidence of both rock

---

410 Estes (1991: 171)
411 Guenther (1999)
412 As described by Marshall (1999) and McGranaghan (2015).

ELEPHANTS AND RAIN 203

Figure 5.10: The Dancing Kudu panel at !Ui-!!aes, with the kudu in flat polish technique. The arcuate forms encircled by cupules (top right) represent women's initiation shelters surrounded by dancers.

Figure 5.11: Remains of woman's initiation seclusion shelter with entrance facing the Dancing Kudu engraving.

art and archaeological remains from this site provide the first concrete example of women's initiation.

In this context, it is conceivable that the nearby vestibule with the painted female kudu was related to the performance of initiation rites at the Dancing Kudu by serving as a place of secluded preparation for the shaman officiating at the initiation ritual. The emergence of the shaman from the vestibule would thus serve as an essential revelatory step in the ritual performance, a transformation which would have been paralleled by the shaman from the seclusion shelter at the Rainman site. These two steps in ritual performance are also evident at the Dancing Kudu site in another form, where the initiates would remain concealed within their shelters and then emerge at the appropriate time. The same precepts of occultation and emergence were evident from the ritual assemblage at Falls Rock Shelter where shamanic paraphernalia were concealed and then revealed, in the same way that the moth would emerge from its cocoon, with its wings resembling the animal skin cloak of the shaman. The flat polishing technique used in the Dancing Kudu engraving provides an important clue indicating the likely dating of the initiation site and the socio-economic context of women's initiation in the Namib Desert to within the last millenium.

During the last one thousand years the widespread use of pottery in the Namib Desert is closely associated with intensive exploitation of wild grass seed which was ground to meal on convenient granitic outcrops, leaving highly polished surfaces. Chapter 6 explores the occurrence and function of these features in more detail, referring to evidence that in order to produce the grinding surfaces, it was necessary to kneel on the rock, adopting a posture like that shown in the engraving of the Dancing Kudu at ǀUi-ǁaes. The engraving which we have considered here combines postural characteristics of the kudu in oestrus with the use of an engraving technique that is not applied in any other context. The polished engraving is therefore a reference to the grinding of grass seed and points to an association between this activity and the paragon of womanly qualities, the female kudu. The association of subject matter and technique is clearly deliberate and intended to combine elements of female activity and ideology.

Before exploring the implications of women's initiation for intensified exploitation of wild plant foods in the next chapter, we first examine further evidence from the site of |Ui-||aes, for the institution of men's initiation, a practice which also had profound consequences for desert subsistence, including both large scale communal hunting and the adoption of certain precepts that are fundamental to pastoralism. In addition to the main rock engravings site at |Ui-||aes there are several isolated groups of engraved boulders. One of these lies about 2.5 km to the north-west and consists of sandstone blocks up to 5 m in height. These are covered with more than one hundred engravings including giraffe, zebra and ostrich, although the most unusual and noteworthy are disembodied penises, of which there are altogether 33 clear examples. The penises are moreover closely associated with representations of *mankala* boards (Fig. 5.12), a traditional game of strategy played mainly by men[413] and known in Khoekhoegowab as *||hūs*.[414] Etched onto the near-vertical rock, the boards are clearly symbolic rather than functional; they are of varying length and configuration, ranging between three and five ranks of cupules. One board, together with several penises, is on an open rockface at the natural point of access to the site, which leads through a narrow passageway into a sheltered area between the boulders. One of the boulders has up to ten *||hūs* boards on its vertical surface, above and adjacent to a small vestibule approximately 3 m in depth, with a total of twelve penises immediately above the entrance.[415] This feature parallels

---

413 Townshend (1979) uses the generic Arabic term *mankala* in general discussion of this widespread and highly variable game.

414 Townshend (1976); Schmidt (1975)

415 Although the rock engravings are well preserved, the site has been incorporated within the entrance of a tourist establishment, thus destroying its unique *genius loci*.

ELEPHANTS AND RAIN 207

Figure 5.12: Men's initiation site at |Ui-||aes, showing penis (below) and a typical four-rank //hūs (*mankala*) board.

both the vestibule below the Dancing Kudu and the vestibule at the Rainman Shelter.

No other concentrations of disembodied penises are known in the rock art of the Namib Desert. //Hūs boards comprising parallel linear ranks of cupules are also largely absent, although single cupules and disordered swarms of cupules are not uncommon.[416] The only known concentration of engraved //hūs boards is in the |Khomas area[417] of the upper !Khuiseb River catchment, 350 km to the south-east where they are associated

---

416 *Mankala* boards found in association with hunter-gatherer rock art sites elsewhere in southern Africa have been erroneously attributed to the game of *morabaraba* (Deacon & Mazel 2010: 17; Eastwood & Blundell 1999). The game of *morabaraba* resembles that of Nine Men's Morris and may have been introduced by English settlers.
417 This is confirmed by the regional survey of rock engravings in Namibia by Scherz (1970).

with copper-smelting sites dating to within the last 400 years.[418] The ǀKhomas copper-working sites, which are described in Chapter 9, are generally small secluded settlements with abundant painted rock art including human figures and a range of animal species. The engraved ǁhūs boards are clustered around the remains of copper-smelting furnaces although many examples occur in isolated spots well away from the open encampment sites and rock shelters that form a common feature of the upper ǃKhuiseb River catchment.

In a broader African context, *mankala* is intimately connected with the transformative process of men's initiation and the inculcation of male values, which are imparted in a secluded place, outside the residential setting. These values include cunning, vigilance, foresight, resilience, perseverance, discretion, memory and self-control.[419] In the context of the site at ǀUi-ǁaes, it appears that a process of physical passage and instruction took place, and that this involved a period of seclusion using the vestibule shelter within the site (Fig. 5.13). Thus, the initiate would be removed from normal society and taken to this isolated site, passing through a ritualized transformation, including a stage of occultation in the naturally dark vestibule interior, and emerging as a fully adult man imbued with the requisite social values.

From the evidence at this site, it may be surmised that groups of young males would experience initiation at the same time, possibly resulting in the emergence of age cohorts with bonds extending beyond those of the immediate social network and forming the basis of a new cooperative group. It is also important to note that stone or seed counters used in the game are traditionally referred to as cattle (Khoekhoegowab *gomati*), thus confirming a link between *mankala*, men's initiation and pastoralism.[420] The evidence from ǀUi-ǁaes provides the first recorded example of a men's initiation from the late Holocene record, combining both

---

418 Kinahan & Vogel (1982); see detailed description in Chapter 9.
419 Townshend (1979: 795)
420 Townshend (1979)

Figure 5.13: Men's initiation site at |Ui-||aes, showing vestibule shelter (right) with extended //hūs board (left).

rock art and archaeological evidence. Although it is apparent that the practice of both men's and women's initiation at |Ui-||aes dates to within the last one thousand years, the details of men's initiation involving *mankala* point to the adoption of new cultural values derived from pastoral society, and thus represent concrete evidence for interaction between pastoralists and hunter-gatherer society in the Namib Desert.

We have seen that mid-Holocene aridification in the Namib Desert prompted the occupation of refugia sites such as the Dâures massif, where significant concentrations of rock art are associated with both intensified ritual activity and the rise of specialist shamanism. The introduction of domestic sheep about two thousand years ago and described in the previous chapter, is linked to shamanic ritual practice through the inclusion of bone splinters suspected to be from sheep and found in what appears to be a ritual assemblage. Rain-making, one of the most clearly depicted shamanic activities in the rock art of the Dâures massif, may have served as a link with pastoral communities who spread into the region during this period. Pre-colonial copper production is closely linked with *mankala* in the process of hunter-gatherer adoption of livestock and pastoralism. Evidence of copper production is discussed in Chapter 9.

The Otjohorongo rain-making site described in this chapter was a special purpose ritual site rather than a domestic shelter such as Falls Rock Shelter or Snake Rock. The site lacks the diverse occupation debris of domestic sites; it is also secluded and largely in permanent semi-darkness. Evidence from the site parallels that of shamanic practice exemplified by the ritual assemblage at Falls Rock Shelter and |Ui-||aes, where ritual performance is shown to be preceded by preparatory seclusion, or occultation, alone and in darkness. It thus appears that specialist shamans operated outside the context of the communal trance ritual. The further evidence from |Ui-||aes discussed here supports the likely existence of itinerant specialist shamans in the late Holocene Namib Desert, comparable to ethnographically documented specialists in the Kalahari, as described below.

Evidence of men's and women's initiation in the rock art of |Ui-||aes corroborates the essential elements of ritual activity inferred from the Dâures massif and Otjohorongo sites, by showing that initiation rites were based on the same principles of seclusion followed by shamanic transformation and emergence. The evidence from |Ui-||aes demonstrates, for the first time, the role of specialized rock art sites as sites of ritual performance, where the content and positioning of the rock art directly relates to evidence of how the site was used. In the case of the women's initiation site, the engraving of the Dancing Kudu not only depicts specific values associated with the social role of women, it also includes depictions of what appear to be seclusion shelters, paralleled by the remains of such structures on the site itself. The men's initiation site includes male rock art motifs in the form of penis engravings and *mankala* in the physical context

Table 5.4: The principal features of men's and women's initiation at |Ui-||aes.

Preparation	Occultation	Emergence
Seclusion	Initiation	Integration
MEN: removal from domestic context to dedicated ritual site	Confinement in vestibule; instruction (mankala); possible circumcision (penis engravings)	Age cohorts; hunting parties
WOMEN: removal from domestic context to dedicated ritual site	Confinement in initiation shelter; instruction (social behaviour); Menstruation (womanhood)	Age cohorts; work parties

of a passage and seclusion shelter.[421] The essential principles of initiation as evidenced at |Ui-||aes are summarized in Table 5.4.

The common features of initiation are the removal of initiates from the domestic context, to separate and dedicated men's and women's ritual sites. This is concretely domonstrated by the archaeological evidence of isolated sites with unique rock art motifs linked to gender identity and maturation, and by the presence of special features including the vestibule shelter on the men's initiation site and the perimeter stones of brushwood initiation shelters on the women's initiation site. These features confirm that men's and women's initiation involved physical seclusion and the use of symbolic references as part of an instructional process. Linking initiation to the general principles of shamanic practice outlined in the context of rainmaking earlier in this chapter, is the evidently important role of occultation and emergence. The

---

421 While there is no direct evidence of circumcision, penis adornment, known also as infibulation, is a widespread but enigmatic feature of southern African rock art (Hampson et al. 2002; Willcox 1978).

initiate is transformed from one state, adolescence, to another, that of adulthood, following the same process as shown by the emperor moth, where the pupa emerges from the cocoon as a patently different being. In Chapter 4, we saw multiple references to this process which also revealed the likely symbolic meaning of the shaman's animal skin cloak, or kaross, which resembles the wings of the emergent moth. It is no surprise to find that the same fundamental principles of shamanic experience occur in the process of initiation.

The evidence presented in this chapter goes further than adding a new layer of detail to our understanding of ritual and shamanic art on individual sites, by opening the possibility to locate and define areas of shamanic activity in the wider landscape. Ethnographically documented areas of operation for individual ritual specialists in the Kalahari are comparable in extent with the area encompassed by the Dâures massif, Otjohorongo and |Ui-||aes (Table 5.5). It is therefore conceivable that a small number of individual shamans were operating among these sites, a possibility that is corroborated by similarities in the style and technique of the imagery, and by evident similarities in ritual practice. The fact that this would have been carried out in physical isolation rather than in the setting of a communal trance dance indicates that shamans in this area may have operated alone, perhaps with apprentices or assistants, moving from place to place where specialist ritual services were required. The specialist ritual sites in the Namib suggest an operating range of up to 100 km, covering an area in excess of 16,000 km^2. The ethnographic data show similarities in the operating range and area of activity, despite the fact that conditions in the Kalahari are less harsh.

Such estimates of shamanic areas of operation are indicative and do not at this stage provide a measurement that can be more widely applied. While it is tempting to suggest that the areal extent of shamanic activity might be a function of ecological conditions, the data in Table 5.5 suggest an operational area that is as much socially as ecologically determined. A similar

Table 5.5: Distances of travel and areas of operation for Kalahari ritual specialists, compared with specialized ritual rock art sites at Dâures massif, Otjohorongo and |Ui-||aes. Kalahari values from unpublished field data courtesy of P. Wiessner.

Kalahari ritual specialists	Avg. km between sites (n)	Avg. area covered km²	Range km
A	113 (7)	11,250	40-225
B	58 (10)	10,400	25-83
C	68 (12)	17,920	30-180
D	63 (11)	17,997	25-105
Average (A-D)	76 (10)	14,391	25-225
Namib rock art sites			
Dâures massif, Otjohorongo and |Ui-||aes	89 (3)	16,741	63-103

combination of possibilities is suggested by the ostrich eggshell bead strontium isotope data presented in Chapter 4, where social networks supported by gift exchange might ultimately be limited as much by aridity and ecological productivity, as by the social limitations of maintaining relationships of reciprocity.

In terms of the adaptive cycle model, intensification of ritual activity in the equilibrium K phase under refugium conditions at the Dâures massif, led to the emergence of specialist shamans as part of a release Ω phase involving shamanic rain-making in the context of interaction with pastoral communities, and the adoption of pastoral initiation rites. These represented a syncretic combination of hunter-gatherer and pastoral symbolic references and social precepts. A panarchial interaction of two quite separate socio-cultural systems led to the rise of specialist shamanism, and the adoption of social precepts which formed the basis of a re-organization α phase leading to the emergence of food production and livestock ownership, discussed in the next chapter.

In the next chapter, we see that Namib Desert communities retaining a basic dependence on hunting and gathering achieved a new level of control over their environment, and a degree of food security through reorganized subsistence strategies which involved systematic exploitation of diverse resources including processing and storage of wild plant foods, involving the use of pottery. These new elements of Namib Desert subsistence were common to both hunter-gatherer and in livestock herding communities to be described in Chapter 7, forming a complex social landscape based on shared social practices and linked by extended networks of exchange and interaction. Pottery and livestock are not diagnostic of an exclusively pastoral economy; the evidence to be presented in the next two chapters shows, rather, that pastoralism included a significant reliance on wild plant foods. In the event of a sudden expansion in livestock holdings, client herders would have been drawn from among hunter-gatherer or temporarily impoverished pastoralist communities. The archaeological evidence, together with the clearly unpredictable environmental conditions in the Namib Desert, argue for a high degree of flux and the existence of a complex diversity of hunter-gatherer and pastoralist subsistence strategies.

VI

DESERT GARDEN

Among hunter-gatherers, a fundamental change in subsistence technology such as the adoption of domestic livestock, will affect custom, ideology and ritual practice, the constantly shifting mediators of social change. Food production and the rise of a more complex subsistence economy does not only involve livestock and, possibly, cereal crops acquired from elsewhere; in the Namib Desert the move towards food production was accompanied by fundamental shifts in human relationships with resources that were already being used, both animal and plant species. A process of intensification occurred, in which novel technologies such as pottery were involved in systematic exploitation and storage of wild plant foods, ensuring a degree of food security. The changes in subsistence behaviour explored in this chapter occurred in parallel with the social changes described in Chapter 5, and form the basis of the unique form of pastoral production that arose in the Namib Desert.

Hunter-gatherer populations in southern Africa attained an apex of specialization and adaptive complexity in the late Holocene.[422] A wide range of plant species were intensively exploited and while there are some indications of small scale processing and

---

422 Mitchell (2002: 161 ff)

storage, none were cultivated; neither were any animal species in this region suitable for domestication.[423] Southern African archaeology has conventionally represented the late Holocene as a point of stasis, or 'ethnographic present',[424] such that the arrival and spread of pastoralist and farming economies in the first millennium AD served only to drive hunter-gatherer peoples to the margins. This approach is based on an essentialist view, once widely held among archaeologists, that egalitarian hunter-gatherer social values could not accommodate the contradictory principles of ownership and husbandry.[425] Even rock art as evidence of shamanic mediation of the ideological and existential, appeared to represent a static, unchanging canon of egalitarian social values.[426]

The escalating complexity of ritual practice described in the previous chapter suggests a different social evolutionary trajectory in the Namib Desert, with evidence for the adoption of social values drawn from intensive and prolonged interaction with food-producing communities on the edges of the Namib Desert.[427] This interaction initiated a number of developments that appear to be unique to the late Holocene archaeology of the Namib Desert, although there could be hitherto unrecognized parallels elsewhere in southern Africa. In the desert, at least, new social precepts, inculcated through rites of initiation, provided the social framework for an enhanced control of food resources involving a high level of cooperation in communal hunting, and in the harvesting, processing and storage of plant foods. While the social values evident in initiation practice are clearly reflective of interaction with pastoral and farming peoples during the last

---

423 H. Deacon (1972); Mitchell (2002: 190)
424 Deacon (1984)
425 e.g. Smith (1999)
426 e.g. Lewis-Williams (1984)
427 There is widespread evidence of such interaction in southern African rock art (e.g. Jolly 2006) but few indications of its consequences for the social economy of hunter-gatherer communities have been found in the archaeological record.

two thousand years, the subsistence practices described here are clearly a local development, for the plant species concerned are endemic to the Namib Desert and the practices involved in their use appear equally unique. In terms of the adaptive cycle model described in Chapter 1, we therefore see both a feedback response to external influences, and an internal memory response based on existing knowledge of the desert environment.[428]

In the first part of this chapter we examine evidence of enhanced or intensified exploitation and control of food resources in the Namib Desert, emerging in tandem with social changes outlined in the previous chapter. We begin with the evidence for large-scale communal hunting, a practice which first appears just a few centuries ago, involving large numbers of hunters and a higher degree of coordination than that of small mobile hunting parties, and presumably resulting in a far higher meat yield.[429] Communal hunting represents a clear example of a re-organization α phase, and successful hunts would have supported social cohesion through occasions such as large communal feasts, while dried meat could also be stored and thus help to maintain short-term food security. This shift in the organization and strategy of hunting chronologically follows the adoption of men's initiation rites as described in the previous chapter. Although it is not possible to demonstrate that age cohorts among initiates necessarily formed the social basis of coordinated hunting, there is compelling evidence, also considered here, for a ritual component in these events, with communal hunts possibly timed to coincide with men's initiation rites.

The onset of a re-organization α phase in which Namib Desert hunter-gatherer society adopted values and practices reflecting their interaction with pastoral and farming communities led to intensified and systematic use of food plants, exemplified by the use of wild grass seed. The parallel practice of !nara *Acanthosicyos*

---

428 Bradtmöller et al. (2017), Freeman et al. (2017)
429 Stone enclosures resembling the eponymous 'desert kites' of Asia Minor have been reported by Lombard & Badenhorst (2019) in the South African Karoo, although these have not been dated.

horridus exploitation sketched in outline here, is described in detail in Chapter 8 as part of a specific set of subsistence practices on the Namib coast. The archaeological evidence points to a significant investment of time and energy in plant food exploitation which, in the case of grass seed, required extended expeditions to remote desert locations, probably by parties of women. The nutritional importance of !nara and grass seed for the provision of food security among desert communities is set out in Table 6.1 which presents a comparison of these wild plant resources with that of pearl millet *Pennisetum glaucum*, the staple cereal crop introduced to northern Namibia by Bantu-speaking farming communities in the first millennium AD.[430] This comparison serves to show that availability of high value food sources, together with the possibility for storage, was not limited to areas suitable for rain-fed cereal cultivation. In the Namib Desert, food security based on particular plant foods became possible only after the introduction and widespread adoption of pottery, a development discussed in the second part of this chapter. This chapter presents evidence for a significant expansion of subsistence activities such as grass seed exploitation, with a large increase in the number of sites and in the extent of occupation in the Namib Desert. On the basis of this evidence it is clear that hunter-gatherer and emergent pastoral communities entered an expansion *r* phase in the adaptive cycle.

Table 6.1 shows that although millet has a higher carbohydrate content, concentrations of fats and oils, as well as protein are higher in !nara and grass seed. In terms of metabolizable energy, the wild plant food sources are comparable with millet, and although !nara concentrate has a lower energy content than the grain foods represented by millet and wild grass seed, it may be stored almost indefinitely.[431] The significance of a comparison among these foods lies in the fact that the wild plant foods which offer comparable nutritional value to cultivated pearl millet were

---

430 Harlan (1993: 57)
431 Budack (1977), Dentlinger (1977), Henschel (2004), Van den Eynden et al. (1992)

Table 6.1: Nutritional analysis of the staple domestic cereal pearl millet *Pennisetum glaucum*, compared with wild !nara melon and grass seed from the Namib Desert.

Plant food	Fats & oils g/100g	Protein g/100g	Carbohydrate g/100g	Energy kJ/100g
Pearl millet	3.7	8.2	74.0	1525.0
Grass seeds	6.3	12.0	59.0	1430.0
!Nara concentrate	6.4	31.0	10.0	942.0
Dried seeds	33.0	24.0	4.0	1669.0

gathered, processed and stored on a systematic basis that afforded a degree of food security to Namib Desert communities that were until then dependent on relatively short-term availability of food sources which could not be processed or stored in large quantities. The change in consumer and resource relations brought about by these innovations was of fundamental significance.

In parallel with the rise of age cohortism among initiated men, there is, as this chapter will show, an equally fundamental shift in the social and subsistence behaviour of women, most clearly apparent in the context of grass seed harvesting. Although pottery is conventionally associated with the spread of pastoralism in southern Africa, the evidence from the Namib Desert shows that it is more closely tied to conditions of intensified use of wild plant resources than to any aspect of animal husbandry. Sustainable dependence on wild plant foods would have required some form of regulated control over these resources. This, together with control over storage and use of accumulated food represent the most important social conditions for food production based on domesticated crops. Wild plant food exploitation, however systematic, does not meet the biological requirement that domesticated organisms must be dependent on human agency for their survival.[432] Grass seed and !nara exploitation involved an advanced degree of husbandry, and evidence for the use of wild tobacco in the Namib Desert shows that this was not confined to food plants alone.

Wild tobacco *Nicotiana africana* is an uncommon and localized endemic found only in the central and northern Namib Desert[433] where its distribution is limited to desert inselbergen such as the Dâures massif. It occurs as isolated plants, usually growing in deep sheltered rock clefts (Fig. 6.1). In every instance, wild tobacco plants are found in the near vicinity of late pre-colonial sites, usually pastoral encampments, and on many of these sites there is some evidence of smoking pipes, made from bone, pottery or stone. Although the sites offer no direct evidence for the cultivation of wild tobacco, early missionary accounts mention that tobacco was planted in shallow pits on the fringes of some settlements.[434] Thus, the association of wild tobacco with recent settlement in the desert is clear, as is the evidence of smoking. Whether the properties of wild tobacco were discovered independently is uncertain, as the evidence of smoking is from approximately the period in which domesticated tobacco *Nicotiana tabacum* was first brought by European visitors to the coast.[435]

Although the alkaloid composition of wild tobacco differs from that of the domesticated species which has a far higher nicotine content in the leaf, the minor alkaloids nornicotine, anabasine and anatabine (Table 6.2)[436] occur in higher concentrations in wild

---

432 Clutton-Brock (1992)
433 Craven (2009: 145); Goodspeed (1954); Merxmuller & Büttler (1975). The specimen database of the National Herbarium of Namibia records only 19 collecting localities for the species, with a single additional record at the Bolus Herbarium, University of Cape Town.
434 Vigne (1991); Vedder (1966: 232)
435 The evidently recent use of *Nicotiana africana* at first suggested that the plant might be an early cultivar of *N. tabacum* (Kinahan 2001a: 85), a possibility now dismissed by molecular phylogeny (Clarkson et al. 2004; Olmstead et al. 2008).
436 Data from Symon (2005)

Figure 6.1: Habit and florescence of *Nicotiana africana*. Illustration reproduced with permission of Botanischen Staatssammlung München.

tobacco, where they mimic or enhance the effects of nicotine.[437] As in other situations where wild tobacco species were used and to some degree cultivated prior to historical contact,[438] the introduced domestic *Nicotiana tabacum* eventually displaced the use of indigenous varieties. The close association of wild tobacco with human settlement in the Namib Desert, together with the fact that the plants were cultivated, provides circumstantial evidence of *Nicotiana africana* as an unusual instance of semi-domestication of an indigenous plant species in southern Africa.[439]

Table 6.2: Alkaloid content of *Nicotiana tabacum* and *Nicotiana africana*, represented as percentage of dry weight.

Species	Part	Nicotine	Nornicotine	Anabasine	Anatabine
N. tabacum	leaves	94.8	0.3	0.2	0.7
N. africana	leaves	4.7	92.4	0.3	2.6
N. africana	roots	45.0	45.1	1.0	8.9

Communal hunting

The long hiatus of occupation at Gorrasis Rock Shelter following the onset of late Holocene aridification discussed in Chapter 3, ended in the last one thousand years with a series of three brief occupations between 1300 and 1800 AD. These events coincided, broadly, with the germination of camelthorn trees described in Chapter 5, indicating human occupation in response to a general improvement in biotic productivity following the Medieval Warm Epoch and consequent episodes of desert rainfall. The recovery of

---

437 Harris et al. (2015)
438 Symon (2005)
439 It is possible that tobacco was used as a narcotic in ritual contexts, as was dagga *Cannabis sativa* elsewhere in southern Africa (Deacon 1994; Katz 1982; Prins 1990), although there is no direct evidence that the use of tobacco extended beyond the recreational in the Namib Desert.

vegetation in the southern Namib would have been associated with an increased population of antelope and other huntable species. Rainfall in the desert allows migratory antelope to disperse over the landscape, and deep into the dune sea in the case of oryx *Oryx gazella* which is able to survive independently of water.[440]

As the nutritional quality of ephemeral desert grasses declines quite rapidly with the onset of the dry season, oryx are obliged to move inland to find suitable pastures, thus following a semi-nomadic cycle. In the southern Namib, this movement is to some extent constrained by topography, and the oryx follow habitual routes between the desert and escarpment, using narrow mountain valleys.[441] Herds tend to be stable groups of 25 or less, often led by a dominant male. Although their movements are highly predictable, oryx are vigilant and difficult to approach. In the Gorrasis-Awasib area, like most of the southern Namib, the difficulty of approach is exacerbated by an almost complete lack of natural concealment for the hunter. The inland movement of oryx in search of dry season pastures takes place within a short time, and even if one or two were brought down, the remainder of the herd would disperse, leaving the gravel plains near Gorrasis Rock Shelter empty of game, and with little water for human use.

To exploit the limited hunting opportunity of the oryx migration period, hunter-gatherer groups reoccupying the Namib during the last one thousand years adopted methods of communal ambush hunting. This strategy followed the natural movement of the oryx and, apparently, deflected their routes towards particular sites that were to the hunters' advantage. Figure 6.2 shows the distribution of ambush hunting sites between the edge of the dune

---

440 Estes (1991: 128)
441 A wildlife field census recorded more than 1,000 mortalities, mainly oryx, along a fence-line that bisects the Awasib-Gorrasis area (unpublished wildlife census data from W. Killian, 2000). A large number of animals had evidently died attempting to enter the series of valleys in which the hunting blinds are sited, thus confirming that this was a habitual route of migration.

sea at Awasib and the gravel plains around Gorrasis. The largest of these (Site F, Fig. 6.2) consists of 51 arcuate stone blinds, each measuring approximately 3 m across, arranged over the whole extent of a low saddle between two hills (Fig. 6.3). These, like all other blinds in the area, are oriented so as to conceal the hunter from animals moving from west to east, thus confirming that the strategy of hunting was to intercept animals migrating inland in search of pasture.

Considering the absence of cover on the open plains, the hunting strategy in all likelihood involved a coordinated effort in which people were positioned at distant points from which to drive the herd in the manner of a *battue* towards the chosen ambush site. This inferred strategy, together with the number of blinds indicating sizeable parties of hunters, provides circumstantial evidence for a level of organization greater than that of the small hunting groups which characterized earlier, mid-Holocene occupation of the same area. The sophistication of the communal hunting strategy is shown at the largest site by the fact that the stone blinds are so positioned as to be below the horizon of the approaching herd until it is within a distance of little more than 30 m. Furthermore, more than one hundred small stone cairns that once held upright lengths of wood[442] were positioned along the approaching game-trails, with the likely purpose of deflecting the animals' direction of movement into the ambush and of forcing the animals into moving abreast rather than in single file, thus increasing the number of potential targets at the critical moment.

In ecological terms, communal hunting maximized the potential yield of food in a density independent situation where water rather than huntable game was the main limiting factor. The orchestrated communal ambush clearly shows that this strategy forced the maximum possible yield into the smallest window

---

442 An AMS date for the stump of one wooden post has a maximum age of 240 years which falls within the range of OSL dates for hunting blinds listed in Table 6.3.

DESERT GARDEN 225

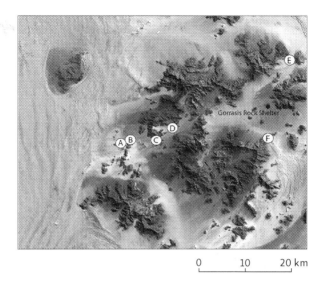

Figure 6.2: Communal ambush hunting sites (labelled A–F), in the vicinity of Gorrasis Rock Shelter.

of opportunity. It is indeed plausible that the oryx migration afforded only one such opportunity, making careful planning and preparation essential for its success.

Ambush hunting such as described here would have most likely been carried out with spears rather than bow and arrow as it was necessary to inflict a mortal wound at close quarters. Due to the fact that the hunting blinds contain no dateable organic material, windblown sand trapped beneath the rock in two of the blinds was dated by optically stimulated luminescence (OSL). OSL dates for Gorrasis Site F ranged between the late 1700s and early 1800s AD, by which time iron-tipped spears were widely available, as exemplified by the spear point from the Rainman Shelter at Otjohorongo described in Chapter 5. Notably, the hunting blind dates fall within the range for recent occupation events at Gorrasis Rock Shelter discussed in Chapter 3 (Table 3.2). Further OSL dates from the early 1700s AD were obtained from a set of hunting blinds elsewhere in the Namib at Husab

226 NAMIB

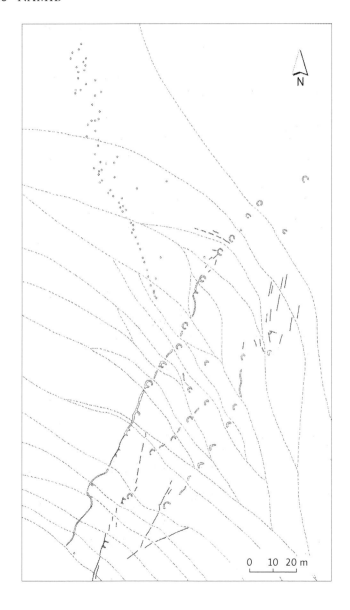

Figure 6.3: Layout of communal hunting Site F (see Fig. 6.2). Hollow lines delineate walling and hunting blinds; solid lines are outcropping dolerite; circles are small cairns; dashed lines indicate game paths.

Table 6.3: Late Holocene Optically Stimulated Luminescence (OSL) dating of windblown quartz sand samples from two sets of Namib Desert hunting blinds.

Site	Dose (Gy)	Dose rate (Gy/ka)	Age (years)
Gorrasis	0.34±0.04	2.40±0.12	140±20
	1.14±0.13	3.00±0.15	380±50
Husab	0.28±0.03	4.01±0.38	260±50
	0.28±0.03	5.38±0.51	230±60
	0.28±0.03	6.05±0.63	240±60

(Table 6.3)[443] and there are numerous undated ambush hunting sites throughout the desert. Considering the importance of communal hunting at the time of the reoccupation of Gorrasis Rock Shelter, it is noteworthy that faunal remains from the site presented in Chapter 3 included no direct evidence of oryx. It is likely that oryx or other large animals obtained in communal hunts were butchered and consumed at temporary camps near the ambush sites rather than at the rock shelter. This exemplifies the importance of linking evidence from rock shelter excavations with evidence of specialized activities on the same landscape.

The level of collaboration required for up to one hundred or more people to drive the animals, and to bring down a number commensurate with such a large group undertaking apparently did not exist prior to the last few centuries. It is therefore arguable that communal hunting on this scale was a consequence of fundamental social changes such as the adoption of men's initiation. This could have formed the basis of cooperation among hunters drawn from different local bands. In all likelihood, a communal hunt would

---

443 OSL ages were determined at Risø Laboratory, Denmark (Gorrasis samples) and the Luminescence Dating Facility, University of Melbourne (Husab samples), and calculated using models of Galbraith et al. (1999) and Olley et al. (2006).

have required the involvement of every available able-bodied person, including not only the hunters who manned the ambush sites but also women, children and older men who could no longer hunt, to serve as beaters and decoys.

Some insight into the organization of communal hunts is provided by a series of otherwise enigmatic radiating stone alignments, one of these being directly associated with the westernmost point of the Awasib-Gorrasis hunting blinds. There are a further two examples located near the Husab hunting blinds shown in Table 6.3 as approximately the same age. All of the radiating stone alignment sites (Fig. 6.4) are located on rising ground and are generally isolated from encampment sites or other evidence of occupation. The Tinkas site comprises more than 500 m of discontinuous rough stone alignment radiating from the crest of an isolated hill overlooking the desert plains. The alignments at Arechademab radiate from the ridge of an isolated hill and are associated with a circular stone arrangement which has similarities to those on the Awasib-Gorrasis site. The stone alignments on the latter site also radiate from the slopes of an isolated eminence. Whereas the strategic function of hunting blind sites is generally obvious, the Tinkas and Arechademab sites do not have any such value. This, together with their isolation and the absence of occupation debris raises the possibility that they were sites of ritual preparation for communal hunts. The scale of these installations, as well as their relative isolation, and their proximity to hunting blind sites, would support the inference that hunters from different local groups might have secluded themselves for this purpose. Given the high degree of coordination required, and the prospect of a dangerous close quarters encounter with their prey, the communal hunt was clearly quite different from more solitary hunting of smaller animals.

Communal hunts could only have occurred under specific conditions such as after rainfall that allowed oryx to disperse into the desert, with the certainty of their return following known habitual migration routes. These hunts required a degree of

Figure 6.4: Stone alignments associated with communal hunting sites, from left to right: Arechademab, Tinkas and Awasib-Gorrasis. Solid lines indicate stone alignments and shaded circles indicate enclosures. All three examples have a maximum extent of approximately 500 m.

collaboration and coordination that was based on close association and familiarity among social groups that were ordinarily dispersed over a wide area. The success of the hunt would have depended on the hunters' ability to act in concert, and it is therefore likely that the relationships forming the basis of this cooperation were forged in advance, with men's initiation as a likely common formative experience.

The social relationships required for the successful organization of communal hunts may well have existed before, as is exemplified by the evidence of ostrich eggshell bead exchange networks discussed in Chapter 4. However, initiation and its attendant reorganization of hunter-gatherer society made it possible to exercise a greater degree of control over resources such as migratory oryx, taking cooperation among hunters to a more advanced level than the maintenance of social networks through gift exchange. Evidence has emerged of mass hunting of migratory antelope elsewhere in southern Africa during the late Holocene[444] and it is therefore plausible that the shift in hunter-gatherer social organization observed in the Namib Desert was a more widespread phenomenon.

---

444 Dewar et al. (2005); Van der Walt & Lombard (2018); see also Hitchcock et al. (2019)

Harvesting grass seed

There is evidence throughout the length of the Namib Desert for systematic harvesting of wild grass seed during the last one thousand years. Physical traces of seed harvesting are visible in the form of diggings to expose the underground seed caches of harvester ants, commonly *Messor tropicorum* which form an important part of the desert grassland ecosystem.[445] Several kilograms of seed (*sâun*) and husks may be obtained from a single nest, depending on its size. Seed harvesting is back-breaking work, walking from nest to nest in the sun, still practised today in remote areas, although on a small scale.[446] A praise poem or *arus* (rhythmic song) to this resource and the ants defending their nests from intruding hands, is still current among ǂNūkhoen in the northern Namib Desert:[447]

ǁGaises ai ge sâu-e ra ǁgarahe.	At ǁGaises we winnow grass seed.
!Oaxaseb ge ǀnanuba ra lawi,	The rain that we've been longing for is falling,
ǀnanub ge ra lawi.	The rain is falling.
Khoetoma, taebas ta aba?	Khoetoma, why are you crying?
Xoaǂgā ta ra hâ tao danaba da !gau	Collecting the seed is making my head break
!nara ta ra hâ tao danaba da !gau.	Moving from place to place is making my back break.
!Naidadama ǁnae so re!	The Giraffe-Damara (nation) are singing!
Hō-ai!	Ouch!

---

445 Marsh (1987); Marsh (1986) reviews the relationship between seed harvesting species abundance and rainfall in the Namib Desert.
446 Sullivan (1998, 1999) notes that grass seed was obtained by such methods as well as being plucked directly from the stem.
447 !Narab and Purros Damara rhythmic song (*arus*) recorded in Sesfontein by Sullivan (1999: 4–5); orthography adjusted by W. Haacke.

Although unable to fully exploit the seed caches of the harvester ant until the acquisition of pottery made this possible, there should be no doubt that the behaviour of these creatures was long known to the inhabitants of the Namib, just as it was to those of other desert regions where they present an example of industry and forward planning in the natural world that was clearly relevant to the challenges of human survival, thus: "Go to the ant, thou sluggard; consider her ways and be wise: which having no guide, overseer or ruler, provideth her meat in the summer, and gathereth her food in the harvest."[448]

The distribution of seed harvesting sites in the Namib Desert is patchy, however, with significant concentrations in areas of optimal grass cover and within reach of ephemeral water sources. Evidence for the exploitation of harvester ant seed caches is most apparent along the inland edge of the desert, declining towards the west as annual species diminish before vanishing completely within 50 km of the desert coast. Grasses of the genera *Eragrostis* spp., and *Stipagrostis* spp. predominate on the Namib plains,[449] and two species, *S. ciliata*, and *S. uniplumis*, are of particular importance. There is a direct relationship between grass standing crop and rainfall, and the zero intercept of grass germination has been demonstrated to lie at 11 mm rainfall received within a period of one week.[450] Thus, even very low levels of precipitation can rapidly initiate significant grass cover. Figure 6.5 provides an example of the local distribution pattern of sites related to seed harvesting in one part of the central Namib.

Standing pools of rainwater allow access to remote areas of grassland but these may last only a few weeks. This does not allow sufficient time for annual grasses to grow and produce seed, nor for the seed to be stripped from the grass, husked and carried underground by the harvester ants. It may also be that if no rain has fallen in a particular area for some years, the harvester ant

---

448 Proverbs 6: 6–8, Authorized King James Bible.
449 Henschel et al. (2005)
450 Günster (1992); Seely (1978); Seely & Louw (1980)

232 NAMIB

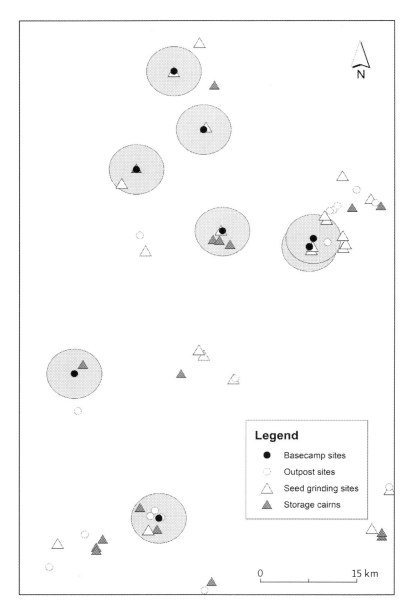

Figure 6.5: Local distribution of seed harvesting sites near Ganab in the central Namib Desert. Basecamp sites at waterholes are shown with a 4 km radius (ca 50 km^2) of intensive seed digging activity.

population may itself need at least one season to recover.[451] This means that seed is not likely to be available for human use in the same year that it is gathered by the ants. As a consequence, the seed excavated from the nests will have been gathered by the harvester ants one or more years previously.

Places with suitable water catchments were evidently well known and repeatedly visited. Harvesting was limited by the availability of water rather than seed and was therefore in ecological terms density independent in the same way as communal hunting. In both cases, however, intensified exploitation in the form of potentially higher yields of oryx meat and grass seed respectively, maximized the opportunity and would have provided a measure of food security at the start of the dry season. It is important to note that evidence of seed harvesting is generally not found in the larger rock shelter sites that have formed the main focus of late Holocene archaeological investigations in the Namib Desert[452] and it has consequently escaped the notice of previous research.[453] Seed harvesting, like communal antelope hunting, shows the importance of spatially dispersed subsistence strategies in the Namib Desert and highlights the necessity to integrate evidence from activities not represented in the evidence recovered from rock shelter excavations.

Field evidence indicates that seed digging was concentrated within a radius of 4 km (or about one hour's walk) from available water, usually in the form of small ponds forming on weathered rock outcrops after localized rain showers. The data presented in Table 6.4[454] show the greatest density of seed diggings per square kilometre lies at the foot of the escarpment, slightly over 100 km

---

451 Marsh (1987) notes that harvester ant populations may take up to five months to recover following a period of food scarcity.
452 e.g. Albrecht et al. (2001); Sandelowsky (1977); Smith & Jacobson (1995)
453 Nic Eoin (2016) has suggested that archaeological evidence of seed harvesting might be found elsewhere in southern Africa although this remains unconfirmed.
454 Rainfall data from Mendelsohn et al. (2002)

inland from the coast. In this zone, the approximately 50 km² area surrounding a basecamp site at water may have a cumulative density of more than 10,000 digging sites. Their distribution on the landscape is uneven, however, and average densities within this zone are closer to half that number. The table also shows that there is a steep decline towards the coast in the local density of seed digging sites. Although rainfall is extremely low and unpredictable throughout the area, it is marginally higher at the foot of the escarpment. Low rainfall and relatively high soil salinity in the coastal fog zone (Na>100mg/kg) extending approximately 50 km inland appears to exclude annual grasses and harvester ants alike.

Table 6.4: The relationship between distance from the coast, rainfall and the local density of seed digging sites.

Distance from coast km	Days >1mm rain^{y-1}	CV Rainfall^{y-1}	Mean number seed diggings per km²	SD seed diggings per km²
<50	5-10	>100	30	10
100	10-15	90-100	150	36
>100	15-20	80-90	529	55

Seed diggings are commonly found on coarse calcareous soils and weathered granitic bedrock, as small roughly circular areas of disturbance up to 3 m in diameter and occurring in dense local concentrations. Seed diggings are characterized by the presence of manuports, brought from neighbouring outcrops of dolerite and other hard rocks used to break open the surface, and by chunks of bedrock, overturned in the process of digging and showing patches of caliche which is formed on the underside of near-surface rock. Basecamp sites associated with concentrations of diggings comprise small groups of windbreaks or semi-circular arrangements of stone about 2.5 m in diameter. Grinding surfaces on outcropping granite are frequently found on or near these sites.

Table 6.5: Comparison of internal dimensions of storage cairns and external dimensions of pottery vessels.

		Storage cairns (n=15) Internal dimensions	Pottery vessels (n=82) External dimensions
Depth mm	maximum	800	620
	minimum	300	125
	average	466	284
Width mm	maximum	750	430
	minimum	250	135
	average	384	241

Storage cairns are also a common feature of both basecamp and isolated seed digging sites (Fig. 6.6). Some of these structures have been found containing whole pots which were evidently used as storage containers. Table 6.5 compares the internal dimensions of storage cairns and the external dimensions of pottery vessels and shows that this was probably the main purpose of these features.

Direct evidence for the processing of grass seed on grinding surfaces is available from a large granitic syenite outcrop located several hundred meters from Gorrasis Rock Shelter. Two rainwater ponds are visible on the outcrop itself, and an adjacent rock fissure has a capacity of approximately 3 m^3. The outcrop is about 50 m in diameter and bears traces of at least 105 grinding surfaces (Fig. 6.7a,b). The grinding surfaces are not deeply hollowed but are recognizable from their glossy siliceous veneer. Photomicrographs of the grinding surfaces revealed the presence of parallel, subparallel and intersecting striations which indicate grinding rather than any natural weathering process (Fig. 6.8). Furthermore, fine cracks in the grinding surfaces yielded an array of phytoliths representative of several grasses that produce seed suitable for grinding, including *Eragrostis* spp. and *Stipagrostis* spp. (Fig. 6.9). The cracks containing the phytoliths also contained a range of

Figure 6.6: Example of a storage cairn at a seed harvesting basecamp site.

diatoms associated with pond flora (Fig. 6.10), thus indicating the presence of standing water in the vicinity of the grinding surfaces.[455]

The Dancing Kudu engraving described in Chapter 5 provides important further insights into the use of communal seed grinding sites such as at Gorrasis. Measurements on this and similar well preserved grinding surfaces yielded a mean length of 0.63 m (SD 0.08 m; n=40). Assuming that stroke-length of grinding surfaces is proportional to human stature,[456] the grinding surfaces yield an estimated mean stature of 1.49 m (SD 0.12 m; n=40). This is comparable to estimates based on human female skeletal remains from the Namib Desert, indicating a mean stature of 1.51 m (SD

---

455 The investigation of use-wear on the grinding surfaces and the recovery of phytoliths followed protocols suggested by Fullagar & Wallis (2012).
456 cf. Mohanty et al. (2001)

DESERT GARDEN 237

Figure 6.7a: Seed grinding site at Gorrasis viewed from the south.

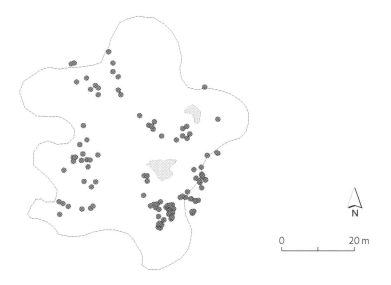

Figure 6.7b: Plan of rock outcrop with grinding surfaces and rainwater ponds at Gorrasis.

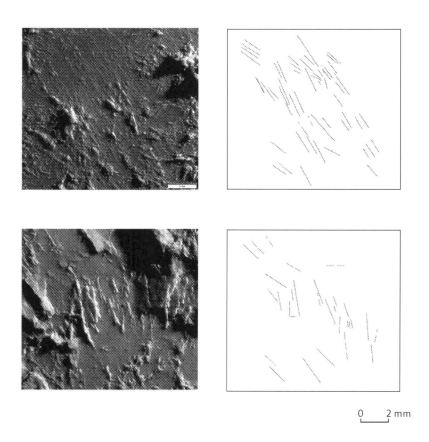

Figure 6.8: Photomicrographs (left) of grinding surfaces at Gorrasis, with grinding scars (right).

DESERT GARDEN 239

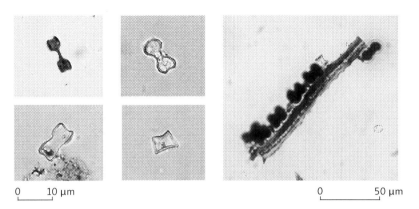

Figure 6.9: Phytoliths from grinding surfaces at Gorrasis, including various Poaceae. Bilobate forms at left attributable to *Aristida* and *Stipagrostis* (upper left and right), *Eragrostis* (lower left), with unidentified Poaceae rondel form (lower right). The image on the right shows bilobate Poaceae phytoliths in articulation. Phytolith morphology terms follow Madella et al. (2005) and provisional identifications follow Piperno (2006: Fig. 2.2).

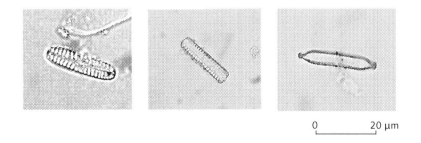

Figure 6.10: Diatoms from grinding surfaces at Gorrasis, with Chrysophyta diatom (left) indicative of aquatic pond flora.

Figure 6.11: Inferred all-fours posture and range of movement required to reproduce the stroke-length of seed-grinding surfaces in the Namib Desert.

0.04 m; n=7)[457] (Table 6.6). Importantly, the stroke-length measured on the grinding surfaces requires an all-fours position, in which the back is hollowed; at full stretch the pelvis is raised (Fig. 6.11), thereby reproducing the posture of the sexually receptive female kudu, both in life and as depicted in the Dancing Kudu.

Table 6.6: Comparative human stature estimates based on skeletal samples from the Namib Desert, and from the stroke-length of seed grinding surfaces at Gorrasis.

Stature estimates* (n)	Median	Mean	SD	Upper mean	Lower mean
All skeletons (20)	158.5	158.9	9.16	163.2	154.6
Male skeletons (13)	162.5	162.0	9.13	167.5	156.5
Female skeletons (7)	154.2	153.1	6.26	158.9	147.3
Grinding surfaces (40)	149.8	146.0	11.8	149.8	142.2

* Methods of stature estimation based on Wilson and Lundy (1994) for skeletal remains and Mohanty et al. (2001) for the grinding surfaces are set out in Kinahan (2013a).

---

457 Kinahan (2013a)

Grinding sites offer other suggestive parallels to the Dancing Kudu engraving as a component of female initiation and the customary role of women. Initiation sites are secluded, partly so that men can avoid contact with menstrual blood;[458] the grinding sites, similarly, are several hundred metres from evidence of encampment and are thus secluded or separated from the encampment, possibly as places reserved for women. The body of the Dancing Kudu engraving lies at an acute angle and could not have been used for grinding, but it is suggestive of a grinding surface; the use of the polished engraving technique on kudu but on no other engravings thus strongly implies a link between the habits of the female kudu, the particular technique of engraving employed, and women's initiation in the Namib Desert.

In the vicinity of seed diggings there are occasionally small rock shelters which have a few loose grindstones, as well as ostrich eggshell with some indications of bead manufacture, and pottery. As a general rule these sites have no hearth, and neither do they have stone artefacts or flaking debris, and no evidence of butchery. It is likely that these sites were used by women on seed harvesting expeditions. It is noteworthy that these sites are often littered with pellets of kudu dung, while the back wall of the shelter sometimes has a glossy polish from kudu rubbing against the rock while sheltering from the desert winds. Significantly, kudu seen in the vicinity of these sites are almost exclusively groups of females and young,[459] providing a remarkable parallel to the activity of women themselves, and a reprise of the role of the female kudu in women's initiation. That one of these sites has within it a painting of a female kudu (Fig. 6.12) provides circumstantial evidence that at least some rock art was produced by women. In this particular case, the image of the female kudu is painted directly above a large grinding hollow in the bedrock of the shelter floor.

---

458 Marshall (1999)
459 Kudu females habitually form small troops while males are often solitary (Estes 1991).

Figure 6.12: Monochrome female kudu from a women's seed harvesting shelter in the Chuos Mountains.

The archaeological evidence discussed here points to a formalization of men's and women's roles among recent Namib Desert hunter-gatherers. Evidence of seed harvesting and associated processing shows that women's activities were localized in their focus on areas with high densities of harvester ant nests. Seed harvesting included a strong emphasis on storage, and co-operation among adjacent groups. There is also an element of seclusion in women's activities shown by the location of communal seed-grinding sites away from basecamp sites, and the use of isolated shelters where seed processing and other tasks were carried out. In contrast, men's use of the landscape appears to have been more extensive and strategic, with an emphasis on linear features such as game trails, and expeditions to isolated resources such as bee's nests and hunting lookout sites. Broad-based co-operation in communal hunts was probably a consequence of formalized social precepts reinforced through initiation.

A simplified structural opposition of late Holocene men's and women's roles is set out in Table 6.7. The opposition of gender roles suggested here does not pre-suppose gender segregation, but merely a difference in the focus of these roles, rooted in the transformative process of initiation. There can be no doubt that men may have participated in seed harvesting work, as they may have done in rituals of women's initiation.[460] Likewise, women would have certainly played a role in communal hunts because of their detailed knowledge of the landscape and the movement of animals observed while seed harvesting. Nonetheless, it does appear that a fundamental shift in social organization was achieved during the last one thousand years in the Namib Desert, with the result that food supply was greatly improved, and through storage, a degree of food security was achieved. Pottery played a fundamental role in the technology of food production.

Table 6.7: Suggested structural opposition of gender roles and activities among late Holocene hunter-gatherers in the Namib Desert

Women	Men
Co-operative	Strategic
Localized	Expeditionary
Circular (ant nests)	Linear (routes/game trails)
Storage cairns	Hunting blinds
Shelters (secluded)	Lookouts (prominent)

Pottery style, dating and function

Pottery is almost ubiquitous on late Holocene archaeological sites in the Namib Desert although it usually occurs as small numbers of scattered sherds. Whole vessels are uncommon and relatively few pottery finds are securely dated. However, it is clear from

---

460 Kinahan (2017b)

excavated finds that pottery first appeared in the Namib Desert about 2,000 years ago, as shown in Chapter 4. Surface finds are dated mainly to within the last one thousand years from the dating of soot coating on the outside of the vessel or where tree resin has been used to effect repairs. The evidence is clear that pottery became common and widely used especially in the last one thousand years, when it is closely associated with exploitation of !nara and wild grass seed, as described above.

Beyond the Namib Desert, there is evidence for the arrival of pottery with farming communities[461] in the first millennium AD, and its rapid spread in the wider hunter-gatherer economy. There is evidence that hunter-gatherer communities initially selected particular vessel size and shape classes useful to tasks such as the collecting and storage of honey.[462] Also, pottery was evidently acquired from multiple sources and vessels appear to have been retained for extended periods, so that hunter-gatherer pottery assemblages sometimes show unusual combinations of vessels with differing ages and affinities.[463] The fact that pottery was sometimes acquired and circulated as single sherds[464] also suggests that it was imbued with magical as well as purely utilitarian value.[465] As in the case of livestock acquisition described in Chapter 4, it seems that pottery, too, entered the hunter-gatherer world through the filter of the supernatural and the domain of ritual. Clearly, though, the technology of potting was effectively transferred by the middle of the second millennium AD,[466] taking a stylistically distinctive local form with functional characteristics closely adapted to the exploitation of wild plant foods.

In general, pottery from the Namib Desert shows considerable variation in shape and decoration, such that most attributes of style

---

461 Kose (2009); Richter (2005); Sandelowsky (1979)
462 Kinahan (1986)
463 Kinahan (2013b)
464 Musonda (1987)
465 Kinahan (2001b); Mitchell et al. (2008)
466 Kinahan (2013b)

are widely distributed and pottery within any particular group of sites shows little or no indication of localized styles. This is illustrated by the simple average cluster analysis of 78 vessels with reliable provenance data presented in Figure 6.13. The analysis, based on attributes of shape, decoration, rim profile, lug types and size, identifies only one discrete cluster, comprising necked, burnished vessels which I shall call Group A. Alongside these are less well-defined combinations of attributes characterizing bag-shaped, coarse tempered vessels of Group B.

Group A vessels are generally small, with a burnished surface, a constricted mouth and sometimes a spout, as well as elaborate incised or punctate decoration on the upper body and rim. These vessels resemble pottery from the region to the south of the Orange River.[467] Many appear to have been used for the storage of prestige materials such as cosmetic ochre and haematite.[468] Such vessels rarely show indications of soot from cooking fires. In contrast, Group B vessels are usually twice as large, with wide mouths and less elaborate decoration comprising rows of incisions or fingernail impressions below the rim. Many of these vessels are thickly coated with soot and evidence of repair is common, often in the form of fibre stitching with holes drilled for this purpose on either side of large cracks that would otherwise render the pot useless. The two groups of vessels are clearly different in appearance and in function but the essential similarities of the pointed base and the presence of lugs indicate that Group A is ancestral to Group B.[469]

The available dating of Namib Desert pottery indicates a chronological continuity from the first appearance of pottery until it fell from use during the historic period. Figure 6.14 shows that the earliest dated pottery finds (Group Aa) from rock

---

467 Rudner (1968)
468 e.g. Beaumont (1973); Jacobson (1977); Sydow (1967). Beaumont and Boshier (1974) have documented evidence dated to 830 AD for mining of cosmetic haematite in the northern Cape.
469 Kinahan (2001a: 72–6)

shelter excavations have dates ranging between 2,300 and 1,500 years BP. The earliest pottery finds include no whole vessels and are therefore not included in the Figure 6.13 cluster analysis. However, this pottery is in every instance burnished and the vessel mouth is usually constricted. On the basis of these attributes, and the common presence of fine decoration around the rim, the earliest pottery may be grouped with the necked, burnished vessels indicated in Figure 6.13 as Group A. Available dates for three necked, burnished vessels (indicated as Group A in Figure 6.14[470]) are continuous with those of Group Aa and intermediary with the dating of bag-shaped, coarse tempered vessels (Group B) which are consistently younger than vessels of Group Aa and A.

Table 6.8: Simplified comparison of early and recent Namib Desert pottery groups

Group A	Group B
>1000 years BP	<1000 years BP
<5.0 litres capacity	>5.0 litres capacity
Burnished fabric	Coarse fabric
Constricted mouth	Wide mouth
Internally-reinforced lugs	Externally-applied lugs
Elaborate decoration	Simple or no decoration
Prestige materials	Food storage & preparation

---

470 Uncalibrated radiocarbon dates in years BP: 130±30 (Beta-291541); 150±70 (Pta-1867); 150±40 (Beta-278552); 170±40 (Beta-278551); 180±40 (Beta-278550); 190±30 (Beta-291540); 230±40 (Beta-278548); 250±40 (Beta-278544); 260±30 (Beta-291542); 270±40 (Beta-278543); 290±40 (Beta-278549); 300±50 (Pta-2264); 310±20 (Pta-1801); 350±50 (Beta-235938); 400±50 (Pta-2296); 410±50 (KN-3600); 420±140 (Pta-2645); 490±50 (Pta-2295); 620±50 (KN-3599); 640±100 (KN-3596); 840±50 (Pta-3925); 970±50 (Pta-3926); 1,170±30 (Beta-450170); 1,370±35 (Hd-25103); 1,460±55 (KN-1.846); 1,550±50 (Pta-1535); 1,640±70 (Wits-1249); 1,745±35 (GrN-5297); 1,840±50 (Pta-2886); 1,880±50 (Pta-2927); 2,040±50 (Pta-2930); 2,100±50 (Pta-2929); 2,140±50 (Pta-2552); 2,190±40 (KN-1.732).

DESERT GARDEN 247

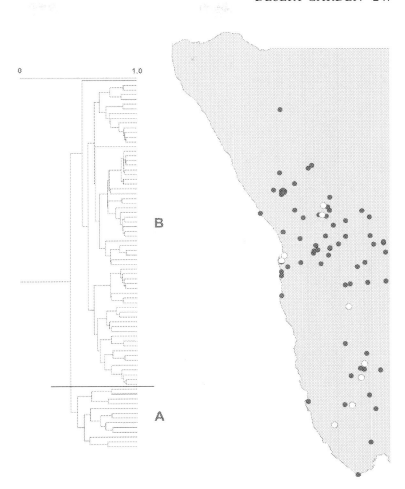

Figure 6.13: Simple average cluster analysis of Namib Desert pottery attribute combinations. The first-order cluster represents Group A necked, burnished vessels and their distribution is indicated by the white map symbols. Bag-shaped, coarse tempered vessels of Group B are represented by other attribute combinations and by the dark grey map symbols.

248 NAMIB

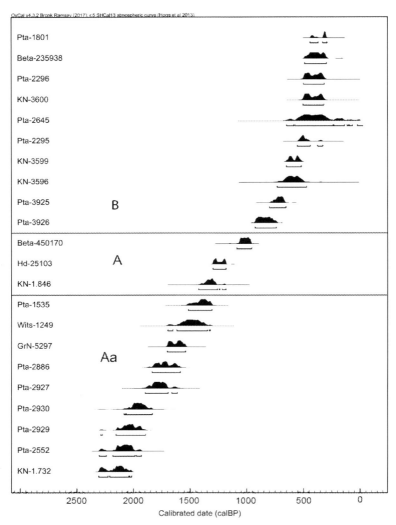

Figure 6.14: Radiocarbon dating of Namib Desert pottery, showing rock shelter finds (Aa), necked, burnished vessels (A) and bag-shaped, coarse tempered vessels (B). The Aa pottery is highly fragmented and therefore excluded from the attribute cluster analysis in Figure 6.13 (see explanation in Notes to the Reader: Archaeological age determination, xvii).

A simplified comparison of these broad stylistic and temporal pottery groups is set out in Table 6.8. There are many examples of continuity between the two groups, such as occasional internally-reinforced lugs, characteristic of Group A, in assemblages of later pottery, although it is rarely the case that externally reinforced lugs, characteristic of Group B, occur in assemblages of earlier pottery. Attribute combinations such as the spout and elaborate decoration are found exclusively in Group A and appear to represent an extension into the Namib Desert from the south, of the pottery style associated with recent Khoe-speaking pastoralists in the arid western parts of southern Africa.[471] Examples of Group A and B pottery from the Namib Desert are illustrated in Figures 6.15 and 6.16, respectively. The stylistic and dating evidence suggests a local development of Group B, based on the adaptation of Group Aa and A style and function, towards the systematic exploitation of plant foods that do not occur outside the Namib Desert. The great majority of Group B vessels found so far (roughly 80%) are from the central Namib between the !Khuiseb River and the Dâures massif, and inland to the escarpment. This is the area in which !nara and grass seed were most intensively exploited. Of the 48 dated pottery finds from within this area, 64% are younger than 1,000 years and belong to Group B, indicating a marked increase in the use of pottery for the purpose of wild plant food processing and storage.

Although early first millennium pottery from Falls Rock Shelter described in Chapter 4 shares some characteristics with Group A (Fig. 6.15), such as surface burnishing and a narrow-necked profile, it also shows a degree of stylistic diversity, suggesting that pottery may have been acquired from more than one source within a stylistically diversified cultural setting. To test this possibility, strontium isotope analyses were carried out on eleven sherds from Falls Rock Shelter (Aa Group) and nine sherds from Group A vessels found elsewhere in the Namib Desert. The $^{87}Sr/^{86}Sr$ results shown in Figure 6.17 confirm that Group A vessels have a diverse

---

471 Rudner (1968); Sadr (2008a); Sadr & Sampson (2011); Sadr & Smith (1991)

250 NAMIB

Figure 6.15: Typical example of 1st millennium AD pottery from the Namib Desert (Group A) showing burnished surface, constricted mouth, spout and decorated above the shoulder with a band of incised, interlocking triangles. From the Sydow Collection, Swakopmund Museum.

DESERT GARDEN 251

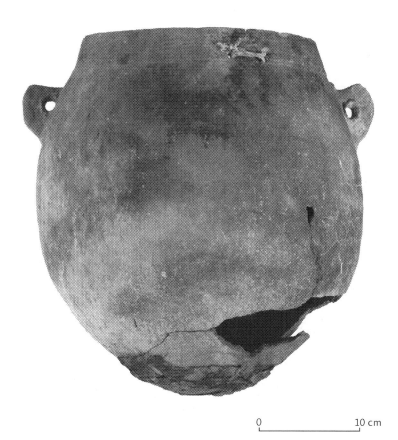

Figure 6.16: Typical example of 2nd millennium AD pottery from the Namib Desert (Group B) showing characteristic bag-shaped profile with pointed base, externally-applied lugs, wide mouth, coarse fabric, soot encrustation and evidence of repair. The rim is decorated with columns of fingernail impressions. From the Kuhne Collection, Swakopmund Museum.

Table 6.9: Elemental composition of ochre and haematite in Group A necked, burnished vessels from the Namib Desert

Elemental composition ‰*	Cu	Zn	Mn	Fe	Pb
Arusis	0.076	0.67	0.73	183	0.24
Barby	<0.05	0.54	1.77	205	0.21
Orumbo	<0.05	0.45	0.78	133	0.21
Aruab 1	0.55	0.73	0.62	172	0.62
Aruab 2	0.05	0.79	0.19	182	0.56

* Method reference: Nitric acid – perchloric acid digestion 2:1 (cf. Rashid 1986)

isotopic signature indicating that they represent potting clays from isotopically distinct and, it is presumed, geographically dispersed locations. Corroborating this is the evidence from cosmetic ochre and specular haematite in Group A vessels found as buried caches in various parts of the Namib Desert. Assays of material from these caches are presented in Table 6.9, which shows large variation in the minor element composition of these high-grade iron ores.

The Aruab cache from Group A, dated to 1170 cal. BP (Fig. 6.14) comprised two vessels, and their contents are shown in Table 6.9 to have large differences in copper, manganese and lead content, which implies that cosmetic ochre was derived from different sources.[472] None of the caches in Table 6.9 are from localities with natural iron ore deposits, showing that this valuable material was transported over considerable distances. The association of Group Aa pottery with early evidence of sheep at Falls Rock Shelter (described in Chapter 4), suggests that complex exchange networks extended deep into the Namib Desert during the first millennium. This could reflect a regional expansion of pastoralism

---

[472] In contrast to an abundance of evidence from South Africa (Mitchell 2003), there are no records of precolonial mining at any of the specular haematite sources in the Namib Desert.

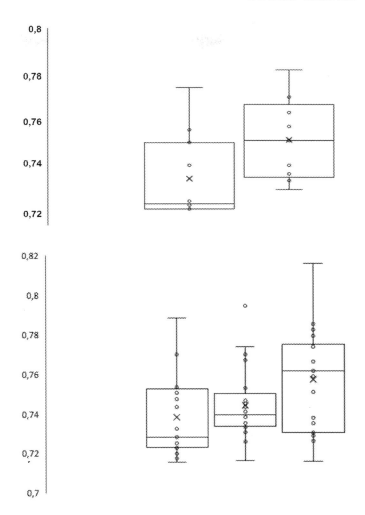

Figure 6.17: Box-and-whisker plots showing distribution of $^{87}Sr/^{86}Sr$ values for first and second millennium pottery from the Namib Desert. The upper diagram compares first millennium Group Aa pottery from Falls Rock Shelter (left) with Group A vessels associated with buried caches of ochre and specular haematite. The lower diagram compares second millennium Group B pottery assemblages (left to right) from the Hungorob Ravine, ǂKhîsa-ǁgubus on the !Khuiseb Delta, and Habis.

in response to improved rainfall and pasture conditions during the Medieval Warm Epoch.[473] Evidence of climatic amelioration during this period was presented in Chapter 5. Furthermore, evidence discussed in the next chapter points to the likelihood of inter-group conflict arising from pastoral expansion as the Namib Desert landscape became more densely populated and its resources subject to increasing competition. The archaeological evidence is that while pottery does occur on many sites with livestock, the bag-shaped, wide-mouthed design of Group B vessels represents a specific adaptation to the systematic exploitation of wild plant foods, a practice that arose with the expansion of pastoralism as part of a diversified subsistence economy. These developments represent a local response to changes in the broader social landscape of the Namib Desert in which Group A vessels associated with the storage of prestige materials such as specular haematite, gave way to the manufacture of wide-mouthed bag-shaped Group B vessels suitable for processing and storage of wild plant foods after the acquisition of potting technology.

Most Group B pottery style attributes are generally distributed throughout the Namib Desert. Pottery design, based on a limited and relatively simple style repertoire may have varied among households or potters rather than between geographically separate communities, but the apparent absence of local style clusters (Fig. 6.13) could also have resulted from the circulation, or local exchange of vessels, among a mobile population. Conceivably, groups of women harvesting grass seed in remote areas could have met and worked together with affines and kin from other parts of the desert, temporarily drawn together while dependent on the same water source. Pots may have been exchanged as gifts or carried to other sites on social visits, and left there, so that eventually all local variation was lost, even if the work of individual potters was known and recognized.

Circulation and exchange of pottery could, however, be reflected in the level of variation in the composition of clays,

---

473 Gil-Romera et al. (2006); Sletten et al. (2013)

thus providing another application of strontium isotope analysis. Sample results from three major concentrations of pottery are shown in Figure 6.17. Pottery from the three sites all belongs to Group B and dates to within the last three hundred and fifty years. The sites lie at an average distance of 160 km apart. The Hungorob pottery is from a dense cluster of pastoral aggregation encampment sites where seed harvesting was carried out on a large scale. The archaeological setting of the sites is described in detail in the next chapter. The pottery from Habis hill is also implicated in seed harvesting, and comprised more than twenty five vessels cached in a series of small caves at the foot of the inland escarpment. The third group of samples is from ǂKhîsa-ǁgubus, an 18th century pastoral encampment which is described in detail in Chapter 8. In this case the pottery would have been primarily used in the processing of !nara melons.

The data presented in Figure 6.17 show that the three Group B pottery assemblages have a comparable range of $^{87}Sr/^{86}Sr$ values, indicating that all include vessels made from clays representing diverse and probably dispersed sources. This would support an argument that pottery assemblages reflect the spatial diversity of social networks in areas such as represented by the three sites. However, in the Hungorob, nearly half of the samples fall within a narrow range around 0.725 $^{87}Sr/^{86}Sr$, implying that pottery in this assemblage might be dominated by clays from one locality. The Habis assemblage is the most diverse, showing little internal clustering, while that of ǂKhîsa-ǁgubus shows a comparable pattern to the Hungorob. More rigorous testing of these inferences would require detailed isoscape data which are not yet available.

Weathered granites with associated clay banks occur along the Ugab River in the vicinity of the Hungorob, while ǂKhîsa-ǁgubus lies within the !Khuiseb Delta which also has clay sources. It is therefore possible that these assemblages have a component of locally produced pottery, represented by clustered $^{87}Sr/^{86}Sr$ values in both groups. Thus, on the one hand, the strontium analyses confirm that pottery assemblages comprise vessels from a number of clay sources, most likely obtained through exchange in the normal course of cooperative gathering and processing of plant foods. On the other, the same assemblages show some internal clustering, suggesting that relatively stable local sources were also important. A combination of localized and dispersed sources for pottery parallels the essential binary components of pastoral settlement in this region: the homestead, a customary focus of settlement, in ecological terms a primary resource site, and the stock-post, one of several alternative temporary encampments usually located on a secondary resource site. These elements of the Namib Desert pastoral settlement and land-use pattern are explored further in the next chapter.

In this chapter, we have seen that changes in social organization and subsistence behaviour during the last two thousand years were more complex than envisioned by conventional accounts of the introduction of domestic livestock and pottery into southern Africa. The adoption of men's and women's initiation accompanied the rise of cooperative hunting and systematic exploitation of wild plant foods. Of these innovations, the processing and storage of wild plant foods would have brought a degree of food security. Although a detailed exploration is beyond the scope of our discussion here, the availability of plant foods such as !nara and wild grass seed, with comparable food value to domestic cereals such as pearl millet, would in all likelihood have helped to ensure stability of family groups and an improved survival of children.

Archaeological investigations usually privilege the evidence of directly visible technological changes over changes in social behaviour that are less easily observed. The adoption of pottery in the Namib Desert is a fundamentally important technological innovation. The evidence presented here shows that pottery with a discrete stylistic identity (Group Aa), but apparently derived from diverse sources on the basis of strontium isotope evidence, spread through the desert in the first millennium AD, more or less coincident with the arrival of domestic sheep. However, Group A pottery was associated with the storage of cosmetic haematite and does not appear to have been integral to herd production and management. Neither was Group B pottery, which was evidently derived from the earlier ware but used instead for plant food processing and storage.

While the pastoral innovation added domestic livestock to the subsistence economy from outside the Namib Desert, pottery was adapted to an enhanced utilization of food sources that are endemic to the Namib Desert. It is likely that this intensified use of plant foods was at least partly a consequence of increased competition for food resources following the widespread adoption of livestock husbandry described in the next chapter. Competition for the control of food resources may have arisen as a consequence of increased food security and with it, an increase in the human population of the Namib Desert. If population increase and resource competition were partly responsible for the intensification of food production and social networking suggested by the evidence presented here, this would indicate that the rise of livestock keeping and food production brought the expansion r phase of the desert economy to the onset of an equilibrium K phase by the middle of the second millennium AD. The introduction and expansion of the livestock economy appears therefore to span a period of approximately one and a half thousand years.

VII

THE FAMILY HERD

The parable observes that the shepherd knows his sheep, that he goes before them and they follow him, for they know his voice.[474] Thus, the essence of pastoralism is in its social relations, not only within and among the households of herd-owners, but between the herdsman and his flock. Genealogy, which determines the pastoralist's place in the social universe of descent and filiation, is mirrored in the blood-lines of the herd, and just as intimately known. Pastoral herds thus exist as a parallel dimension in human society, and are implicated in both its biological reproduction, as a source of food, and in every facet of its social reproduction, from marriage in this world, to that of the afterlife, where cattle are just as much part of pastoral life. So, pastoralism is more than mere food production and its archaeology must therefore address much wider concerns than the bones of domestic stock.

Evidence of pastoralism in the form of livestock bone appears, as we observed in Chapter 4, quite suddenly through much of the arid western parts of southern Africa by the early first millennium AD. The rapid dispersal of livestock and of pottery was at first taken by archaeologists to represent the arrival, as an immigrant

---

474 The Gospel of St. John 10: 3–5, Authorized King James Bible.

Figure 7.1: Painting of Sanga cattle, Spitzkoppe

THE FAMILY HERD 261

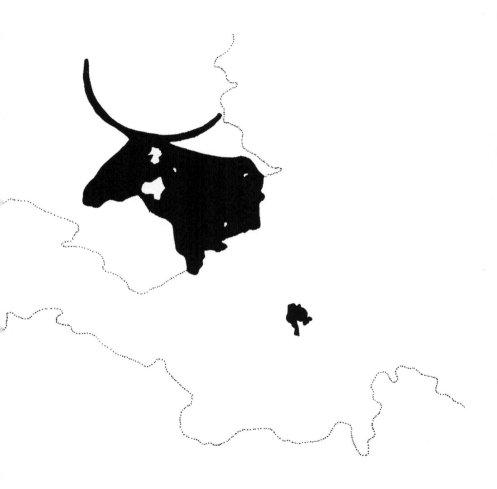

0 ──────────── 25 cm

population, of the Khoe-speaking herders encountered later by the first European visitors to the Cape.[475] Problematically, pastoralists, due to their mobile settlement pattern, appear to be almost invisible archaeologically, and it has therefore proven difficult to identify and trace the movement of pastoralists over the landscape.[476] A view has begun to emerge from re-appraisals of the evidence that pastoral communities in the Cape arose from an extended and more complex social evolutionary process than previously suspected.[477]

Debates surrounding the introduction and spread of pastoralism at first favoured a point of origin in the northern Kalahari, with a number of radiating routes of dispersal.[478] One of these indicated a westward movement following the Orange River where it divided, with one stream entering the western Cape while another turned north into the southern Namib Desert.[479] This model has gained support from studies that attribute one particular rock art genre in this region to the pastoral Khoe,[480] and from archaeological remains of cattle in Namaqualand dating to the first millennium AD.[481] The evidence of early pottery in the Namib Desert discussed in the previous chapter concurs with this, indicating some similarities of pottery style and dating.[482] A northward expansion from south of the Orange River could help to explain several lines of evidence, including pottery, as

---

475 Kinahan (2019)
476 Arthur (2008)
477 Sadr (2008b); for a comprehensive critique of linguistic, genetic and archaeological approaches to the introduction of pastoralism, see Guillemard (2020).
478 Archaeological corroboration is provided by evidence from Toteng (Robbins et al. 2005)
479 Elphick (1985); see also Dewar & Marsh (2018), Orton (2012)
480 Smith & Ouzman (2004)
481 Orton et al. (2013)
482 The spread of pottery into the Namib Desert may have co-incided with a climatic amelioration in the late Holocene, as described by Gil-Romera et al. (2006); Sletten et al. (2013).

well as the early appearance of sheep remains in archaeological context, and the so far undated presence of livestock, including cattle, in the rock art of the Namib Desert (Fig. 7.1).[483]

A northward pulse of pastoral expansion might also explain evidence of encampments in the northern Namib Desert near the mouth of the Uniab River in the first millennium AD.[484] These sites contain circles roughly 4 m in diameter, of anchor stones which could be the remains of mat house encampments. Such dwellings comprised a framework of curved poles which was overlaid by reed mats; the structure could be disassembled and transported on the backs of oxen.[485] However, the evidence discussed in the preceding chapters is of multiple influences on hunter-gatherer society, including innovations from the southward expansion of farming communities, and of autochthonous developments in food production. The acquisition of pottery linked to an expansion of pastoralism from south of the Orange River adds yet another dimension to the emergence of a livestock-keeping economy in the Namib Desert. A comprehensive explanation of these different lines of evidence would require more detailed investigation.

The expansion r phase of complex, intensified hunter-gatherer subsistence and emergent pastoralism in the Namib Desert parallels the regional evidence for the spread of pastoralism through southern Africa in the first millennium AD. The Namib Desert evidence to be presented here is of a rapid expansion of pastoralism, with a systematic pasture management regime based on autonomous households as productive units which moved between annual and perennial grazing areas in a well-established and regulated fashion. This pattern of settlement and land-use which appears to cover the full extent of viable pasture areas in the Namib Desert suggests that swift expansion led rapidly to the establishment of a managed equilibrium K phase. Further evidence in support of this interpretation to be presented in this chapter includes the

---

483 Kinahan (1990)
484 Blümel et al. (2009)
485 See further discussion of this topic in Chapter 9.

conversion of surplus livestock into copper and other redeemable commodities, and that of direct competition between pastoral communities. Such evidence suggests that by at least the middle of the second millennium AD pastoral expansion had approached the limits of sustainable grazing and of stable social organization.

This chapter begins on the margins of the northern Namib Desert, with a general description of modern pastoral Ovahimba social organization and settlement, based on published ethnography and direct observation of some surviving practices that cast valuable light on the broader archaeological record, including land-use strategies used to manage the inherent risks to herd management. Thereafter, we turn to the unique evidence of a late first millennium AD massacre site in the same area, possibly exemplifying the extreme consequences that may have arisen from competition over the resources of a hyper-arid environment. The discussion then addresses the archaeological evidence of semi-nomadic pastoral movement in response to rainfall and the availability of pasture in the central Namib based on evidence from the Hungorob Ravine.

The pastoral Ovahimba

Archaeological investigations of pastoralism and its spread in southern Africa rely to a very large extent on the early colonial ethnography of the Cape, partly because independent pastoral communities no longer exist over most of the region. In Namibia, however, traditional herding does survive, and to gain insight into this practice while it was still possible I worked among the pastoral Ovahimba from the mid-1990s over a period of five years, moving with my family into the homestead of Kapokoro Tjiramba, near Okandombo on the Kunene River. The extended family at Okandombo was in a constant but amiable state of flux, with a few moments of high drama. The centre of life was the cattle enclosure *otjunda*, each evening a milling throng of beasts, impenetrable dust and the noise of people, cattle, goats and dogs, only falling silent in the chill of darkness.

Due to their remote location pastoralists in the north-west of Namibia remained largely unscathed by early colonial conflict.[486] The Ovahimba are semi-nomadic cattle and small stock pastoralists who inhabit the arid fringes of the northern escarpment and desert country to the west. Widely known as one of the last remaining traditional pastoralist societies in Africa, the Ovahimba are cut off from lucrative commercial cattle markets by the imposition of veterinary disease control measures. This has had the effect of sustaining complex traditional social structures,[487] and a rich array of cultural norms and material cultural features such as the visually striking use among women of cosmetic ochre, liberally applied to the body,[488] clothing and domestic utensils. It can be truly said that the touch of Ovahimba women leaves an enduring mark on the pastoral landscape and all who pass through it (Fig. 7.2).

Ovahimba practise an unusual system of dual descent linking each person to two lineages: a patrilineal group *oruzo* and a matrilineal group *eanda*, both having entirely separate functions.[489] Residence patterns, religious observance and secular authority resort under the patrilineage, while the control and inheritance of moveable wealth resort under the matrilineage.[490] One simple and immediate consequence of this system is that while residence is patrilocal, cattle are acquired through the matrilineage, usually the mother's brother.[491] A common Ovahimba cultural practice that is archaeologically attested in this and subsequent chapters is that of *okuhiua*,[492] the mutilation or ablation of the central incisors, sometimes said to be essential for preferred

---

486 Bollig (1997a); Bollig & Gewald (2000)
487 See Van Warmelo (1951) for a basic ethnography of the Ovahimba, Crandall (2000) for a detailed account of social organization, custom and material culture, and Bollig (2020) for an authoritative social history of Kaoko.
488 Rifkin et al. (2015)
489 Gibson (2009)
490 Crandall (1996)
491 Malan (1995)
492 Briedenhann & Van Reenen (1985); Virimuje Kahuure (2020, pers comm.)

Figure 7.2: Ovahimba family, Okandombo, north-western Namibia.

pronunciation in Otjiherero. Among Ovahimba, this operation is performed at puberty using a sharpened sliver of wood. Once extracted, the broken teeth are wrapped in a leaf and given to the child who casts them away, saying as he does so, *Mayo wandje yaruka kotjirongo kumba kwaterwa*.[493]

Because a man does not acquire cattle from his father's line, his status as a herd owner is immediately, if nominally, independent of the patrilocal residence group to which he belongs. The residence group is centred on the homestead *onganda* of the senior male representative of the *oruzo*. The homestead is located in an area of dry season or reserve grazing and immediately after rain has fallen the herds are driven away to temporary stock-posts *ohambo*, of which there may be several under the control of a single residence group. Consumption of timber and heavy browsing of shrubs in the vicinity of the homestead and its associated wells and other water points contributes to a piosphere effect which

---

493 Literally: "My teeth, go back to the place where I have been born", translation Jekura Kavari (6.04.2020, in litt.)

results in long-term changes in vegetation structure. Stock-posts, in comparison, have small brushwood enclosures and huts that quickly vanish from view as the vegetation recovers.

In the north-west of Namibia rainfall is uncertain but generally occurs in the months between January and March. Grass cover which forms the most essential and widespread food source for livestock responds quickly to rainfall, and temporary stock-posts *ohambo* are established where grass is found within grazing distance of water. However, the nutritional value of pasture grasses, particularly annual species, declines rapidly and livestock have to be moved to dry season pastures, often in the near vicinity of the homestead *onganda*. During the dry season livestock may depend almost entirely on non-grass forage such as tree pods. The nutritional comparison of grass and tree pods presented in Figure 7.3 shows that the optimum food value of grass pastures is limited to the months immediately following the peak rains, while that of tree pods is greatest at the onset of the dry season and remains at a high level for the whole year. The comparison shown in Figure 7.3 includes only one species *Faidherbia albida* (Otjiherero *omue*) among thirteen commonly consumed by Ovahimba livestock and all showing broadly similar patterns of nutritional availability.

The *onganda* is generally occupied for the lifetime of the lineage head, in practical terms for a period of at least thirty years extending from his majority to his eventual death. The site is abandoned at this point although the new lineage head may establish himself in the same locality, resulting in a palimpsest of adjacent and overlapping settlements both occupied and abandoned. The dispersal of animals to temporary stock-posts serves to conserve grazing in core areas near to water and under ideal circumstances cattle will remain at successive stock-posts for most of the year, leaving a small number of milk cows and their calves at the homestead. The number of animals kept at an Ovahimba homestead in no way reflects the full pastoral wealth of the herd owner. Wealth and status are a matter of

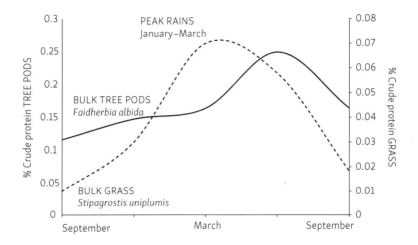

Figure 7.3: Nutritional value of livestock food resources in relation to seasonality of rainfall. Nutritional analyses by the Agricultural Laboratory of the Government of Namibia Ministry of Agriculture, Water and Rural Development on field samples for the period September 2000 to September 2001.

common knowledge and do not need to be manifested at the residence site by the presence of large herds. Although it may remain virtually empty for much of the year, a large timber cattle enclosure *otjunda* is a central feature of the lineage residence. Construction of the enclosure may require the felling of several hundred trees.

Figure 7.4 illustrates the impact of Ovahimba timber consumption based on measurements of spacing and diameter in mopane *Colophospermum mopane* woodland. Three sample plots each 1 ha in extent were assessed in the vicinity of Okandombo, where Ovahimba people have been continuously resident for at least one hundred years. These plots are compared with three sample plots, each 1 ha in extent located in the vicinity of Otjovasandu which lies within the Etosha National Park, from

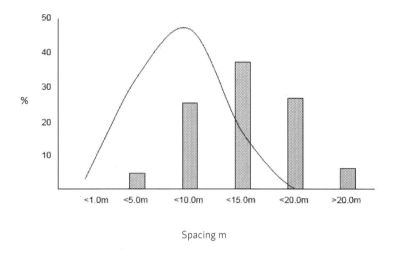

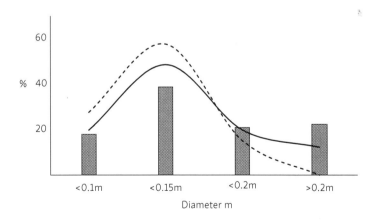

Figure 7.4: The impact of Ovahimba timber consumption on mopane woodland. Tree spacing, above, is more dense in natural woodland (solid black line) than in areas with settlement (vertical bars), but size distribution, below, is similar, and not visibly affected by selection of trees for construction of cattle enclosures (dashed line).

which traditional pastoralists have been excluded for approximately one hundred years. The Okandombo and Otjovasandu sample plots contained an average of 456 and 584 trees per hectare, respectively, indicating a consistently lower density of trees in areas with human settlement. Figure 7.4 shows that trees are more widely spaced in areas of established settlement, although the size distribution of trees in four diameter classes is generally similar. The median diameter class of between 0.1 and 0.15 m is the most heavily used in construction of cattle enclosures. Trees in this size class, however, are usually coppiced about 0.8 m above ground and produce multiple stems from the same stump, thus improving the availability of construction timber.

Ovahimba thus practise a conservative approach to woodland consumption, with relatively little clear-felling. A proportion of coppiced trees fail to recover, thus increasing spacing of trees near settlements, where browsing by small stock also inhibits vegetation recovery and contributes to a piosphere of cleared and heavily browsed vegetation with a diameter of approximately 200 m. While the undisturbed structure of mopane woodland in this environment results mainly from natural self-thinning, timber consumption results in greater spacing of trees while maintaining a similar size distribution. Together with this, settlement piospheres help to create a patchy distribution in the wider woodland environment, characterized by limited survival of seedlings and the presence of widely spaced older trees which are valued for the shade they provide. Large isolated trees are often destroyed by elephants both within areas of settlement and where there is no settlement, thus reducing the number of large specimens in the woodland population.

The layout of the Ovahimba homestead provides a formalized expression of relations between lines of descent and filiation, between the living and the dead, between people and livestock, and between the ordered world of the *onganda* and the disordered world or wilderness *mokuti*, beyond the perimeter *kavepo* of the settlement (see Fig. 7.5). The yard *orupanda* is swept clean and

THE FAMILY HERD 271

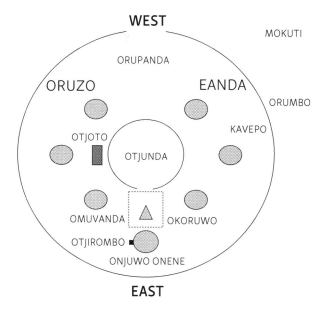

Figure 7.5: Schematic layout of an Ovahimba homestead, *onganda*.

forms the main focus of social life, while the space immediately outside *orumbo* is often dotted with ash middens and household refuse. As a general rule, the *onganda* is oriented to the west,[494] and so placed that it receives the first rays of dawn and the last rays of sundown. It is, in addition, preferentially located on a gentle gradient, cattle being reluctant to walk up steeper slopes in the late dry season when they are often in poor condition.[495]

The dwelling *onjuwo onene* of the lineage head faces the entrance of the cattle enclosure *otjunda* with a small enclosure *otjoto* for calves. A corridor between the entrance of the cattle enclosure and that of the dwelling occupied by the lineage head is a ritual precinct *omuvanda* containing the ancestral fire

---

494 Orientation angle averaged 287° on a sample of 30 *omuvanda* alignments.
495 Slope gradients averaged less than 3° on a sample of 30 *onganda* sites.

okuruwo which is placed in a semi-circle of stones and contains a single permanently smouldering stump of wood that is stirred into flame only when important rituals are performed. A small shelter *otjirombo* is located against the outside of the dwelling and used for special ritual functions. To the left are the houses of the *oruzo* members, including the successor of the lineage head, while to the right are ranked those of the *eanda*. On the ground, these structural principles of Ovahimba society may not be readily apparent to the uninitiated; for example, the *omuvanda* which may not be crossed between the *onjuwo onene* and the entrance of the *otjunda* has no physical demarcation. However, the relationships expressed in this way are played out in every aspect of daily life, including most importantly the management of the herd which is also subject to specific prohibitions governing the ownership of cattle according to combinations of colour and pattern.[496]

The physical dimensions of Ovahimba settlements are fairly consistent. For example, the average diameter of the *orumbo* which is the space enclosed by the *kavepo* perimeter fence is approximately 65 m, while that of the *otjunda*, the cattle enclosure at its centre, is usually about 15 m. The fact that *onganda* homestead sites in areas with suitable dry season browse are on average less than 1 km apart contributes to a patchiness of woodland vegetation cover that is clearly anthropogenic in its structure.

Animal husbandry is at the heart of Ovahimba social life and it is therefore no surprise that at the homestead and the stockpost men will often gather to play *mankala*,[497] known in Otjiherero as *onyune*. This is the game described earlier in Chapter 5 as the rock art metaphor of pastoral values that was adopted by hunter-gatherer groups in the transition to herding and incorporated in men's initiation rites. Among the Ovahimba, livestock are slaughtered for a variety of social

---

496 Hangara et al. (2020)
497 Crandall (2000: 137)

purposes: traditional fines are paid in cattle, as is bride-wealth, and animals are slaughtered on occasions such as to celebrate puberty or to welcome a new bride. A wealthy man will choose to be buried in the hide of his favourite ox which could be one of many slaughtered to provide for his funeral feast.[498]

There is unverified oral testimony regarding the number of cattle slaughtered at a single funeral, with more than ten animals slaughtered at the funeral of very prominent individuals. However, the meat of sacrificial cattle may not be eaten by members of the same patriclan as the deceased, and in general, there are strict provisions for the distribution of meat from different parts of the carcase. For example, the upper hind leg *etumbo nokurama* is reserved for the most senior male *ovya tate*, while the lower leg *epindi* is reserved for the senior wife of the lineage head *omukazendu omuini wonganda*. Nearly every part of the animal carcase is either consumed or used, including hides, horn and hooves.[499]

The most visible concentration of cattle remains is found at the grave site of a lineage head where the skulls of oxen from his ancestral herd are displayed on wooden posts *orumbango* after the funeral feast (Fig. 7.6). Graves are not located within settlements but usually on customary routes between them, often in a secluded place and surrounded by a timber fence *otjimbandwangoma*. The grave site is a sacred place where lineal descendants commune with the deceased and seek their guidance.[500] Ideally, patrilineal relatives live together and will be buried at the same place, so that the cemetery will in time mirror the kinship group that lived on the surrounding landscape.[501]

---

498 Bollig (1997a: 40) relates the story of an elderly Ovahimba man who refused to die until his favourite ox could be brought from Angola to provide his burial shroud. The ox which provides the hide used as a funeral shroud is referred to as *ondara*, a term derived from the verb *rara* to sleep (Hangara et al. 2020: xiv).
499 Hangara et al. (2020)
500 Bollig (1997a)
501 Crandall (1991)

Figure 7.6: Grave of Ovahimba lineage head at Omuramba, with cattle skulls on timber posts (left), and ancestral sacrificial oxen of Ovahimba lineage head at Okandombo (right).

Traditionally, the grave site of a lineage head was furnished with a trumpet *ondjembo yozongombe*, made from oryx horn and fitted with a large bulbous sound cavity modelled from beeswax. The trumpet is blown to accompany chants in praise of ancestral oxen or in recollection of heroic cattle raids.[502] Commemoration rituals involve smearing the grave with butterfat and milk from ancestral cattle and the kindling of the ancestral fire at the grave

---

502 Gibson (1962)

itself, symbolizing the harmonious relationship between the living and the dead.[503]

Livestock bone is rarely seen on Ovahimba settlement sites no matter how wealthy its inhabitants may be. At the homestead, bone as well as discarded hide, horns and hooves, are assiduously collected and disposed of where they cannot be eaten by cattle. This is in response to the fact that Ovahimba pastures, in common with most southern African arid zone grazing areas, are phosphorus deficient. As a consequence, cattle develop a pica syndrome, or osteophagia, and will eat livestock bone or even the carcases of small rodents and other animals to assuage their mineral deficiency.[504] Animal bones host the exotoxin *Clostridium botulinum*, and the generally fatal results of botulism are well known to the Ovahimba as *omutjise wombindu*. Disposal of bone or the grinding of bone to a fine meal which can be used as a mineral supplement for cattle, reduces or even eliminates an important potential source of archaeological evidence.

Dairy products are important to Ovahimba diet and include both goat's and cow's milk, usually fermented as *omaere*.[505] Fermentation employs wooden containers and gourds in which residues of previous fermentation provide back-slopping together with the addition of selected plant roots.[506] Extreme aridity affects both milk yield and livestock fertility, and milch pastoralism is not therefore a constant element of Ovahimba food security. Lactation declines with poor nutritional status and milk offtake contributes to reduced ovulation and fertility.[507] The availability

---

503 The natural world is believed to lie between the spiritual world of Ndjambi, Mukuru and the Ovakuru, where the departed souls of noble human beings reside, and the underworld of evil, disorder and misfortune. It is possible for the dead to return, bringing with them their cattle and other possessions, as well as their earthly nature which combines elements of both worlds (Kavari 2001; J.H.A. Kinahan 2004).
504 Cameron (2009)
505 Van Warmelo (1951)
506 Misihairabgwi & Cheikhyoussef (2017)
507 Berry et al. (2016)

of dairy products among pastoralists such as the Ovahimba or any other arid zone herd-owning peoples in southern Africa is limited to periods of relatively good rainfall and the availability of high value pasture grasses.[508]

The fact that pottery is not used by the Ovahimba relates to the cultural importance of dairy products rather than grain in the diet; conversely, the importance of pottery used in the preparation of plant foods among other groups described in this chapter may indicate that milk production was relatively unimportant among Namib Desert pastoralists.

Another aspect of mineral deficiency in arid zone pastures which has archaeological consequences is the presence of highly persistent phosphorus concentrations within stock enclosures. Over time, the dung of cattle returning to the homestead results in a significant accumulation of phosphorus within the livestock enclosure. This has been observed on the south-eastern margins of the Kalahari Desert where patches of phosphorus tolerant grasses provide clear botanical evidence of ancient settlements.[509] In some situations, phosphorus anomalies are so clearly delineated that they may be used to determine the actual dimensions of livestock enclosures.[510]

In north-western Namibia, background soil phosphorus concentrations are commonly 300 ppm or less. The local woody vegetation, dominated by *Colophospermum mopane* readily germinates in these soils and in the vicinity of homestead sites where phosphorus concentrations reach 1,000 ppm. However, phosphorus concentrations in a livestock enclosure itself may exceed 3,000 ppm and most woody species cannot germinate

---

[508] Bollig (1997a) Although Lombard and Parsons (2015) and Parsons and Lombard (2017) correctly point out that dairy production among southern African pastoralists has been overlooked by archaeologists (see also Russell 2020), they overestimate its importance in relation to environmental limiting factors such as rainfall and pasture quality under arid conditions.
[509] Denbow (1979)
[510] Kinahan (2000c)

on these sites, with the result that the core area occupied by the cattle enclosure will remain bare for an indefinite period.[511] Old livestock enclosures are usually colonized by pioneer species such as the terrestrial creeper *Tribulus campestris*.[512] Another important exception is the perennial grass species *Cenchrus ciliaris* which is tolerant of high soil phosphorus levels and grows abundantly in old cattle enclosures. Cattle are attracted to these patches of highly nutritious grazing.

Ovahimba herding practices show that the uncertainties of arid zone pastoralism require multiple strategies to mitigate against risks of livestock losses. A simplified model of pastoral risk is presented in Table 7.1[513] which opposes the predictability of risk to its spatial scale. Thus, degradation of pasture is a highly predictable risk which is offset by strictly enforced rules of access, as opposed to the less predictable risks of cattle raiding. Both of these risks have spatially limited consequences, in contrast to displacement of communities which, like the effects of drought and famine, can affect large areas and multiple communities. Displacement is a highly predictable result of pasture degradation, unlike drought and consequent famine which pose an ever-present risk to Ovahimba pastoralists.

Table 7.1 Dimensions of risk among Ovahimba pastoralists

Predictability	HIGH	Degradation	Displacement
	LOW	Raids & epidemic	Drought & famine
Spatial scale		LOW	HIGH

One important risk management strategy is the dispersal of livestock through the mechanism of stock loans.[514] The advantages

---

511 Kinahan (2001b)
512 The seeds of *Tribulus camprestris* are introduced to the site most successfully entangled in the fleece of sheep returning from pasture.
513 Based on Bollig (1997b: Table 1)
514 Bollig (1997b)

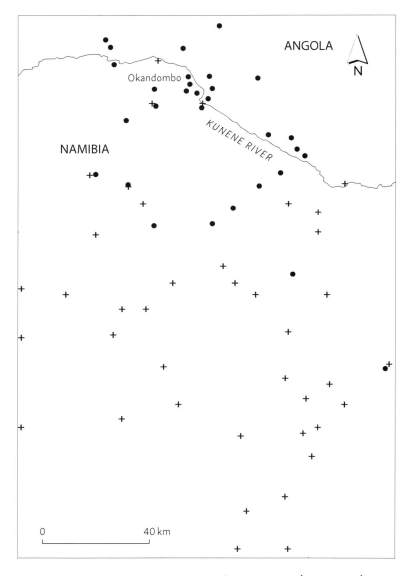

Figure 7.7: The geographical extent of cattle loans (black dots) from one owner at Okandombo on the Kunene River. Note the apparent avoidance of botulism outbreak sites (plus signs) in the same area. Cattle loan data from author field records; botulism outbreak areas from Government of Namibia Ministry of Agriculture, Veterinary Services.

of stock loans as a risk management strategy are twofold: livestock are relocated to areas of higher grazing value, and this serves to maintain alliances between stock owners over a wide kin-based network, sometimes extending over 100 km in any direction. Dispersal of livestock militates against the highly predictable and localized risks of pasture degradation, as well as the less predictable risks of raiding and disease. Figure 7.7 indicates the geographical spread of stock loans from one owner at Okandombo on the Kunene River. Loans may link owners of similar means but can also establish relationships with client herders who benefit from milk and meat offtake. A submerged class of generally impoverished people, the Ovatjimba, often serve as client herders for wealthy pastoralists.

If the labour capacity of a stock owner and his loan partners is exceeded by the size of the herd, Ovahimba convert some livestock into equivalent value commodities. Traditionally, Ovahimba women are adorned with copper and iron jewellery which serves as heirloom wealth that can be redeemed as livestock in the event of need. Human labour is an important requirement in any pastoral economy, not least that of the Ovahimba. Herd management, including such tasks as moving animals to pasture, guarding them against predators, constructing and maintaining enclosures and wells, milking and processing of milk products, are among the myriad labour requirements of the pastoral household. These, however, are generally overlooked in archaeological discussions of pastoralism which emphasize rainfall and the availability of grazing as the major limiting factors in the pastoral economy. Ovahimba herding practices show a fine subsistence balance between the labour needs for herd production and the nutritional needs of the household that must be maintained primarily through the reproduction of the family herd.

Central to Ovahimba risk management is the need to maintain the breeding potential of the herd through judicious slaughter of surplus male stock so that the herd can recover quickly from losses due to drought, disease or, in the past, raiding. An

280 NAMIB

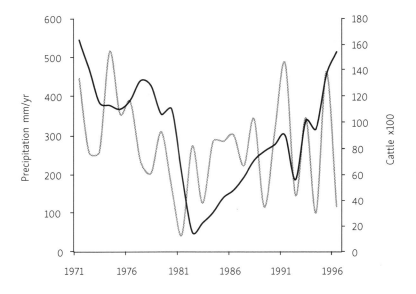

Figure 7.8: The relationship between rainfall (grey) and Ovahimba cattle numbers (black) 1971–1996. Cattle census data from Government of Namibia Ministry of Agriculture, Veterinary Services; rainfall records from Namibia Police, Kamanjab and Meteorological Services, Namibia.

illustrative example of rapid herd growth is the recovery of Ovahimba livestock numbers in north-western Namibia following the extreme drought of the early 1980s which resulted in the mortality of approximately 90% of cattle. Figure 7.8 shows a precipitous drop in cattle numbers caused by successive dry years, followed by a steady recovery with improved rainfall, bringing herds to their former level within little more than ten years. This growth was achieved by maintaining a high ratio of breeding female stock so that the aggregate reproductive potential of the herd was maximized.[515] Wild ungulate populations which also diminish as a result of drought conditions recover far more slowly

---

515 cf. Dahl & Hjort (1976)

due to their lower natural ratio of breeding females to males. The oft-cited reluctance of traditional pastoralists to slaughter their livestock is based on a misunderstanding of the function of slaughter in the maintenance of the growth potential of the herd, most especially in the hyper-arid pasture environment of the Ovahimba.

Ovahimba pastoralists form stable kin-based hierarchies, and household groups average about 8.5 members, with widely varying degrees of wealth in livestock. The ratio of people to livestock ranges from 1:1 to 1:9, with household livestock numbers sometimes exceeding 200 head. Pasture carrying capacity, however, is generally low, and within the area inhabited by the Ovahimba stocking density averages 2.5 cattle/km². Historical census data show wide variation in livestock numbers and it can be assumed that the vagaries of climate have resulted in repeated expansion and contraction of pastoral settlement.[516] While short-term climatic variation might result in small-scale local shifts in grazing patterns, larger scale climatic variation could lead to significant changes in the geographical extent of pastoral settlement. The evidence presented below concerns the massacre of at least sixteen adults, probably an entire homestead. This event, dated to the 10th century AD, coincides with the Medieval Warm Epoch described in Chapter 5 as a period of higher than normal rainfall in the Namib Desert. These conditions can enable pastoral communities to expand rapidly, encroaching on the pastures of adjacent groups in otherwise less optimal areas.

The arid southern margin of the highland and escarpment area most favoured by Ovahimba pastoralists is a marginal zone dominated by sparse scrub vegetation with few permanent water sources. The site of Khorixa-ams, located in this marginal zone, is a large cave formed by a solution cavity in a low-lying dolomitic limestone anticline; the cave is more than 200 m in length and has only one opening, a vertical fissure issuing

---

516 Bollig & Lang (1999)

282 NAMIB

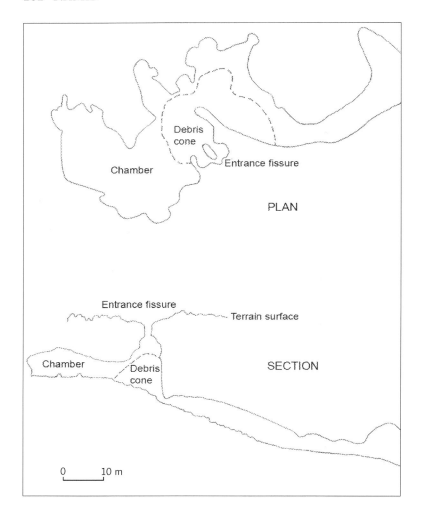

Figure 7.9: Plan and section of Khorixa-ams cave site showing the position and extent of the debris cone associated with the bone accumulation. The underground cavity extends for approximately 190 m beyond the righthand margin of the diagram.

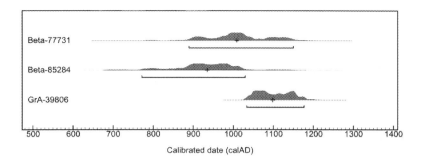

Figure 7.10: Calibrated radiocarbon dates for human skeletal and associated material from Khorixa-ams (see explanation in Notes to the Reader: Archaeological age determination, p. xvii).

into a bell chamber approximately 25 m deep and forming a natural pitfall (Fig. 7.9). A cone of debris from the collapse of the ceiling has filled the space to within 10 m of the surface. Quantities of disarticulated human and animal skeletal remains had accumulated at the foot of the debris cone.[517] Cultural material associated with the human remains included a number of fragmentary elephant ivory bangles, some with paired copper tacks, and a large wooden bowl decorated below the rim with a row of copper strips arranged in a herringbone pattern. Radiocarbon dates indicate that the skeletal and associated material accumulated between 930 and 1100 cal. AD (Fig. 7.10).[518]

A total of 254 human skeletal elements were recovered from the Khorixa-ams site, representing sixteen individuals of which

---

517 Prior to its dating, the unusual nature of the Khorixa-ams site and its human remains initially suggested that it might be of colonial age and it was therefore subject to a detailed forensic analysis (Rossouw 2010). The site plan and general description presented here is based on information provided by J. Irish and E. Marais (SWAKNO 16–17.8.94).
518 Uncalibrated radiocarbon dates in years BP: 1,080±60 (Beta-77731); 1,150±60 (Beta-85284); 970±25 (GrA 39806).

eight were adult, four sub-adult and two of indeterminate age.[519] The skeletons were relatively incomplete due to their dispersal and partial burial or destruction beneath the accumulation of rock debris. Thus, the minimum number of individuals based on post-cranial elements such as femora and humeri did not exceed five individuals in total. Based on cranial features alone, seven individuals were male and five female, the remainder being indeterminate. Cranial features showed that six individuals were over forty years of age at death, while five were under forty years at death. A combination of cranial and post-cranial elements showed that the sample contained six older adult males, two older adult females, one young adult male and two young adult females. Fusion of cranial sutures and epiphyseal elements showed that the sample contained no juvenile individuals.

Apart from some evidence of osteoarthritis and other minor skeletal pathologies, the individuals in the sample appeared to be in good health at the time of death. Stable isotope analyses suggested that these were not agriculturalists but depended on a pastoral diet of meat and milk augmented by gathered plant foods.[520] Comparison of the crania, based on Principal Components Analysis (PCA) with cranial vault reference measurements, showed overwhelmingly Negroid rather than Khoekhoe affinity, particularly in the males. This general affinity is also confirmed by measurements of the facial bones of the crania.[521] Notably, three mandibles from the assemblage showed evidence of dental modification involving deliberate removal or ablation of the central incisors (Fig. 7.11),[522] as described above in the general overview of Ovahimba cultural practices. The likely Ovahimba or Ovaherero affinity of the Khorixa-ams human remains is reinforced by the fact that dental mutilation is not practised by

---

519 See Rossouw (2010)
520 cf. DeNiro (1985)
521 Rossouw (2010: 162–9)
522 cf. Briedenhann & Van Reenen (1985); Buikstra & Uberlaker (1994)

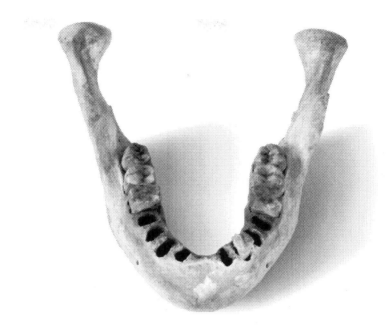

Figure 7.11: Mandible of young adult female from Khorixa-ams showing ablation of anterior incisors and pre-mortem alveolar resorption.

other neighbouring groups such as the Aawambo and ǂNūkhoen.[523]

There is a marked difference between the average estimated living stature of the Khorixa-ams individuals and that derived from human skeletons recovered from burial sites in the central and southern Namib. Table 7.2 summarizes data for eleven individuals at Khorixa-ams and twenty individuals from other Namib Desert burials,[524] which though not directly dated are associated with pastoral site distributions from the last one thousand years, and thus considered to be approximately coeval with Khorixa-ams. There is marked sexual dimorphism in both

---

523 Van Reenen (1986)
524 Kinahan (2013a)

Table 7.2: Comparison of estimated living stature for individuals from Khorixa-ams and other burial sites in the central and southern Namib Desert.

Sample groups	Stature m	
	Khorixa-ams mass grave (n)	Namib Desert burial sites (n)
Adult male stature	1.681 (7)	1.598 (13)
Adult female stature	1.565 (4)	1.506 (7)
Average stature	1.623 (11)	1.552 (20)

samples with adult males from the Khorixa-ams on average 8 cm taller than those from the other Namib sites. Adult females are similarly taller by an average of 6 cm. The absence of dental modification involving removal or ablation of the central incisors among the Namib Desert skeletons further supports a physical and cultural distinction between the Khorixa-ams group and other Namib Desert populations.

The relatively uniform preservation state of the human remains from Khorixa-ams suggests that the site represents a single event rather than deposition over a longer period. This is supported by evidence of injuries visible as peri-mortem blunt force trauma on a number of the crania. Examples of these injuries which in most cases seem to have resulted from single blows to the head and face are illustrated in Figure 7.12. It is noteworthy that none of the skeletons displayed evidence of defence wounds which would normally be found on the forearms,[525] suggesting that the individuals were probably bound or restrained, dispatched with one or more fatal blows from a heavy club and then cast into the pit. Post-cranial fractures found on the lower limbs of several skeletons are consistent with a fall from this height. Taken as a whole, the evidence from the site points to the massacre of a small homestead community such as is typical of modern and historical

---

525 Rossouw (2010: 173)

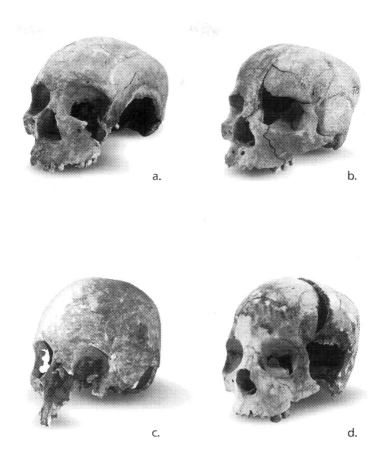

Figure 7.12: Peri-mortem trauma to crania from Khorixa-ams: a. older male with fracture at left temporal and zygomatic arch intersecting left mastoid; b. older female with impact above left orbit, radial fractures through nasal bone and left zygoma; c. older male with fracture through left mastoid, along squamous suture and terminating at mid-point of left zygomatic arch; d. young adult female with parietal bone fractured at base of coronal suture causing separation of the frontal bone, and fracture transecting left mastoid, terminating at left temporal squamous suture.

Ovahimba.[526] The absence of juvenile individuals could indicate that younger members of the household were taken into captivity.

Namib Desert pastoralism

Evidently, pastoralists showing some similarities to the Ovahimba have inhabited the northern fringes of the Namib Desert for at least 1,000 years. South of Khorixa-ams, pasture conditions are relatively marginal, yet the lower reaches of the Huab and Ugab Rivers and the area in between, have high local densities of pastoral settlement remains dating to within the same period.[527] These sites, discussed in detail below, have distinctive archaeological features comprising stone hut circles with associated livestock enclosures, as well as pottery and stone artefact assemblages. They represent a cultural tradition different from that of cattle pastoralist communities further north but share with them some basic features of pastoral social organization which can be discerned from the layout of the sites. This is the archaeological signature of the ǂNūkhoen, ancestors of the modern Damara people who occupied a vast area stretching from the central ǀKhomas highlands to the desert margins and the Hungorob Ravine in the Dâures massif where we find abundant evidence of pastoral settlement.

These sites are significantly concentrated between the 150 mm and 50 mm rainfall isohyets, reflecting opportunistic, short-term use of ephemeral pastures in a land-use pattern based on quasi-seasonal aggregation and dispersal. Large aggregation encampments on desert pastures were evidently tethered to widely spaced water sources including rainfall catchments, occasional springs and subsurface water reached via shallow wells. In contrast, dispersal sites are the remains of isolated and relatively permanent homesteads located along dry river courses

---

526 Bollig & Lang (1999)
527 Kinahan (2001a); see also Speich (2010) and Breunig et al. (2019) for further regional survey data.

THE FAMILY HERD 289

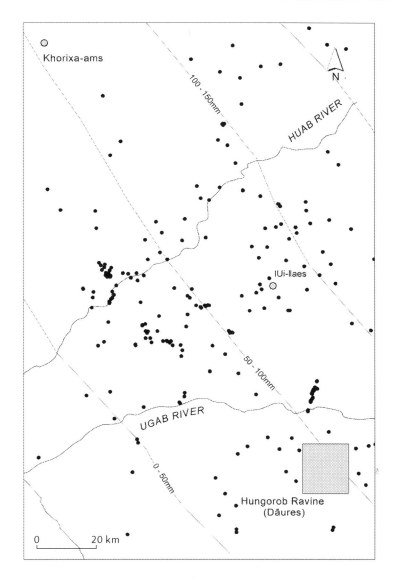

Figure 7.13: The distribution of pastoral settlement sites between the Huab and Ugab Rivers, shown in relation to Khorixa-ams (top left) and !Ui-!laes (centre right) with the position of the Hungorob Ravine survey area also indicated. Isohyets show west-east rainfall gradient (0 to 150 mm/annum).

where livestock could browse perennial tree and shrub vegetation, and high mountain sites with abundant perennial grass.[528] The pattern of settlement and land-use adopted by pastoralists in this hyper-arid zone is exemplified by the unusual concentration of sites in the Hungorob Ravine (Fig. 7.13).

Evidence of wild grass seed exploitation, as described in Chapter 6, is an important component of the pastoral settlement pattern in the area between the Huab and Ugab Rivers. This evidence includes traces of intensive digging in areas of concentrated harvester ant nests, stone storage cells both in isolated locations and within the encampments themselves, as well as associated pottery and stone seed-grinding pestles. Rock art, predominantly engraved, is abundant in the area and the largest concentration of pastoral sites is in close proximity to |Ui-||aes, described in Chapter 5 as a centre for the performance of ritual initiation. The pastoral sites appear to be closely integrated with the changes which involved the transformation of hunter-gatherer society based on existing ritual practices and the adoption of innovations emanating from the spread of food production in the Namib Desert.

Pastoral settlement in the area between the Huab and Ugab Rivers was not confined to the narrow longitudinal strip of marginal rainfall and pasture shown in Figure 7.13. The ephemeral westward-flowing rivers of the Namib served as linear oases allowing access to the Atlantic coast. Large pastoral aggregation sites were established close to the coast in locations such as the Uniab, Huab and Koichab Rivers.

The extent of pastoral movement further to the east is not clear, although evidence of rain-making at Otjohorongo presented in Chapter 5 showed that the wider context of shamanic activity associated with this complex combination of pastoral and hunter-gatherer settlement would have reached at least the western margins of the area occupied by pastoral Ovaherero during the late pre-colonial period.[529] In comparison, rock art is scarce north

---

528 Kinahan (1984b)
529 Werner (1980)

of Khorixa-ams,[530] further suggesting that the area between the Huab and Ugab Rivers represents a particular combination of shamanic rock art and recent pastoralism.

Herding in the Hungorob

To exploit grazing near the western limit of the Namib Desert rainfall gradient shown in Figure 7.13, pastoralists needed to cover considerable distances from primary resource sites, moving to ephemeral secondary resource pastures within reach of water. Because the availability of water would have placed limits on the area of desert pasture that could be used, this grazing strategy was in ecological terms density independent. Much of the grass cover in the desert would lie beyond reach for livestock needing to be watered each day from sparsely distributed springs and wells. The use of perennial pastures was, in contrast, density dependent and required that grazing resources in relatively small areas were carefully conserved until it was possible to move once more out into the desert. Moving to secondary pastures for a short period after rain allowed primary pastures to rest and, depending on the unpredictable distribution of desert rainfall, such movements could have covered distances of up to 100 km or more. This dispersed pattern of land-use is inferred from environmental conditions and is difficult to verify archaeologically. However, an informative exception is found at the Hungorob Ravine, where the range of pastoral transhumance is fortuitously compressed by unusual environmental circumstances.

As described in Chapter 4, the Dâures massif rises almost 2,000 m above the surrounding desert plains, and by virtue of its size and elevation receives localized orographic precipitation which supports a high diversity of plant and animal life. Rainwater runoff collects in rock hollows and feeds numerous semi-permanent springs and seepages. These conditions which provided a unique desert refugium for mid-Holocene hunter-gatherers, attained particular importance for pastoral settlement during the last one thousand

---

530 Lenssen-Erz & Vogelsang (2005); Vogelsang & Eichhorn (2011)

years. Detailed analysis of vegetation structure and density along a transect from the Namib coast to the interior in the vicinity of Omaruru showed that the vegetation characteristics of the upper Hungorob Ravine approximated those of the highland savanna 125 km to the east. By exploiting the altitudinal difference between the desert plains and the high pastures of the massif, pastoralists could move easily and rapidly between pasture environments normally separated by long distances requiring extended and potentially risky movement of herds. The considerable difference in livestock carrying capacity[531] between the desert plains and mountain pastures is shown in Table 7.3.

Table 7.3: Comparison of primary and secondary resource pasture composition and livestock carrying capacity in the Hungorob Ravine

Pasture zone	Elevation masl	Grass biomass kg/ha^{-1}	Grass species spp/ha^{-1}	Carrying capacity ssu/ha^{-1}/ 6 months	Carrying capacity ha^{-1}/ssu/ 6 months
Primary	2,000	7,900	11	12.0	0.08
Secondary	670	130	1	0.2	5.00

The pastures of the gravel plains at the foot of the Dâures massif are dominated by single species stands of Bushman grass *Stipagrostis ciliata,* a palatable and nutritious perennial.[532] Due to low rainfall conditions in the desert, however, these pastures are relatively sparse and do not last; the grass stalks are soon broken and scattered by the dry season winds which leave the gravel plains bare by late summer. In contrast, pastures in the higher parts of the mountain are notably diverse and abundant, dominated by species such as Wool grass *Anthephora pubescens,*

---

531 Calculated on the estimation that 1 small stock unit (ssu) consumes 2.5 kg pasture per day: therefore, available pasture (kg) less 30% (loss by trampling)/ n kg/ pasture days = carrying capacity
532 Van Oudtshoorn (1999: 117)

a high value climax perennial.[533] This species, together with Thimble grass *Fingerhuthia africana*, the Small Panicum *Panicum coloratum* and Red-top grass *Rhynchelytrum villosum*, constitute more than 80% of grass cover in the upper Hungorob Ravine and, together with similarly high value browse shrubs such as *Rhigozum brevispinosum* and *Eriocephalus* spp,[534] provide excellent perennial forage a mere 10 km from the foot of the mountain. Similar grazing conditions are normally found more than 100 km to the east, beyond the 250 mm rainfall isohyet.

Archaeological evidence of a settlement and land-use pattern adapted to these circumstances during the last one thousand years includes dense localized aggregation encampments at the foot of the Hungorob Ravine, and dispersed homestead sites above 2,000 masl in the upper parts of the ravine. The aggregation encampments, which consist of more than four hundred hut circles and related features are concentrated within an area of approximately 50 ha flanking the ravine entrance, in a locality known as !Nau-aib.[535] The site as a whole comprises no less than fifteen relatively discrete clusters. One of these, shown in Figure 7.14, illustrates the distinctive features of pastoral aggregation encampment layout in the Namib Desert. The encampments vary in the number and positioning of features, and in comparison to the circular plan of Ovahimba homesteads described earlier, appear at first disordered in their arrangement. It is unlikely that these sites were occupied at the same time and evidence presented below suggests that they represent successive short-term aggregation encampments.

The encampment in Figure 7.14 consists of about fifty stone hut features in various configurations, circular, arcuate and multi-lobed, as well as a number of storage cairns. The latter are sometimes free-standing, but several are attached to the

---

533 Müller (1984: 54)
534 Curtis & Mannheimer (2005)
535 The term refers to the open, exposed location of the site (E. Eiseb, pers. comm.)

four multi-lobed structures indicated as A to D in the site plan. These features all have at least one hearth and are associated with simpler hut or windbreak features forming groups within the general layout of the encampment. The simple features have two further characteristics that are not shared by the complex huts: they have ashy middens adjacent or close to their outer perimeter, and several are associated with stone seed-grinding pestles. The complex huts and their adjacent features represent household clusters within the larger encampment, and are associated with storage facilities. These huts might have accommodated heads of household groups and were evidently cleaned, the refuse being deposited outside or at the simple huts. The association of seed-grinding pestles with the simple huts suggests that these were occupied by women, indicating a gender-based division of space within a patriarchal household.

Beyond these consistently observable characteristics, no two pastoral aggregation sites are alike in the details of their layout. Such variation probably arises from the fact that the aggregation encampments were a temporary and unique configuration of the social relations within the pastoral alliance. Other, or subsequent aggregations at the foot of the Hungorob Ravine and elsewhere, would have expressed by means of the encampment layout the social relations of those particular alliances. The dispersal of the household groups in the dry season would not necessarily be followed by an identical set of relations in subsequent aggregations, and to properly express these relations would require an entirely new layout. This pattern is of an altogether more dynamic and fluid social organization than that of the Ovahimba, although

Figure 7.14: The layout of a pastoral aggregation encampment at the foot of the Hungorob Ravine. The encampment comprises four family units, each focused on a single complex hut (labelled A–D); storage cairns are labelled S; seed grinding pestles are labelled P, while hearths and ash middens are indicated as black circles and asterisks, respectively.

THE FAMILY HERD 295

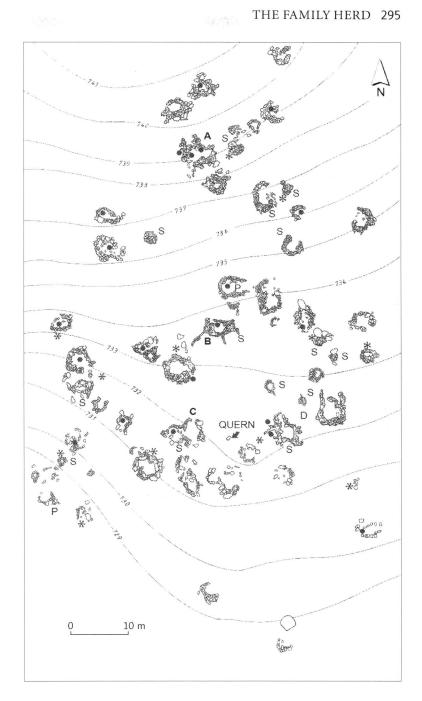

it is based on similar principles of household autonomy and gender differentiation.

Some storage cairns on the Hungorob Ravine aggregation sites had elevated levels of soil phosphorus, indicating that these may have been used to confine lambs or kid goats. The encampments do not have larger livestock enclosures and while it is possible that these were brushwood constructions that have since vanished, there is some evidence of stone enclosures at small waterholes located a few kilometres away. Although waterholes near the foot of the Hungorob Ravine may last into the dry months of the year, grazing range over the desert plains from these sources is limited to less than 10 km. As a result, livestock would have to be moved to dry season pastures in the upper reaches of the ravine or elsewhere. The onset of the dry season would also coincide with optimal exploitation of harvester ant seed caches, providing a source of food that could be carried up the mountain.

The onset of the dry season is also the optimum time for the exploitation of honey from bees' nests in hollow trees and rock crevices around the foot of the ravine. Several bees' nests show clear evidence of this activity, with the remains of climbing scaffolds and peg ladders as well as evidence that the entrances of the nests, enlarged to remove the honeycomb, were repaired by lodging stones in the cavity. Figure 7.15 shows that one section of the ascent to the upper Hungorob required the construction of a rough pathway by removing loose rock and creating short sections of retaining wall. The ravine bed at this point is nearly impassable, its course choked with enormous boulders from the mountainside leaving only a narrow route of access. In some places it would have been necessary to carry or assist livestock

Figure 7.15: Pastoral transhumant pathway (dashed line) located approximately halfway between the upper and lower Hungorob Ravine (streambed arrowed). Sections of retaining wall are indicated as bold lines, waterholes as W, small rock shelters as R, huts as H and livestock enclosures as E. The large stone cairn described in the text is indicated as C.

THE FAMILY HERD 297

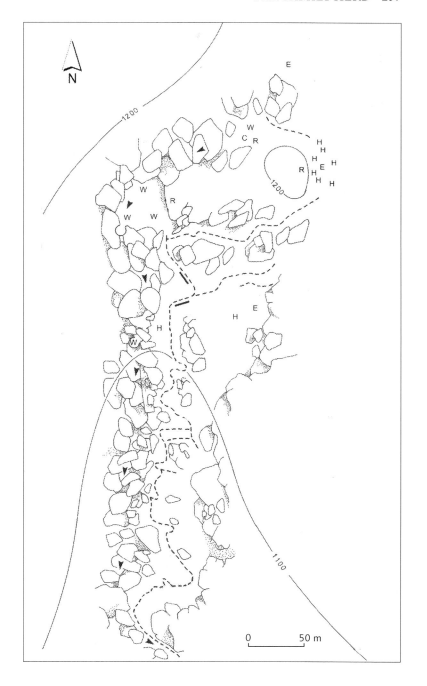

Figure 7.16: View to the south from the upper Hungorob Ravine.

over this section and it is clear that only sheep and goats were taken via this route. Figure 7.16 shows the nature of the terrain. If pastoralists in the Hungorob Ravine had cattle, these were probably taken to dry season pastures elsewhere, such as along the Ugab River immediately to the north of the Dâures massif.

The remains of two small hutted encampments with livestock enclosures shown in Figure 7.15 in all likelihood represent a transhumant waystation. The pathway site has little pasture and is located too far from the lower ravine pastures for daily grazing on the desert plains. A prominent feature of the pathway site is a large stone cairn, one of several located along natural routes following the local drainage. The largest such cairn is at the foot of the Hungorob and measures almost 5 m in diameter. These are also relatively prominent features on possible routes followed by pastoralists in the area between the Huab and Ugab Rivers (Fig. 7.13). While some cairns are probably burials, the largest of these monuments represent metaphorical burial places, *Haitsi‖khōs*, of the mythical trickster deity known in Khoekhoegowab as *Haibeb*. Traditionally, stones were added to the cairn in passing, while shielding the back of the head to prevent the trickster from interfering with the thoughts and intentions of the traveller.

The evidence from the Hungorob Ravine suggests a general model for pastoral settlement and land-use within the wider distribution of archaeological sites presented in Figure 7.13.[536] Figure 7.17 presents a simplified time-geographic[537] model of a pastoral transhumant cycle in the Hungorob Ravine over a hypothetical 18 months. The cycle begins with an aggregation phase in the lower Hungorob lasting approximately three months, the likely duration of palatable and nutritious summer grazing in the lower parts of the ravine. This is followed by a rapid movement to dispersed homestead sites in the upper ravine and a stay of approximately nine months before descending again to the lower ravine. The model accommodates the key features of the archaeological record, such as the formation of new households through marriage and the recruitment of new households by immigration. Converse processes including households leaving the Hungorob for other grazing areas are also accommodated. The model illustrates the short duration of the rains and opposes the dispersed and aggregated patterns of settlement that constitute the quasi-seasonal turning points of the transhumant cycle.

Pastoral settlement in the Namib Desert would have been more complex than this simplified model suggests. For example, if cattle were managed as an auxiliary component depending on other pastures, the dispersal phase of the model would need to reflect movement over a wider area. More importantly, if the transhumant cycle was interrupted by drought, epidemic disease or raiding, the model would need to allow for options to move beyond the Hungorob, with some households remaining in

---

536 Kinahan (1984b)
537 cf. Ellegård & Svedin (2012); Kraak (2003)

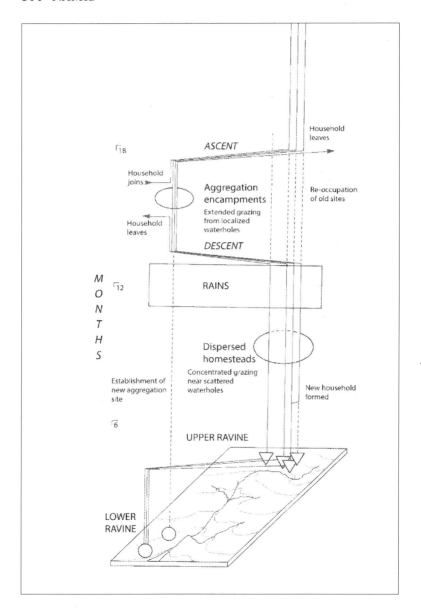

Figure 7.17: Simplified time-geographic model of pastoral transhumance in the Hungorob Ravine.

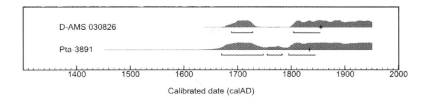

Figure 7.18: Calibrated radiocarbon dates (median dates indicated as +) for the Falls Rock Shelter cache (above) and the pastoral aggregation encampment shown in Figure 7.14 (below).

the ravine and others migrating elsewhere. However, the basic premise of the archaeological interpretation and the transhumant model is that pastoral settlement in the Namib Desert was based on the autonomous stock-owning family unit which entered into opportunistic grazing alliances with related households, operating according to a transhumant cycle between ephemeral desert pastures and perennial dry season pastures.

The buried cache of metal beads and other objects from Falls Rock Shelter mentioned in Chapter 4 is further evidence of interaction through exchange networks extending beyond the Hungorob Ravine and the surrounding desert. The stratigraphic context of the parcel (Fig. 4.3) indicates that it was buried beneath the grass lining of a sleeping hollow and was therefore intended to be stored or concealed. A leather thong fragment from the cache dates to the mid-19th century AD, indicating that it was buried at approximately the same date as the occupation of the pastoral aggregation encampment shown in Figure 7.14. The median values for calibrated radiocarbon dates shown in Figure 7.18[538] corroborate other evidence presented here that the upper and lower ravine areas formed part of a single settlement and land-use system.

The Falls Rock Shelter cache (Fig. 7.19) was wrapped as a parcel in sheets of the papery bark of the *Cyphostemma currorii* tree

---

538 Uncalibrated radiocarbon dates: 143±25 (D-AMS 030826); 150±50 (Pta-3891).

(Khoekhoegowab *kobas*) which is common in the near vicinity of the site. Within the parcel, a bag of finely stitched leather contained a variety of objects including an iron-tipped adze with a bulky resin or mastic socket, as well as a string of iron and copper beads, and twelve cowries *Cypraea annulus*, threaded on a short leather thong. A second, smaller pouch with a drawstring of sinew contained a plum-sized ball of a black tarry substance, which might be arrow poison or mastic, wrapped in a circular patch of leather. The metal beads include 34 large copper beads ranging from 13.5 to 16.3 mm in diameter, one small copper bead 6.2 mm in diameter, 12 large iron beads ranging from 10.4 to 13.8 mm in diameter, and five small iron beads ranging from 4.6 to 6.2 mm in diameter.

Metallographic analyses of the copper beads showed a generally uniform method of fabrication irrespective of size, the metal having been hot-worked into a strip and the ends cut with a chisel, after which the bead itself was formed by bending and annealing, with some evidence of cold hammering. Variations in minor elements such as lead and arsenic suggested that the beads were derived from different sources, and comparison with beads from pastoral encampments in the !Khuiseb Delta and copper-working sites in the |Khomas area in central Namibia[539] showed variation in zinc, silver, lead and arsenic.[540] The evidence thus points to exchange of copper beads from various sources, with a significant cache of beads and other exchange items reaching the Hungorob Ravine, which was evidently an established focus of pastoral settlement.[541]

---

539 Evidence from the !Khuiseb pastoral sites is discussed in Chapter 8 and from the |Khomas copper-working sites in Chapter 9.
540 Miller & Kinahan (1992)
541 Stephens et al. (2020) have shown on the basis of lead isotopes that copper artefacts from early second millennium contexts in north-western Botswana originate from the Copperbelt of Katanga Province in Congo, pointing to the possibility of long distance regional trade in copper artefacts.

THE FAMILY HERD 303

Figure 7.19: Leather bag with cache of copper and iron beads (left), and cowries *Cypraea annulus* (lower right), from Falls Rock Shelter.

While the copper and iron beads, as well as the cowries, presumably reached the Hungorob via exchange networks that existed in the Namib Desert prior to the 19th century, the iron adze blade (Fig. 7.20) may have a different origin. The dimensions of the blade are

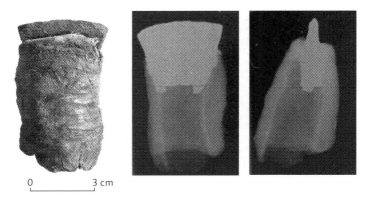

Figure 7.20: Iron-tipped adze (left) with resin or mastic socket from Falls Rock Shelter cache. X-ray images (right) show the shape and mounting position of the blade.

consistent with that of iron hoops used in wooden casks carried on European sailing vessels visiting the Namib coast from at least the 18th century. The width of the blade, at 40 mm, falls within the range for such hoops which varied between 30 mm and 56 mm, depending whether they were placed at the ends or middle of the cask. The thickness of the blade, at 2 mm, is that of a standard cask hoop. An indication of the value attached to even a small fragment of this material is provided by the missionary Archbell who reported in 1824 that "one piece of hoop-iron a foot long can buy a sheep or goat".[542]

The buried cache from Falls Rock Shelter corroborates other evidence from the Hungorob Ravine indicating extensive exchange of commodities in the context of pastoral settlement. Strontium isotope analyses of ostrich eggshell beads from Falls Rock Shelter discussed in Chapter 4 showed that exchange networks linking Namib Desert hunter-gatherer groups continued to exist during

542 Vigne (1991: 34)

the last two thousand years among pastoralist communities. Pastoralism depended on extensive movement of people within an unpredictable environment and employed a range of commodities which served as proxies for livestock within a complex system of animal production and management. In Chapter 6, variations in strontium isotope ratios of pastoral pottery, including one sample group from the Hungorob Ravine, suggested that pottery was exchanged and circulated in the course of harvesting wild grass seed. Earlier evidence indicated the spread of highly decorated and burnished pottery during the first millennium AD, associated with the distribution of haematite as a high value cosmetic substance. Evidence from the pastoral occupation of the Hungorob Ravine adds a further dimension to this development by suggesting that cosmetic haematite was distributed via networks of exchange among recent pastoral communities.

A small rock shelter located in the entrance of the Hungorob Ravine, close to the 19th century pastoral encampment of !Nau-aib described above, has a clearly visible band of red ochre forming a dado about 0.9 m above the floor. The pigment appears on protruding parts of the backwall, on low horizontal shelves which may have been used as seats, and at points where people may have sat with their backs against the wall. Although there are some remnants of figurative paintings at the site it appears that pigment was mainly applied to the rock by contact with human bodies smeared with ochre. Probably coeval with the occupation of !Nau-aib is a granite roof spall (Figure 7.21) from the final occupation of Falls Rock Shelter which was used as a palette to mix an ochre pigment paste, most probably for cosmetic use.[543]

---

[543] Other palettes described from southern African rock art (e.g. Hampson et al. 2002; Yates et al. 1990) might be more correctly described as indistinct or undefined motifs, rather than as surfaces used for the mixing and preparation of pigment.

Figure 7.21: Granite roof spall palette with thickly applied ochre pigment from the final occupation of Falls Rock Shelter

Table 7.4 presents a comparison of the colour[544] and composition of the Hungorob pigments,[545] together with an ethnographic sample of unprocessed Ovahimba cosmetic ochre pigment which had not been adulterated with other minerals, aromatic plant extracts and animal fat in the finished product. The colour of the three pigment samples is similar, although that of the Entrance Shelter dado is weaker, possibly due to its exposure to the elements. It

---

544 Following Munsell (1992)
545 Non-destructive analysis of these and the Ovahimba cosmetic ochre was carried out with a hand-held Niton XL3t XRF analyser, using an Au anode 50kV (200μA) maximum. The values shown in Table 7.4 are averaged.

also has a higher calcium content which might be derived from the calcareous precipitate forming on the walls of the shelter after rain. Lead, zinc and manganese values are similar across the three samples with the exception of the Ovahimba sample where lead concentration was lower than the detection limit of the equipment used. The markedly higher iron concentration in that sample probably reflects the fact that in the final product represented in the other two samples the ochre would be diluted by the addition of other ingredients.[546]

Table 7.4: Colour and composition of cosmetic ochre from Namib Desert pastoral contexts

Sample	Colour	Pb ‰	Zn ‰	Fe ‰	Mn ‰	Ca ‰
Dado: Entrance Shelter	10R 4/4 (weak red)	0.00015	0.00035	2.348	0.0043	15.41
Palette: Falls Rock Shelter	10R 3/6 (dark red)	0.00016	0.00033	2.611	0.0028	1.853
Cosmetic: Okandombo	10R 4/8 (red)	n.d.	0.00102	57.84	0.0053	0.358

Although remote from the increasingly frequent contact on the Namib coast described in the next chapter, two records exist of early European travellers reaching this part of the desert interior. In the 1850s, William Messem made his way inland from Cape Cross, and while there is some doubt that he reached the Hungorob, he reported encountering a sizeable encampment at the foot of a great massif.[547] There is no other mountain comparable in size to the Dâures massif, and the Hungorob has the largest concentration of pastoral settlement in that

---

546 Rifkin (2011); Rifkin et al. (2015)
547 Andersson (1861)

part of the Namib Desert, making it likely that this was the site Messem visited. The people he met apparently had no metal, but a later visit, by Gürich[548] in 1888 observed the manufacture of stone smoking pipes at the Hungorob. Numerous fragments of these pipes which replaced pipes of pottery or made from hollow bones, are found in both the lower and upper reaches of the ravine, and show clear evidence that iron saws, files and drills of European origin were used in their manufacture.[549] On balance, the evidence suggests that both imported and indigenous copper and iron had reached the Hungorob in the 19th and possibly the 18th century.

Sites with evidence of pipe manufacture are closely associated with the occurrence of wild tobacco *Nicotiana africana* plants as described in Chapter 6. The manufacture of stone pipes, like several other activities related to pastoral settlement in the Hungorob Ravine, was carried out at different stages of the transhumant cycle. Wood-shavings from the carving of winnowing trays (Khoekhoegowab *gaub*) used in grass seed processing, occur on the upper ravine or dry season sites. These shavings are mainly from the wood of *Faidherbia albida* which does not grow in the ravine and roughouts for carving these trays were evidently carried up for this purpose. Rough blanks of pipestone are found on sites at the foot of the ravine, as are the sawn-off ends of the blanks. Pipes were evidently taken up the ravine for finishing during the period of relative inactivity during the dry season. Pipes found in the upper ravine are finished articles or fragments of pipes that broke during use or in the final stages of manufacture.

An important point of comparison between the pattern of settlement found in the Hungorob Ravine and among Ovahimba pastoralists is the presence of two essential spatial components represented by the dry season homestead in the upper Hungorob, and the *onganda* or Ovahimba homestead, as opposed to the

---

548 Gürich (1891)
549 Kinahan (2001a: 55)

annual pastures grazing camp at the foot of the Hungorob, and the *ohambo* or temporary grazing camp of the Ovahimba. In both, the homestead is a relatively permanent site which serves in a sense as a family seat, whereas the grazing camp is a more changeable and dynamic component of the settlement system. An important difference is found in the fact that while the Hungorob grazing camp is an aggregation encampment comprising several households, the Ovahimba *ohambo* tends to be spatially dispersed. This is explained by the fact that water sources are fewer and more widely spaced in the Namib itself, such as at the Hungorob, requiring households to share single watering holes, while in the escarpment area favoured by the Ovahimba small springs and seepages are more generally distributed and allow grazing camps to be more widely spread.

In both the Hungorob and Ovahimba situations there is another important settlement and livestock management component: the stock post. At the foot of the Hungorob it appears that livestock were not necessarily kept at the encampment itself, but at stock post sites a short distance away in tributaries of the ravine. This strategy probably served to protect livestock from raiding and from predators, but it also shows that herd owners did not require the presence of their livestock in order that their status would be recognized, for this would have been a matter of common knowledge in the Hungorob as it is among the Ovahimba of today. In the next chapter, we discuss evidence concerning the strategies adopted by pastoralists on the Namib Desert coast in their interactions with European traders, where the stock post was an essential means for the protection of both livestock and women from the depredations of European visitors. Larger pastoral sites on the coast, like those at the foot of the Hungorob, do not have livestock enclosures.[550]

---

[550] Ndobochani (2020) has emphasized the importance of the stock post as a social and economic facet of pastoralism in southern Africa, overlooked in most archaeological discussions.

In this chapter we have reviewed evidence for the establishment of pastoral settlement in the Namib Desert and while showing clear similarities to the archaeology of early pastoralism in the Cape, the evidence here suggests a series of developments at once different from and more complex than the conventional explanation for the spread of pastoralism in southern Africa. Pottery, clearly, was adopted by desert hunter-gatherers and formed an essential part of a specialized plant food exploitation strategy that was the precursor of a fully pastoral economy. Pottery was evidently not employed in food production related to animal husbandry, such as in the processing of milk products, or if it was, dairying was not its principal purpose. However, cattle pastoralism on the northern margins of the Namib Desert did employ a technology of dairy production; this involved the use of wooden milk containers in a material culture repertoire that did not include pottery.

From this evidence it may be inferred that if Namib Desert hunter-gatherer communities did acquire domestic livestock and pottery from the same source, as is suggested by evidence that these were introduced at the same time, they probably formed part of a carnivorous pastoral tradition in which milk consumption played a negligible role due to the low milk yield of animals under conditions of extreme aridity and consequently poor pasture. Evidence of pastoral settlement in the Namib Desert is strongly concentrated in the region between the !Khuiseb and Huab Rivers which Chapter 5 showed to be the core area for the occurrence of Group B pottery associated with wild food plant exploitation. Group A pottery showed a more generalized distribution with apparent links to the south suggesting that pottery, and possibly small stock, were introduced from the south in the early first millennium AD.

Within the core area for the occurrence of Group B pottery associated with pastoral settlement dating to the second millennium AD, however, there is a consistent association with rock art. This association indicates that shamanic interaction between hunter-gatherer and pastoral communities formed the basis for the local emergence of a particular form of pastoralism which retained elements of pre-existing hunter-gatherer social organization and subsistence patterns, while combining these with elements of technology and social organization adopted from other sources. Hunter-gatherers also established intimate links with food producing groups moving into the region from the north. Thus, *mankala* was adopted by Namib Desert hunter-gatherers from pastoral communities such as the Ovahimba, and this in turn, served to establish other links which brought commodities such as copper beads and cowries.

In terms of the adaptive cycle model, these developments illustrate the interaction, or panarchy, of three initially separate but increasingly entangled socio-economic systems, in a process which resulted in the emergence of a Namib Desert pastoral economy combining livestock keeping with a continued reliance on specialized plant food exploitation. The late Holocene hunter-gatherer economy was resilient in the face of environmental uncertainty and showed a high degree of receptiveness to innovation. In adaptive cycle terms it combined the qualities of potential and connectedness which initiated a release Ω phase in the first millennium AD and was followed by a re-orientation α phase which included a transition to livestock keeping and the adoption of pastoral social values and precepts through the medium of initiation. The expansion r phase of pastoralism in the Namib Desert is shown in considerable detail by the evidence presented in this chapter. The central features of pastoralism in the desert approaching an equilibrium K phase include formalized controls over pasture use, regular cycles of herd movement which would ensure rest periods for dry season grazing, and social networks, including both livestock loan and commodity exchange systems. The appearance of precautionary measures such as livestock loans and the use of stock posts suggests that competition over pastures and water sources reached a critical point in the last millennium. Evidence of a massacre at Khorixa-ams indicates that a critical level of competition was reached by the 10th century AD, during the Medieval Warm Epoch.

The next chapter focuses on the interaction between Namib Desert pastoralists and visiting European merchant vessels at Walvis Bay on the !Khuiseb Delta. This evidence shifts discussion from the issues of pastoral social structure and pasture ecology, to that of trade, with the pastoral economy having reached an unstable equilibrium K point that tipped inexorably towards a release Ω phase and the collapse of independent pastoralism on the Namib coast. Two important factors influenced this development: one was the inability of the pastoral economy to maintain control over what were essentially unequal terms of trade; another was the predatory impact of livestock raiding by pastoral groups from the desert interior.

VIII

☙

THE BLACK SWAN

Imagine the surprise and consternation of a Namib Desert pastoralist seeing for the first time a sailing ship at anchor, and the strange figures clambering about in its spider's web of rigging. How might he describe this sight in his village beyond the dunes; what was to be done if these strangers came ashore? Unexpected events are as common today as at any time in the human past, but they simply reflect the limitations of human experience; we are apt to generalize and identify trends, not to rationalize the unexpected. Small deviations from the norm are easily accommodated but something completely outside the bounds of knowledge has a different significance, and may have profound consequences. Such phenomena are met initially with surprise but this is soon overtaken by the human propensity to construe even something entirely new in terms of what we already know, and this is how we make sense of the unexpected. Our hypothetical first arrival of a sailing ship on the desert coast exemplifies what is sometimes known as a Black Swan.[551]

Pastoralists are extremely risk-averse, and we have seen in the last chapter how a complex of measures ranging from settlement

---

551 The term Black Swan was coined by Taleb (2007), in reference to Popper's (1980) principle of falsification.

and marriage patterns, to livestock loans and customary restrictions over access to pastures, all combine to ensure the highest possible degree of stability in an inherently unstable and unpredictable environment. Over time, the lessons of past events are rendered and refined as social customs. But custom is not static, and without constant adjustment it risks redundancy. In previous chapters we saw that ritual, and in the Namib Desert its expression through rock art, played a fundamental role in this mediation between custom, or belief, and contradictory circumstances. In this chapter, we see that pastoral communities on the Namib coast responded to the arrival of European trading vessels by absorbing the visitors into their world, controlling the supply of livestock, limiting access to the interior, and taking the same precautions as they would against a raiding party of their own people.

On the south-western coast of Africa, trading contact between indigenous nomadic pastoralists and European merchant vessels became increasingly common towards the end of the 17th century. Earlier landfalls by 16th century Portuguese navigators do not seem to have involved much contact at all with the local population. Indeed, most maritime traffic between Europe and the Far East passed this coast without pausing to examine it more closely. No trace has been found on coastal or inland indigenous sites of either trade commodities or the large quantities of gold coinage carried by the *Bom Iesus* (litt. Good Jesus), which foundered north of the Orange River ca. 1525 AD.[552] Important though they are in the

---

552 The earliest evidence of contact on the Namib coast is the limestone padrão erected at Angra Pequena (Lüderitz) by Bartolomeu Dias in 1488 (J.H.A. Kinahan 1988b). A skeleton, believed to represent one of the West African women deposited on the Namib coast by Dias (Kinahan, J.H.A. 1988b) to act as emissaries from King João II, has been shown to be a male, probably local and predating the Portuguese voyages by at least two centuries (Wendt 1988). The wreck of the Portuguese trading ship popularly referred to as the *Bom Jesus*, which foundered (post 1525 AD) on the southern Namib coast (Alves 2011; Chirikure et al. 2010; Chirikure & Sinamai 2015) is of the treasure ship genre, unlike that of examples elsewhere in southern Africa (cf. Maggs 1984) where the archaeology of the wreck is closely integrated with that of the coastline and its human history.

field of international maritime history, shipwreck finds apparently cast no light on the recent archaeology of the Namib Desert coast, other than to confirm its relative isolation from merchant trading.

The exchange of cattle for manufactured trade goods, when it began in earnest in the mid-18th century, brought pastoralist communities into a web of intricate relationships that were to their ultimate disadvantage, leading within less than 200 years to colonial rule and the widespread collapse of indigenous society. Almost every place of intensive early contact on the southern African coastline developed from a small trading entrepôt which eventually grew to become a modern port and settlement. In the Cape, urban expansion and large-scale farming transformed the landscape, effectively erasing much of the archaeological record.[553] Only on the Namib Desert coast, and specifically at Walvis Bay (historically !Gomen-ǁgams), does a well preserved archaeological record of this early interaction fortuitously survive.[554] Beside the archaeological record, there are also key eyewitness accounts from which it is possible to identify the specific sites of early contact, such that the history of the ǂAonîn of the !Khuiseb Delta rests on a combination of archaeological and documentary sources that is unique in southern African.[555]

Along the Namib Desert coast, shifting sands driven by a prevailing south-westerly wind regime, alternately cover and expose archaeological sites, mainly surface scatters situated on areas of exposed alluvium lying beneath the dunes. The coastline itself is subject to such dramatic shifts that some recent historical sites have been lost to the sea or engulfed by the advancing dunes,[556] and the attritional force of driven sand is capable of destroying even substantial structures (Figure 8.1). In this chapter the effects of these natural forces, more powerful on the coast than in any

---

553 Elphick (1985); the scale of livestock purchases by early Dutch settlers at the Cape is documented by Ross (2012).
554 See Kinahan, J.H.A. (2000)
555 Kinahan, J.H.A. (2000)
556 Kinahan, J.H.A. (1991)

Figure 8.1: The effect of wind erosion on a brick and mortar structure erected in 1920 at Elizabeth Bay.

other part of the desert, are an important consideration in the interpretation of the archaeological record.

European commercial interests were approaching a peak expansion r phase in the eighteenth century when regular trade was established on the Namib Desert coast with an indigenous pastoral economy that had expanded rapidly over the preceding one thousand years. Contact between the two resulted in a panarchy that is the subject of discussion in this chapter. Events on the Namib coast were to reprise the same process of contact, intensification and subordination that occurred elsewhere in southern Africa[557] and further afield.[558] Trade at the mouth of the !Khuiseb Delta initially favoured the pastoralists, whose strategies maintained an equilibrium K phase in the adaptive cycle. This equilibrial state was based not only on the relationship between pastoral production and the limits of pasture and water, but also on the exchange of surplus livestock for indigenous commodities with an established value within the existing economy. Intensified exchange with visiting European traders soon initiated a collapse or release Ω phase, partly due to the introduction of commodities such as glass trade beads whose production was not coupled to the relationship between livestock and labour in the pastoral economy. Very large quantities of trade goods quickly undermined the livestock equivalence of indigenous commodities, initiating a sharp deflation in the local value of accumulated trade goods. This was but one factor in the rapidly changing circumstances of Namib Desert pastoralists.

There is little detailed evidence of Namib Desert coastal settlement prior to the onset of intensive contact and trade during the last few centuries. The large shell middens at Elizabeth Bay post-dating the mid-Holocene sea level high-stand described in Chapter 3 have apparently no parallel elsewhere on this coastline and most examples of marine food exploitation point to sporadic,

---

557 e.g Meillassoux (1981); Vercruijsse (1984); Wolf (1982)
558 Wolf (1982)

later, events.[559] An unusual example therefore is the remains of an encampment site dating to the early second millennium AD at the mouth of the Ugab River. There is evidence of subsequent occupation of this site in the form of a Spanish 2 *Reales* coin from the Toledo mint of Felipe II (AD 1556–1598).[560] Most prominent at the site were the skeletal remains of 16 Southern Right Whales *Eubalaena australis*, which had evidently beached at the river mouth. The whale bones had been used as the main construction elements for seven substantial dwellings and windbreaks, incorporating 221 ribs, 31 mandibles, and 22 nasal cranial bones. The group of structures also included 22 vertebrae, some evidently positioned as seats. These structures exemplify the whale bone hut settlements described by early European travellers in the southern Namib (Figure 8.2).[561] An 18th century historical map cartouche[562] shows people in one of these settlements near the mouth of the Orange River wearing cloaks of African penguin *Spheniscus demersus* skins, a practice confirmed from evidence of cut-marks on penguin humeri recovered on a southern Namib coastal shell midden.[563] The Ugab Mouth site is the only surviving example of whale bone structures on the southern African coast.

At the Ugab River site, white mussel *Donax serra* was an important subsistence mainstay, and there were more than a dozen middens of discarded shell apparently representing the proceeds of separate gathering trips. The middens each comprised an average of 10,000 mussels and estimates based on comparative material from the same area yielded a mean wet meat mass of 34 kg per midden. This is comparable to the dressed meat yield of a medium sized desert antelope such as the springbuck *Antidorcas*

---

559 Vogelsang & Eichhorn (2011)
560 Kinahan & Kinahan (1984)
561 Kinahan & Kinahan (2016)
562 Gordon (1779)
563 Avery (1985)

Figure 8.2: Remains of an encampment at the mouth of the Ugab River constructed from ribs and mandibles of the Southern Right Whale *Eubalaena australis*.

marsupialis at 28 to 31 kg.[564] In energy content, the average Ugab River midden represents about 80,000 kilojoules, or slightly in excess of 8 kilojoule man-days, sufficient for a group of eight people for one day.[565] The collecting strategy at the Ugab River seemed consistently to favour smaller mussels which formed a relatively minor component of the population from which the comparative sample was derived.[566] Based on the estimated proportional selection of three shellfish size classes (see Figure 8.3), 16 middens at the Ugab River represented a total of over 120,000 shellfish, or about 440 kg wet meat (Table 8.1). The !Khuiseb Delta sites described below occupied a far more diverse

---

564 Kroukamp (2004)
565 Following Meehan (1982)
566 Kinahan & Kinahan (1984)

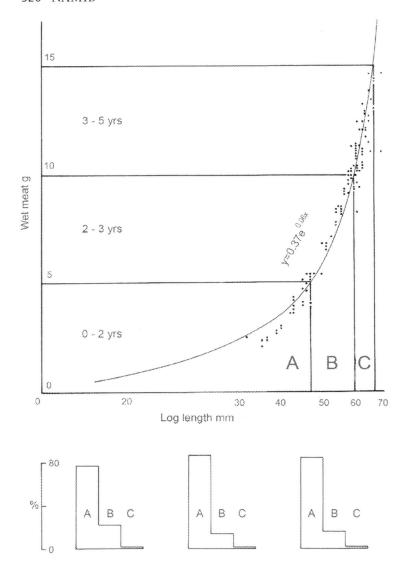

Figure 8.3: The relationship between size and wet meat weight of *Donax serra* from Ugab River shell middens and the distribution of size classes from three sample shell middens. Meat weight: size class relationship based on data from de Villiers (1975).

resource base which provided optimal conditions for sustained occupation following the establishment of regular trade with European merchant vessels.

Table 8.1: Frequency, meat weight and metabolizable energy of shellfish *Donax serra* from Ugab River middens.

Donax serra All middens (n=16)	MNI*	Total meat kg	Total energy kJ
Total	127,859	441.2	1,019,159
Mean	9,835	33.9	78,397
SD	6,295	21.6	49,973
Sample middens (n=3) cf. Figure 8.3			
Size class A	81.6%	5,761	13,311
Size class B	16.3%	3,472	8,021
Size class C	0.6%	220	509

*Minimum Number of Individuals

Pastoralists in the !Khuiseb Delta

The !Khuiseb River delta, like the Hungorob Ravine, presents an anomalous concentration of resources in the Namib Desert. The lower reaches of the !Khuiseb form the northern edge of the Namib sand sea and support a dense corridor of riparian woodland reaching to within less than 20 km of the Atlantic coast. Mobile dunes deflect and impound the episodic flow of the river, maintaining reliable near-surface water sources.[567] Archaeological evidence in the form of scattered shell middens suggests that Holocene occupation of this environment only commenced within the last three thousand years. However, shell middens are subject to intense weathering and aeolian attrition, and evidence of earlier occupation may have been erased by these natural processes.

---

567 Huntley (1985); Stengel (1964)

Attrition of shell midden deposits is illustrated by the example from the !Khuiseb River delta presented in Figure 8.4, where the primary shell accumulations on the site are the same as from the Ugab River sites just described. The shell midden appears as an agglomeration of discrete shell heaps averaging around 0.2 m^3 each, with their margins obscured due to slippage. These accumulations are reduced through gradual removal of shell from the midden by the force of coastal winds reaching a velocity in excess of 36 km/hr.[568] The wind repeatedly lifts and drops midden shell which fragments under attritional impacts until small enough (between 70 and 500 μm) to move by a process of aeolian saltation, leaving the site via a well-defined wind-transport course towards the north. A large proportion of shell midden sites in the !Khuiseb Delta are represented only by an extended narrow streak of such finely comminuted shell on the windward surface of a dune, the primary midden itself having entirely vanished. Shell middens dating to within the last two millennia exhibit strongly developed wind-transport streaks, and this implies that appreciably older middens might no longer exist. Although some older middens may lie beneath the dune cover, the coastal zone in this area is generally very young, much of it having developed in the Late Holocene.[569]

Here we focus primarily on the evidence from a number of sites centring on ǂKhîsa-ǁgubus,[570] an eighteenth century pastoral homestead site that was intimately involved in early contact and trade between traditional ǂAonîn communities and visiting seafarers. The site is located about 4 km inland from the Walvis Bay lagoon, set among high shifting dunes and close to the most westerly freshwater seepages in the !Khuiseb Delta. Within the dunefield there are over one hundred sites considered to be of pre-contact date, and about fifty further sites with evidence of

---

568 Ward & von Brunn (1985)
569 Kinahan & Kinahan (2016); Ward (1987)
570 The site name refers to the fine dust stirred up by cattle on their way to water (E. Eiseb, pers. comm.; Budack 1977).

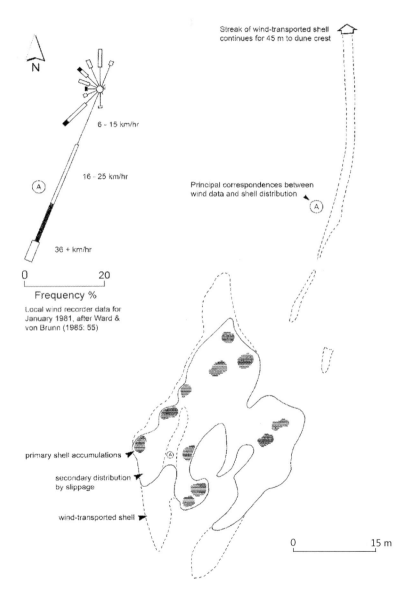

Figure 8.4: The effects of attrition and wind transport leading to the eventual dispersal of a !Khuiseb Delta shell midden.

trade in the form of glass beads, imported ceramics and metal artefacts indicating an increasing intensity of contact with the Western world between the late eighteenth and late nineteenth centuries. Largest by far, ǂKhîsa-ǁgubus covers almost 4,000 m² and has a dense scatter of pottery representing more than seventy vessels of the Group B variety described in Chapter 6. Pottery and other archaeological remains were concentrated around the remains of about seven dwellings. These were identifiable from the stumps of wooden posts forming the perimeter of circular hut structures between two and three metres in diameter. Rootstocks indicated that the structures were built within the shelter of a small grove of tamarisk *Tamarix usneoides* trees.[571] Altogether fourteen human burials were present on the site, most lying partially exposed on the surface due to wind erosion of the silt.

Although it was well known to European seafarers as a safe anchorage since the seventeenth century,[572] there are few detailed accounts of early visits to Walvis Bay. An invaluable record therefore is the narrative of Thomas Bolden Thompson, commander of HMS *Nautilus*, sent to investigate the Namib coast in 1786.[573] In contrast to his experiences further south on the coast, Thompson found the people at Walvis Bay friendly, and accepted an invitation to visit their village. After walking several miles through the dunes, Thompson and his party reached a small encampment set among stunted trees: this was ǂKhîsa-ǁgubus.

Thompson noted the evident importance of the !nara melon in the local diet but saw little trace of livestock other than spoor. He augmented his written account with a series of detailed watercolour sketches and his portrait of a woman at Walvis Bay reproduced in Figure 8.5a is the earliest known image of an indigenous inhabitant of the Namib Desert as seen by a visitor from the outside world. The combination of a contemporary eyewitness account and the well preserved archaeology of ǂKhîsa-ǁgubus

---

571 Kinahan, J.H.A. (2000)
572 Kinahan, J.H.A. (2000); Moritz (1915)
573 Kinahan, J.H.A. (1990)

is one of several such examples which distinguish the evidence from the Namib Desert in the archaeology of early interaction between European explorers and the indigenous peoples of the southern African coastline.

Subsistence and diet

The abundant evidence of human diet at ǂKhîsa-ǁgubus includes large concentrations of marine shell and fish bone, as well as a significant assemblage of domestic animal remains, including cattle and sheep/goat. At least two dogs are represented at the site, one by an almost complete articulated skeleton which suggests that the animal was intentionally buried.[574] The vegetable component of the diet is indirectly represented by the large quantities of pottery, their pattern of distribution on the site and their association with bone knives (Fig. 8.5b) known from historical accounts[575] to have been used in the processing of !nara *Acanthosicyos horridus* melons. The !nara plant, a Namib Desert endemic,[576] grows abundantly in the !Khuiseb Delta (Fig. 8.6).

The !nara bushes are traditionally owned and controlled by ǂAonîn family groups.[577] Ethnographers have observed that rights of access and ownership over the !nara and its fruits are held by women and inherited in the female line,[578] a phenomenon that a more recent study has considered in the wider context of traditional property relations in ǂAonîn society.[579]

---

574 The antiquity of dogs in the Namib Desert is not known but they were probably introduced at the same time as sheep, and widely adopted during the last 2,000 years (see Mitchell 2014).
575 Kinahan, J.H.A. (1990)
576 Curtis & Mannheimer (2005: 626)
577 See Henschel (2004), Van den Eynden et al. (1992); Dentlinger (1977) asserts on the basis of !nara seeds dated at Mirabib Shelter that human use of the plant began at least 8,000 years ago (Sandelowsky 1977). Intensive exploitation of the !nara depends on the use of pottery and therefore could only have arisen within the last 1,000 years (Kinahan 2001a).
578 Budack (1977)
579 Widlok (2001)

Figure 8.5a: Watercolour sketch from the journal of Captain Thomas Bolden Thompson, HMS *Nautilus*, 1786. The woman wears a sealskin cloak, has glass trade beads woven into her hair and an earring made from a Royal Navy tunic button with fouled anchor motif. Suspended from her neck are a bone bodkin and !nara knife (see Fig. 8.5b). Image titled "Woman in Walwich Bay, Caffraria", T.B. Thompson (1786), reproduced courtesy of Quentin Keynes; see Kinahan, J.H.A. (1990: Fig. 7)

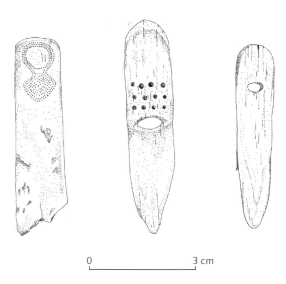

Figure 8.5b: Bone !nara melon knives from ǂKhîsa-ǁgubus including an example with punctate decoration and hole for suspension (see Fig. 8.5a).

Figure 8.6: Ripe !Nara *Acanthosicyos horridus* melon, approximately 1 kg.

The strong female associations of the !nara are expressed in a traditional praise poem still recited by the ǂAonîn.[580]

!Gubu ǂûse	You round food
ǁkhūxaǀkhāse	with many thorns
ǂguisammese	you many-breasted
ǂAonîǀgôan di kaikai-aose	foster-mother of the ǂAonî children
!nūse ta ga hā	even if I am far away
xawe ta nî ǂâi si	I will think of you
Ti ǁnaon ǂûse	you food of my ancestors
ǀuru si ta tide	I will never forget you
Sas khemi ge daisikhoes a ǀkhai	There is no wet nurse like you

Processing of the ripe melons entails removing the rind and rendering the flesh in large pots over a low fire while separating the seeds for drying. The resultant melon extract is cast out on a patch of clean sand as a thin soup and left to dry, after which the seeds and the nutritious preserve can be stored for later consumption. The fact that pottery at ǂKhîsa-ǁgubus is concentrated around hearths adjacent to the huts and also on the margins of encroaching dunes is consistent with this process. Nutritional data presented in Table 6.1 shows that !nara, both as dried flesh and as seeds, is comparable in food value to both wild grass seed extensively used in the Namib Desert at that time, as well as pearl millet, the major cereal crop introduced to northern Namibia by farming communities in the first millennium AD.

Marine food remains from the site include whale, dolphin, fur seal *Arctocephalus pusillus*, a variety of seabirds of which only African penguin *Speniscus demersus* was identifiable with certainty, and white mussel *Donax serra*. The majority of marine

---

580 Budack (1977: 9); Kooitjie, S. (1997) cited by Widlok (2001); orthography corrected by W. Haacke.

food remains were, however, from a limited array of fish species including sea barbel *Galeichthys feliceps*, the salmon-like cob *Argyrosomus hololepidotus*, and hake *Merluccius capensis*. These occurred in the approximate ratio of 150:2:1, with a total estimate of 2,466 sea barbel. Identifications are based on otoliths as are estimates of abundance. Otoliths were found as 23 localized concentrations, each representing an average of 54 fish. Using otoliths as an index of size,[581] sea barbel had a mean mass of 0.6 kg (SD 0.2 kg), while cob had a mean mass of 27.3 kg (SD 5.8 kg). These near-shore and pelagic species were probably obtained not by using fishing lines or nets, but from mass mortality events such as result from periodic eruptions of sulphuretted hydrogen from the floor of the Walvis Bay lagoon.[582] Cartilaginous lagoon species which leave no direct archaeological trace were probably caught with spears (Fig. 8.7), represented on the site by numerous bone points ranging between 60 mm and 150 mm in length, found in the fishbone middens.[583]

The intimate relationship of ǂAonîn and the sea is expressed in a traditional praise poem:[584]

Hurítse, hurítse, kai ǁgamtse	Sea, oh sea, you great water
Sida ǂAonîda ǁgamtse!	Master of our ǂAonî people
Kare re, huriba, ǂAonîlgôado!	Praise the sea, you ǂAonî children
...Dâu re, ǁnuitse!	...Flow, oh fat
Dâu re ǁganxa!nâ ǁgamtse!	Flow, you flesh-rich water!

---

581 cf. Metin & Ilkyaz (2008)
582 Ohde & Mohrholz (2011); Weeks et al. (2004). Historical incidents of sulphur eruption are recorded in the Journal of the Resident Magistrate of Walvis Bay, March 1890.
583 These double-pointed bone artefacts, probably barbs from fishing spears, are considerably larger than the fish gorges found on South African coastal sites where they appear to have been used for line-fishing (Bradfield 2019).
584 Following Budack (1977); orthography corrected by W. Haacke.

Figure 8.7: "Topnaar Hottentots spearing fish", Thomas Baines, November 1864, Walvis Bay. The fish shown are probably sandsharks *Rhinobates blochi*. Painting reproduced courtesy of Museum Africa, Johannesburg (MA 6336).

While !nara melon processing and storage ensured a degree of food security, this resource was clearly augmented by marine foods, most of which represent what were probably unexpected windfalls from mass mortalities. Alongside the evidence for the exploitation of marine resources, a general scatter of cattle and sheep/goat bone lay across most of the site. A large proportion of the livestock bone was found in twelve small, tightly packed heaps. Significantly, these contained only bone and appeared to be the contents of disposal pits in sediments since removed by the action of the wind. As such, these heaps probably represent direct archaeological evidence of measures to prevent livestock from consuming potentially harmful botulin-infected bone, described in the previous chapter as a livestock disease control measure among Ovahimba pastoralists.

Small stock and cattle occurred in the approximate ratio of 6:1, based on minimum number estimates of 28 and five individuals, respectively. Analysis of the sheep/goat remains comprising 761 identifiable bones shows distinct biases in the preservation of particular skeletal elements (Fig. 8.8), with mandibles and pelvic bones relatively well represented in comparison to elements such as proximal humerus, tibia and femur. The distal epiphyses of the humerus and tibia are more commonly represented than proximal ends of the same elements due to differential epiphyseal fusion and the fact that these elements generally consist of less robust bony material. Two other influences on the relative survival of skeletal elements are butchery practices and the age of the slaughtered animal. Butchery practices among traditional ǂAonî communities in the !Khuiseb River result in skeletal assemblages that are largely comparable to those of ǂKhîsa-ǁgubus.[585] For example, ǂAonî butchery commences with the removal of the horns with an axe, and sheep/goat cranial fragments from ǂKhîsa-ǁgubus show clear evidence of this; ǂAonî butchery tends to preserve the scapula and pelvic bones intact, also evident from the ǂKhîsa-ǁgubus assemblage.

The age distribution of sheep/goat from the assemblage (Table 8.2)[586] shows a preference for slaughter in year 2, with a steep decline in the slaughter of older animals. Animals in year 1 could be under-represented due to the relative fragility of these bones, but in this age group several key skeletal elements have similar survival characteristics as in older animals, and the age distribution is therefore assumed to be approximately representative of slaughter patterns.[587] Although the sex of the animals is not determined, this pattern indicates that the pastoralists at ǂKhîsa-ǁgubus used a management strategy that maximized the potential for herd growth by slaughtering excess stock, which were primarily young

---

585 Brain (1967, 1969)
586 Dental age is based on eruption and wear criteria of Silver (1969), Noddle (1974) and Bullock and Rackham (1982). Epiphyseal fusion ages are based on Silver (1969) and Schweitzer (1974).
587 cf. Lambacher et al. (2016).

Table 8.2: Slaughter age distribution of sheep/goat at ╪Khîsa-ǁgubus

Skeletal Element	Year 1 MNI (%)	Year 2 MNI (%)	Year 3 MNI (%)	Year 4/> MNI (%)	MNI
Cranial and dental	2 (9.5)	14 (66.6)	3 (14.2)	2 (9.5)	21
Humerus distal epiphyses	1 (6.6)	11 (73.3)	3 (20.0)	nd	15
Femur distal epiphyses	nd	8 (66.0)	3 (25.0)	1 (8.3)	12
Total individuals per age group (Average %)	3 (8.0)	33 (68.0)	9 (19.7)	3 (5.9)	
Ratio of age groups	1	11	3	1	

males. This, together with the evidence for disposal of waste bone on the site shows that two key elements of herd management practised by Ovahimba pastoralists as described in Chapter 7, were fundamental to Namib Desert pastoralism in the past.

A further intriguing similarity is provided by a pendant of a single sheep/goat 2nd phalange associated with an eighteenth century female burial in a dune valley adjacent to ╪Khîsa-ǁgubus (Fig. 8.9). Pendants such as these are given to newly married Ovaherero women and known as *omaṭupa wonjova*, the four 2nd phalanges of the animal each representing a future child.[588] While it appears therefore that this practice was also known to the !Khuiseb pastoralists, historical records mention the presence of other groups, including pastoral Ovaherero, living in the !Khuiseb River,[589] although they were sometimes in conflict with the ╪Aonîn, who were historically the dominant group[590] and the most likely inhabitants of ╪Khîsa-ǁgubus.

A third component of herd management earlier noted in the evidence from the Hungorob Ravine is the use of stock-posts

---

588 Jekura Kavari (pers. comm.); Crandall (2000: 121) uses the term *okanatje* for the bridal necklace made from these bones.
589 Vigne (1991: 32) citing the unpublished 1823 account of James Archbell.
590 Alexander (1967)

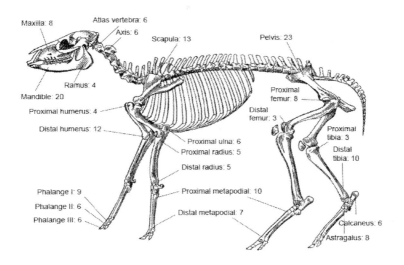

Figure 8.8: Minimum number of individuals (MNI) for sheep/goat at ǂKhîsa-ǁgubus calculated using different skeletal elements shows a bias in preservation due to butchery practices and slaughter age of livestock.

with adequate water and pasture located at sites away from the homestead. The relatively small number of animals represented in the ǂKhîsa-ǁgubus assemblage is unsurprising given the paucity of grazing in the near-coastal dune fields, and there is evidence to be discussed below that livestock were kept further up the !Khuiseb River, for purposes of grazing and for security as the pastoralists were drawn into trading relations with ships calling at Walvis Bay.

An indication of the relative importance of food sources consumed by !Khuiseb pastoralists is provided by stable isotope analysis of bone from six of the burials at ǂKhîsa-ǁgubus. Table

8.3[591] presents data from carbon and nitrogen isotope analyses of bone collagen and carbon isotope analyses of bone apatite. The collagen values refer to the photosynthetic basis of the diet which in these samples indicates an emphasis on animals that feed by browsing, although grazing was evidently also important. On this basis the skeletons fall within the range attributed to mixed cattle and sheep pastoralism with some consumption of food crops,[592] in this case represented by the !nara. The apatite-collagen ratio indicates the trophic level of the diet, in this case consumed as meat rather than milk. While the marine component appears less significant than the archaeological evidence would suggest, in arid environments nitrogen isotopes do not provide a precise separation of marine and terrestrial components of the diet.[593]

Table 8.3: Stable isotope data for human remains from ǂKhîsa-ǁgubus

Sex	n.d.	M	F	F	F	F
Age	infant	36	50	45	40	48
Δ13C ap	-8.7	-8,2	-11.3	-6.8	-4.4	-9.1
Δ13C coll	-12.0	-14.9	-14.0	-11.3	-7.4	-13.8
Δap-coll	3.3	6.7	2.7	4.6	3.0	4.6
Δ15N	15.3	15.9	16.8	15.5	13.6	16.2

Contact and trade

Remarking on the people he met at ǂKhîsa-ǁgubus at the time of his visit in 1786, Thompson noted that men predominated,

---

591 Isotope ratios are expressed as Δ values, where Δ*X = [[(*X/X) sample/ (*X/X) standard]-1] x 1000%. For carbon *X/X is 13C/12C and the standard is P.D.B. carbonate; for nitrogen *X/X is 15N/14N and the standard is atmospheric A.I.R. nitrogen. Analyses by J. Lee-Thorp, Archaeometry Laboratory, University of Cape Town.
592 Ambrose & DeNiro (1986: 322)
593 J. Sealy (pers. comm.)

Figure 8.9: Pendant from sheep/goat 2nd phalange associated with eighteenth century female burial in the !Khuiseb Delta.

most being armed with bows and poisoned arrows, as well as wooden clubs and spears tipped with either antelope horn or iron. Men as well as the two women present wore aprons and sandals, and some of the men affected caps with small antelope horns attached. In their hair the people wore glass beads and shells, with thickly applied grease and a powdering of haematite which Thompson likened to brick dust.[594] Thompson was unable to see for himself the waterholes in the dunes which, on the day before leaving, he 'penetrated…tho' not without much murmuring among the Natives'.[595]

The general description provided by Thompson as to the setting and appearance of the encampment closely matches that of ǂKhîsa-ǁgubus which was the main pastoral encampment at

---

594 Thompson's observations corroborate the evidence presented in Chapter 7 for the use of ochre as a cosmetic in the Hungorob Ravine and among the Ovahimba.
595 Kinahan, J.H.A. (1990: 44)

Walvis Bay in the late eighteenth century. A low denomination Dutch coin, or *duit*, from the site confirms its occupation after the middle of the eighteenth century[596] or at the time of Thompson's visit in 1786, as does an assemblage of 1,399 glass trade beads which points to a calendar age range of 1702–1780 AD[597] (Fig. 8.10). Other trade items included fragments of a European bisque tobacco pipe, buttons and small quantities of imported ceramics and fragments of Dutch "case" gin bottle glass. Larger and more diverse assemblages of European objects occur on nineteenth century sites within the dunefield, indicating a subsequent intensification of exchange. European ceramics acquired through trading contact during the nineteenth century typically included Scottish sponge-printed bowls (Fig. 8.11) that seem to have been particularly favoured over other ceramics such as plates and cups. The absence from ǂKhîsa-ǁgubus of more recent glass trade beads and other exotic imports confirms that the site represents a single sustained occupation during the early phase of trading contact. In addition to the imported items from the site, an array of iron and copper beads, as well as cowrie *Cypraea annulus* shells confirms that ǂKhîsa-ǁgubus formed part of an extensive regional exchange network.

Thompson noted that the people wore bone knives suspended from the neck and waist, similar to the !nara knives shown in Figure 8.5b. He also inferred that they must have met Europeans before, and wondered if their beads had been acquired more indirectly, perhaps through inland peoples in contact with Portuguese settlements to the north of the Kunene River.[598] This would include groups such as the Ovahimba and others on the

---

596 L. Meltzer, South African Cultural History Museum, Cape Town, (in litt.); Kinahan, J.H.A. (1988b: Figs 3 & 4).
597 Kinahan (2001a: 120)
598 Kose (2009) discusses evidence for the widespread distribution of ceramics from farming communities in northern Namibia, with some items reaching the !Khuiseb Delta during the late pre-colonial period, as described by Kinahan, J.H.A. (2000).

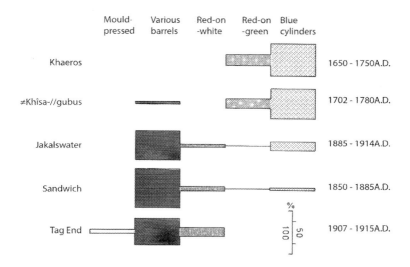

Figure 8.10: Seriation sequence for glass trade beads from the !Khuiseb Delta, showing eighteenth century imports dominated by red-on-green and blue cylinder beads and the augmentation of assemblages by more recent innovations, including mould-pressed beads which were first introduced at the end of the nineteenth century.

borderlands of what is now Angola. Along with the general absence of women, Thompson was puzzled to find so little evidence of livestock, an observation that was corroborated by a subsequent event in 1796 when the crew of a visiting ship were made to wait several days for cattle to be brought for trade.[599] Further evidence from ǂKhîsa-ǁgubus and other sites in the !Khuiseb Delta offers an explanation for this delay as well as for the absence of women, and casts important new light on the developing relationship between pastoral communities and visiting Europeans in the eighteenth century.

At ǂKhîsa-ǁgubus an exposed surface of alluvial silt on the northern edge of the site preserves the spoor of small stock being

---

599 Kinahan (2014)

Figure 8.11: Imported ceramic bowls including Scottish sponge-printed (left) and annular ware (right) from nineteenth century trading contact sites on the !Khuiseb Delta. The vessel on the left measures 165 mm in diameter and 83 mm in height, while the vessel on the right measures 150 mm in diameter and 75 mm in height. Photograph by M. Weiss, reproduced courtesy of Jill Kinahan (2000: Figure 8.6).

driven into the encampment as a compact flock. Similar exposures of silt at Khaeros, approximately 25 km away, preserve the spoor of cattle at a floodwater pond among the dunes. The silts also preserve a variety of other animal tracks including elephant, black rhinoceros, mountain zebra and ostrich. Organic flood debris trapped in the silt deposit, and bark samples from a dead camelthorn tree in the area of the pond yielded radiocarbon dates between mid-seventeenth and late eighteenth centuries[600] (Fig. 8.12).[601] These dates are corroborated by a small glass trade bead assemblage from the site which shows that ǂKhîsa-ǁgubus and Khaeros were contemporaneous (cf. Fig. 8.10). The latter site probably served as an inland stock-post. Visitors such as

---

600 Kinahan et al. (1991)
601 Uncalibrated radiocarbon dates in years BP: 280±35 (Pta-4619); 240±35 (Pta-4726).

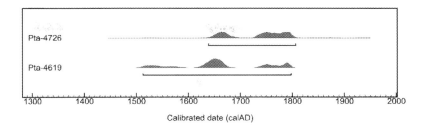

Figure 8.12: Calibrated radiocarbon dates for flood debris and tree bark at Khaeros (see explanation in Notes to the Reader: Archaeological age determination, p. xvii).

Thompson could not have known of the lush desert pastures in the dune valleys near Khaeros, which produce up to six tonnes of fodder per hectare.[602] The dominant grass in these dune valleys is *Stipagrostis ciliata*, a hardy and highly nutritious species,[603] sustained by sea fog and occasional light showers of rain.

More evidence of human and animal tracks is found on hardened surfaces of tidal mud deposits adjacent to the Walvis Bay lagoon. These deposits result from the combination of a prevailing wind regime which transports dune sand from the south west,[604] and occasional north-westerly winds which drive tidal surges into the entrance of the lagoon to create areas of impoundment between the mobile dunes. Repeated surges replenish this ponded seawater which is also subject to high rates of evaporation, thus producing a saturated saline solution containing gypsum, anhydrite and a range of related minerals. The mud formed in this way is dimensionally stable and retains faithful impressions, even of relatively light, medium-sized birds walking across the surface, provided it has not set. Coastal conditions promote case-hardening of the exposures, further

---

602 Nel & Opperman (1985: 124)
603 Müller (1984)
604 Ward & von Brunn (1985)

increasing their durability and resulting in the formation of a siliceous rind, or varnish.[605]

Hardened sediment surfaces bearing human and animal tracks vary in extent from less than 25 m² up to 150 m², the remnants of far larger surfaces of at least 1 km² extent that have been extensively deflated by wind erosion. Wind erosion tends to undermine and collapse sediment exposures presenting a sheer face to the prevailing south-westerly wind. It is therefore clear that the surviving surfaces represent only a small part of a rapidly disappearing sedimentary phenomenon. Where tracks do survive, they are found in great profusion, those of cattle, especially near to the seepages, suggesting a throng of milling beasts. Interspersed among the cattle tracks, which generally predominate, are the tracks of small stock as well as dogs, and of course, people, with elephant, giraffe and hyaena as the most easily recognised wild fauna visiting the same water sources. One particular individual, an adult male with a toe deformed by a poorly healed break, left a recognizable track that could be followed for several hundred metres across the hardened silt. An example of a human footprint is shown in Figure 8.13, while Figure 8.14 illustrates a surface which preserves the tracks of cattle and small stock being mustered by people assisted by a dog.

Crossing the same surfaces are shallow linear paths, and of thirteen examined, two were in excess of 35 m in length, the others being less than 15 m in length. A sample of 25 random width measurements of these pathways yielded a mean of 305 mm (SD 29.8), nearly identical to that of modern cattle paths, both in terms of width, reflecting the single-file nose-to-tail movement of cattle, and the characteristically sinuous trails so produced. The paths were relatively smooth with a mean depth of 37 mm (SD 10.2) below the roughly trampled surrounding surface. Repeated animal traffic, such as in following a pathway, would have accelerated compaction of the surface to the point where passing animals would leave little or no further impression. The effect

---

605 Conca & Rossman (1982); Larsen & Chilingar (1983)

THE BLACK SWAN 341

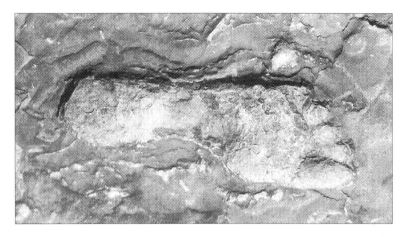

Figure 8.13: Human footprint in case-hardened lagoon silt deposit, Walvis Bay.

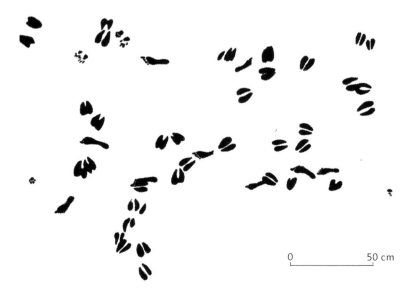

Figure 8.14: Hardened lagoon silt surface with an assemblage of tracks apparently representing the mustering of cattle by people with dogs.

of this process, which does not occur under natural conditions of hardening due to exposure alone, is reflected by measurable differences in the shear strength of surfaces within and adjacent to the paths. Five samples of the surface adjacent to the paths and without discernible tracks yielded a mean breaking strength value of 83.8 kPa (SD 10.6). A corresponding five samples taken from the central depression of the paths yielded a mean value of 126 kPa (SD 11.1). This difference in excess of 34% shear strength is most likely to have been caused by compaction resulting from the movement of cattle.[606]

The general orientation of the cattle paths is north–south, towards the historical anchorage at Walvis Bay[607] from the direction of the !Khuiseb River; there are no paths leading in the direction of ǂKhîsa-ǁgubus which lies to the north-east. This agrees with the absence of cattle at the site described by Thompson and the direction of the paths suggests that cattle were brought to the shore by a different route. An American whaler in 1803[608] wishing to barter for cattle, reports that:

> ...after a little time someone made a noise like the lowing of cattle, and then laid her head on her hand shutting her eyes imitating sleep, then pointing and following the sun 'til down, ... and when the sun arose the third day, the bullocks, sheep and goats would be there. True to the signs they came.

The distance from Khaeros to the cattle path sites following the !Khuiseb River is approximately 25 km. From the cattle path sites the animals would have appeared at the landing place without

---

606 A Pilcon™ hand vane tester was employed to measure the shear strength of the near-surface sediment within the paths and on adjacent surfaces. The instrument comprises a torque head with a direct-reading scale graduated in kiloPascals(kPa), measuring pressure required to break the surface against a 19 mm stainless steel vane head (Kinahan 2014a).
607 As shown in the hydrographic map of Owen (1833) reproduced in Kinahan (2014).
608 Gardner (1803); cited in Kinahan (2014a: 101); full transcript in Kinahan, J.H.A. (1990: 50).

the traders gaining any precise information as to where they were kept or how much stock the pastoralists really had.

This combination of documentary and archaeological evidence provides unique insights into the way in which !Khuiseb pastoralists were initially able to control trading relations without compromising the security of the herds. Herd-owners needed almost no adjustment to their established pattern of settlement using homestead sites and stock-posts in order to dominate trade at Walvis Bay. In this sense, European traders were drawn into the indigenous economy and were for all practical purposes subject to the values, customs and preferences of pastoral society. The evidence of the footprints preserved in the lagoon deposits may also help to explain why Thompson on visiting the pastoral encampment noted "a great disproportion in the sexes, the whole village consisting of 8 women, 3 female children, 49 men and 25 boys, under 10 years of age."[609] It is likely that previous encounters with visiting seamen lead the pastoralists to conceal their cattle and ensure that vulnerable women were out of sight.

Stature estimates based on twenty human skeletons from the Namib Desert dating to within the last one thousand years confirm the marked sexual dimorphism noted among similar samples from elsewhere in southern Africa.[610] The Namib Desert skeletons yield a mean adult male stature of 1.62 m (SD 0.913 m) and a mean adult female stature of 1.53 m (SD 0.626 m).[611] Calculated stature based on the length of forty footprints at Walvis Bay yields a mean stature of 1.47 m (SD 0.927). Upper and lower mean stature values based on the footprints are 1.51 m and 1.44 m, indicating that a significant proportion of the footprints associated with the sites where cattle were mustered probably

---

609 Kinahan, J.H.A. (1990: 40)
610 Kinahan (2013a); Wilson & Lundy (1994); Sealy & Pfeiffer (2000)
611 Following Lundy & Feldesman (1987); Wilson & Lundy (1994)

represent women.[612] This provides strong circumstantial evidence to show that !Khuiseb pastoralists responded to the overtures of visiting Europeans by providing livestock for trade while at the same time protecting both livestock and women, using the same strategies they would employ against pastoralist raiding parties.

The concentration of human burials at ǂKhîsa-ǁgubus and their close proximity to the living area at the site is unusual in the Namib Desert, where most burials occur singly and in relatively isolated locations. To this, Thompson's narrative may present an explanation, for he notes in several places that the crew of the *Nautilus* were taken ill with "ague", or fever, before reaching Walvis Bay. The most badly afflicted were recovering when the ship regained Spithead in England, but it is possible that by then ǂKhîsa-ǁgubus had been hastily abandoned by the survivors of whatever contagion the sailors had brought. This may also help to explain why a subsequent visit by a British Navy vessel found the people less approachable.[613]

In their trade with European and American vessels calling at Walvis Bay, pastoral communities appear to have favoured items that had functional or value equivalence in the indigenous economy. Glass beads, initially red-on-green and blue cylinder beads, were obtained in significant quantities, and the inland distribution of these beads helps to define extensive networks among Namib Desert pastoralists. The glass beads augmented an existing trade in copper beads, the production of which was linked to pastoral groups on the interior escarpment, where beads

---

612 Kinahan (2013a), using criteria for determination of age and sex in human skeletons (Brothwell 1981; Buikstra & Uberlaker 1994; Walrath et al. 2004). Estimation of stature based on foot impression follows Robbins (1986). For detailed investigation of the Walvis Bay human footprints, see Morse et al. (2013).

613 Remarks, HMS *Star*, Captain Alexander, 1795 (Kinahan, J.H.A. 1992). Mortality through contagious disease occurred in a number of such contact situations, one well documented example being the Tierra del Fuego region of South America (Delaunay et al. 2017).

held an established livestock value equivalence.[614] Beads, both copper and subsequently glass could therefore be used as a means to convert livestock into redeemable commodities, serving as an essential component of herd management along with the role of client herders as a means to disperse livestock and so reduce losses through raiding, disease and shortage of suitable pasture.

Historical accounts identify two main groups among the ǂAonîn: the !Khuisenin, who were livestock owners, and the Hurinin, said mainly to live from what they could gather along the seashore.[615] However, the archaeology of the !Khuiseb Delta does not support this distinction, showing that encampments with livestock were situated close to the shore and that the diet of people on these sites included large quantities of marine foods. It is therefore conceivable that the Hurinin represented an economic underclass of people on the periphery of the pastoral economy rather than a culturally distinct group. It is these people who may have served as client herders, with some acquiring sufficient livestock to become independent pastoralists. The increasing importance of trade may have had the result that livestock were preferentially exchanged for beads and other commodities. This would have reduced opportunities for client herders, leaving larger numbers of people without livestock and thus leading to a more numerous Hurinin social class. With the eventual collapse of the pastoral economy in the nineteenth century, the delta community as a whole was reduced to poverty[616] and the people of the !Khuiseb were generally referred to as "*strandlopers*", or beach rangers.

---

614 Kinahan (1980); Kinahan & Vogel (1982); the presence of cowrie *Cypraea annulus* shells at ǂKhîsa-Ilgubus (Kinahan, J.H.A. 2000) supports the contention of the nineteenth century missionary James Archbell (Vigne 1991: 30) that Namib Desert pastoralists participated in trading networks that may have extended to the east coast of the subcontinent.
615 Budack (1977)
616 Kinahan, J.H.A. (2000)

Bearing in mind the destructive effects of natural processes on the survival of shell midden sites as discussed at the beginning of this chapter, there are some notable and potentially informative anomalies in the archaeology of coastal settlement. The very large shell middens at Elizabeth Bay are unique on the Namib coast; their initial accumulation coincides with evidence of hyper-aridity in the late Holocene presented in Chapter 3 and it is possible that being situated close to one of the very few reliable sources of artesian water in that region, Elizabeth Bay may have served as a refugium in the same way as did the Dâures massif for hunter-gatherers in the central parts of the Namib Desert, both sites providing a sustainable resource of small-sized, easily procured sources of food. Later Holocene hunter-gatherer sites in the desert interior, however, have relatively little evidence for the use of coastal resources and show a consistent emphasis on plains antelope until the appearance in the last two millennia, of shell middens near the mouths of a few desert rivers.

While the possible use of Elizabeth Bay as a refugium site indicates an ecological imperative driven by increasing aridity, the later Holocene use of coastal resources suggests two other, closely linked imperatives: competition over scarce resources, and cooperation in the control of access to scarce resources. In Chapter 7, the evidence from Khorixa-ams points to conflict resulting from pastoral expansion, and that from the Hungorob, to regulated control over livestock pastures, both indicative of a pastoral equilibrium *K* phase. The appearance of settlements such as at the Ugab River mouth described in this chapter suggests that there may have been a shift towards the use of less highly valued marine resources in response to competition in the interior. At the same time, the exploitation of wild grass seed, as described in Chapter 6, became widespread in the Namib, pointing to the broadening of the subsistence base. Evidence from the storage of grass seed in Group B pottery vessels reveals a degree of coordination and cooperation in this activity, through indications of possible pottery exchange and circulation shown by patterns in strontium isotope ratios.

Clearly, the !Khuiseb Delta is the most productive primary resource site on the Namib coast and its importance is unsurprising, especially as Walvis Bay provided the rare possibility of secure and sheltered anchorage for merchant vessels requiring supplies of meat and drinking water. It is striking that historical records indicate only one major site during the late 18th and early 19th centuries.[617] While the archaeological evidence indicates that there were between one and three encampments, these may not have been in use at the same time. On the one hand, the delta, combining abundant marine and terrestrial resources, could conceivably have supported a number of encampment sites and a larger human population than is indicated by historical and archaeological evidence; on the other, the archaeological evidence is of a pastoral settlement system combining fixed homestead encampments such as ǂKhîsa-ǁgubus with stock-post sites such as Khaeros, in a more complex settlement model.

It is likely that available resources in the lower !Khuiseb limited the number of stock-post sites, and without stock-posts to supply animals to the encampments in the delta, it would not have been possible to conduct regular trade with vessels calling at Walvis Bay. The small number of encampment sites therefore reflects livestock pasture requirements as well as competition among pastoral communities for control over trading opportunities. Semi-permanent occupation of such sites was arguably based as much on trade as it was on the resource base of the !Khuiseb Delta itself.

The presence at the !Khuiseb Delta of an underclass without livestock, the Hurinin, parallels the situation of the Ovatjimba mentioned in the previous chapter as occasionally serving as client herders to the Ovahimba. This uneven distribution of wealth due to the concentration of livestock in the hands of successful

---

617 e.g. Kinahan, J.H.A. (1990) citing the description of Thompson, HMS *Nautilus* in 1786; Kinahan (2014) citing Alexander, HMS *Star* in 1795.

herders thus appears to be a widespread feature of an economy in which the risks of loss are relatively high and the possibilities of a recovery in wealth and social standing not out of reach. Indeed, in the early twentieth century, the anthropologist Winifred Hoernlé while working among the increasingly Christianized ǂAonîn in the !Khuiseb Delta, reported their great affection for the Old Testament story of Job, whose travails so well reflect the vicissitudes of pastoral life.[618]

Unequal trading relations with merchant vessels visiting Walvis Bay certainly contributed to the decline of independent pastoralism in the Namib Desert. One missionary at Walvis Bay remarked in 1845 "exceptionally many ships have come here, six to nine at once; they came from Ichaboe and purchased oxen here."[619] However, Orlam raiding parties from the interior had an equal if not greater impact. The rise of the Orlam raiding economy, described in the next chapter, directly affected pastoralists in the !Khuiseb Delta, and in one incident in 1844, a group under Willem Swartbooi captured most of their livestock, carried away their women and children, and forced the men into service as client herders.[620] Missionaries visiting Walvis Bay at the time observed that the ǂAonîn had no livestock of their own and were reduced to poverty.[621]

This chapter has shown that the expansion *r* phase of the adaptive cycle reached an equilibrium *K* phase towards the end of the eighteenth and early nineteenth centuries when !Khuiseb Delta pastoralists were able to maintain their herds while participating in coastal trade. The equilibrium in trading relations tipped inexorably to favour European traders, who eventually bypassed the ǂAonîn to gain control of the livestock from the interior. This supply of livestock was derived from an emergent raiding economy that was

---

618 Carstens, Klinghardt & West (1987)
619 Kienetz (1977: 558) citing Moritz (1915: 238)
620 Tindall (1959)
621 Dentlinger (1983); Moritz (1916)

also to collapse in the face of increasing European domination. The decline in pastoral fortunes both on the coast and inland, represents the onset of a collapse Ω phase in the adaptive cycle, signalling the demise of the pastoral economy.

However, while a local decline in pastoral fortunes did occur in the !Khuiseb, in the wider context of Namib Desert pastoralism, there was an unexpected, if short-lived response in which pastoral communities were able to initiate a reorganization α phase, resisting for several decades the spectre of colonial rule. This development is described in the next chapter.

IX

MEN IN HATS

A bow wave of European expansion from the Cape Colony reached northward to the Orange River in the late eighteenth century, pushing before it displaced and dispossessed Khoe pastoralists. These communities fell under the depredations of frontier settlers who were effectively beyond the reach of colonial control in a largely lawless zone where cattle raiding served to feed the Cape market.[622] Khoe on the margins of settler society became increasingly accustomed to European ways: Dutch was widely spoken, and horses,[623] firearms and other innovations were quickly adopted.[624] A degree of literacy and nominal Christianity accompanied these changes, although European settlers were generally hostile to the presence of missionaries among the Khoe, where acculturated communities earned the sobriquet Orlam, or people knowledgeable in European

---

[622] Penn (2005); Legassick (1989: 361); the late 19th century missionary Joseph Tindall (1959) described the frontier as a twilight zone of European influence spreading in advance of colonial power.

[623] Horses were widely adopted by pastoralist communities in Namibia (see Mitchell 2017) where they were used to great tactical advantage during livestock raids, rather than as a means to control and manage grazing herds.

[624] Kienetz (1977)

ways.[625] Khoe living beyond the Orange River learned to fear these increasingly adept raiders, whom they knew as the "hat wearers".[626]

Here, we follow the migration of the Orlam northwards, skirting the eastern interior to the central highlands, where missionary activity, trade and mining set in train further developments which had profound consequences in this region. In a sense, the Orlam were travelling backwards in time: the panarchial interaction of indigenous and settler society was much further advanced in the Cape, so that when Orlam raiders eventually reached the Namib Desert and fell upon pastoral communities there, the people they preyed on were in a situation quite similar to their own, but a generation before. As with other regional-scale examples of historical economic integration, there is both a chronological and a chorological[627] aspect to the changing fortunes of Khoe-speaking pastoralists during the last two centuries. The first part of this chapter deals with the northward expansion of the Orlam, and the second with its consequences both in the interior and on the Namib Desert coast.

The rapid spread of European settlement in the Cape Colony initiated a collapse or release Ω phase in the Khoe pastoral economy. Their displacement across the Orange River and beyond the boundaries of the colony is characterized by a fundamental re-organization α phase associated with the emergence of a new social order under Orlam control. This chapter shows that the rapid expansion r phase of the Orlam and the emergence of powerful warlords among the Afrikaner clan and later under Hendrik !Nanseb Witbooi, represents a significant adaptive development in the pastoral and political economy of the region.

---

625 Du Bruyn (1981)
626 Lau (1987)
627 cf. Entrikin (2008)

A moving frontier

The Orlam were for practical purposes the vanguard of colonial expansion into Namibia, raiding cattle pastoralists as far as southern Angola, and driving their booty to the Cape Colony where they established lucrative trading relationships. This development affected the wider pastoral economy in a number of ways: Khoe communities were transformed into armed chieftaincies and the cattle-rich Ovaherero were placed under increasing pressure to do the same, having moved steadily southward in search of new pastures. The Orlam warlord, Jonker Afrikaner, gained control over the cattle trade to the Namib coast at Walvis Bay, building a wagon route, known as the Bay Road, to facilitate the movement of goods to the interior.[628] European traders intervened on the side of the Ovaherero, and missionaries began actively to participate in trading enterprises, including the supply of guns and ammunition. In this newly emergent social order, the Orlam may be seen as essentially an encapsulated element of the colonial mercantile economy.

Documentary sources on this phase of frontier history primarily reflect the concerns and perspectives of European traders, missionaries and settlers[629] and until now, scant attention has been focused on indigenous responses to early colonial and mercantile expansion. Here, we first consider the archaeology of Khoe refuge settlement on the north bank of the Orange River at !Nabas, before turning to the site of the first Orlam encampment at ǁKhauxaǃnas. The evidence from these sites confirms the interpretation presented in the previous two chapters based on autonomous household units as archaeologically definitive of pastoral settlement. ǁKhauxaǃnas, moreover, shows that this social organization was transformed into an hierarchical structure supporting the institution of chieftaincy which became characteristic of Orlam responses to early colonial intervention. The transformation of Orlam social

---
628 Dierks (1992)
629 Wallace & Kinahan (2011)

relations in the re-orientation α phase is clearly expressed in the architecture and layout of ǁKhauxaǃnas.

ǃNabas is situated in a secluded embayment of rocky outcrops a short distance upstream from the historical wagon crossing on the Orange River at *Compagniesdrift*, a name which most likely refers to its use by agents of the Dutch East India Company, known by the acronym VOC.[630] The river afforded relatively few safe crossing points, and while ǃNabas was protected from direct approach by a deep and fast-flowing stretch of the river, its inhabitants nonetheless posted lookouts at defensive positions overlooking the south bank. This pattern of settlement combined with defence structures, sometimes with embrasures or firing loopholes, is widespread on the north bank of the river and attests to the insecurity of the frontier.[631] The course of the river at this point, as well as the surrounding terrain and the location of Khoe settlements, is shown on a map drawn by Hendrik Wikar (Fig. 9.1a), a fugitive from the VOC who negotiated a pardon in exchange for details of his wanderings along the Orange River between 1775 and 1778.[632]

Figure 9.1b shows the layout of the site at ǃNabas which consists of a stock enclosure represented by an area of discoloured soil approximately 10 m in diameter, partly surrounded by circles of small anchor stones indicating the margins of four dwellings, as well as the collapsed remains of three small corbelled structures which probably served as storage facilities. The roughly semi-circular layout of the site corresponds with that shown in historical depictions of Cape Khoe encampments.[633] Although characteristic of Khoe settlement throughout the Cape Colony, no archaeological examples of such sites have been thus far reported south of the Orange River. Excavation at ǃNabas revealed several fragments of

---

630 Vereenigde Oostindische Compagnie (VOC), founded in 1602 (Gelderblom et al. 2013)
631 Penn (2005)
632 Mossop (1935)
633 e.g. Burchell (1824)

MEN IN HATS 355

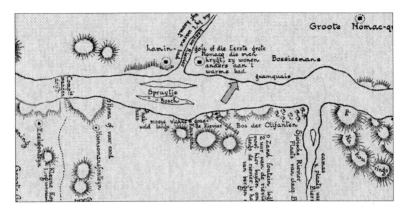

Figure 9.1a: The approximate location of !Nabas (arrowed) on Hendrik Wikar's map of 1779. From *The Journal of Hendrik Jacob Wikar, 1779* (Van Riebeeck Society, Cape Town, 1935). Edited by E.E. Mossop.

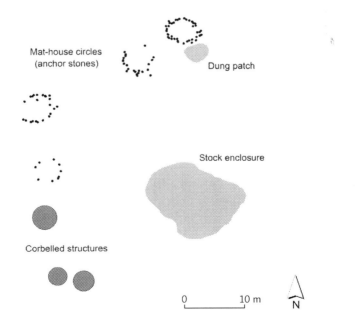

Figure 9.1b: Layout of nineteenth century pastoral encampment at !Nabas (arrowed in Fig. 9.1a) showing anchor stones of portable mat houses encircling stock enclosure and adjacent to corbelled structures.

imported hand-painted sponged earthenware bowls suggesting occupation in the early to mid-nineteenth century.[634]

The anchor stones shown in the site plan mark the positions of mat-houses which consisted of reed mats covering a framework of light poles. These structures were portable but bulky, requiring the use of pack animals as shown in Figure 9.2, a contemporary view painted in the first decade of the nineteenth century. In the absence of domestic animal bone or other remains, the remains of mat-houses is proxy evidence for the presence of cattle, specifically pack oxen, at the site. The corbelled structures provide further evidence for late eighteenth or early nineteenth century occupation. This form of construction, using overlapping flat stones to create unsupported dome-like structures was widespread among Sotho-speaking communities in parts of South Africa and it is possible that this practice was adopted by the Khoe, becoming more widespread in the process. The same technique, however, is found in the vernacular building methods of Europe and it is equally possible that it was adopted by the Khoe from French Huguenot settlers at the Cape.[635] The site of !Nabas therefore presents a particular syncretism of influences within pastoral nomadic Khoe society on the frontier of the Cape Colony.

At the end of the eighteenth century, escalating conflict with settlers prompted one Cape Khoe clan, under Klaas Afrikaner, to move well beyond the frontier where they established a stronghold at ǁKhauxa!nas. The site consists of an elaborate drystone walled enclosure, strategically situated to overlook a rare dependable waterhole on a bend in the Bak River. Their occupation of the site was to prove short-lived, however, perhaps on account of the poor grazing in this area. The Afrikaner Orlam soon moved north, first to Nai-ais,[636] near present-day Rehoboth, finally establishing themselves in 1840 at Windhoek,[637] so named

---

634 Kelly (1993); Kinahan, J.H.A. (2000)
635 cf. Kramer (2012)
636 Also given as !Nao-as by Heywood and Maasdorp (1989: 17).
637 Simon (1983)

Figure 9.2: Painting by Samuel Daniell in 1805 titled "Kora-Khoikhoi preparing to remove." Samuel Daniell, CC0, via Wikimedia Commons.

because the surrounding mountain ranges reminded them of their original home among the Winterhoek Mountains of the Cape.[638] Ovaherero pastoralists, who had recently reached the same place in their expansion from the north, called it Otjomuise, after the hot mineral springs that emerged in the valley.

‖Khauxa!nas is a unique surviving example of Orlam settlement combining residential and elaborate defensive architecture.[639] The main feature of the site is a perimeter wall almost 700 m in length circling the top of the hill (Fig. 9.3). To raise the wall, stones up to 2 m in length were laid on the surface of the ground in parallel rows, and further courses were added without levelling or mortar (Fig. 9.4), while the cavity between was filled with rubble and soil. Over most of its length, the wall is little more than 1 m in height so that through-band stones were needed only at the various points

---

638 Lau (1987)
639 Kinahan (1996b)

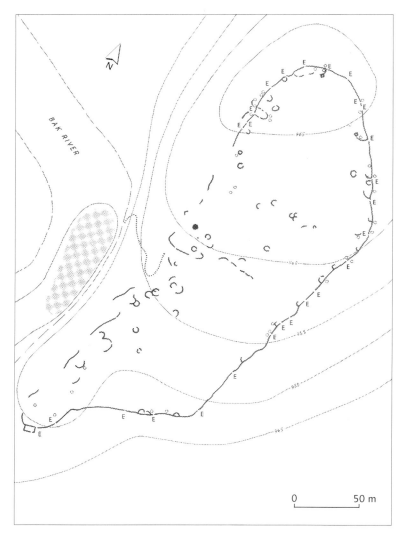

Figure 9.3: Plan of ǁKhauxa!nas with walling indicated as bold lines, entrances marked E and middens as open circles. The pathway to the waterhole is indicated as a dotted line.

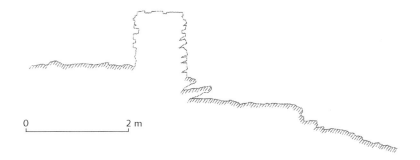

Figure 9.4: Section of ǁKhauxa!nas perimeter wall showing construction on exposed bedrock.

of entry to create a well finished appearance. Some of the stones weigh several tons and would have probably required the use of strong chains and well-trained oxen to move them into place. At some points along the perimeter, exceptionally long stones were placed in an upright position and while these are an impressive embellishment, they do not add to the strength of the wall or its effectiveness as a line of defence.[640]

The method of construction reflects the use of colonial building techniques by the Orlam as coursed, rubble-filled walling is not found on earlier indigenous sites. Other innovations include several rectangular structures; these are clearly contemporaneous since they are keyed into the perimeter and internal walls. There are also drains or weep-holes at several points, providing a further example of European-style construction, evidently used to demonstrate familiarity with colonial technology rather than to drain the site, which lies in a zone of extremely low rainfall. Gunflints found within the perimeter wall suggest the use of smoothbore muskets of the type that were in general use on the

---

640 Upright stones, often more than 1 m in height, are a distinctive feature of more elaborate pre-colonial burials in the southern parts of Namibia.

frontier.[641] These were of limited range and accuracy,[642] but the positioning of the wall had the advantage that its approach from the south was via a natural *glacis* which would have added to the effectiveness of the defences, besides making the wall appear higher than it really was. When the missionary Ridsdale visited the abandoned site in 1847 he remarked:

> Here they [had] resolved upon making a stand… [and within]… this entrenchment…considered themselves able to defy all their enemies. They seemed scarcely able to conceive of a valour that would proceed in the face of their bullets, scale their fort… [and]…drive them over the fearful precipice on the opposite side, [to] plunge them into the abyss of black waters beneath. The opportunity of defending themselves in their impregnable fortification…never occurred, as the commandos of Boers from the Colony pursued them no farther than Nisbett Bath.[643]

But there is more to the site than fortification, for its layout clearly incorporates the same principles of social organization as those described in the previous two chapters, where individual household units are identifiable within larger pastoral encampments. The walling along the northern perimeter of the site forms an integral part of a series of residential structures including circles of loose stones and associated lengths of walling (Fig. 9.3). These groups of structures are relatively discrete household units, facing towards the central part of the greater enclosure and with one or more private entrances at the rear, through the common perimeter wall. Several of the entrances abut semi-circular screening walls and these are associated with stone mortars and pestles as well as ashy middens, suggesting that they served as cooking shelters adjacent to the dwellings. The positioning of the ashy middens

---

641 Berkovitch (1976: 9–13)
642 Swenson (1972)
643 Ridsdale (1883: 264); Nisbett Bath is present-day Warmbad in southern Namibia, nearly 150 km south-west of ǁKhauxa!nas.

immediately outside the entrances indicates that the perimeter wall served as the rear of the household dwelling area. Some of the structures may have had rudimentary roofing but portable mat houses were probably the main form of shelter within the enclosure, as is indicated by circular arrangements of anchor stones similar to those found at !Nabas. Although it is difficult to estimate the number of residential features, there were probably no more than 30, grouped in up to five separate household clusters. These would conservatively suggest that between 50 and 100 people lived on the site.

There is less evidence of residential features in the vicinity of the southern perimeter. This is corroborated by the greater distance between entrances along this section of the wall and the smaller number of ashy middens. The implication is that while the northern perimeter was formed as a series of contiguous individual household clusters, the southern perimeter wall served as a communal boundary for the site as a whole. The importance of this distinction lies in the fact that the expected direction of approach by visitors or attackers from the colonial frontier was from the southern quadrant. Only from this aspect does the site present a complete line of defence (Fig. 9.5). Significantly, the entrance of the rectangular walled feature on the southern perimeter faces outward and has no communicating entrance to the main enclosure, indicating that this feature served as a

Figure 9.5: Elevation view of ǁKhauxa!nas perimeter wall from the south-east.

reception or waiting area for visitors to the site. The overall layout of the site favours the existence of a formal, public approach from the south, as distinct from the private household entrances elsewhere on the periphery of the site.

The combination of a communal southern perimeter with a dedicated point of entry, and a rear perimeter of the site formed by separate residential units, is suggestive of hierarchical organization. With the rectangular reception building on the outer southern perimeter serving to control access to the site and the leadership of ǁKhauxa!nas, at least one level of stratification is implied. The same pattern, however, is repeated in a more rudimentary form among the residential units, two of which have attached to their screening walls small but otherwise similar rectangular structures. These could represent a further level of stratification requiring controlled access to particular households. The fact that none of the other residential units had such structures suggests that there were three levels of seniority in this community: a clan leader or chieftain, two lieutenants, and beneath that a stratum of allied households. The presence of two lieutenants rather than one would imply that the organization of the site was based on principles of kinship and genealogical seniority. Since it was the Orlam chieftain Klaas Afrikaner who established the site, it is reasonable to infer that the basic design of the site was determined by the patriarchal relationship between Klaas and his two sons, Jager and Titus.

Jager, the younger of the two brothers, succeeded Klaas as chieftain, or *kaptein*, of the Afrikaner clan. He was invited to Cape Town where he received an ox wagon as a gift from the Governor of the Cape Colony.[644] Ox wagons were essential for the transport of ivory from the interior and this acquisition marks a further degree of Orlam integration in the colonial economy. Significantly, none of the entrances of ǁKhauxa!nas is wide enough to admit a wagon, and since something as valuable as this in terms of both economic utility and status would not

---

644 Penn (2005)

be left outside the walled enclosure, it may be inferred that the Afrikaners only acquired wagons after they had moved on from ‖Khauxa!nas. On his visit to Cape Town, Jager was accompanied by his son Jonker who was to succeed him in 1823 and lead the Afrikaners northward.[645] Jonker is estimated to have been born in 1790[646] and would therefore have spent at least part of his boyhood at the walled encampment of ‖Khauxa!nas, if he had not in fact been born there.

The spatial organization of ‖Khauxa!nas may be compared to that of earlier pre-colonial aggregation encampments by the technique of permeability analysis[647] using a graphical representation of access to controlled space, from the perspective of a visitor to the settlement. The basic premise is that observable spatial patterns can be explained in social terms with reference to historical and ethnographic evidence.[648] The permeability map in Figure 9.6 shows the accessibility of household units within a pre-colonial encampment with no restricted entry and no evidence of social rank. A visitor to the encampment has equal access to all household units, each centring on the dwelling of the household head. While the visitor would presumably approach members of the household through the household head, members of households within the encampment would probably have free access to all parts of the site on the basis of kinship ties. According to this analysis there are two levels of permeability: that of the space occupied by the household head and that of the space occupied by the rest of the household.

In contrast, ‖Khauxa!nas shows at least five levels of permeability (Fig. 9.6). The outer reception building, representing the first level, provides access to the enclosed area occupied by the household of the community head, located at the second level.

---

645 Grimm (1929) referred to Jonker Afrikaner as the "Hottentot Napoleon" in recognition of his regional influence.
646 Galton (1889)
647 Hillier & Hanson (1984)
648 Boast & Yiannouli (1986)

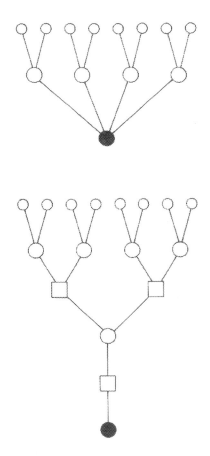

Figure 9.6: Access analysis of pre-colonial pastoral aggregation encampments (above) and the site of ǁKhauxa!nas (below) from the perspective of a visitor (solid black circle). The large open circles represent household heads while the smaller circles represent members of the household. The open squares represent levels of access at ǁKhauxa!nas marked by the use of rectangular reception buildings.

The third level is represented by the two reception buildings situated among the household units at the northern end of the site. These and the remaining household units would contain the fourth and fifth levels of permeability, equivalent to that of a pre-colonial aggregation encampment. Here, too, residents of the site would presumably have had unrestricted access within the fourth and fifth levels, while the two household heads at the third level (putatively Jager and Titus Afrikaner) may have enjoyed more open access to the most senior household (their father Klaas), located at the second level of permeability. Seen in this way, ǁKhauxaǃnas represents a permutation of the pattern of pastoral settlement described in the previous two chapters and therefore exemplifies a critical aspect of the re-organization α phase in the Orlam economy.

The evidence from the Namib Desert showed that autonomous households were able to aggregate and disperse according to the availability of pasture, and that the archaeology of aggregated settlements shows no formal indication of seniority within the pastoral alliance. This fluid combination of domestic autonomy and communal resource management, characteristic of pastoral settlement,[649] when taken together with the evidence from ǁKhauxaǃnas accommodates both the relative autonomy of households and a higher order of community leadership. The fact that the layout of the site reflects the principles of indigenous pastoral society contradicts arguments that Khoe society simply disintegrated to form an underclass of colonial settler society.[650] Instead, the evidence from this site exemplifies the particular resilience of indigenous communities and the re-organization α phase in which the Orlam emerged as a formidable force, first in their domination of the regional economy and then in their effective resistance to German colonial rule.

---

649 Bonte (1981); Lefébure (1979)
650 Lau (1987); Smith (1990)

Figure 9.7: Otjikango Otjinene (Neu Barmen) Rhenish mission station in 1860. The mission residence is on the right, with the church to the left. Visible on the far left are several dwellings, probably of Ovaherero congregants.

Missionaries, merchants, miners

Once established at Windhoek, Jonker Afrikaner invited missionaries to settle among his people, not only as a means to consolidate his authority and trading interests but also to induce allied Orlam groups to move northward and join him there. Mission societies were compelled by the colonial government, under pressure from European settlers, to operate beyond the Orange River frontier[651] and a number of relatively stable mission communities were established early in the nineteenth century.[652] Missionary efforts further north were initially less fruitful, partly due to the instability of the new frontier created by the Orlam. Wesleyan missionaries arrived at Windhoek in 1842. In 1844,

---

651 Penn (2005)
652 cf. Wallace & Kinahan (2011). Missions in this area introduced wheat cultivation and several mission settlement sites have surviving evidence of threshing floors.

the Rhenish mission established its first station further north at Otjikango Otjinene,[653] later renamed Neu Barmen,[654] to work among the Ovaherero (Fig. 9.7). However, persistent raiding kept the Ovaherero constantly on the move, as did the grazing requirements of their cattle during a period of recurrent drought.[655] Carl Hugo Hahn and a succession of later missionaries persisted, despite the station itself being sacked several times, but it was eventually abandoned in 1904.[656]

Archaeological excavation of the mission residence (Fig. 9.8) revealed a simple structure of sundried mudbrick resting on a foundation of undressed stone, mortared with mud. Collapsed sections of the exterior walls lay on disaggregated mudbrick, preserving parts of the roof structure which consisted of heavy beams cut from riverine thorn trees, probably *Faidherbia albida*, covered by reed thatch, presumably cut from stands of *Phragmites australis* growing in the vicinity of the nearby spring. Cultural material recovered from the excavations included a small assemblage of domestic porcelain, brass brackets from window frames and doors, as well as quantities of windowpane glass. Also found in the excavation was a locally manufactured serpentinite pipe, imitating the style of imported white bisque clay pipes such as found among the debris of trading sites on the Namib coast. The excavated assemblage included items such

---

653 Literally "a weak spring running over rocky ground", Mossolow (1993)

654 The practice of domesticating the landscape by imposing European place-names was widespread among missionaries in Africa (see Ashley 2018). Rhenish missionaries in Namibia renamed settlements and geographical features as if they were in Germany; thus, Windhoek was renamed Elberfeldt, Okahandja Schmelens Verwachtung, and the Swakop River as the Rhine. These names did not endure. Others, such as the London Mission Society, named their stations after places of biblical significance such as Bethanie (Bethany) and Berseba (Beersheba) and these are still in use.

655 The period between 1880 and 1890 was marked by recurrent drought in central Namibia (Grab & Zumthurm 2020).

656 Hahn, *Tagebücher* 1837–1860; Mossolow (1993)

Figure 9.8: Otjikango Otjinene (Neu Barmen) Rhenish mission residence showing exposed stone foundations and collapsed sections of mudbrick walling. The rectangular front section of the building matches that of the contemporary sketch in Figure 9.7.

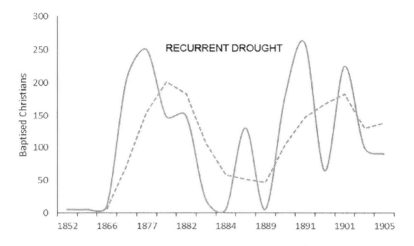

Figure 9.9: Fluctuations in the number of congregants present at Otjikango Otjinene (solid line), with 3 year moving average (dashed line) showing two major peaks; population data from Mossolow (1993), and historical rainfall data indicating a period of recurrent drought between 1877 and 1890, from Grab & Zumthurm (2020).

as nails and hoop iron, as well as both cattle and sheep/goat bones. On the southern periphery of the site lay the remains of what were probably Ovaherero encampments, marked by stone circles, discarded grindstones, and an array of European debris dominated by green bottle glass sherds that had been used as cutting and scraping implements.

Archival records from the mission at Otjikango Otjinene show large fluctuations in the number of congregants and other residents (Fig. 9.9). The number of Ovaherero families grew from about twenty to about sixty in 1844 but all had left by the next year; two years later, there were about 24 families, but all left the same year. When the mission church was built in 1849 it was fully attended by about 50 worshippers, but again all had left within the year. Numbers increased in 1851 following an outbreak of conflict between Jonker Afrikaner and the Ovaherero chief Kahijene and there were approximately 420 people at the mission, of whom about one quarter attended church services, with about 70 children attending religious instruction. Numbers plummeted to less than ten adults the same year, continuing thus through 1852. In 1854 the mission was pillaged while temporarily abandoned. Fluctuations such as these characterize the entire history of the mission which illustrates its failure as an attempt to create among the Ovaherero a form of settlement and a way of life that was entirely alien.[657]

Throughout this time the number of Europeans slowly increased, bringing cattle traders, ivory hunters and prospectors who travelled to the interior from Walvis Bay. When copper prospectors reached Otjikango Otjinene in 1855, the mission church became a dance hall.[658] Their operations moved to the upper drainage of the !Khuiseb River where production began at the short-lived Matchless Mine.[659] Mining was confined to the relatively shallow high-grade oxide zone[660] and the copper ore was concentrated by hand before being transported to the coast via ox wagon.[661] Traffic in goods along the so-called Bay Road was subject to a lucrative tax imposed by Jonker Afrikaner[662] who strictly limited movement of livestock by other routes, ostensibly to control the spread of stock disease. Copper-mining was nonetheless profitable, and several shiploads went to the Cape before the mine closed in 1860.[663]

There is archaeological evidence that the Matchless ore-body was exploited for several centuries (Fig. 9.10) before the arrival

---

657 See Comaroff and Comaroff (1986), and King and McGranaghan (2018) for recent studies on the archaeology of mission activity in southern Africa.
658 Mossolow (1993)
659 Lau (1987)
660 Adamson & Teichmann (1986)
661 Dierks (1992)
662 Dierks (1992)
663 Kinahan, J.H.A. (1991)

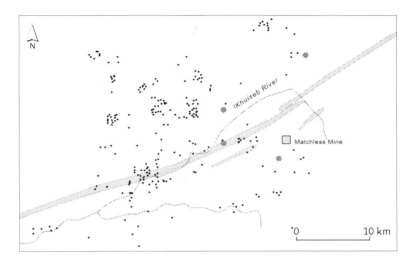

Figure 9.10: Matchless Mine (1855–1860) in relation to earlier indigenous copper-smelting sites (grey circles) and the Matchless ortho-amphibolite belt, which hosts several copper-bearing ore bodies. Related archaeological sites in the upper !Khuiseb drainage are indicated as black dots.

of European miners (Fig. 9.11).[664] Copper-smelting sites in the upper !Khuiseb drainage are associated with the only known concentration of engraved *mankala* boards, described in Chapter 5 as an integral component of men's initiation rites at |Ui-||aes. The association of *mankala* with copper smelting suggests that the technology of copper production was acquired through interaction with farming communities who settled in the northern parts of Namibia during the last two millennia. Almost all of the *mankala* boards are of the 4-rank variety and therefore tentatively linked to southern Zambia,[665] indicating a local adoption of copper

---

664 Uncalibrated radiocarbon dates in years BP: 420±50 (Pta-2573); 350±45 (Pta-2903); 320±45 (Pta-3436); 275±40 (Pta-2559); 230±45 (Pta-2904);190±45 (Pta-3428). See also Kinahan & Vogel (1982)
665 Townshend (1979)

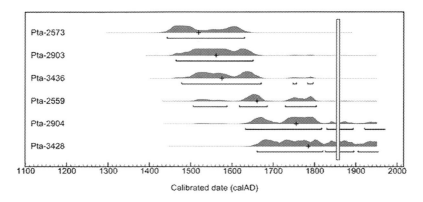

Figure 9.11: Calibrated radiocarbon dates for copper-smelting furnaces in the upper !Khuiseb drainage (see explanation in Notes to the Reader: Archaeological age determination, p. xvii). Median dates (indicated +) indicate production commenced in the early 16th century and ceased in the late 18th century, half a century before the arrival of European miners. The vertical bar indicates the period of European operations at Matchless Mine from 1855 to 1860.

working together with its related symbolic referents. Most of the *mankala* boards are engraved on inclined and near-vertical rock surfaces; at least one example is painted, indicating that this motif was absorbed within the corpus of rock art found on these sites. It therefore appears that *mankala* was implicated in a shamanic process of transformation from ore to metal. The acquisition of copper production technology in the second millennium AD coincides with the adoption of initiation rites as described in Chapter 5 and therefore indicates a widespread phenomenon of α phase re-organization in hunter-gatherer society in the process of a transition to food production.

The upper !Khuiseb sites were one of the major sources of copper beads which formed part of the internal exchange and risk management strategy of Namib Desert pastoral communities described in Chapters 7 and 8. Copper production was thus closely integrated with the pre-colonial pastoral economy.[666] However, the advent of trade with European merchant vessels at Walvis Bay described in the previous chapter introduced a variety of commodities including glass trade beads which augmented and eventually displaced copper beads from circulation. It is apparent from the dating of indigenous copper furnaces in the upper !Khuiseb that production ceased after the late 18th century. Its demise may be linked both to the effects of Orlam raiding and to the advent of intensive trade with European merchants at Walvis Bay, at least fifty years prior to the establishment of Matchless Mine as an early colonial enterprise (Fig. 9.11). A contemporary account of copper production in this region records that:

> [T]hey made a kind of charcoal from the wood of a certain mimosa. ...they break the ore into small pieces....thus prepared they lay the material in alternate strata, within a small enclosure of stone... They set fire to the charcoal, and blow it with several bellows, each made from the skin of a gemsbok converted into a sock, with the horn of the same animal fixed to one end for the pipe. This is all that is necessary to procure the metal from the sort of ore they make use of... being vitreous copper ore.[667]

Archaeological examples of copper-smelting furnaces excavated in the vicinity of the Matchless Mine ore body consist of roughly circular areas of burnt earth about 50 cm in diameter and surrounded by the partially dispersed remains of upright stone enclosures (Fig. 9.12). Some of the stones bear adhering slag, while the furnace site itself is strewn with finely broken slag and informal hammer-stones. Also associated with the furnace sites

---

666 In the 18th century Wikar (Kinahan 1980) observed that copper production was valued in terms of livestock, and this was later confirmed by Andersson who reported that "a yard of [copper] beads [was] the regular price of an ox" (1861: 173).

667 Barrow (1801); Kinahan (1980)

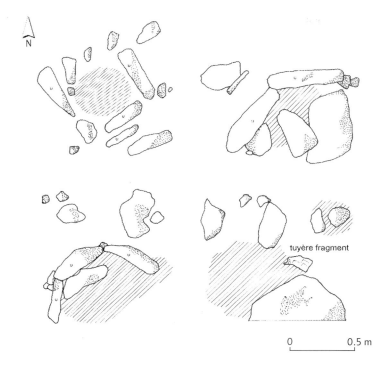

Figure 9.12: Four examples of |Khomas copper smelting furnaces. Areas of burnt earth are hatched; upright stones are marked "u", and slag adhesions are stippled. Note fragment of stone tuyère, lower right furnace.

were fragments of re-usable *tuyères* made from serpentinite schist quarried from the Matchless amphibolite.[668]

The potential yield of |Khomas copper furnaces was determined through a series of experimental smelts.[669] Four successful experimental smelts using an average charge of 7.5 kg of hand-concentrated ore, and up to 10 kg of charcoal, produced an average of 2.1 kg of slag with an average yield of 90.7 g metallic copper

---

668 Kinahan & Vogel (1982)
669 Kettis & Enflo (1996)

Table 9.1: Mineral assay results for hand-concentrated Matchless Mine oxide ore and archaeological slag

Elemental composition ‰	Cu	Pb	Zn	Fe	Mn	Ca
Concentrated ore	67.0	0.583	3.6	72.9	0.870	0.128
Archaeological slag	91.0	0.271	3.8	145.0	0.302	0.160

in the form of small prills trapped within the slag. The furnaces achieved and maintained a working temperature of 1100°C with the use of two bellows. Assay results for archaeological slags from one of the ǀKhomas furnaces are set out in Table 9.1, together with those of hand-concentrated copper oxide ore from the Matchless Mine ore body. The results indicate that a relatively poor separation was achieved by pre-colonial open-hearth smelting, probably due to inadequate fluxing of the ore charge and over-supply of oxygen via the bellows, rather than insufficiently high smelting temperatures.

Averaged mineral assay results for the experimental smelts are summarized in Table 9.2. These results show a relatively low purity of metallic copper and confirm the poor separation indicated by archaeological slag. It is evident from both the archaeological and experimental results that pre-colonial smelting did not result in a fluid slag that could be tapped from the furnace and that it was necessary to extract the copper by breaking up the slag. This is further confirmed by numerous slag processing dumps and by metallurgical analysis of archaeological copper beads from these sites indicating the use of cold hammering rather than annealing.[670] Copper smelting was therefore highly labour intensive and probably did not result in large production of metallic copper. The implication is that copper beads which were exchanged for livestock had a relatively high scarcity value.[671]

---

670 Miller & Kinahan (1992)
671 Kinahan (1980)

Table 9.2: Mineral assay results for experimental metallic copper and slag from Matchless Mine oxide ore

Elemental composition ‰	Cu	Pb	Zn	Fe	Mn	Ca
Copper	520.5	0.38	0.83	2.09	0.1	2.02
Slag	128.2	0.12	2.25	68.28	0.9	13.35

Towards the mid-19th century the ivory trade had begun to wane,[672] and the movement and export of cattle had fallen entirely under the control of European merchants, to provide a secure supply to the Cape market and the British garrison on the island of St Helena. Whaling, once profitable along the Namib Desert coast was also in decline and attention turned to other commercial ventures such as sealing, fish and fish oil production, and guano.[673] Significant guano deposits were discovered on Ichabo Island, about 2 km from the mainland and this led to the brief but highly profitable "Guano Rage" involving hundreds of ships jostling for anchorage and involving thousands of diggers between 1843 and 1845 (Fig. 9.13). Royal Navy vessels, including HMS *Thunderbolt*, arrived at Ichabo in 1845 to maintain order among the diggers who were confined to their ships after sunset.

Several conflicts arose with local desert communities when diggers landed on the shore in search of water and to bury their dead.[674] Items obtained in trade and scavenged from digger's camps occur up to 100 km inland across the dune sea among the Awasib-Gorrasis sites described in Chapter 6. These items include bottle glass, scrap iron, copper wire, sherds of annular ware and a decorated bisque clay pipe bowl, as well as glass beads similar

---

672 Wilmsen (1989)
673 Kinahan, J.H.A. (2000)
674 About thirty graves were found among the hummock dunes at Douglas Bay on the mainland opposite Ichabo Island. When the guano deposits on Ichabo were exhausted, a smaller, shore-based operation was established at Hottentot Bay, 15 km further north (Kinahan & Kinahan 2009).

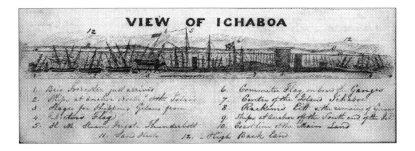

Figure 9.13: Sketch showing ships riding at anchor while collecting guano at Ichabo Island in 1845, viewed from the south-west. From the log of the American brig *Forrester*, January 1845, reproduced by courtesy of Mystic Seaport Museum, G. W. Blunt White Library, Manuscripts Collection, Log 508; see also Kinahan & Kinahan (2009: Figure 3)

to those described from Walvis Bay in Chapter 8. The imported items are associated with indigenous pottery, copper beads and !nara *Acanthosicyos horridus* melon seed cases. The occurrence of coastal material so far inland shows that people were able to remain on the periphery of the European presence and retreat from contact with outsiders if expedient.

In the aftermath of the "Guano Rage", attention shifted to Sandwich Harbour (historically Anixab)[675] where on-shore fish processing operations were established. These involved more sustained contact with local communities. Sandwich Harbour was serviced by a regular traffic of coasting vessels between Walvis Bay and Cape Town, carrying supplies for European traders and missionaries. Large quantities of dried fish[676] and shark oil were exported from Sandwich Harbour in mixed cargos

---

675 Sandwich Harbour first appears on hydrographic charts in 1791, named after its discovery by the whaler James Shields of the *Sandwich* in 1789 (Kinahan, J.H.A. 1991: 5).

676 Shipping registers show that between 1853 and 1880 over 4,000 tons of dried fish was exported from Sandwich Harbour (Kinahan, J.H.A. 1991: Table 1).

including hides and ivory. Eighteenth century contact and trade at Walvis Bay drew people away from Sandwich Harbour but as the pastoral economy began to collapse by the early nineteenth century, increasing numbers of people gravitated to the fishing operations where they gained seasonal employment as general labourers. The growth of the Hurinin underclass of people without livestock represents the onset of a collapse Ω phase, linked to the on-shore operations of fishing enterprises and their need for casual labour.

Figure 9.14 shows the location of the nineteenth century fish processing sites at Sandwich Harbour. These comprised simple wood and iron sheds, with suspended wire lines for drying the fish and tryworks for rendering oil, initially from sharks, until these had been fished out. Storage facilities included the iron barque *Eagle*, beached in 1861 when no longer seaworthy. Fishbone and shellfish middens with indigenous items such as pottery show that local people lived on the site during and between fishing seasons. Figure 9.14 also shows the location of a pastoral encampment about 4 km north of Sandwich Harbour at ǂGorogos. The site, which includes evidence of cattle and small stock, as well as the exploitation of !nara and shellfish, indicates that the pastoral economy was relatively intact in the early phase of fishing operations at Sandwich Harbour. Contemporaneity of the fish processing sites and the ǂGorogos site assemblage is shown by the presence of glass trade beads and shreds of European clothing, including British military tunic buttons.[677]

Towards the end of the nineteenth century, local communities began to complain of frequent abuse and forced labour demands by German traders and officials. When the German Imperial District Officer visited ǂGorogos *en route* to Sandwich Harbour in 1908, he was surprised that although potable water was

---

[677] Kinahan, J.H.A. (1991); buttons from ǂGorogos include those of the 9th (East Norfolk) Regiment of Foot and the 99th (Lanarkshire) Regiment of Foot (Kinahan, J.H.A. 2000: 48).

MEN IN HATS 379

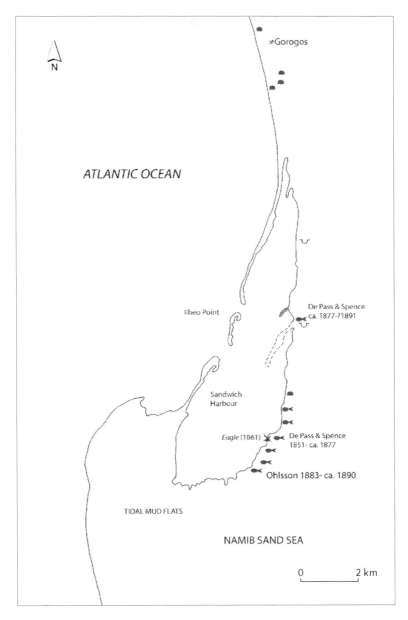

Figure 9.14: Historical fishery sites at Sandwich Harbour in relation to the pastoral settlement at ǂGorogos.

available at springs in the dunes nearby, the site was deserted. It was at about this time, following the imposition of German colonial rule in 1884, that the fisheries at Sandwich Harbour were abandoned. An attempt by the *Deutsch-Westafrikanische Kompanie* in 1888 to establish a meat-canning plant at Sandwich Harbour failed within three years.[678] In the interior, conflict had broken out between the Germans and both Ovaherero and Nama chieftaincies who resisted pressure to enter into "protection" treaties that limited their authority and required their services in military campaigns to secure the pacification of the new colony. Most prominent in this resistance was the Nama leader Hendrik !Nanseb Witbooi, who acquiesced only after a series of campaigns left his forces exhausted and without sufficient arms and ammunition to continue.[679]

Witbooi was an avowed Christian, believing that his divinely ordained mission was to unite the Ovaherero and Nama people against the forces of German colonialism.[680] This ambition was thwarted by colonial strategies of divide-and-rule which left Witbooi isolated and vulnerable when the Ovaherero under Samuel Maharero accepted direct colonial rule. The Ovaherero had been weakened by the erosion of their pastoral wealth through mendacious trading practices and the alienation of land, both sanctioned by the colonial authorities. Since cattle were the *de facto* currency of the indigenous economy and essential for the purchase of supplies and arms, the trade in cattle reduced pastoral livestock holdings as well as control over grazing and water. Moreover, German military posts at watering points effectively cut off independent movement across the desert to trading establishments at the coast.

Links between the interior and the Namib coast were entirely dependent on ox wagon transport following the Bay Road

---

678 Bridgeford (2008: 50)
679 Drechsler (1980)
680 Gugelberger (1984); Hardung (2014)

established by Jonker Afrikaner, and this veritable lifeline was disrupted by the outbreak of the *Rinderpest* (Paramyxovirus) epidemic in 1897.[681] The epidemic devastated Ovaherero herds, resulting in an estimated 90% mortality although a campaign of inoculation saved at least half of settler herds. Nonetheless, a critical shortage of draught oxen for wagon transport left the German settlements in the interior without essential supplies which accumulated at their depots in Swakopmund. The Bay Road was abandoned and the building of a railway line to the interior, described in the next chapter, became an urgent priority. Archaeological traces of the Bay Road are still visible, especially on the waterless section crossing the central Namib Desert from the Swakop River to Walvis Bay.[682]

Where the Bay Road leaves the Swakop River near Riet, the boulder-strewn banks were cleared to a little more than the width of an ox wagon. On the calcrete and gravel plains to the south-west, the spoor of cattle, horses and small stock are still clearly visible, more than 120 years later, together with the impressions of wagon wheels, in a swathe up to 50 m broad. Along the route, items discarded or lost on the trek include remnants of pocket knives, pipe stems and the occasional harmonica reed-plate. Due to the lack of water, there were no outspan places on the route which was probably completed in one – possibly overnight – stage. There is, however, at least one campsite with the abandoned remains of a cast iron cooking pot such as was commonly slung beneath the wagon chassis. Evidence that wagons were guided or accompanied by people from local communities is provided by scattered !nara bushes

---

681 The Bay Road formed part of an extensive network of trading and cattle droving links across the interior (Wilmsen 1989) which served as a major vector for the spread of the epidemic (see Schneider 2012).
682 This section required approximately 16 hours' travel by ox wagon, according to the missionary Carl Hugo Hahn (Dierks 1992: 34) and was probably completed as a single stage.

which probably germinated from seeds carried as provisions.[683]

To conclude this chapter, a broader regional perspective on the early colonial experience of Khoe-speaking pastoralists in the Cape corroborates the documentary evidence of social disintegration, but also shows that some remnant communities were able to reorganize themselves and become a major economic force in Namibia during the whole of the 19th century. In terms of the adaptive cycle model, an economic equilibrium *K* phase, of indigenous and settler communities at the Cape tilted against the Khoe, resulting in their rapid decline, and the onset of a release Ω phase. Escaping beyond the colonial frontier initiated a re-orientation α phase, accompanied by the rise of hierarchical social structures and a significant concentration of political power in the hands of leaders such as Jonker Afrikaner and Hendrik Witbooi, under whom the Orlam experienced a significant growth and expansion *r* phase in their regional influence.

The exposure of the Cape Khoe to intensive interaction with European settlers commenced in the first half of the 17th century; by the end of the 18th century the Afrikaner clan had moved across the Orange River. The chronology of their transition from equilibrium to decline spans only 150 years, and their re-emergence and rise to regional prominence, no more than 100 years. These processes did not occur in synchrony over the region, and the passage of events clearly shows a series of chorological responses in which some pastoral communities were transformed into tributary Orlam clans. At the same time, Ovaherero were expanding in the central part of the country and became bitter rivals to the Orlam, who maintained control over the regional livestock economy in which they were effectively the agents of mercantile capitalism, and their influence was arguably greater

---

683 Describing people on the Namib coast near Walvis Bay setting out into the desert, Alexander (1838) notes that "for provisions they carried at their backs nets containing half-a-dozen of the ripe !naras fruit, which served them for food and water" (Alexander 1967: Vol 2, p. 72).

than that exercised by European traders in their first forays along the Namib Desert coast. Orlam raiders approaching Walvis Bay from the interior were armed horsemen, wearing European clothes and having adopted, selectively, the customs and material culture of early colonial settlers at the Cape. The "hat wearers" were thus able to dominate the regional economy and to resist for almost twenty years Germany's territorial designs in the region.

Endgame?

In 1878, Britain annexed Walvis Bay and a small surrounding enclave of dunes and gravel plains,[684] without doubt one of the bleakest outposts of the Empire. Here, as British Resident Magistrate during the closing years of the nineteenth century, John Cleverly[685] maintained an extensive intelligence network, recording the ever-increasing number of atrocities committed against the indigenous population of the newly proclaimed *Schutzgebiet*, or protectorate of German South West Africa.[686] Cleverly exchanged regular correspondence with Hendrik Witbooi who had established himself at Hornkranz on the desert escarpment, from where he raided the cattle of the Ovaherero with impunity, captured wagon freight on the Bay Road and adeptly outmaneuvered pursuing columns sent by Lieutenant Curt von Francois.

Witbooi is often described as a guerrilla leader of rare genius and his reputation is well earned.[687] But the success of his long campaign must also be weighed against the military ineptitude of his opponents who had no understanding of irregular warfare and were unable to counter him until guided to his Hornkranz encampment by spies in the pay of von Francois. As hostilities escalated, Cleverly heard 200 km away in Walvis Bay, "that Hendri[c]k Wit[te]booi has had a dream that he was fighting with

---

684 Berat (1990)
685 *Journal of the Resident Magistrate, Walvis Bay*
686 Wallace & Kinahan (2011)
687 Wallace & Kinahan (2011)

the Germans. (Henri[c]k's dreams be it noted generally come true)".[688] Witbooi and his most trusted followers survived the attack on 12 April 1893 in which more than eighty people, mainly women and children, were killed.[689] He withdrew to Gibeon in the south, regrouped, forged alliances with other warlords, and continued his resistance until 1905 when, at the age of 75, he was fatally wounded in a battle with German forces at Vaalgras. Throughout, Witbooi kept detailed campaign diaries; a number of these were captured at Hornkranz and later published,[690] while his Bible and riding crop, carried away with other looted items, were eventually repatriated to Namibia in 2019.[691]

---

688 *Journal* 15th July 1891.
689 Drechsler (1980)
690 Gugelberger (1984)
691 Köβler (2019)

X
☙
THE DEATH OF MEMORY

In the late 19th century, little of Africa was left unclaimed by the expansionist powers of Europe, but for the arid and politically unstable region between the British administered Cape Colony, south of the Orange River, and Portuguese Angola, north of the Kunene River (see map inside back cover). The trader Adolph Lüderitz and his agent Heinrich Vogelsang acquired the whole extent of the Namib Desert coast and its immediate hinterland in a series of deliberately fraudulent transactions.[692] Lacking the capital to develop the land, the traders sold it off in 1885 to the newly formed *Deutsche Kolonialgesellschaft für Südwestafrika*, which proceeded to acquire yet further extensive tracts of land. Indigenous leaders were generally contemptuous of German authority, even when Hauptmann Curt von François – introduced in the previous chapter – was dispatched to the new colony in 1889.

A statue of von François still stands near the centre of the modern capital, Windhoek, marking what was claimed to be the

---

692 The traders did not explain to the Nama chieftain with whom they concluded the land purchase that the unit of measurement was not the familiar English mile, equivalent to 1.6 km, but the *geographical* mile, equivalent to 7.4 km (Wallace & Kinahan 2011: 117).

end of his arduous compass march into the interior to establish the centre of European settlement.[693] As we have seen in the previous chapter, however, there was a well constructed and busy wagon road over the entire route from the coast, and the settlement which was to become the colonial seat of government had already been in existence for half a century, established by the Orlam warlords who occupied the central highlands of the territory. Von François' journey of exploration was but one among many strange conceits which characterized the thirty years of German rule. Some were comical, such as urban buildings mimicking the half-timbered Bavarian style, with roofs pitched to shed snow which never fell on the African colony. But the grand design, to establish a Germanic agrarian idyll based on the ideology of settler *lebensraum*,[694] was decidedly less benign. For this to be achieved, the indigenous peoples of Namibia were to surrender all rights to the land and live under the near-feudal authority of colonial rule.

In terms of the adaptive cycle, Ovaherero and Orlam occupation of the prime grazing lands in the central parts of Namibia in the early nineteenth century represented an unstable equilibrium *K* phase. This eventually collapsed under the influence of European traders who at first favoured the Ovaherero as economic and political allies. The rising dominance of European traders in the region was related to the expansion *r* phase of merchant capitalism which first made its presence felt on the Namib coast in the late eighteenth century. Merchant and indigenous economies became entangled in a panarchy of two adaptive cycles; to this was added a third intersecting cycle with the era of German colonial settlement. In this chapter we see that colonial rule in an exceptionally brutal form led to the collapse Ω phase of Ovaherero pastoralism.

---

693 The stone obelisk and commemorative plaque marking the supposed terminus of the compass march has been removed.

694 The concept of *lebensraum* is attributed to Friedrich Ratzel and the *Volkisch* movement which sought an agrarian solution to the increasing urbanization and perceived social decay of Germany at the end of the 19th century (Smith 1980).

THE DEATH OF MEMORY

This chapter has two parts, the first dealing with the Ovaherero revolt and the second with the World War I invasion by an allied British and South African force which brought German rule to an end, and introduced yet another era of colonial rule. My object here is not to provide a comprehensive account of these events for which there is a considerable literature,[695] including a number of general overviews of the early anti-colonial struggle.[696] Instead, my focus is the German genocidal campaign and its consequences for the Ovaherero, with particular attention to archaeological evidence which sheds new light on some key moments in the Ovaherero revolt that are usually considered only on the basis of the archival documentary record. A similar examination of the Nama revolt after 1904 would certainly provide equivalent examples,[697] although that is beyond the scope of this study.

First, we consider direct evidence of Ovaherero settlement in the east of the country where the revolt was finally extinguished, and then turn to both direct and indirect evidence of the Ovaherero experience as captives and slave labourers in the Namib Desert. The second part of the chapter focuses on archaeological evidence of the Allied invasion campaign in which the Namib Desert presents an exceptionally well-preserved theatre of conflict in World War I. Here again, events that are generally understood on the sole basis of documentary records, left on the desert landscape physical traces that cast new light on the events of this period.

They dig no wells[698]

The southward expansion of the Ovaherero mentioned in the previous chapter was probably a response to conditions of

---

695 See Bley (1996); Drechsler (1980); Wallace & Kinahan (2011)
696 e.g. Wallace & Kinahan (2011)
697 Drechsler (1980)
698 One commonly held justification for the appropriation of Ovaherero land is expressed in Gustav Frenssen's (1906) colonial era novel *Peter Moors Fahrt nach Südwest: Ein Feldzugbericht*: "These blacks have deserved death before God and man ... because they have built no houses and dug no wells", cited in Baer (2018: 57).

increasing aridity between 1300 and 1800 AD, described in Chapter 5 as the Little Ice Age. By the mid-19th century there were no less than five loosely allied Ovaherero chieftaincies established in central Namibia. This confederation had developed into a number of permanent settlement nodes towards the end of the century and the advent of German colonial rule.[699] As the threat posed by Orlam cattle-raiders began to decline, the Ovaherero came to play a central role in long distance cattle droving between the Kalahari and trading posts on the Namib Desert coast. It was this very network of interlinked routes connecting essential waterholes that also ensured the rapid and catastrophic spread of the *Rinderpest* epidemic described in the previous chapter. Cattle production was the economic basis of Ovaherero political organization and the decimation of the herds brought poverty and famine, thus weakening chiefly authority based in large part on wealth in livestock.

In these circumstances a combination of factors led to the outbreak of the Ovaherero revolt in 1904.[700] German traders had extended credit to Ovaherero chiefs who became irreversibly indebted, losing first their remaining cattle and then large swathes of land to speculators, so that even as their herds began to recover in the aftermath of the epidemic, they no longer controlled the land on which they were temporarily allowed to remain. Missionaries and the colonial governor at the time, Theodor Leutwein, attempted unsuccessfully to halt the alienation of Ovaherero land. As the authority of Ovaherero leaders declined, settlers and military alike began to demand all the land of the Ovaherero, often using the specious argument that a people who built no houses and dug no wells did not husband the land and therefore did not deserve to retain it; they were to make way for German colonialism.[701]

---

699 Gewald (1999)
700 Bridgeman (1981)
701 For a detailed discussion of Ovaherero landuse and the use of wells, see Henrichsen (1997)

Hostilities broke out first at Okahandja, near the settlement of the paramount chief Samuel Maharero at Osona, and quickly spread to other centres. Leutwein launched an offensive campaign but continued to negotiate in the hope of a settlement that would preserve the Ovaherero role in an emergent colonial economy. The colonial forces suffered a number of humiliating reverses[702] and Berlin summarily rescinded Leutwein's military authority, dispatching General Lothar von Trotha to prosecute the campaign.[703] For several months while German forces assembled, the Ovaherero havered; failing to press the advantage they had held until then, they gathered at Hamakari under the shadow of the Waterberg. Using an encircling strategy and supported by field artillery, von Trotha's army routed the Ovaherero, forcing the survivors to retreat into the Omaheke, a vast area of thorn-scrub on the margins of the Kalahari. The pursuing German forces caught up with the Ovaherero on the Omuramba Eiseb and again put them to flight with a decisive artillery barrage. By late 1904 the offensive campaign was over, one contemporary observer reporting that the routes followed by the fugitives were littered with dead Ovaherero and their livestock, and the waterpoints, poisoned by the Germans, were choked with corpses.[704]

In October 1904 at Ozombu zo Vindimba, about 25 km northeast of present-day Otjinene, von Trotha issued his infamous *Vernichtungsbefehl*, the extermination order in which he pledged to kill all Ovaherero, men, women and children, whether armed

---

702 see Drechsler (1980); Burden (2017) reviews a number of detailed contemporary newspaper reports on these incidents.
703 Lothar von Trotha, 1848–1920, was a Prussian officer and devotee of von Clausewitz's concept of Total War which aimed not just to defeat the opponent militarily but to destroy their capacity to resist. It is unsurprising therefore that he was known among Ovaherero as *omuzepe*, 'the killer' or alternatively *omukorokohe womaṭupa* 'skeleton killer' (Katjivena 2020: 23; see also Becker 2020).
704 Rohrbach (1907); Katjivena (2020) presents a first hand account of these events.

or not, and to drive any survivors into the waterless Kalahari.[705] Although the revolt and the genocide that followed are well documented, little attention has been paid to the landscape setting in which these events occurred and the possibility that this might shed further light on Ovaherero settlement and land-use at the end of the nineteenth century. Archaeological evidence from the Omuramba Eiseb shows that contrary to the opinion of settlers, the Ovaherero did indeed dig wells and did so on a hitherto unsuspected scale. This evidence corroborates historical accounts of centralized political organization among the Ovaherero and points to a sophisticated land and water management system.[706]

Although German military maps record waterpoints in the vicinity of settlements from which Ovaherero fugitives were evicted during the campaign, these reflect only a small fraction of the wells that existed along the Omuramba Eiseb at that time. Figure 10.1 shows the distribution of wells indicated on the relevant campaign map,[707] together with a far larger number located in the course of field survey and analysis of satellite remote sensing data, which indicated wells of two broad types. First, a field survey mainly concentrated around Otjinene located a large number of shaft wells between 1.8 and 2.0 m in diameter and up to 6 m deep. These wells, of which many have detailed oral histories, date mainly to the Ovaherero re-occupation of the area some decades after the cessation of hostilities, and reflect on the existence of a highly domesticated landscape, intimately linked with social history. The wells are in this sense documents of settlement history in this area, imprinted on the stories attached to the landscape and its features,[708] adding significantly to its importance.[709]

---

705 Hull (2005); Gewald (1999: 172)
706 Henrichsen (1997)
707 Deutsch-Südwestafrika Vorläufige Ausgabe Blatt 17 Gobabis, Bearbeitet in der Topographischen Abteilung Landesaufnahme Berlin November 1910.
708 Gewald (1999)
709 Lindholm (2006)

In contrast to the shaft wells just described are those of a second type, comprising numerous large wells. These, up to 50 m in diameter and 3 to 5 m deep, were revealed by further survey of a more extensive area within the Omuramba Eiseb basin. The large wells are circular in shape and, in addition to their shape and size, are also characterized by an outer spoil-heap up to 4 m in height, increasing the outer diameter of the feature as a whole to as much as 140 m. Further confirming that these are artificial rather than natural features are steps cut into the sides of the excavation, grooves worn by ropes used to haul water, and passages cut through the spoil-heaps to bring livestock to water. The approximately 250 wells shown in Figure 10.1 probably represent an underestimate of about 20%, allowing for low visibility of some features due to erosion and bush encroachment.

The bed of such well excavations contains no vegetation, while the spoil-heap usually supports a relatively dense growth of trees and shrubs, thus presenting a characteristic doughnut shaped feature that is plainly visible on satellite imagery. In the generally featureless Omaheke landscape, the wells are almost impossible to see until stumbled upon in the dense bush. Natural features of similar shape but of clearly natural origin, occur in the Otjinene area as dolines, where calcrete surface layers are undermined by fluctuations in near-surface groundwater. These have no spoil-heap, however, and the doline itself usually has a dense thicket of vegetation within rather than surrounding it.

Because the large wells appear to pre-date the shaft wells there seem to be two broad phases of water management on the Omuramba Eiseb. Whereas the shaft wells can water only small numbers of livestock at the same time, the large wells could be used for co-ordinated watering of large herds. Shaft wells, on the other hand, appear from the oral history associated with them to have been the property of specific individuals and were probably excavated and maintained by the members of a single family. There are no comparable records for the large wells which therefore probably pre-date the Ovaherero revolt; these

392 NAMIB

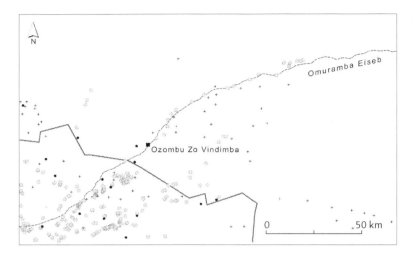

Figure 10.1a: The distribution of wells in the vicinity of Ozombu zo Vindimba on the Omuramba Eiseb, located during archaeological field survey (grey circles). Also shown are permanent wells (black dots) and temporary wells (crosses) as indicated on German colonial military maps. The solid line indicates the boundary of the settler farming area. Map data from Deutsch-Südwestafrika Vorläufige Ausgabe Blatt 17 Gobabis, Bearbeitet in der Topographischen Abteilung Landesaufnahme Berlin November 1910, with additional data from Lindholm (2006).

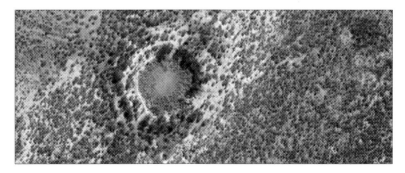

Figure 10.1b: Aerial view of a typical large well feature on the Omuramba Eiseb, in this instance having an external diameter of 140 m.

wells represent a significant investment of labour and their size alone suggests a relatively centralized polity. The excavation, maintenance and use of large wells therefore points to a level of organization and authority above that of the family and clan in the management of grazing access and water use. This evidence concurs with historical accounts cited earlier for the existence of several loosely allied Ovaherero chieftaincies in central Namibia, one of them being centred at Otjinene.

The distribution of wells in Figure 10.1a shows a major concentration of shaft wells to the south-west of Ozombu zo Vindimba. Many of these wells are higher than the main course of the Omuramba Eiseb and suggest that perched water in the unsaturated zone lying above the water table, could be accessed within this area which also contains the most productive grazing.[710] Such wells probably mark the area of greatest settlement density and may have been used for domestic water supply. In contrast, the largest wells lie mainly along the course of the Omuramba Eiseb to the north-east; these were probably on open pastures on the periphery of the main area of settlement and suggest that cattle were kept at stock posts and watered at communal wells. This would indicate a pattern of dispersed grazing similar to that described in Chapters 7 and 8. Figure 10.1a also shows the eastern boundary of settler farmland allocated in many instances to demobilized German military personnel. The farms clearly occupy the area with the most reliable water and pasture, the former centre of Ovaherero settlement in this region.

Considering the fact that settler farms in this area were awarded as early as 1910, it is clear that the acquisition of land for settler farming under the policy of *lebensraum* was a major factor driving the German campaign against the Ovaherero. This was in addition to the large tracts of land already acquired by state sponsored agricultural enterprises, a process which was well underway in 1896 under the administration of Theodor

---

710 Mendelsohn et al. (2002)

Figure 10.2: Enamelled sign erected by the *Deutschesfarmgesellschaft* in the ǃKhomas region of central Namibia, stating that it is a punishable offence to leave the gate open.

Leutwein.[711] Among measures adopted to break down "tribal cohesion", people were removed by decree from large parts of central Namibia,[712] to make way for the extensive land-holdings granted to the *Deutschesfarmgesellschaft*[713] (see Figure 10.2). A remarkable illustration of this strategy is apparent in the fact that while the German colonial *Kriegskarte* or war maps, published at the outbreak of the Ovaherero Revolt in 1904 clearly indicate the areas occupied by tribal groups throughout the country, there is no trace of them on the maps issued by the *Topographischen Abteilung Landesaufnahme* Berlin in November 1910; the indigenous people of the colony had been literally expunged from the landscape.

Profound social consequences followed the expulsion of the Ovaherero, and these extended beyond the mere re-drawing of land

---

711 De Vries (1978: 191); Leutwein (1906)
712 Gann & Duignan (1977: 75)
713 Esterhuyse (1968: 178); Sarkin (2011); Wallace & Kinahan (2011)

ownership boundaries. Ovaherero society and land-use centred on the authority of local chiefs whose legitimacy was derived from descent in specific lineages which represented a line of continuity from ancestral figures and carried responsibilities towards present and future generations. These responsibilities extended over the entire landscape via an intricate web of social integration and interdependence.[714] Ovaherero chiefs were expected to be great men *omuhona*, showing the same generosity and compassion as the supreme deity *Mukuru*, the overseer of all human affairs.[715] Now, the Ovaherero chief was replaced by a new *beau idéal* with essentially opposite attributes: the settler farmer.[716] The former communal landscape of Ovaherero society was at once divided into bounded freehold properties, with the settler farmer emerging as an almost mythic hero figure who exemplified individuality and independence, in a pioneering spirit that was given to accumulation rather than distribution, exclusivity rather than inclusivity, and rigid notions of private ownership as opposed to customs of socially negotiated access to resources. Religious sanctions governing the decisions of the chief gave way to an avowedly secular *weltanschauung* ruled by the provisions of colonial law.

In addition to the social consequences of land appropriation there were fundamental ecological consequences, involving a shift in the nature of the pastoral environment that remains visible more than a century later. Pre-colonial pastoral range management as described in Chapter 7 involved intensive localized exploitation of ephemeral pastures during rest and growth periods for perennial dry season pastures, following a cycle that directly and cumulatively affected key ecosystem components. Pastoral settlement and land-use exert various dynamic forces on

---

714 The social organization and land use system of the Ovahimba described in Chapter 7 provides some indication of Ovaherero settlement and land management practices as they may have existed in the central parts of the country at the time of the revolt.
715 Crandall (2000: 187-8); Kavari (2001)
716 see Zollmann (2020)

rangeland environments, such as, for example, in the construction of livestock enclosures which involves large-scale consumption of timber, creating a piosphere of reduced vegetation cover that is maintained by continuous browsing of palatable species and harvesting of re-growth from coppiced trees. Also, the concentration of phosphorus through dung accumulation in livestock enclosures influenced re-growth in abandoned settlement sites, thus promoting an open parkland vegetation structure combined with a grass cover species mosaic reflecting variations in soil nutrient levels.

Under the relatively passive range management imposed by colonial land-use practices, livestock are not actively herded and graze selectively on highly palatable grasses in fenced paddocks. This system promotes succession of less palatable species as well as leading to dense thickening of woody vegetation which markedly reduces the area available for pasture. Resulting mainly from a drastic reduction in the number of people associated with livestock production, colonial range management practices exclude consumption of timber for construction of livestock enclosures, building and fuel. As a result of dense vegetation thickening under colonial range management practices, grazing area is greatly reduced, and access to pasture sometimes requires mechanical clearing of cut-lines, or industrial-scale clearing to restore the optimal parkland structure of pre-colonial land management. This comparison illustrates the differing impacts on semi-arid savanna vegetation under two alternative land management regimes. Pre-colonial and colonial pastoral strategies are both therefore effective forces of niche construction. However, they are not entirely ecological in character, resting as they do on two fundamentally different cultural ideologies.

Events following the military defeat of the Ovaherero at Otjinene and elsewhere in the colony show a clear shift in the nature of the German campaign, from defeat and land appropriation, to genocide. The officer tasked with the pursuit of the Ovaherero into the Omaheke noted:

It was a policy which was equally gruesome as senseless, to hammer the people so much, we could have still saved many of them and their rich herds, if we had pardoned and taken them up again, they had been punished enough. I suggested this to General von Trotha but he wanted their total extermination.[717]

One reflection of the impact these actions had on Ovaherero society is found in the widespread adoption of Christianity. As shown in Chapter 9, missionary evangelization enjoyed little success in the nineteenth century, when Ovaherero were economically predominant. The catastrophe visited upon them by the German military offensive so fragmented Ovaherero communities and weakened their customary institutions that large numbers turned to the Christian faith as a means to understand the dramatic change in their circumstances.[718] Ovaherero identity and institutions were to be gradually rebuilt in the decades following the genocide.[719]

The settler occupation of core grazing areas that were essential to transhumant pastoralism in the Otjinene area was only one example of a widespread strategy of land expropriation that rendered the Ovaherero unable to support themselves through livestock production. The military campaign concluded with a series of attempts to coax scattered communities to assembly points in central Namibia, sometimes using the humanitarian efforts of missionaries who provided food, clothing and rudimentary

---

717 From von Estorff (1979: 117), cited in Silvester and Gewald (2003: xxi). Grawe (2019) has argued that Von Trotha had a free hand in the campaign against the Ovaherero, and was shielded from public criticism of his extreme measures by the Prusso-German General Staff who were to a large extent complicit in the genocide.
718 An illustration of this is provided by the execution of Zacharias Kukuri, *omuhona* of Otjosazu who was transported to the gallows on an ox-cart, and remarked somewhat drily to the missionary Meier who accompanied him "Muhonge, like Elias [i.e. Elijah] I too travel to heaven in a wagon [i.e. chariot]" (Gewald 1999: 198).
719 Krüger and Henrichsen (1996) add that elaborate burial practices among the Ovaherero also contributed to the re-establishment of traditional structures.

medical attention. Missionary accounts record that many fugitives were so weakened by the journey that they quickly succumbed. In reality, the assembly points were holding pens where leaders and combatants were identified for summary execution, and those found fit for work were assigned to settler farms[720] and construction projects. Although many escaped to the north and east, this final phase of the war effectively destroyed the fabric of Ovaherero society.

We now turn to archaeological evidence concerning the mass transportation from 1904 of Ovaherero prisoners across the Namib Desert to the German port settlement of Swakopmund.[721] Prisoners were conveyed to the coast on the narrow-gauge railway commissioned in 1902 as an alternative to ox wagon transport following the *Rinderpest* epidemic. Many Ovaherero and other people were involved in the construction of the railway as forced labour. Following the war, however, the basis of this involvement changed in that people were not merely providing their labour; they had in effect become the property of the colonial state and were therefore slaves, kept in confinement and deprived of all recourse. In this sense, the labour needs of the German colonial economy were based on slavery rather than coercion, and this distinguishes it among African colonies controlled by other world powers at the time.[722]

The narrow-gauge railway was the essential link between the Namib Desert coast and the interior, reaching both Windhoek

---

720 Katjivena (2020) presents a unique description of a young Ovaherero woman's experience of this.

721 Known in Otjiherero as Otjozondjii, "a place of shells", Jekura Kavari (27.01.2020, in litt.).

722 A detailed study of indigenous slavery in colonial and pre-colonial Namibia by Zollmann (2010) does not recognize this particular shift in the social relations of labour under German rule. However, Muschalek (2020) describes a labour system in which indigenous people were treated as productive assets of the colonial state and distributed among settler farmers and other enterprises without respect to family relations or juvenile dependency.

THE DEATH OF MEMORY 399

and the northern mining area around Otavi.[723] The railway provided an efficient and punctual service, with regular stations and sidings to provide water and fuel for the locomotives. Little remains of the railway line in the Namib Desert beyond its earth embankments and the ruins of some sidings. Found occasionally along the railway line are coal pellets approximately the size and shape of a slightly flattened goose egg; in the absence of local fuel, these were shipped from Germany where they were manufactured from high quality coal waste processed through a mandrel press, resulting in a compact, smooth surfaced pellet with a clearly visible lateral seam. One siding, Welwitsch, is situated on the desert plains between the Khan and Swakop Rivers. When the line was decommissioned in 1913, Welwitsch Siding was sold to a salvage contractor to be entirely removed,[724] and although this instruction was dutifully observed, revealing evidence of station life remains on the site.

Figure 10.3a shows a view of the siding after its completion in 1902 by Hauptmann Pophal, when it was praised as a fine example in the *Gebäudezusammenfassung der Kaiserliche Eisenbahnkommissariat*. The photograph is carefully posed to represent the ideal of cleanliness and order espoused by the colonial project.[725] However, this intended image is belied by the archaeological evidence shown in the accompanying site plan. At Welwitsch Siding the earth embankments of the railway are flanked by a broad surficial deposit of cinders and coal waste, with the remains of discarded lubricant containers and other refuse relating to the maintenance of the locomotives. Beyond

---

723 Bravenboer & Rusch (1997)
724 The siding was sold to a certain Herr Küstner of Swakopmund for a sum of 200 Marks with the condition that the purchaser should demolish the buildings entirely and remove all trace of them, so that *"keine Spuren oder Übereste auf die Bebauung hindeuten"* (National Archives of Namibia ZBU 2197 L.3.4.A.).
725 Carefully posed colonial photography (e.g. Hartmann et al. 1999) consistently exemplifies the German cliché *Ordnung muss sein* (litt. 'There must be order').

400 NAMIB

Figure 10.3a: Contemporary view of Welwitsch Siding. Image 01870 reproduced by courtesy of the National Archives of Namibia.

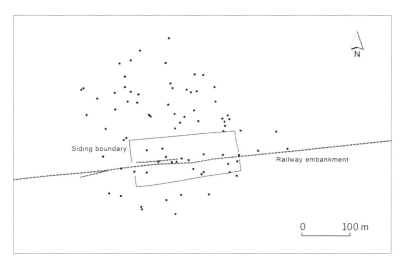

Figure 10.3b: Archaeological plan of Welwitsch Siding showing bottle dumps.

the perimeter of the siding which is marked by an irregular rectangle of anchor stones for an enclosing fence, are forty-four refuse dumps comprising pits and open scatters which range between 1 m and 3 m in diameter.

The dumps lie within easy walking distance of the siding; they are randomly scattered and there is no indication of orderly garbage disposal. Refuse from the dumps is completely dominated by thousands of green glass bottles, such that in archaeological terms, Welwitsch, like many other stations along the narrow-gauge line, is characterized by alcohol consumption rather than by any other activity.[726] It is of particular interest that although the railway line project was overseen by a railway construction unit or *Eisenbahnkompanie* of the German army and used throughout the period of the Ovaherero revolt for the transport of troops and matériel, there is little indication of a military presence beyond a few cartridge cases, carbine clips and food cans. Taken as a whole, the evidence from Welwitsch Siding seems to suggest the transport of a poorly trained and undisciplined military force to the Namibian interior.[727]

A burial located on the desert plains approximately 700 m south of the site adds a further dimension to the archaeology of Welwitsch Siding.[728] Although it was somewhat disturbed and less than complete, a bias in the preservation of skeletal parts suggests that the individual was buried in an extended position and lying on the right side in a shallow grave. Some machine-stitched shoe-leather and two pine boards found with the remains indicate an historical date and the possibility that the burial may have been marked with a wooden cross, implying that the individual was

---

726 Ovaherero fugitives were able to recognize German military bivouac sites from the evidence of discarded bottles (Katjivena 2020).
727 See Gewald (1999: 141ff); Lau (1989) has shown that a large proportion of German troops shipped to Namibia were unfit for service.
728 The Husab burial was unintentionally exposed by earthmoving machinery in the course of civil engineering works and the analysis reported here is based on surviving fragments of the skeleton.

either a baptized Christian or was afforded a Christian burial.[729] On the basis of standard criteria for the determination of sex and age,[730] the skeleton is that of a young adult male, between 21 and 25 years of age, showing no obvious signs of perimortem pathology or injury.

Supporting this inference, the sciatic notch of the right pelvic bone had an internal angle of 52°, as is characteristic of the adult male, with further confirmation from the broad medial ridge and the absence of sub-pubic concavity. Male characteristics of the cranial bones included the strongly developed mental eminence of the mandible, and the pronounced mastoid process on the surviving left temporal. The frontal cranium also exhibited further strongly male characteristics, including a sharply defined supra-orbital margin, and pronounced glabella. Full dental eruption, including M^3 and M_3 shows the individual to be over the age of 21 years, while attrition of the occlusal surfaces of the teeth indicates an age of 20 to 24 years for the maxilliary dentition, and 18 to 22 years on the basis of the mandibular dentition.[731] This agrees with the evidence of epiphyseal fusion pointing to an age at death of between 20 and 25 years, on the basis of the unfused sternal epiphysis of the clavicle.[732] Skeletal height of the individual calculated from the absolute length of the femur is 1.55 ± 0.24 m. Estimated living stature, obtained by adding 0.105 m to skeletal height[733] is therefore 1.66 m.

Evidence of cultural identity is shown in this case by dental modification involving deliberate removal or ablation of the central mandibular incisors (Fig. 10.4a), the specifically Ovaherero practice[734] known as *okuhiua*.[735] On this basis the Welwitsch Siding

---

[729] In traditional pre-Christian context the dead were buried in the flexed rather than extended position (Kinahan 2014b).
[730] Following Buikstra & Ubelaker (1994)
[731] Lovejoy (1985)
[732] White & Folkens (2005)
[733] Lundy & Feldesman (1987)
[734] Briedenhann & van Reenen (1985)
[735] Virimuje Kahuure (pers comm.)

individual shares the same Ovaherero cultural identity as the skeletons from Khorixa-ams described in Chapter 7. Given that tooth mutilation was performed at puberty as part of initiation rites, it is significant that the individual from Welwitsch Siding was both an initiated man and at the same time possibly Christian, thus reflecting the collapse and disintegration of Ovaherero society and religious practices during the 1904 revolt. This combination of traditional and Christian attributes suggests that he came to Welwitsch Siding following the revolt rather than some years earlier as a labourer on the construction of the narrow-gauge railway.

Aged in his mid-20s, the young man from Welwitsch Siding would have been initiated before the outbreak of the war when Ovaherero society and cultural practices were still intact; he came of age and it is therefore likely that as a healthy individual he would have served as a warrior before falling captive to the Germans. At some stage in this process he would have been Christianized or formed part of a group that fell under missionary influence. His death at Welwitsch Siding, probably en route to Swakopmund, may have been the result of illness, exhaustion or starvation since the skeletal remains show no evidence of traumatic injury. It is noteworthy that in spite of the fact that at least 100,000 people died in the course of the colonial genocide[736], these are the only documented *in situ* skeletal remains of an Ovaherero captive from the 1904 revolt.[737] The skeleton from Welwitsch Siding exemplifies at the level of an individual person the broader collapse Ω phase of the indigenous economy.

At Swakopmund, captives were placed in a concentration camp and put to work on the development of the town as well as stevedoring and other tasks.[738] With this source of labour available

---

736 Drechsler (1980)
737 Faber-Jonker (2018) describes the repatriation of cranial material exported to Germany for use in racial science research at the time of the genocide; see also Shigwedha (2018).
738 The site of the concentration camp at Swakopmund, now a luxury residential area, overlooks the cemetery where prisoners were buried.

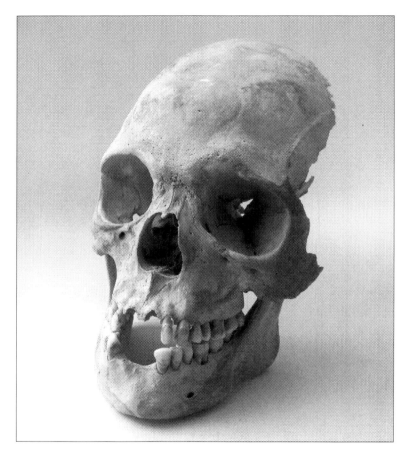

Figure 10.4a: Frontal view of cranium and mandible from Welwitsch Siding burial, showing *okuhiua* ablation of lower incisors.

the town grew rapidly in the years immediately following the suppression of the Ovaherero revolt. Conditions were extremely harsh in concentration camps at Swakopmund and elsewhere, most particularly on Shark Island at Lüderitzbucht (Angra Pequena, historically !Namiǂnūs). Captives had virtually no shelter and even with clothing, food and rudimentary medical attention provided mainly by missionaries, the rate of mortality was extremely high. One missionary eyewitness observed that:

Figure 10.4b: Narrow gauge railway transportation of prisoners under German military guard. Image reproduced by courtesy of the National Archives of Namibia

> They were placed behind double rows of barbed wire fencing, [...] and housed in pathetic [*jammerlichen*] structures constructed out of simple sacking and planks [...]. From early morning until late at night, [...] they had to work under the clubs of raw overseers [*Knutteln roher Aufseher*], until they broke down [*zusammenbrachen*]. [...]. Like cattle hundreds were driven to death and like cattle they were buried.[739]

Data from the cemeteries of Swakopmund are summarized in Table 10.1. Approximately 4,500 prisoners were interred between the end of the Ovaherero revolt in 1904 and the closure of the

---

739 Silvester and Gewald (2003: xxi), citing from Heinrich Vedder documents, Evangelical Lutheran Church in the Republic of Namibia (ELCRN), V. Ortschroniken Swakopmund, translated by J-B Gewald.

concentration camps in 1908.[740] Their graves lie outside the European cemetery which contains sixty-four graves from the same period. Based on these numbers, prisoner deaths were therefore about seventy times higher than European deaths, the majority of which were soldiers from the Swakopmund *kaserne*, or barracks. More than half of the soldiers buried at Swakopmund during this period died in 1905, the year immediately following the mass arrival of Ovaherero prisoners. Disease was rife among the prisoners, and dysentery, being effectively transmitted by direct physical contact, probably spread among the German soldiery[741] as a result of their sexual abuse of female captives.[742]

Table 10.1: Comparison of settler and prisoner interment rates at Swakopmund, 1904–08.

Cemetery	Graves	Burials/year
Settlers	64	13
Prisoners	4,500 (est.)	900 (est.)

Ovaherero mortalities at Swakopmund were meticulously recorded; death certificates from the German medical authorities contained a pre-printed statement to the effect that death was the result of *"Entkräftung und Entbehrungen"*, literally, exhaustion and starvation, indicating that it was intended for the prisoners to be worked to death. Occasional annotations indicate other causes of death including scurvy and heart failure, its likely result. While cause of death among captives points to the consequences of sustained deprivation during and after the revolt, data from the official camp records also cast further light on the situation at Swakopmund. The fact that women outnumbered men among

---

740 Ovaherero burials at Swakopmund are typically Christian, being elongate in plan and east-west in orientation.
741 Gewald (1999); Muschalek (2020); Silvester & Gewald (2003)
742 Baer (2020) has commented on the role of alcohol consumption in the historical record of sexual violence under German colonial rule.

the dead, shows that captives were not exclusively combatants. This, together with a numerical preponderance of individuals over the age of twenty years, suggests that Ovaherero were sent to Swakopmund not simply as prisoners of war, but as labourers (see Fig. 10.5a).[743]

The trajectory of growth in Swakopmund during the same period is illustrated in Figure 10.5b which is based on an analysis of 403 documented building projects on surveyed residential, commercial and government properties. The data show a peak in building following the end of the revolt and the arrival of captives in Swakopmund. This is followed by a steep decline in building activity after the closure of the concentration camps in 1908. The buildings dating from the aftermath of the revolt have given Swakopmund an enduring German character and many examples have been preserved as national monuments or listed as structures of outstanding architectural and historical significance (Fig. 10.6).[744] The use of slave labour is not acknowledged at the national monuments themselves,[745] and the buildings are generally perceived as showing the energy, initiative and civilizing benefits of colonial rule.

---

743 Data from Werner Hillebrecht (2020, in litt.) Gefangenen-Todesstatistik Swakopmund, manuscript in progress.
744 A catalogue of national monuments (Vogt 2004) reflects a strong bias towards the memorialization of colonial sites, without remarking on the absence of sites relating to indigenous resistance to colonial rule. See also Silvester and Gewald (2003: xiv) and Tunbridge and Ashworth (1996).
745 A monument erected by indigenous groups at the prisoner cemetery in Swakopmund states: "Nama and Ovaherero Genocide Monument 1904–08, in honour and loving memory of thousands of Ovaherero and Nama men, women and children who perished at this sacred site. They died in concentration camps of hunger, slave labour, sexual abuse, disease, fatigue and adverse weather conditions at the hands of German soldiers. Their remains were buried in shallow graves by fellow inmates. Our ancestral lands and restorative justice remain the inspiration for our struggle today, tomorrow and forever. Inaugurated by the late Dr Kuaima Riruako (Ovaherero Paramount Chief) and the late Chief Christian Zerua (Zerua Royal House) 31.03.2007."

Figure 10.5a: Female prisoners hauling cargo from the jetty in Swakopmund after the Ovaherero revolt. Image in public domain, copied from https://en.wikipedia.org/wiki/File:Erichsen_slave_labour_p._83_v2.jpg

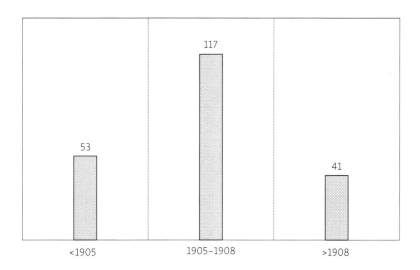

Figure 10.5b: Frequency of building projects in Swakopmund before and after the Ovaherero revolt, based on data from the records of the Namibian Institute of Architects, E. Schoedder and K. Brandt.

Figure 10.6: The Hohenzollern Building in Swakopmund, a neo-baroque relic of the German colonial era erected immediately after the Ovaherero revolt, and a proclaimed national monument. National Monument proclamation in Official Gazette 4786 No. AG 109 (1983).

After the closure of the concentration camps in 1908, indigenous people were subject to stringent controls over their movement and were required to wear numbered metal tags indicating the magisterial district in which they lived and worked, allocated to government and civilian enterprises[746] (Fig. 10.7). The military campaigns to counter the Ovaherero and subsequent Nama insurrections resulted in large-scale population displacement, and many people sought to avoid continued mistreatment by moving to Walvis Bay.[747] To counter this loss of productive labour, in 1907 the German Governor Friedrich von Lindequist[748] established a *cordon sanitaire* around the British enclave at Walvis Bay, creating a zone in which free movement of indigenous people was forbidden, and thereby attempting to prevent escape of the labour needed by the settler colony.

The combination of documentary and archaeological evidence presented here adds a material and landscape dimension to historical appraisals of the 1904 Ovaherero revolt and its aftermath. The analysis of wells and water infrastructure in the Otjinene area described in the first part of this chapter demonstrates that settler demands for *lebensraum* were motivated by a false narrative regarding indigenous land-use. The appropriation of core settlement and grazing areas, as exemplified by the data from Otjinene, effectively destroyed the economic basis of Ovaherero society. The enslavement and transportation of captives to centres such as Swakopmund greatly accelerated the colonial project, as seen from the analysis of building activity, which was accompanied by high rates of prisoner mortality. These observations contribute a degree of materiality that has been notably absent from critical analysis of the German colonial period.

---

746 A group of 52 graves at the Khan Mine near Welwitsch Siding probably represents captive labourers.
747 Gewald (1999) describes the recruitment of Ovaherero fugitives at Walvis Bay for work on the South African gold mines, while Katjivena (2020) relates an unusual but temporary escape to safety in north-western Namibia.
748 This was gazetted as a "game reserve" (Bridgeford 2008), suggesting that its real purpose had to be concealed.

Figure 10.7: Numbered metal pass tag, length 5 cm, to be worn about the neck. The tag bears the crown of the German Emperor Kaiser Wilhelm II and the name of the magisterial district, Swakopmund, in which the wearer is permitted to reside.

Fire on the desert[749]

With the outbreak of World War I in 1914, Germany assumed that overseas possessions would not be involved in the conflict, and with troops thinly scattered, was therefore unprepared for an invasion of the colony. Although an allied British and South African land assault across the Orange River was quickly repulsed by the German colonial forces, this was soon followed by an almost unopposed landing at Lüderitz which led to the capture of the railway linking the port with the interior, and a rapid northward

---

749 From the title of a paper by Saunders and Faulkner (2010) describing the archaeology of the contemporaneous Arab Revolt.

advance. Under the command of General Louis Botha[750] a second bridgehead was established when Swakopmund was captured after a naval barrage destroyed radio communication with Berlin. Botha massed his troops and engaged the German forces with a series of tactical moves that resulted in their defeat and unconditional surrender. Like so many that had gone before them, the men under Botha's command were confronted by what seemed to be "one of the most awful scenes of desolation to be found on the face of the globe.... For miles and miles it stretches, a great empty expanse of grey plain, with a thin sandy surface crust covered with small pebbles", marching over "dreary sandy wastes out of which arise, in a variety of heights and a confusion of order, unscaleable granite rocks of massive proportion, intermingled with smaller series of serrated barren ridges. Not a drop of water, not a sign of life". In the words of a war correspondent attached to Botha's staff, the campaign was "...one prolonged wallow in the dessicated dregs of an abominable hell".[751]

There was a considerable disparity in the size of the German and Allied forces due to the fact that following the Ovaherero and subsequent Nama revolt, indigenous groups largely declined to honour the German "protection treaties" under which they were required to furnish both men under arms as well as support units when called upon. The South African component of the invasion force was in contrast almost entirely made up of volunteers and these were supported by an estimated 30,000 further volunteers of primarily African labourers and support personnel drawn from British southern African colonies and possessions.[752] Within the German colony, disaffected communities either engaged the German forces in skirmishing and distracted their attention, or joined the invasion force as scouts, thus contributing valuable

---

750 General Louis Botha, a renowned guerrilla leader in the Anglo Boer War (1899–1902), was the Prime Minister of South Africa when he led the 1915 invasion of the German colony.
751 Comments cited by Steyn (2018: 224–6).
752 MacGregor & Goldbeck (2014)

THE DEATH OF MEMORY 413

Figure 10.8: Ovaherero scouts attached to General Botha's invasion force. The man on the left, identified as Wilhelm, wears a British-issue tunic, while Isaac, to the right, wears a German-issue tunic. Image used with permission Library, Parliament of South Africa, 18891 (66).

local knowledge linked to an extensive informal intelligence network (Fig. 10.8).

Here, we examine archaeological and landscape evidence that sheds new light on the conflict in the central Namib Desert. The campaign, which was mobilized in January 1915, comprised essentially two prongs: an advance along the new broad-gauge railway towards Karibib, under Colonel Skinner, and an encircling southern advance along the Swakop River under the direct command of General Botha.[753] Skinner's advance which is not discussed in detail here had a number of novel elements, including a fleet of converted Rolls Royce sedan cars fitted with armour plating and Vickers machine guns, manned by a unit of the Royal Navy.[754] Skinner established a series of posts at isolated points along the railway and the units at these points, who were largely idle, constructed elaborate stone arrangements depicting their regimental insignia, thus leaving an enduring landscape record of their presence (see Fig. 10.9), along with machine gun emplacements, heliograph signal stations and other installations.

General Botha's group, consisting of motorized infantry, field artillery units and mounted infantry, also included mounted Boer commandos who were to play a decisive role at many points in the campaign. Botha moved up the Swakop River valley following a section of the historical Bay Road described in the previous chapter. After a series of minor skirmishes at Goanikontes and other pockets of German resistance, he encamped at Husab to prepare for an assault on the strongly-held German position at Jakalswater which he intended to reach by crossing the Swakop River at Riet. Here he met more determined resistance before dispatching a flying column of Boer commandos to attack

---

753 Detailed accounts of the ensuing engagements are given by L'Ange (1991) and MacGregor and Goldbeck (2014).
754 Royal Navy insignia comprising pebbles arranged in the initials RN and the iconic "fouled anchor" symbol occur at several sites where these units bivouacked on the desert plains.

Figure 10.9: South African regimental insignia on a gravel hillside in the Namib Desert (height ca. 20 m). Insignia of the 2nd Battalion, Kimberley Rifles is above that of D Company, 2nd Battalion, Durban Light Infantry. 'Tit-bit' is the name of the regimental mascot, a billy-goat, so named because of his taste for army rations.

Jakalswater from the west via Pforte.[755] The remains of Botha's camp at Husab and the battlefield at Riet, both described below, are relatively well preserved and provide illuminating insights into the field tactics of the two adversaries.

Figure 10.10a shows a field plan of Botha's camp, occupying a shallow bowl-like depression, or "dead ground" in military terms, being situated below the immediate horizon and to some extent concealed from view. The site flanks the old Bay Road where a track descends to the Swakop River, essential for the water and

---

755 This was the occasion of a formal complaint addressed to General Botha by the German officer commanding the battery at Pforte, *Leutnant* Weiherr, who considered the skirmishing tactics of the attacking Boer horsemen too informal (Reitz 1994).

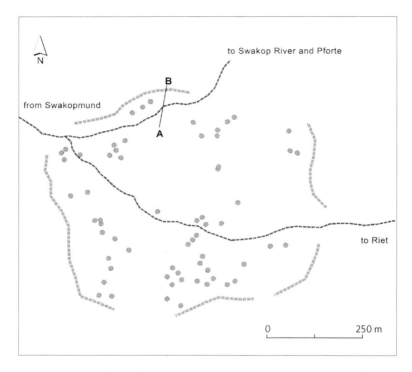

Figure 10.10a: Plan of General Botha's encampment at Husab, the arrangement of tent circles and other features within the concealing hollow, including features A and B.

rough grazing needs of cavalry mounts and the draught oxen used to pull field artillery pieces. The rim of the depression bears the remains of numerous *sangars* or defensive firing positions sometimes with rough stone screens, a practice first adopted by the British during their mid-19th century campaigns in Afghanistan. Within the site perimeter are circular areas of cleared ground approximately 4 m in diameter, marking the positions of small clusters of standard British army bell-tents. Among these are various discarded items including dense scatters of nails, probably from ammunition crates used as fuel, and bundles of wire used in the baling of horse fodder. It is a possible reflection on the

Figure 10.10b: General Botha's breakfast table conference, probably on the eve of his advance on Riet. The position of the rock cairn (B) on the horizon is shown in Fig. 10.10a which also indicates the position of the breakfast table (A) shown in the photograph. Image 06896 reproduced by courtesy of the National Archives of Namibia.

scarcity of grazing that the tethers on the horse lines were of wire rather than hemp rope which would have been eaten by the cavalry mounts. Among other interesting features of the site are numerous small scatters of rifle cartridge cases which include both the British army .303 and the Portuguese Mauser 6.5 mm calibre issued to the Boer commandos.

Figure 10.10b shows General Botha gesturing while consulting his staff at Husab, seated at what appears to be a breakfast table. A stone cairn visible on the right horizon of the photograph (labelled 'B' in Fig. 10.10a) is still in place and allows the position of the breakfast conference to be approximately determined on the ground, as shown on the site plan. This is a slightly elevated spot on the northern side of the encampment and has a small rectangular drystone structure that appears to have formed part of the command post. Immediately behind the group of figures is the open gravel bed of the tributary stream leading down

Figure 10.11a: Botha's attack on Riet, showing obstructed line of sight between the encampment at Husab and the German observation point on the Langer Heinrich mountain.

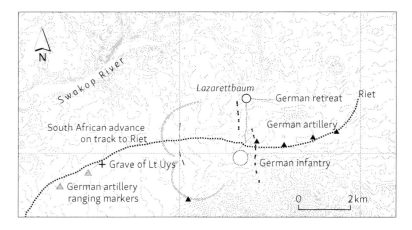

Figure 10.11b: The approach to Riet, showing German artillery positions (black triangles), artillery sighting markers (grey triangles), grave of Lieut. Uys killed by shell-burst (cross), German infantry entrenchments (large hollow circle) and German first aid post *Lazarettbaum*.

to the Swakop River. The youthful officers standing behind General Botha are wearing pith helmets and jodhpurs (one has a riding crop) and these are probably soldiers of the Imperial Light Horse, while the figure on the right who appears to be older, may be from one of the Boer commandos. This informal photograph was probably taken on the eve of General Botha's advance towards Riet.

The line-of-sight diagram in Figure 10.11a shows that the Husab encampment would not have been directly visible from the German observation point near the summit of the Langer Heinrich Mountain on the right of the diagram. General Botha was therefore able to advance unseen until his column entered the valley leading down to the Swakop River at Riet. It is, however, possible that the dust of the approaching column was visible and that the size and disposition of Botha's column could have been determined by scouts observing from the hills near the Husab encampment. As it was, on 20th March 1915 Botha's men entered the Riet valley to be met by carefully sighted German artillery which brought them under converging fire from two points: a single artillery piece on the northern footslopes of the Langer Heinrich and a group of up to five artillery pieces positioned below the visible horizon to the east.[756] Remains of the artillery positions and what appear to be ranging markers near the track attest to the preparations made by the German gun-layers (Fig. 10.11b).

Also overlooking the track is a line of shallow entrenchments or *schutzengraben* from which German infantry intended to enfilade the approaching column with rifle and heavy machine-gun fire. However, it appears that this position was quickly overrun by mounted Boer commandos after the barrage commenced. Certainly, the site had no traces of spent ammunition to indicate that Botha's column was fired upon from this position. Botha's artillery was brought forward and the main German artillery group retreated in stages towards the Swakop River. German wounded were evacuated towards Jakalswater along a narrow gully to the north and assembled at a point known as the *Lazarettbaum*, or hospital tree. The lower trunk of the tree bears the names and initials of several individuals, including that of a South African officer of the Rand Rifles Regiment patrolling the area after the conflict.

---

756 Lieut. Uys was killed at this point and buried at the side of the track (see Figure 10.11).

Botha's column and the Boer flying column approaching Jakalswater from the west converged, and after further exchanges of fire the German forces withdrew towards Karibib which was soon taken by Botha's forces. Botha advanced steadily eastwards meeting little resistance. Realizing that defeat was inevitable, the German forces under Major Franke began a general retreat. It was rumoured that they might attempt to break out to the north with the possibility of joining the master strategist Colonel Von Lettow Vorbeck who had throughout the initial stages of the war tied up a large force of British and Indian troops in German East Africa, now Tanzania.[757] Botha dispatched an encircling force to be positioned along the railway line north of Otavi and in due course accepted the German surrender at a point on the railway known as Kilo 500.[758] The campaign was concluded and German rule brought to an end.

Although there are a great many more World War I sites in the Namib Desert, those discussed here provide an adequate reflection of the archaeology of mobile warfare at that time, equalled only by the well documented traces of the contemporaneous Arab Revolt in which British forces and Bedouin allies fought occupying Turkish forces for the control of the Jordan valley and its hinterland.[759] The main theatres of conflict in Western Europe were in comparative stalemate for long periods with opposing forces occupying static lines. The sheer numbers of combatants and the great quantities of matériel involved have left enduring traces. Although in comparison the mobile warfare seen in the Namib and Jordanian deserts was a fleeting phenomenon and its archaeology more subtle, it is nonetheless a valuable adjunct to the documentary record.

At the close of hostilities in Namibia, German combatants were confined to internment camps for the remainder of the war

---

757 L'Ange (1991: 264) citing Collyer (2013: 121).
758 L'Ange (1991: 322)
759 Saunders & Faulkner (2010)

in Europe. Under South African administration German settlers retained land they had acquired under colonial rule and were allowed to continue largely unhindered in their economic activities. However, the Treaty of Versailles under which Germany lost some of its expanded territory in Europe, also saw the Kaiser stripped of his colonies; Namibia was given over to South Africa in 1920 under League of Nations mandate to be prepared for eventual independence. The deep resentment engendered by these decisions was instrumental in the rise, less than two decades later, of the Third Reich which nurtured not only the ambition to expand Germany's borders in Europe, but also to regain the lost colonies held in great sentimental attachment, most notably German South West Africa.

Prior to World War I, Britain had refrained from interference in the administration of the German colony, despite frequent complaints by indigenous leaders and the publication of eye-witness reports describing large-scale atrocities. Immediately after the war, and to justify the confiscation of German territorial possessions under the Treaty of Versailles, the occupying British and South African forces compiled a detailed report, the so-called Blue Book, on Germany's treatment of indigenous peoples in German South West Africa.[760] The report lifted the veil of silence that had descended on the colony following the suppression of the Ovaherero and Nama revolts[761] and in doing so provoked

---

760 The conduct of German troops, officials and settlers towards indigenous people in Namibia was documented in detail in the official British Imperial publication *Report On the Natives of Southwest Africa and Their Treatment by Germany* (O'Reilly 1918), informally known as the Blue Book. The name derives from the blue covers which distinguished all colonial reports published by H. M. Stationery Office. See also Silvester and Gewald (2003) for comprehensive references to colonial apologist responses to this documentation.

761 It is noteworthy that German colonial "amnesia" concerning the genocide was paralleled by a form of aphasia among Ovaherero who had escaped from the colony and retained little cultural memory of these traumatic events (Alnaes 1989). Katjivena (2020) provides a highly unusual example of documented oral testimony.

the ire of Germany and its colonial settler community. None of the crimes documented in the report were ever prosecuted, but its publication was held to impugn German honour. The report contained direct testimony of indigenous people who had witnessed and experienced brutal abuse and atrocities, which Germany dismissed as unreliable. However, the report rested very largely on Germany's own colonial records captured during the campaign, and these were not easily refuted.

Many German settlers were declared prohibited immigrants and deported, but South Africa wished to gain the support of the settler community and agreed in 1926 to withdraw the Blue Book from circulation, and to destroy all available copies. German settlers were granted South African citizenship and became enfranchised voters; their support in 1948 was instrumental in the narrow electoral victory of the South African Nationalist Party, which led to the establishment of apartheid rule and its imposition in South West Africa. During the inter-War years, the rise of the Nazi Party enjoyed widespread support in South West Africa because it held the promise of a return to German rule. But the organization was proscribed in the country and its activities were therefore carried out in secrecy, for the most part hidden from the gaze of outside observers.

However, in 1939 an American journalist reported that while

> ...Crouching behind a tamarisk bush late at night I watched [as] flames crackled and spiralled across a course formed by long ranks of boys and girls. Voices chanted, softly at first, then shriller, *"Ein Reich, Ein Volk, Ein Führer"*...Gasps of pain gave way to cries of triumph – they had survived the "Ordeal by Fire".[762]

Such accounts, which illustrate the Nazi para-militarization of the German settler youth in the former colony, might be considered

---

762 Olusoga & Erichsen (2010: 317), citing Bennett (1939). Similar events were recorded by Barron (1978).

THE DEATH OF MEMORY 423

Figure 10.12: Nazi ceremonial gathering site on the plains of the central Namib Desert, with the date "1938" picked out in white quartz pebbles below.

apocryphal were it not for the discovery of one archaeological site in the Namib Desert that directly attests to Nazi ceremonies carried out at isolated places and in apparent secrecy. The site, situated on a low rocky ridge providing slight relief on the gravel plains of the desert, lies approximately 60 km due east of Swakopmund. It consists of stone letters in black dolerite about 1 m in height spelling out the words *"Heil Hitler"* with a large *hakenkreuz*, or swastika. Above the lettering is a small stone construction that may have formed the footing of a flagpole or a podium from which to address those assembled at the site. The presence of slow-growing desert lichens on the exposed surfaces of the stones seems to be consistent with the date of 1938 which is picked out in white quartz pebbles beneath the lettering (Fig. 10.12).

The dating of the site to the eve of World War II is significant because it follows the establishment of the *Reichskolonialbund*, or German Colonial League, which by 1938 represented an influential pressure group. The League was founded by von Epp who had served in the campaign against the Ovaherero and with his deputy, Wilhelm Rümann, cultivated close ties with prominent settlers still resident in the former colony. The patron of the League was the future *Reichsmarschall* Hermann Göring, an enthusiastic proponent of the *lebensraum* principle who had spent part of his youth in German South West Africa during his father's term as the first Reich Commissioner to the colony.[763] This otherwise insignificant site serves to show that archaeological and landscape evidence can corroborate documentary accounts that might otherwise be dismissed. The desert is in this sense an unforgiving witness to history.

Gazing on Emptiness

To bring this chapter to a close, I now return, after the extended review of the archaeological evidence for the last one million years that has occupied the whole of this book, to the paradox raised on the first page of the first chapter: the colonial insistence on the concept of *terra nullius*, or emptiness, in the face of overwhelming evidence to the contrary. While the Namib Desert and its immediate hinterland did appear to be empty of people to the earliest European visitors, regular contact with indigenous communities ensued in the two centuries before the advent of colonial occupation. As I have described in this chapter, the indigenous population was decimated under early colonial rule, and the largely deserted landscape then became a neutral backdrop in the theatre of colonial conceit.

---

[763] Olusoga & Erichsen (2010: 291) have pointed out that the uniforms of the *Sturmabteilung*, or eponymous Brown Shirts were surplus colonial *Schutztruppen* issue, thus providing a further link between the rise of the Third Reich and the romantic allure of the lost colony. The importance of the link with Hermann Göring rather than his father Heinrich, is shown by the fact that a street in the central business district of the colonial capital, Windhoek, bore his name until shortly after national independence in 1990.

One reflection of this development was the rise of a remarkable tradition of landscape art, much of it in the German Romantic style, which emphasized the harmony and clarity of pure, untouched nature, and the spiritual experience of communing with the landscape.[764] This movement arose from the example of Fritz Behn, Wilhelm Kuhnert and Ernst Vollbehr, who set out in the first three decades of the 20th century to document "a romantic Africa, depicted with a longing eye, [...] an Africa that never existed, but still lingered in European fantasies...".[765] A prominent example in Namibia was Adolph Jentsch (1888–1977) who used techniques of spare brushwork, strict adherence to the golden mean and a balance of positive and negative space.[766] Jentsch and other artists portrayed the landscape as if it were at rest, silent and virgin. The desert came to exemplify openness and purity in a natural wilderness devoid of people, in a style that became an entrenched and enduring colonial trope.[767] This is in marked contrast to colonial era landscape art elsewhere, where people, albeit romanticized, are a constant element of composition[768] (see Fig. 10.13).

The concept of a wilderness as an area to be conserved undisturbed by human presence, has a long history in Namibia, much of the central Namib Desert having been proclaimed a game reserve by the German Governor Friedrich von Lindequist,[769]

---

764 See Lilienthal (1997). The term is loosely applied here, not as an art historical tradition but as a set of social attitudes (cf. Wilke 2006) that were expressed through art and literature, arising from the earlier *Sturm und Drang* movement. In the Namibian context there are no restless landscapes and the colonial art seems to follow the example of Fritz Strich in striving for calm, balance and perfection.
765 Wilke (2006)
766 Levinson (1973); Meaker (1984)
767 Colonial photography at first depicted the landscape "as a terrain awaiting or fulfilling the colonizers enterprise..." but diverged later to present a more critical perspective (Brandt 2020: 45, 61; Kinahan & Kinahan 2021).
768 e.g. Macneil (2001); Tobin (1999); Trench (1986)
769 Bridgeford (2008)

Figure 10.13: Adolph Jentsch at work in the Namib Desert. Image reproduced by courtesy of Orde Levinson.

significantly in 1907, following the suppression of the Ovaherero Revolt. Under South African rule a series of national parks was proclaimed, covering almost the entire Namib Desert, with the addition of the former diamond mining *Sperrgebiet,* or Forbidden Zone, closing all but a few small areas of settlement to human occupation on the Namib coast.[770] The supposedly most pristine part, the Namib Sand Sea was inscribed on the UNESCO World Heritage List in 2012, with the nomination dossier containing the remarkable statement that:

> ... all archaeologists stress that linking these disparate lines of [archaeological] evidence with the ethnographic present is tenuous. No clear historiographical evidence,

---

[770] After 1990, community-based conservation programs were implemented in many rural areas, restoring some traditional land and resource rights, but not within the proclaimed national parks (Republic of Namibia 2013).

whether oral, subsistence practice, or historical records, links modern Namibian peoples with those past practices. People were found living along the coast... by early explorers from Europe, but they were not the direct ancestors of the modern inhabitants.[771]

There is no factual basis whatsoever for this statement which elides the many archaeological, ethnographic and historical studies available at the time of its writing. It is also entirely contradicted by the evidence presented in this book.

---

771 Republic of Namibia (2012: 77)

EPILOGUE

'We shall not cease from exploration, and the end of all our exploring will be to arrive where we started, and know the place for the first time.'
T.S. Eliot, *Four Quartets*

The human history of the Namib Desert is a tangled skein, and coaxing its threads apart, we find recurrent combinations of particular artefacts or materials, their dating, and the ecological or landscape setting in which they were employed. This is the pattern of the past, a complex set of relationships, of articulations to be laid out almost as a skeleton.[772] Such is our first and most simple purpose, of description and functional linkage between site, assemblage and environment. But in this book, our object in carefully following out the lines of evidence before us has been to go beyond description and pattern to try and discover the processes that lie beneath the appearance of things.[773]

Exploring the archaeological evidence with this purpose in mind, I found it helpful to pay out a metaphorical length of string as I went along, so that I (and the reader) could always retreat and look for another way. So, in the manner of Ariadne's mythological thread, I marked my course using the adaptive cycle, or Holling loop, explained in the opening chapter. There I set out the particular advantages of this approach, based on the non-linear landscape-based relationships between human and natural systems, in the general framework of human ecodynamics.[774] I hope that in the preceding chapters I have shown that this has some advantages over the traditional antiquarian approach to archaeology in Namibia, while also

---

772 In the manner of Giddens' (1984) notion of structuration; see also Johnson (2010).
773 Charlton (2008) in appreciation of Gregory Bateson.
774 Fitzhugh et al. (2019)

presenting a promising alternative to other current approaches to the archaeology of the wider region.

The evidence from the Namib Desert provides many examples of systemic interactions, a panarchy of nested and intersecting adaptive cycles. These interactions occurred on multiple scales, ranging from local settlement patterns to sub-regional systems of social networks and exchange. The evidence also shows how these interactions operated at different rates, ranging from the millennial to the decadal, and of persistence or continuity in both occupation sequences and patterns of resource dependence. The Namib Desert has provided many examples that illustrate the usefulness of the adaptive cycle approach. Of these, I propose to review briefly only a few in this closing discussion.

One example, emerging from critiques of the conventional notion that the archaeological record is best understood in terms of the identity and actions of larger social units, is that of analysis focusing on the behaviour of individuals as agents of social action and change.[775] In the Namib Desert this is particularly well exemplified by the rise of specialist shamans who become identifiable as individual actors, itinerant ritual practitioners who played a fundamental role in the transformation of hunter-gatherer society. These individuals initiated systematic plant food exploitation and livestock keeping, as well as a complex assembly of customary practices, technology and land-use drawn from pre-existing hunter-gatherer adaptations as well as those acquired and adapted from both indigenous and colonial interactions.

We have seen in the evidence from the Namib Desert many other examples of the individual as an actor in the wider cultural drama, ranging from the pastoralist with the broken toe, immortalized by his footprint preserved in the hardened tidal mud at Walvis Bay (Chapter 8), to the boyhood home of the warlord Jonker Afrikaner at ǁKhauxaǃnas (Chapter 9), to the remains of an anonymous Ovaherero warrior buried in a shallow grave en route to what would have been a short life of slavery in the German

---

[775] Dobres & Robb (2000); Fitzhugh (2000)

port settlement of Swakopmund (Chapter 10). Throughout this research I have found it important to dig to the layer below that of cultural identity; certainly in my work among the Ovahimba of north-western Namibia, I saw countless examples of the way in which pastoral life was a constant interplay between deeply held cultural values and individual action. Among the Ovahimba individual acts of courage and foolishness live on in oral history more vividly than the generalities of custom.[776]

A second area in which the adaptive cycle or ecodynamic approach has proved useful is in the analysis of what are sometimes known – clumsily – as "place-based" histories of change, where human interactions with natural systems produce legacies of cumulative effects.[777] In the Namib Desert, it is clear that climatic variation and the generally sparse distribution of food and water had a decisive influence on human ecological responses at the level of the actual site and its immediate landscape setting. We see this in evidence that responses occurred at different temporal and spatial scales, and in the rise of highly localized specializations, such as an apparently sustainable local cropping of rock hyrax on refugium sites, and in the form of large scale communal

---

[776] This is exemplified by the fact that the Ovahimba, who do not follow the Gregorian calendar, instead maintain an informal narrative of epochs named according to events such as droughts or floods, disease outbreaks, or in the past, the inexplicable and often amusing decisions of colonial officialdom. Gibson (1977) recorded eight event years between 1941 and 1969, including 1954 *ongaha ya omasitu*, or "the year of getting in", when Chief Kasita travelled to Opuwo in the vehicle of the District Commissioner. My own fieldwork yielded 11 event years between 1970 and 1997. Examples include 1975 "the year of flies", a year of high rainfall (22 days of rain); 1980 "the year of guns" when war broke out along the Kunene River; 1984 "the year of mice", a year of exceptional rain (33 days of rain), as was 1985 "the year of injury between the hooves of goats" when *Tribulus campestris* thorns covered the landscape; 1981 *ombura yotjita*, the year of drought when cattle numbers had dropped by almost half from 1975; 1989 *ombura yo Undaka*, referring to the United Nations Transitional Assistance Group (UNTAG) which prepared Namibia for independence.

[777] Fitzhugh et al. (2019)

hunting of migratory antelope in the late Holocene. These and other subsistence adaptations in the Namib Desert were tied to a particular set of ecological consumer and resource relations involving alternation between primary resource sites such as refugia, based on density dependent dynamics, and on short-lived events, such as antelope migrations, where the resource relationship was based on secondary resource sites subject to density independent dynamics.

The nature of the relationship between people and their environment is elusive and the certainties of ecological modelling seem arbitrary and flimsy when faced with evidence of connection and exchange through vast regional networks linking communities that in all probability would never actually meet. Likewise, the subtlety of relations between people and animals is a constant quality of the rock art, but finds expression in the landscape through the example of women's shelters used on seed gathering expeditions also being used by parties of female kudu for the same purpose of retreat from the desert wind (Chapter 6). This interleaving of human and animal behaviour points to a degree of harmony on the landscape that is essentially absent from the conventional archaeology of hunter-gatherers, including the more nuanced field of rock art studies. With the advent of pastoralism and the social integration of the herd and its keepers, this more complex relationship is quite absent from the archaeology of pastoralism which has rendered the animals simply as meat.

Table 11.1 attempts a summary of the archaeological sequence as discussed in this book, extending from the terminal Pleistocene, to the Holocene arid phase, the transition to pastoralism, the late pre-colonial period and the colonial period. The table provides a generalized chronological sequence matched to the defining climatic conditions of each stage in the sequence. More detailed dating and discussion of climatic data have been presented in each chapter with the relevant archaeological evidence. The table is intended to show that climate, while a major driver of human adaptation, is not an overarching determinant. Climate and the environmental conditions it sustains form the boundaries of permission and constraint for human survival in the Namib Desert. The parallel record presented in the table, of sequence and adaptive cycle phase, summarizes the more detailed processes described in the text. In essence, the sequence is of hunter-gatherer expansion and response to environmental constraint leading to a series of increasingly complex and inventive adaptations, one of these being the adoption of pastoralism and the establishment of an advanced measure of food security under conditions of climatic instability and structural limitations on social organization.

As we follow the Namib Desert archaeological sequence through time we find the evidence becoming more abundant, more diverse and better preserved, especially within the last five thousand years. This evidence, placed in the context of a large and reasonably well dated sub-regional distribution of archaeological sites, and viewed within the framework of a general theoretical perspective, allows a range of new insights. Some of these emerge from the discovery of new and unique evidence such as of ritual paraphernalia (Chapter 4), men's and women's initiation (Chapter 5), the semi-domestication of wild tobacco (Chapter 6), and the remains of internecine conflict (Chapter 7). These are a few examples of evidence from the Namib Desert that casts new light on questions of much broader relevance in southern African archaeology. But our interest here does not lie with the antiquarian urge to find the first or the oldest, whether of ritual paraphernalia, rock art, pottery or the bones of sheep. Instead, we are concerned above all with finding the dynamic relations between these things. It should be said, though, that the many examples of unique evidence emerging from the archaeology of the Namib Desert is no mere accident of preservation; instead, it is the consequence of a fundamental difference in research perspective.

An important development that emerges in this way is the apparent path from the adoption of pastoralism and the rise of food production to an orderly and regulated allocation of resources, which suggests steadily increasing competition among desert communities (Chapter 8). It is likely that the measure of food security obtained through livestock production and the systematic exploitation of wild plant foods resulted in some increase in the human population of the Namib Desert. Certainly, food security would have helped to mitigate the seasonal famines that beset most desert communities and would therefore have ensured an improved survival of infants, but also of the elderly, the living memory of past events, of resources and social relationships. Under pastoralism, livestock production requires labour as much as it does pasture, and maintaining the balance of livestock numbers and human capacity in an unpredictable environment poses particular challenges for the adaptive resilience and social integration of desert communities.

We have seen that risk management lay behind many pastoral strategies, from the use of stock-posts to the conversion of surplus animals into redeemable commodities such as copper beads. The evidence also points towards the emergence of an impoverished underclass as a consequence of pastoral expansion. In the last two centuries we see that the potential instability of the pastoral economy could result in a collapse into poverty and servitude, or a re-organization such as occurred among the Orlam (Chapter 9). This development, leading to the emergence of a formidable class of warlord raiders illustrates the extraordinary resilience of the indigenous pastoral economy. The depredations of Orlam raiding parties operating as far as southern Angola successfully challenged both the Ovaherero and the German colonists, extending competition over the control of desert resources to its uttermost limits (Chapter 10).

Competition over resources and the uneven accumulation of pastoral wealth and social dominance were established features of the desert economy at the time of early contact and the first European attempts at ethnographic documentation. The ethnography of the ǂAonîn (Chapter 8) recognizes the !Khuisenin as livestock owners, and the Hurinin, said mainly to live from what they could scavange along the shore and in the dunes of the !Khuiseb Delta.[778] Revisionist scholars have argued that the Kalahari peoples documented by modern ethnographers were not untouched survivors of Palaeolithic hunter-gatherer life, but impoverished communities living on the periphery of a complex late precolonial economic landscape characterized by great inequalities in wealth and access to resources.[779] The ǂAonîn of the Namib coast may therefore represent a unique example combining archaeological, ethnographic and historical evidence relevant to this most important controversy in the study of southern African precolonial society: the Kalahari Debate.[780]

Archaeological evidence from the Namib Desert is also particularly relevant to the issue of niche construction[781] which relates directly to the adaptive cycle or ecodynamic approach.[782] As it implies, this concept departs from the conventional idea of adaptation to pre-existing ecological niches, towards one in which the organism, in our case humanity, shapes the niche it occupies through dynamic interaction. The rise of intensive and systematic exploitation of wild plant foods in the Namib during the last one thousand years provides several instances of niche construction and manipulation, involving the active conservation of harvester ant nests, propagation of !nara melons and, in the case of wild tobacco, a relationship that might be described as semi-domestication. Active tending of wild bees' nests in the same areas provides a further example of niche construction through the provision and maintenance of viable nest sites. To this should of course be added the metaphysical intervention through the work of specialist rainmakers.

---

778 Budack (1977)
779 Denbow (1983); Denbow & Wilmsen (1986); Wilmsen (1989)
780 Barnard (1992a)
781 Laland & O'Brien (2011); Parsons (2015) presents an application of niche construction concepts in southern African archaeology.
782 Fitzhugh et al. (2019)

Table 11.1: Summary of Namib Desert terminal Pleistocene and Holocene climatic and adaptive cycle sequence.

Years BP	Climate	Sequence stage
EARLY COLONIAL		
150 BP (ca.1880–1904)	Variable with episodes of extreme drought	Pastoral decline
LATE PRE-COLONIAL		
200 BP (ca.1790–1810 AD)	Warm/wet	Pastoral equilibrium Pastoral expansion
250 BP (ca.1675–1780 AD)	Cool/dry (Little Ice Age)	Pastoral displacement
500 BP (ca.1500–1675 AD)	Warm/wet	Mixed pastoralism and systematic use of plant foods
PASTORAL TRANSITION		
650 BP (ca.1300–1500 AD)	Cool/dry	Itinerant shamanism and transition to pastoralism
1,000 BP (ca.900–1300 AD)	Warm/wet (Medieval Warm Epoch)	Pastoral expansion
HOLOCENE ARID PHASE		
2,000 BP	Warm/wet	Hunter-gatherer pastoral interaction
3,000–4,000 BP	Cool/dry	Rise of specialist shamans
6,000–8,000 BP	Warm/wet (Holocene Optimum)	Hunter-gatherer expansion
TERMINAL PLEISTOCENE		
12,000 BP	Warm/wet (onset of Holocene)	Hunter-gatherer expansion
20,000–30,000 BP	Cool/dry (peak Glacial Maximum)	

Adaptive Phase	Key events and sites
Ω	Colonial rule, Ovaherero and Nama uprisings, genocide
r-K	Intensive trade contact on the Namib coast at ǂKhîsa-ǁgubus
Ω-α	Northward migration of Orlam from ǁKhauxa!nas
r-K	Southward migration of Ovaherero into central Namibia
α-r	Re-occupation of Namib; extensive regional trade; widespread use of pottery
α	Initiation at ǀUi-ǁaes Rain-making at Otjohorongo
r	Massacre at Khorixa-ams
Ω-α	Introduction of pottery and domestic stock at Falls Rock Shelter
K	Occupation of refugium sites in Dâures massif
r	Occupation of desert hunting sites including Gorrasis Rock Shelter
α	Increased hunter-gatherer mobility
Ω	Escarpment ecotone sites Rock art at Apollo 11

An elementary form of niche construction is also found in the evidence of communal hunting of migratory antelope which involves the use of the landscape to deflect the movement of the antelope to the site that is most advantageous to the hunter. This involves two forms of interaction with the animal and the terrain: the use of *battue* beaters approximating the role of predators encircling their prey, and the use of carefully positioned hunting blinds which are sited according to the needs of the hunter rather than the habits of their prey. More systematic and intensive niche construction is found in pastoral land use where the structure of woodland is modified with enduring effects, including the alteration of soil chemistry through the accumulation of cattle dung.

The most remarkable example of niche construction is of course the use of wells to provide water for livestock where no natural springs or surface waters exist. Conventional approaches to the archaeology of pastoralism in southern Africa do not consider an interaction with the pastoral environment that might leave enduring features on the landscape itself. Indeed, the general approach to both hunter-gatherer and pastoral ecology is one in which the environment is a given, rather than a more malleable and porous niche where detailed knowledge of ecological processes would have allowed a degree of manipulation, allowing sustainable conservation of some resources through informed social sanctions. The interaction of hunter-gatherers with plant resources especially in the vicinity of sustained occupation sites would have an enduring effect on plant diversity and vegetation structure, so that the resource base of Holocene occupation may have been in this respect quite different from the floral community as it appears today, untouched by the harvesting hand for many generations. In southern Africa generally, human impacts on natural systems are often seen in terms of negative disturbance rather than as formative influences shaping the environment over extended periods of time.

In this book I have argued against the practice of attempting to infer human ecological responses such as subsistence strategies, from the environment itself, by assuming a simple determinative or functional relationship between the two. I have supported my view with reference to folkloric explanations and through the rock art of the Namib Desert which provides abundant evidence of a hunter-gatherer ideology of supernatural causation. There is, however, something of a paradox here, in that southern African hunter-gatherers, including those of the Namib Desert, combined a belief in supernatural causation with an extraordinarily sophisticated knowledge of ecosystem function.[783] The archaeology of southern African hunter-gatherers does not yet provide a satisfactory emic understanding of their human ecology.

I was made to reconsider my own assumptions regarding the differences between a traditional pastoralist understanding of dryland ecology and my own, one hot afternoon on the banks of the Kunene River, with a small group of Ovahimba debating whether it would be safe to retrieve a dead cow from the crocodile-infested water. By way of distraction I held forth on a paper which had just appeared in the journal *Ecological Applications* by Andrew Illius of Edinburgh University, setting out what was to become for me a fundamentally useful perspective on the alternation of density dependent and density independent consumer resource relations in pastoral grazing systems. I wanted to know if this idea made sense to a herdsman in the remotest corner of Kaoko.

Our conversation drew several helpful passersby who offered their translation services for the possibility of meat from the somewhat bloated carcase, now drifting towards a patch of reeds, and in my mind an almost certain lurking crocodile. At this point, Kapokoro Tjiramba, the patriarch, who was reclining in

---

[783] The interaction between these two contrasting frames of reference has an obvious parallel in Western thought, with the reconciliation of reason and faith, by an unbroken line of scholarship beginning with St Thomas Aquinas (ca 1274 AD). A similar dichotomy persists in secular thought, with the opposition between classical, observable reality and theoretical, or quantum, reality.

the shade of a palm tree, engaged his son, asking what we had been talking about so animatedly. I watched Tjiramba as he drew his snuff spoon and probed thoughtfully among the folds of his headcloth; Ngaututwe summarized, and his father shook his head slowly, gesturing towards me and asking the assembled listeners in genuine puzzlement, "Didn't he know that?" Clearly, Ovahimba understanding of practical rangeland ecology provides a conceptually advanced framework for cattle production within an ideology that accommodates both secular and supernatural agency, while remaining highly resilient to change.

None of the changes observed in the palaeoenvironmental record for the last one million years in the Namib Desert can be described as catastrophic in either scale or intensity. However, one change in the archaeological and historical sequence that approaches a catastrophe in its social consequences is the genocide described in the previous chapter. Another is the somewhat earlier advent of trading contact. Yet even here, a process that did ultimately result in the destruction of the indigenous economy exemplifies the resilience of social systems that evolved in this environment. Thus, we saw in the development of desert pastoralism a complex of risk management strategies that were used to distribute animals over pasture zones, to mitigate outbreaks of disease, to convert animals into redeemable commodities and to disperse vulnerable herds to isolated stock-posts. While the arrival of European traders presents an apt example of a Black Swan phenomenon in its unexpectedness and potentially severe impact, the response of the risk-averse pastoralist was to construe this event in terms of a traditional cattle raid, adroitly averting catastrophe, if only for the moment.

It is necessary that archaeologists should strive to integrate the material record of at least the more recent pre-colonial past, with the historical perspective of both conventional and critical accounts of the colonial era in southern Africa. The evidence from the Namib Desert presents multiple examples where the material archaeological record and the documentary historical record can be compared to useful advantage. Historians in particular should be encouraged by these insights to see the archaeological record, including the environmental and landscape setting of past human settlement, as constituting historical documents in their own right. Archaeologically, it is remarkable that the period of early interaction between colonial settlers and indigenous communities in the Cape is represented almost entirely by the documentary records and surviving architecture and material culture of *settler* society, with an almost negligible body of material evidence for the indigenous response to early contact. There is in contrast, abundant archaeological evidence from the Namib Desert and the adjacent interior, representing the colonial period from its inception to the recent past, showing both the settler and the indigenous response. This evidence, as we have seen, provides a very strong basis from which to evaluate historical accounts based on the colonial record alone.

Ecologists and archaeologists both maintain a strong interest in processes and consequences of environmental disturbance, or perturbation. Severe, and occasionally rapid climatic changes and their consequences are well illustrated by the links explored in this book between the human occupation record in the Namib Desert and the evidence of shifts in rainfall, temperature and biotic productivity. The archaeological evidence examined through the framework of the adaptive cycle approach provides multiple examples of human resilience, while the palaeoenvironmental evidence illustrates a high potential for the recovery of ecosystem function with climatic amelioration. However, just as the archaeological evidence points to a pattern of response towards ever-increasing complexity in subsistence and other adaptations, the environmental evidence suggests a comparable series of cumulative, stochastic and non-linear shifts towards new states, rather than a return to a previous equilibrium state. Over the span of the last one million years in the Namib Desert, both human and natural systems are therefore contingent on historical events, with successive system responses and states.

Although there have been important changes towards a rural community-oriented conservation model in Namibia, these do not extend to the national parks in the Namib Desert, but for a single, quite unintended exception. The British annexation of Walvis Bay in 1878 included a treaty with the ǂAonîn (Topnaar) chief Piet Haibeb which recognized his people's right to live in the lower !Khuiseb.[784] These rights were fortuitously preserved through successive changes in the political status of Walvis Bay, and the ǂAonîn retained–precariously–limited usufruct rights within the Namib-Naukluft National Park, outside the Namib Sand Sea World Heritage Site. The continuity of occupation of this area over several thousand years, by a mixed pastoral and hunter-gatherer community with well-developed marine resource dependence is remarkable, and in the southern African context, quite unique. The evidence from the !Khuiseb provides a direct and unbroken record of human settlement from the pre-contact period to the present day, which is entirely unmatched by any other location of early historical trading contact on the southern African coastline. The archaeological evidence from the !Khuiseb, which closely corroborates a wealth of contemporaneous documentary evidence cited in this book, offers an unambiguous rebuttal of the statement contained in the World Heritage nomination cited in the last chapter, which appears to deny a historical ǂAonîn right to live on the !Khuiseb.

The conservation management of the Namib Desert environment has been historically based on the maintenance of an equilibrium state, in keeping with global approaches to environmental conservation which generally consider the human presence, especially in the form of permanent indigenous settlement, as incompatible with the ideal of wilderness.[785] This approach also allows for the harvesting of "nature's *excess*

---

784 Berat (1990); Budack (1977); Kinahan, J.H.A. (2000)
785 Adams & McShane (1996)

production with as little fluctuation as possible",[786] promoting the notion of maximum sustainability and, with it, the now ubiquitous commoditization of ecosystem productivity through activities such as tourism. The ecodynamic approach, and the principles of resilience theory, relate to a major shift in ecological thinking among conservationists in Namibia and elsewhere, questioning not only the idea of desert ecosystems as equilibrium-seeking, but also that of sustainable off-take from an unpredictable environment.[787] The extended timescale of the archaeological and environmental records favours a different perspective, one in which the human presence, both past and present, is intrinsic to an understanding of ecosystem function, something abundantly demonstrated by this book. The shift in conservation thinking now apparent in Namibia is towards a more holistic understanding of the desert than existed a generation ago.

In summary, then, our hominin ancestors made their way down the escarpment and into the Namib Desert, moving as far west as they could with the permission of global climate at the time. Until the late Pleistocene, they seem to have advanced and retreated like an arhythmic tide, honing ever more sophisticated desert survival skills until, around the dawn of the Holocene era, they were able to live permanently in this place. We have seen the emergence of several uniquely specialized strategies which developed hand in hand with a range of social institutions serving the same fundamental requirements. Thus, ritual sanctions promoted basic social harmony under conditions of extreme scarcity of food and water; these ritual practices evolved to ease interaction with farming communities pressing at the margins of the desert in the last two thousand years. The intensity of this interaction was sufficient to initiate a major shift in hunter-gatherer social organization and the rise of a highly adapted form of Namib Desert pastoralism. In the last one thousand years, pressure on resources led to the appearance of social institutions

---

786 Holling (1973: 21) [my emphasis]; see Sullivan (2009).
787 Sullivan (2013)

of negotiated access to pasture and water as critical conditions of pastoral risk management.

All of this – the movement of people over the landscape, the finely tuned, geographically extended networks of social connection, and the only environmentally sustainable system of settlement and subsistence that has ever existed here – was completely invisible to early visitors who saw only *terra nullius*. In the colonial era, these extraordinary achievements were beneath the notice of Western experts who apparently had nothing to learn from the practical land management of indigenous society. We have seen in the final chapters of this book that the first casualty in the succession from pre-colonial to colonial land-use was the socially negotiated system of access to resources, which was replaced by the institution of private freehold tenure. Colonial land administration rests on the foundation of a cadastre system that developed in tandem with the imposition of German colonial rule, making it possible to accurately determine the boundaries of state and freehold land parcels. This fundamental shift in the way that land and resources are conceptualized, apportioned and understood is one of the most important changes brought by the colonial era, and one that has had most enduring consequences.

There are multiple examples to illustrate the fragmentation of the Namib Desert landscape during the last two centuries, including both freehold farm ownership and the early delineation of state controlled conservation areas. Mineral exploration and mining provide another example, one that has direct implications for the archaeological record in this region. Figure 11.1 illustrates the degree of land and resource fragmentation associated with this industry. A very large proportion of such holdings are merely speculative and in many cases there is no visible evidence of exploration or mining activity as these holdings exist only on paper. However, large-scale exploration is potentially destructive in this sensitive environment, as is actual mining due to the fact that ore grades are generally low. Although mining therefore has a major impact on the archaeological record at the landscape scale,

EPILOGUE 445

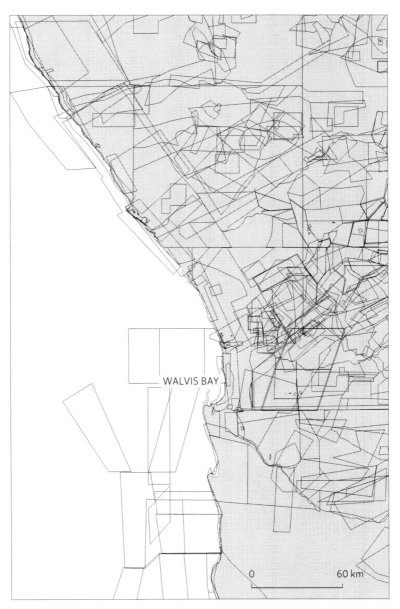

Figure 11.1: The delineation of mineral exploration licence areas in the Namib Desert, based on spatial data from the Government of Namibia, Ministry of Mines and Energy.

the impact on specific and often highly significant archaeological sites is comparatively low. This is a consequence of the now established practice in Namibia of archaeological assessment in the early stages of large scale exploration and mining projects. A significant proportion of the archaeological field survey evidence discussed in this book results from investigations by the Namib Desert Archaeological Survey on behalf of such projects.

A diametrically opposite situation exists with regard to tourism activities: tourism operators place a high opportunity value on pristine desert landscapes, so their landscape impact is generally low in comparison to mining. However, the impact of tourism on specific archaeological sites is disproportionately high, due to the cumulative effects of poorly controlled access to such sites as visitor attractions. Tourism has by far the greater direct negative impact on archaeological sites, sometimes leading to the irreparable degradation of globally important sites. Tourism is less rigorously managed than the mining industry and this is associated with a generally lower level of awareness in both established commercial operations and in community-level tourism. It is generally not realized within the tourism sector that archaeological sites, primarily rock art sites, were never intended to serve this purpose. Most are too fragile to withstand even moderate visitor traffic, and some, as we have seen in the examples discussed in this book, are places of ritual seclusion which are not appropriate to use as places of recreation and amusement. The entrance of the tourist lodge at ǀUi-ǁaes World Heritage Site, incorporating what would have been a secret men's initiation site, is the worst example of this practice.

The degradation of archaeological sites is such that some, once the focus of important archaeological research, can no longer be recommended as visitor attractions. Fortunately, however, some key examples such as the Maack Shelter, site of the infamous "White Lady" painting at the Dâures massif, have been the focus of significant interventions to create sustainable

Figure 11.2: The destruction of a Holocene rock art site through quarrying of low value granite dimension stone.

community-based archaeological tourism ventures with effective site conservation measures in place. The ǀUi-ǁaes engraving site, despite a long history of neglect and poor management has been largely rescued as a further example of successful community-based archaeological tourism in partnership with both commercial tourism ventures and the National Heritage Council, existing alongside ongoing research programmes.

There is of course no prospect of restoring the Namib Desert to its historical occupants. After all, we have seen that shifts in the circumstances of desert communities, driven by climatic and other forces, do not result in a return to some previous state when conditions improve, for change is cumulative and irreversible. However, the extraordinary archaeological record of this landscape provides insights into the long-term human experience in extremely hostile environments. It is a scientific delusion I believe, to attempt to understand the Namib Desert without systematic reference to the evolution of what is arguably its most influential biotic component, or at least one of its most critical ecosystem drivers: humankind. Understanding human responses to conditions of hyper-aridity is also especially important in the light of global concerns regarding climate change because it provides crucial insight into the likely threshold of human tolerance for long term environmental variation in the past.

Despite the high conservation value of the Namib Desert environment and a general appreciation of its aesthetic beauty, there is still little effective protection of archaeological remains on this landscape, and the results of their neglect have been catastrophic. Many sites have been damaged or destroyed, some inadvertently but most through a careless and ignorant disregard of their importance. Entire outcrops of granite, often containing the most exquisite rock art, are quarried for the decorative stone facings of monstrous corporate buildings in Europe and Asia. Large expanses of the desert have been destroyed for short-lived commercial gain, leaving a landscape irreparably scarred and littered with abandoned mines. Misguided attempts to rehabilitate the landscape by raking and other methods, only succeed in more completely erasing the archaeological record from ancient gravel surfaces. Archaeological sites fortunate to avoid this fate may survive only by providing local interest to safari establishments bent on recreating the romance of colonial Africa rather than providing what should be a salutary glimpse into a far deeper and more ancient past than any of the countries from which their tourist clients originate.

In the post-Modern era of moral relativism and an eclectic approach to context and meaning, the desert is used to project a vision quite different from that which guided the sentimentalism of colonial landscape art with its allusions to a tranquillity and elemental beauty, undisturbed by the human presence. Looming ever larger today is the dystopian vision of a world without tranquillity and without beauty, one dominated by humanity in the grip of dark and destructive impulses. Whether or not mankind might ever descend to the level of brutality depicted in movies such as *Mad Max – Fury Road* (Fig. 11.3), set in the Namib Desert, there is evidently some vicarious pleasure in contemplating a world of violence and chaos. The Namib has become a sought-after location for such movies,[788] where people have been restored once more but to a landscape disassociated from its real history to serve as a mere backdrop, a world without life, water or sustenance. The desert is seen as a place of emptiness, *terra nullius*, its people desperate and sub-human.

The archaeology of the Namib Desert reveals a world in which the human response to adversity and climatic unpredictability could hardly be more different from this. In the late Pleistocene, when conditions were driest and food extremely scarce, we see the first material evidence of ritual behaviour concerned with reducing hostility within groups, and with this the emergence of landscape-scale networks promoting social interdependence through gift exchange. In the early Holocene we see an enhanced, intensified development of these forms of behaviour occurring alongside inventive improvements in subsistence technology. Cultural interaction brought a range of innovations to the desert and helped to initiate a series of complex social changes. These were linked

---

788 Other recent examples of violent fantasy productions filmed at least partly in the Namib Desert include The Mummy (2017); Generation Kill (2008); The Fall (2006); The Cell (2000).

Figure 11.3: A still image from *Mad Max – Fury Road* in which the Namib Desert is used to portray a dystopian vision in which mankind is reduced to a state of brutality in a hostile environment. With permission from Alamy/Gallo Images.

to a florescence of art 5,000 years ago, which has no parallel in the modern era of western art genres in Namibia.

There is also much to be learned from the archaeological record, of sustainable food production based on a foundation of negotiated access, rather than exclusive ownership of resources. The stakes were sometimes high, and direct conflict not unknown; but the overall impression of the late pre-colonial pastoral economy is of interdependence and risk avoidance rather than isolation and narrow strategies aiming at high, short-term yields. The linkage, or articulation of indigenous and early colonial social economies had profoundly transformative consequences. Predatory warlord formations arose but did not endure: on the one hand their depredations undermined the very social fabric which sustained them, while on the other their success alone turned them into adversaries of a colonial enterprise that was bent on the destruction of all that opposed it.

Namibia has an irreplaceable wealth of archaeological evidence that is essential to the understanding and appreciation of our common human past. It is therefore important that the notion of *heritage* should carry this broader human implication, engendering a sense of responsibility and custodianship, rather than a narrow nationalism, based on ownership and entitlement. The significance of the archaeological record in this country, exemplified here by the Namib Desert, should be a matter of great pride, for one of the youngest nation states of Africa has at the same time an extraordinary depth of history, reaching as far back as the dawn of our common humanity.

Sit finis libri, nil finis quaerendi.

GLOSSARY

aeolian	Arising from the action of the wind
anticline	A geological fold in the form of an arch
breccia	Rock containing fragments cemented by fine calcareous material
chorological	Causal link between geographically separated phenomena
cohort	A similar-aged segment of a population
corbel	Unsupported masonry arch or dome
ecotone	Zone of transition or overlap between two biomes
edaphic	Determined by soil conditions rather than climate
emic	From the perspective of the subject rather than that of the observer
endoreic	Drainage basin with no outflow
erg	A large expanse of sand dunes with little or no vegetation
eustatic	Relating to global changes in sea level
homeostatic	Tending towards a relatively stable equilibrium
inselberg	Isolated rocky mountain rising abruptly from a plain
manuport	Object moved by human agency from its natural context
palimpsest	Successive occupation events on the same surface
panarchy	Co-existence of stability and change in complex systems
phytolith	A microscopic silica structure found in plant tissue
piosphere	The zone of vegetation influenced by grazing
riparian	Vegetated zone flanking a drainage system
sexual dimorphism	Differences between male and female of the same species
syncretic	Combining two or more cultures or belief systems
taphonomy	The processes affecting the survival of skeletal remains
Tertiary	The first part of the Cenozoic Era, between 66 and 2.6 million years

BIBLIOGRAPHY

Adams, J.S. & McShane, T.O. 1996. *The myth of wild Africa: Conservation without illusion*. Berkeley: University of California Press.

Adamson, R.G. & Teichmann, R.F.H. 1986. The Matchless cupreous pyrite deposit, South West Africa/Namibia. *Mineral Deposits of Southern Africa* 2: 1755–60.

Albrecht, M., Berke, H., Eichorn, B., Frank, T., Kuper, R., Prill, S., Vogelsang, R. & Wenzel, S. 2001. Oruwanje 95/1: A late Holocene stratigraphy in northwestern Namibia. *Cimbebasia* 17: 1–22.

Alexander, J.E. 1967. *An Expedition of Discovery into the Interior of Africa*. Two volumes. Facsimile reprint, Cape Town: C. Struik.

Alnaes, K. 1989. Living with the Past: The Songs of the Herero in Botswana. *Africa: Journal of the International African Institute* 59(3): 267–299.

Alves, F.J.S. 2011. *The 16th Century Portuguese Shipwreck of Oranjemund, Namibia*. Lisbon: Ministério dos Negócios Estrangeiros.

Ambrose, S.H. & DeNiro, M.J. 1986. Reconstruction of African human diet using bone collagen carbon and nitrogen isotope ratios. *Nature* 319: 321–24.

Andersson, C.J. 1861. *The Okavango River: A Narrative of Travel, Exploration and Adventure*. New York: John Murray.

Arthur, C. 2008. The Archaeology of Indigenous Herders in the Western Cape of Southern Africa. *Southern African Humanities* 20: 205–220.

Ashley, C. 2018. (Re)making Landscape and Place: An archaeology of the Lake Ngami Mission (1893–96), Khwebe Hills, Botswana. *Journal of Southern African Studies* 44 (4): 703–22.

Avery, G. 1985. Late Holocene use of penguin skins: Evidence from a coastal shell midden at Steenbras Bay, Lüderitz peninsula, SWA/Namibia. *Annals of the South African Museum* 96: 55–65.

Baer, E. 2018. *The Genocidal Gaze: From German South West Africa to the Third Reich*. Windhoek: University of Namibia Press.

Baer, E. 2020. A Reconsideration of Sexual Violence in German Colonial and Nazi Ideology and Its Representation in Holocaust Texts. In Aarons, V. & Lassner, P. eds *The Palgrave Handbook of Holocaust Literature and Culture*. Palgrave Macmillan, pp. 651–8.

Bahn, P.G. 2001. Save the last trance for me: An assessment of the misuse of shamanism in rock art studies. In Francfort, H.P., Hamayon, R.N. & Bahn, P.G. eds *The concept of shamanism: Uses and abuses*. Budapest: Akadémiai Kiado, pp. 51–94.

Bahn, P.G. 2010. *Prehistoric rock art: Polemics and Progress*. Cambridge: Cambridge University Press.

Barham, L. 1989. *The Later Stone Age of Swaziland*. Unpublished PhD thesis, University of Pennsylvania. *Dissertations available from ProQuest*. AAI8922465. https://repository.upenn.edu/dissertations/AAI8922465

Barham, L. 2013. *From Hand to Handle: The first Industrial Revolution*. Oxford: Oxford University Press.

Barham, L. & Mitchell, P. 2008. *The first Africans: African archaeology from the earliest toolmakers to most recent foragers*. Cambridge: Cambridge University Press.

Barnard, A. 1979. Nharo Bushmen medicine and medicine men. *Africa* 49: 68–80.

Barnard, A. 1992a. *The Kalahari Debate: A bibliographical essay*. Edinburgh: Centre for African Studies, University of Edinburgh.

Barnard, A. 1992b. *Hunters and Herders of Southern Africa: A Comparative Ethnography of the Khoisan Peoples*. Cambridge: Cambridge University Press.

Barron, L.S. 1978. *The Nazis in Africa*. Documentary Publications. ISBN-13: 978-0897120760.

Barrow, J. 1801. *Travels Into the Interior of Southern Africa: In which are Described the Character and the Condition of the Dutch Colonists of the Cape of Good Hope, and of the Several Tribes of Natives Beyond Its Limits, the Natural History of Such Subjects as Occurred in the Animal, Mineral, and Vegetable Kingdoms, and the Geography of the Southern Extremity of Africa*. Vol. 2. London: T. Cadell Jun. and W. Davies.

Beaumont, P. 1973. The ancient pigment mines of southern Africa. *South African Journal of Science* 69: 140–6.

Beaumont, P. & Boshier, A. 1974. Report on test excavations in a prehistoric pigment mine near Postmasburg, northern Cape. *South African Archaeological Bulletin* 29: 49–59.

Beavon, K.S.O. & Hall, A.V. 1972. A geotaxonomic approach to classification in urban and regional studies. *Geographic Analysis* 4: 407–15.

Becker, H. 2020. Writing genocide: Fiction, biography and oral history of the German colonial genocide in Namibia, 1904–1908. *Matatu* 50: 361–395.

Bednarik, R. 1990. On Neuropsychology and Shamanism in Rock Art. *Current Anthropology* 31 (1): 77–80.

Berat, L. 1990. *Walvis Bay: The Last Frontier.* New Haven and London: Radix.

Berger, L.R., Hawks, J., Dirks, P.H., Elliott, M. & Roberts, E.M. 2017. *Homo naledi* and Pleistocene hominin evolution in subequatorial Africa. *Elife* 6: e24234.

Berkovitch, B.M. 1976. *The Cape Gunsmith.* Stellenbosch: Museum Stellenbosch.

Berry, D.P., Friggins, N.C., Lucy, M. & Roche, J.R. 2016. Milk production and fertility in cattle. *Annual Review of Animal Biosciences* 4: 269–90.

Biesele, M. 1993. *Women like meat: The folklore and foraging ecology of the Kalahari Jul'hoan.* Johannesburg: Witwatersrand University Press.

Binneman, J.N.F. 1982. *Mikrogebruikstekens op steenwerktuie: Eksperimentele waarnemings en 'n studie van werktuie afkomstig van Boomplaasgrot.* Unpublished MA thesis, University of Stellenbosch, Stellenbosch.

Blackwell, L., Bradfield, J., Karlson, K.J., Jashashvili, T., Wadley, L. & d'Errico, F. 2018. The antiquity of bow-and-arrow technology: Evidence from Middle Stone Age layers at Sibudu Cave. *Antiquity* 92: 289–303.

Bleek, D.F. 1933. Beliefs and customs of the |Xam Bushmen, Part VI: Rain-making. *Bantu Studies* 7: 375–92.

Blench, R. 1993. Recent developments in African language classification and their implications for prehistory. In Shaw, T., Sinclair, P.J., Andah, B. & Okpoko, A. eds *The archaeology of Africa: Food, Metals and Towns.* London: Routledge, pp. 126–38.

Bley, H. 1996. *Namibia under German rule.* Studien zur Afrikanischen Geschichte Bd. 5. Hamburg: Lit Verlag.

Blum, J.D., Taliaferro, E.H., Weisse, M.T. & Holmes, R.T. 2000. Changes in Sr/Ca, Ba/Ca and ^{87}Sr/^{86}Sr ratios between two forest ecosystems in the north-eastern USA. *Biogeochemistry* 49: 87–101.

Blümel, W.D., Eberle, J., Hüser, K. & Eitel, B. 2009. Holozäne Klima- und Landschaftswandel in der Namib? *Acta Nova Leopoldina* NF 108, 373: 125–49.

Boast, R. & Yiannoulis, E. 1986. Creating space. *Archaeological Review from Cambridge* 5 (2): 136–40.

Bollig, M. 1997a. Contested places: Graves and Graveyards in Himba Culture. *Anthropos* 92: 35–50.

Bollig, M. 1997b. Risk and Risk Minimization among Himba pastoralists in north-western Namibia. *Nomadic Peoples* 1 (1): 66–89.

Bollig, M. 2020. *Shaping the African savanna: From Capitalist Frontier to Arid Eden in Namibia*. Cambridge: Cambridge University Press.

Bollig, M. & Gewald, J-B. 2000. People, Cattle and Land: Transformations of a Pastoral Society in Southwestern Africa. *In People, Cattle and Land: Transformations of a Pastoral Society in Southwestern Africa*. Cologne: Köppe.

Bollig, M. & Lang, H. 1999. Demographic growth and resource exploitation in two pastoral communities. *Nomadic Peoples* 3 (2): 16–34.

Bonneau, A., Brock, F., Higham, T.F.G., Pearce, D.G. & Pollard, A.M. 2011. An improved pretreatment protocol for radiocarbon dating black pigments in San rock art. *Radiocarbon* 53: 419–28.

Bonneau, A., Pearce, D.G. & Pollard, A.M. 2012. A multi-technique characterization and provenance study of the pigments used in San rock art, South Africa. *Journal of Archaeological Science* 39: 287–94.

Bonneau, A., Staff, R.A., Arthur, C. & Brock, F. 2017. The earliest directly dated rock paintings from southern Africa: New AMS radiocarbon dates. *Antiquity* 91: 322–33.

Bonte, P. 1981. Marxist theory and anthropological analysis: The study of nomadic pastoralist societies. In Kahn, J.S. & Llobera, J.R. eds *The Anthropology of Pre-capitalist Societies*. London: Macmillan, pp. 22–56.

Borror, D., DeLong, D. & Triplehorn, C. 2004. *Introduction to the Study of Insects*. New York: Holt, Rinehart and Winston.

Bousman, C.B. & Brink, J.S. 2018. The emergence, spread, and termination of the Early Later Stone Age event in South Africa and southern Namibia. *Quaternary International* 495: 116–35.

Bradfield, J. 2019. Fishing with gorges: Testing a functional hypothesis. *Journal of Archaeological Science (Reports)* 24: 593–607.

Bradtmöller, M., Grimm, S. & Riel-Salvatore, J. 2017. Resilience theory in archaeological practice – an annotated review. *Quaternary International* 446: 3–16.

Brain, C.K. 1967. Hottentot food remains and their bearing on the interpretation of fossil bone assemblages. *Scientific Papers of the Namib Desert Research Station* 32.

Brain, C.K. 1969. The contribution of Namib Desert Hottentots to an understanding of Australopithecine bone accumulations. *Scientific Papers of the Namib Desert Research Station* 39.

Brain, C.K. 1981. *The hunters or the hunted? An introduction to African cave taphonomy.* Chicago: University of Chicago Press.

Brain, C.K. & Brain, V. 1977. Microfaunal remains from Mirabib: Some evidence of palaeoecological changes in the Namib. *Madoqua* 10 (4): 285–93.

Branch, M. & Branch, G. 1981. *The Living Shores of Southern Africa.* Cape Town: Struik.

Brandt, N. 2020. *Landscapes between then and now: Recent histories in southern African photography, performance and video art.* London: Bloomsbury Visual Arts.

Bravenboer, B. & Rusch, K. 1997. *First one hundred years of state railways in Namibia.* Windhoek: TransNamib Museum.

Breuil, H. 1955. *The White Lady of the Brandberg.* London: Trianon Press.

Breunig, P. 1985. New excavations in the Brandberg provide clues to the age of the rock paintings. *The Digging Stick* 2 (3): 3.

Breunig, P. 1986. *Ernst-Rudolf Scherz, Felsbilder in Südwest-Afrika Vol. 3. Die Malereien.* Zusammenfassungen. Köln Wien: Böhlau Verlag.

Breunig, P. 2003. *Der Brandberg – untersuchungen zur Besiedlungsgeschichte eines Hochgebirges in Namibia.* Köln: Afrika Praehistorica 17.

Breunig, P., Behringer, H., Fels, M. & Maidhof, J. 2019. West of the Best. Rock art and archaeological discoveries in the Doro!nawas region of northwest Namibia. *Acta Archaeologica* 89: 99–118.

Bridgeford, P. 2008. One hundred years of conservation: From Game Reserve No. 3 to Namib-Naukluft Park. *Journal Namibia Wissenschaftliche Gesellschaft* 56: 45–62.

Bridgeman, J.M. 1981. *The Revolt of the Hereros*. Berkeley and Los Angeles: University of California Press.

Briedenhann, S.J. & Van Reenen, J.F. 1985. Tooth extraction and tooth mutilating practices amongst the Herero-speaking peoples of South West Africa (Namibia). *Journal of the Dental Association of South Africa* 40 (9): 531–536.

Bronk Ramsey, C. 2016. *OxCal Program v4. 2.4*. Oxford: Radiocarbon Accelerator Unit, Oxford University.

Brook, G., Srivastava, P. & Marais, E. 2006. Characteristics and OSL minimum ages of relict fluvial deposits near Sossus Vlei, Tsauchab River, Namibia, and a regional climate record for the last 30 ka. *Journal of Quaternary Science* 21 (4): 347–62.

Brook, G., Marais, E., Srivastava, P. & Jordan, T. 2007. Timing of lake-level changes in Etosha Pan, Namibia, since the middle Holocene from OSL ages of relict shorelines in the Okondeka region. *Quaternary International* 175: 29–40.

Brothwell, D.R. 1981. *Digging Up Bones*. 3rd edn. London: Oxford University Press.

Buch, M.W. 1996. Geochrono-Geomorphostratigraphie der Etosha Region, Nord-Namibia. *Die Erde* 127: 1–22.

Budack, K.F.R. 1977. The ǂAonîn or Topnaar of the lower !Khuiseb valley and the sea. *Khoisan Linguistic Studies* 3: 1–42.

Buikstra, J. & Uberlaker, D.H. 1994. *Standards for data collection from human skeletal remains*. Fayetteville: Arkansas Archaeological Survey Research Series: 4.

Bullock, D. & Rackham, J. 1982. Ephiseal fusion and tooth eruption of feral goats from Moffatdale, Dumfries and Galloway, Scotland. In Wilson, B., Grigson, C. & Payne, S. eds *Ageing and sexing animal bones from archaeological sites*. British Archaeological Reports 109: 73–80.

Burchell, W.J. 1824. *Travels in the Interior of Africa*. (2 vols). London: Longman, Hurst, Rees, Orme, Brown and Green.

Burden, T. 2017. Rivers of Blood and Money: The Herero Genocide in German Southwest Africa. *The Student Researcher: A Phi Alpha Theta Publication* 2, Article 2.

Burfeindt, C. 1970. *Der Weg zum Brandberg*. Windhoek: Selbstverlag.

Burroughs, W.J. 2005. *Climate Change in Prehistory: The End of the Reign of Chaos*. Cambridge: Cambridge University Press.

Cameron, C.M. 2009. A Brief History of Botulism in South Africa. *Onderstepoort Journal of Veterinary Research* 76: 11–12.

Carstens, P., Klinghardt, G. & West, M. 1987. *Trails in the Thirstland: The anthropological field diaries of Winifred Hoernlé*. Cape Town: Centre for African Studies, Communications No. 14.

Carter, P.L., Mitchell, P.J. & Vinnicombe, P. 1988. *Sehonghong: The Middle and Later Stone Age industrial sequence at a Lesotho rock shelter*. Oxford: British Archaeological Reports, S.406.

Cashdan, E.A. 1985. Coping with risk: Reciprocity among the Basarwa of northern Botswana. *Man* (N.S.) 20: 454–74.

Chami, F.A. 2006. *The Unity of African History, 3000BC to AD500*. Dar es Salaam: E&D.

Charlton, N.G. 2008. *Understanding Gregory Bateson: Mind, beauty and the sacred earth*. New York: State University of New York Press.

Chase, B. & Meadows, M. 2007. Late Quaternary dynamics of southern Africa's winter rainfall zone. *Earth Science Reviews* 84: 103–138.

Chase, B., Meadows, M., Scott, L., Thomas, D.S.G., Marais, E., Sealy, J. & Reimer, P.J. 2009. A record of rapid Holocene climate change preserved in hyrax middens from southwestern Africa. *Geology* 37 (8): 703–706.

Chase, B.M. 2010. South African palaeoenvironments during marine oxygen isotope stage 4: A context for the Howiesons Poort and Still Bay industries. *Journal of Archaeological Science* 37: 1359–66.

Chase, B.M., Tyler Faith, J., Mackay, A., Chevalier, M., Carr, A.S., Boom, A., Lim, S. & Reimer, P.J. 2018. Climatic controls on Later Stone Age human adaptations in Africa's southern Cape. *Journal of Human Evolution* 114: 35–44.

Chazan, M. 2017. Toward a Long Prehistory of Fire. *Current Anthropology* 58: 351–9.

Chirikure, S. & Sinamai, A. 2015. World History from the Seabed: Rescuing a Portuguese Shipwreck off the Coast of Namibia. *Shipwreck Around the World. Revelations of the Past*. New Delhi: Delta Book World, pp. 114–29.

Chirikure, S., Sinamai, A., Goagoses, E., Mubusisi, M. & Ndoro, W. 2010. Maritime archaeology and trans-oceanic trade: A case study of the Oranjemund shipwreck cargo, Namibia. *Journal of Maritime Archaeology* 5: 37–55.

Clarence-Smith, W.G. 1979. *Slaves, Peasants and Capitalists in Southern Angola, 1840–1926*. Cambridge: Cambridge University Press.

Clark, J.D.G. 1969. *Kalambo Falls Prehistoric Site Volume 1: The Geology, Palaeoecology and Detailed Stratigraphy of the Excavations*. Cambridge: Cambridge University Press.

Clarkson, J.J., Knapp, S., Garcia, V.F., Olmstead, R.G., Leitch, A.R. & Chase, M.W. 2004. Phylogenetic relationships in *Nicotiana* (Solanaceae) inferred from multiple plastid DNA regions. *Molecular Phylogenetics and Evolution* 33: 75–90.

Cohen, K.M. & Gibbard, P.L. 2019. Global chronostratigraphical correlation table for the last 2.7 million years, version 2019 QI-500. *Quaternary International* 500: 20–31.

Collyer, J. 2013. *The Campaign in German South West Africa, 1914–1915*. London: Naval and Military Press.

Comaroff, J. & Comaroff, J. 1986. Christianity and colonialism in South Africa. *American Ethnologist* 13 (1): 1–22.

Compton, J. 2006. The mid-Holocene sea-level highstand at Bogenfels Pan on the southwest coast of Namibia. *Quaternary Research* 66: 303–10.

Compton, J. 2007. Holocene evolution of the Anichab Pan on the southwest coast of Namibia. *Sedimentology* 54: 55–70.

Conard, N.J., Breunig, P., Gonska, H. & Marinetti, G. 1988. The feasibility of dating rock paintings from Brandberg, Namibia, with C-14. *Journal of Archaeological Science* 15: 463–6.

Conca, J.L. & Rossman, G.R. 1982. Case hardening of sandstone. *Geology* 10 (10): 520–23.

Conroy, G.C., Pickford, M., Senut, B., Van Couvering, J. & Mein, P. 1992. *Otavipithecus namibiensis*, first Miocene hominoid from southern Africa. *Nature* 356: 144–8.

Corvinus, G. 1983. *The Raised Beaches of the West Coast of South West Africa/Namibia: An Interpretation of their Archaeological and Palaeontological Data*. Forschungen zur Allgemeinen und Vergleichenden Archäologie, 5, München: C.H. Beck.

Cowling, R.M., Richardson, D.M., Schultze, R.E., Hoffman, M.T., Midgley, J.J. & Hilton-Taylor, C. 1997. Species diversity at the regional scale. In Cowling, R.M., Richardson, D.M. & Pierce,

S.M. eds *Vegetation of Southern Africa*. Cambridge: Cambridge University Press, pp. 447–73.

Craffert, P.F. 2011. Shamanism and the shamanic complex. *Biblical Theology Bulletin* 41 (2): 59–67.

Crandall, D. 1991. The strength of the OvaHimba patrilineage. *Cimbebasia* 13: 45–51.

Crandall, D. 1996. Female over male or left over right: Solving a classificatory puzzle among the OvaHimba. *Africa* 66: 327–48.

Crandall, D. 2000. *The Place of Stunted Ironwood Trees*. New York: Continuum.

Craven, P. 2009. *Phytogeographic study of the Kaokoveld centre of endemism*. Unpublished PhD thesis, University of Stellenbosch, Stellenbosch.

Cruz-Uribe, K. & Klein, R.G. 1983. Faunal remains from some Middle and Late Stone Age archaeological sites in South West Africa. *Journal of the South West Africa Scientific Society* 36/7: 91–114.

Curtis, B. & Mannheimer, C. 2005. *Tree Atlas of Namibia*. Windhoek: National Botanical Research Institute.

Dahl, G. & Hjort, A. 1976. *Pastoral Herd Growth and Household Economy*. 1st edn. Stockholm: Stockholm Studies in Social Anthropology, 2.

Davis, W. 1990. The study of rock art in Africa. In Robertshaw, P.T. ed. *A History of African Archaeology*. London: James Currey, pp. 271–95.

Deacon, H. 1974. A Review of the post-Pleistocene in South Africa. *South African Archaeological Society Goodwin Series* 1: 26–45.

Deacon, H. 1976. *Where hunters gathered: A study of Holocene Stone Age peoples in the Eastern Cape*. Claremont: South African Archaeological Society.

Deacon, H. & Wurz, S. 2001. Middle Pleistocene populations of southern Africa and the emergence of modern behavior. In Barham, L. & Robson-Brown, K. eds *Human roots: Africa and Asia in the Middle Pleistocene*. Bristol: Western Academic and Specialist Press, pp. 55–63.

Deacon, J. 1984. *The Later Stone Age of southernmost Africa*. Oxford: British Archaeological Reports International Series 213.

Deacon, J. 1994. Rock engravings and the folklore of Bleek and Lloyd's |Xam San informants. In Dowson, T. & Lewis-Williams, J.D. eds

Contested images: Diversity in southern African rock art research. Johannesburg: Witwatersrand University Press, pp. 237–56.

Deacon, J. & Lancaster, N. 1988. *Late Quaternary palaeoenvironments of southern Africa.* Oxford: Oxford University Press.

Deacon, J. & Mazel, A. 2010. uKhahlamba Drakensberg and Mapungubwe: Contrasts in South Africa's World Heritage rock art sites. *Adoranten* 2010: 5–23.

DeAngelis, D.L. & Waterhouse, J.C. 1987. Equilibrium and non-equilibrium concepts in ecological models. *Ecological Monographs* 57: 1–21.

Delaunay, A.N., Belardi, J.B., Marina, F.C. Saletta, M.J. & De Angelis, H. 2017. Glass and stoneware knapped tools among southern continental Patagonian and Fuegian hunter-gatherers from the late sixteenth to the twentieth century. *Antiquity* 91: 1330–43.

Denbow, J.R. 1979. *Cenchrus ciliaris*: An ecological indicator of Iron Age middens using aerial photography in Eastern Botswana. *South African Journal of Science* 75: 405–9.

Denbow, J.R. 1983. *Iron Age economics: Herding, wealth and politics along the fringes of the Kalahari Desert during the Early Iron Age.* Unpublished Ph.D thesis, Bloomington, Indiana.

Denbow, J.R. 1984. Prehistoric herders and foragers of the Kalahari: The evidence of 1500 years of interaction. In Schrire, C. ed. *Past and present in hunter-gatherer studies.* Orlando, Academic Press, pp. 175–93.

Denbow, J.R. 1986. A new look at the later prehistory of the Kalahari. *Journal of African History* 27: 3–28.

Denbow, J.R. 1990. Congo to Kalahari: Data and hypotheses about the political economy of the western stream of the early Iron Age. *African Archaeological Review* 8: 139–76.

Denbow, J.R. & Wilmsen, E.N. 1986. Advent and course of pastoralism in the Kalahari. *Science* 234: 1509–15.

DeNiro, M.J. 1985. Postmortem preservation and alteration of *in vivo* collagen isotope ratios in relation to palaeodietary reconstruction. *Nature* 317: 806–809.

Dentlinger, U. 1977. *The !nara plant in the Topnaar Hottentot culture of Namibia: Ethnobotanical clues to an 8000 year old tradition.* Munger Africana Library Notes 38.

Dentlinger, U. 1983. *Social and spatial mobility along the !Khuiseb River in the Namib Desert*. Unpublished MA thesis, University of Cape Town, Cape Town.

d'Errico, F., Henshilwood, C.S. & Nilssen, P. 2001. An engraved bone fragment from ca. 75 kyr Middle Stone Age levels at Blombos Cave, South Africa: Implications for the origin of symbolism and language. *Antiquity* 75: 309–18.

d'Errico, F., Henshilwood, C.S., Vanhaeren, M. & van Niekerk, K. 2005. *Nassarius kraussianus* shell beads from Blombos Cave: Evidence for symbolic behaviour in the Middle Stone Age. *Journal of Human Evolution* 48: 2–14.

De Villiers, G. 1975. Growth, population dynamics, a mass mortality and arrangement of White Sand Mussels *Donax serra* Röding, on beaches in the southwestern Cape Province. *Investigative Reports Sea Fisheries Branch of South Africa* 109: 1–31.

De Villiers, P.A. & Kok, O.B. 1984. Verspreidingspatrone van olifante (*Loxodonta africana*) in Suidwes-Afrika met spesiale verwysing na die Nasionale Etoshawildtuin. *Madoqua* 13: 281–96.

De Vries, L. 1978. *Mission and colonialism in Namibia*. Johannesburg: Ravan Press.

Dewar, G., Halkett, D., Hart, T., Orton, J. & Sealy, J. 2005. Implications of a mass kill site of springbok (*Antidorcas marsupialis*) in South Africa: Hunting practices, gender relations and sharing in the Later Stone Age. *Journal of Archaeological Science* 33: 1266–75.

Dewar, G. & Marsh, E.J. 2018. The comings and goings of sheep and pottery in the coastal desert of Namaqualand, South Africa. *Journal of Island and Coastal Archaeology* 14: 17–45.

Diehl, M. 1990. *Geology, mineralogy, geochemistry and hydrothermal alteration of the Brandberg alkaline complex, Namibia*. Geological Survey of Namibia Memoir 10.

Dierks, K. 1992. *Namibian roads in history: From the 13th century till today*. Johann Wolfgang Goethe Universität, Frankfurt am Main: Frankfurter Wirtschafts- und Sozialgeographische Schriften.

Dobres, M.A. & Robb, J.E. eds 2000. *Agency in Archaeology*. New York: Routledge.

Drechsler, H. 1980. *Let us die fighting: The struggle of the Herero and Nama against German imperialism*. London: Zed Press.

Du Bruyn, J. 1981. The Oorlam Afrikaners: From dependence to dominance c. 1760–1823. Unpublished paper, University of South Africa, Pretoria.

Dudley, J.P. 1999. Seed dispersal of *Acacia erioloba* by African bush elephants in Hwange National Park, Zimbabwe. *African Journal of Ecology* 37: 375–85.

Dusseldorp, G.L. 2010. Prey choice during the South African Middle Stone Age: Avoiding dangerous prey or maximising returns? *African Archaeological Review* 27: 107–33.

Dusseldorp, G., Lombard, M. & Wurz, S. 2013. Pleistocene Homo and the updated Stone Age sequence of South Africa. *South African Journal of Science* 109 (5–6): 1–7.

Eastwood, E. 2006. Animals behaving like people: San rock paintings of kudu in the central Limpopo basin, southern Africa. *South African Archaeological Bulletin* 61: 26–39.

Eastwood, E. 2008. Networks of supernatural potency: San rock paintings of loincloths and aprons in the Central Limpopo Basin, southern Africa. *South African Archaeological Bulletin* 63: 130–43.

Eastwood, E. & Blundell, G. 1999. Re-discovering the rock art of the Limpopo-Shashi confluence area. *Southern African Field Archaeology* 8 (1): 17–27.

Eastwood, E. & Eastwood, C. 2006. *Capturing the Spoor: An Exploration of Southern African Rock Art*. Cape Town: David Philip.

Eisenmann, S., Bánffy, E., van Dommelen, P., Hofmann, K., Maran, J., Lazarides, I., Mittnik, A., McCormick, M., Krause, J., Reich, D. & Stockhammer, P. 2018. Reconciling material cultures in archaeology with genetic data: The nomenclature of clusters emerging from archaeogenomic analysis. *Nature (Scientific Reports)* 8: 13003.

Eitel, B. 2005. Environmental history of the Namib Desert. In Smith, M. & Hesse, P. eds. *23 Degrees South: Archaeology and environmental history of the southern deserts*. Canberra: National Museum of Australia Press, pp. 45–55.

Ellegård, K. & Svedin, U. 2012. Torsten Hägerstrand's time-geography as the cradle of the activity approach in transport geography. *Journal of Transport Geography* 23: 17–25.

Entrikin, J.N. ed. 2008. *Regions: Critical essays in human geography*. London: Routledge.

Elphick, R. 1985. *Khoikhoi and the founding of White South Africa*. Johannesburg: Ravan Press.

Eren, M.I. & Lycett, S.J. 2012. Why Levallois? A morphometric comparison of experimental 'preferential' Levallois flakes versus debitage flakes. *PLoS one* 7(1).

Ericson, J.E. 1989. Some problems and potentials for strontium isotope analysis for human and animal ecology. In Rundel, P.W. & Nagy, K.A. eds *Stable isotopes in ecological research*. New York: Springer Verlag, pp. 252-9.

Ervedosa, C. 1980. *Arqueologia Angolana*. República Popular de Angola: Ministerio da Educação.

Esterhuyse, J.H. 1968. *South West Africa 1880-1894*. Cape Town: Struik.

Estes, R.D. 1991. *The behaviour guide to African mammals*. Berkeley: University of California Press.

Faber-Jonker, L. 2018. *More than just an object: A material analysis of the return and retention of Namibian skulls from Germany*. Leiden: African Studies Centre.

Fath, B.D., Dean, C.A. & Katzmair, H. 2015. Navigating the adaptive cycle: An approach to managing the resilience of social systems. *Ecology and Society* 20 (2): 24.

Faure, G. 1986. *Principles of isotope geology*. New York: Springer Verlag.

Fitzhugh, B. 2000. Thoughts on the evolution of social inequality: A paradigmatic analysis. In Kradin, N. ed. *Alternatives to Social Evolution*. Vladivostok: Archaeological Institute of the Russian Far East, pp. 103-16.

Fitzhugh, B., Butler, V.L., Bovy, K.M. & Etnier, M.A. 2019. Human ecodynamics: A perspective for the study of long-term change in socioecological systems. *Journal of Archaeological Science: Reports* 23: 1077-94.

Forsmann, T. & Gutteridge, L. 2012. *Bushman rock art: An interpretative guide*. Johannesburg: 30 Degrees South.

Fox, F.W. & Norwood Young, M.E. 1982. *Food from the veld: Edible wild plants of Southern Africa*. Johannesburg: Delta.

Freeman, J., Hard, R.J. & Mauldin, R.P. 2017. A theory of regime-change on the Texas coastal plain. *Quaternary International* 446: 1-12.

Freundlich, J.C., Schwabedissen, H. & Wendt, W.E. 1980. Köln radiocarbon measurements II. *Radiocarbon* 22 (1): 68-81.

Fullagar, R. & Wallis, L. 2012. Usewear and phytoliths on bedrock grinding patches, Pilbara, north-western Australia. *The Artefact* 35: 75–87.

Galbraith, R.F., Roberts, R.G., Laslett, G.M., Yoshida, H. & Olley, J.M. 1999. Optical dating of single and multiple grains of quartz from Jinmium Rock Shelter, northern Australia: Part I, experimental design and statistical models. *Archaeometry* 41(2): 339–6.

Galton, F. 1889. *Narrative of an Explorer in Tropical South Africa, Being an Account of a Visit to Damaraland in 1851*. London: Ward, Lock & Co.

Gann, L.H. & Duignan, P. 1977. *The Rulers of German Africa 1884–1914*. Stanford: Stanford University Press.

Gardner, E. 1803. Typewritten copy of manuscript journal. Call no. F5.24.10. Cambridge, MA: The Houghton Library, Harvard University.

Garlake, P. 1990. Symbols of potency in the paintings of Zimbabwe. *South African Archaeological Bulletin* 45: 17–27.

Gelderblom, O., De Jong, A. & Jonker, J. 2013. The formative years of the modern corporation: The Dutch East India Company VOC, 1602–1623. *Journal of Economic History* 73: 1050–76.

Gewald, J-B. 1999. *Herero Heroes: A socio-political history of the Herero of Namibia*. London: James Currey.

Gibson, G.D. 1962. The Himba trumpet. *Man* 62: 161–3.

Gibson, G.D. 1977. Himba epochs. *History in Africa* 4: 67–121.

Gibson, G.D. 2009. Double descent and its correlates among the Herero of Ngamiland. *American Anthropologist* 58 (1): 109–39.

Giddens, A. 1984. *The constitution of society: Outline of a theory of structuration*. Berkeley: University of California Press.

Gil-Romera, G., Scott, L., Marais, E. & Brook, G. 2006. Middle- to late-Holocene moisture changes in the desert of northwest Namibia derived from fossil hyrax dung pollen. *The Holocene* 16 (8): 1073–84.

Gingele, F.X. 1996. Holocene climatic optimum in Southwest Africa – evidence from the marine clay mineral record. *Palaeogeography, Palaeoclimatology, Palaeoecology* 122: 77–87.

Gluckman, P.D., Hanson, M.A. & Spencer, H.G. 2005. Predictive adaptive responses and human evolution. *Trends in Ecology and Evolution* 20 (10): 527–33.

Goodspeed, T.H. 1954. *The genus Nicotiana: Origins, relationships and evolution of its species in the light of their distribution, morphology and cytogenetics*. Waltham, Mass.: Chronica Botanica Company.

Gordon, R. 1779. Journal of Col. Robt. Gordon: 1 Oct 1779 to 13 Jan 1780. Cape Archives VC 593. Cape Town: Cape Town Archives Repository.

Goudie, A.S. 1996. Climate: Past and Present. In Adams, W.M., Goudie, A.S. & Orme, A.R. eds *The Physical Geography of Africa*. Oxford: Oxford University Press, pp. 34–59.

Gowlett, J.A.J. 1996. Mental abilities of early *Homo*. In Mellars, P. & Gibson, K. eds *Modelling the early human mind*. Cambridge: MacDonald Institute for Early Human Research, pp. 191–215.

Grab, S. & Zumthurm, T. 2020. 'Everything is scorched by the burning sun': Missionary perspectives and experiences of 19th and early 20th century droughts in semi-arid central Namibia. *Climate of the Past* 16: 679–97.

Grawe, L. 2019. The Prusso-German General Staff and the Herero Genocide. *Central European History* 52: 588–619.

Greenbaum, N., Schwartz, U., Benito, G., Poirat, N., Cloete, G. & Enzel, Y. 2014. Palaeohydrology of extraordinary floods along the Swakop River at the margin of the Namib Desert and their palaeoclimatic implications. *Quaternary Science Reviews* 103: 153–169.

Grimm, H. 1929. *Die dreizen Briefe aus Deutsch Südwestafrika*. Albert Langren: Berlin.

Grine, F.E., Wurz, S. & Marean, C.W. 2017. The Middle Stone Age human fossil record from Klasies River main site. *Journal of Human Evolution* 103: 53–78.

Grün, R., Brink, J.S., Spooner, N.A., Taylor, L., Stringer, C.B., Franciscus, R.G. & Murray, A.S. 1996. Direct dating of Florisbad hominid. *Nature* 382 (6591): 500–1.

Guenther, M.G. 1975. The trance dancer as an agent of social change among the farm Bushmen of the Ghanzi District. *Botswana Notes and Records* 7: 161–6.

Guenther, M.G. 1999. *Tricksters and trancers: Bushman religion and society*. Bloomington: Indiana University Press.

Guenther, M.G. 2020. Experiencing Transformation. In Guenther, M.G. ed. *Human-animal relationships in San and hunter-gatherer cosmology.* (Vol 2) Cham: Palgrave Macmillan, pp. 43–68.

Gunderson, L.H. & Holling, C.S. 2002. *Panarchy: Understanding transformation in human and natural systems.* Washington: Island Press.

Günster, A. 1992. Aerial seed banks in the central Namib: Distribution of serotinous plants in relation to climate and habitat. *Journal of Biogeography* 19: 563–72.

Guérin, G., Murray, A.S., Jain, M., Thomsen, K.J. & Mercier, N. 2013. How confident are we in the chronology of the transition between Howiesons Poort and Still Bay? *Journal of Human Evolution* 64: 314–7.

Gugelberger, G. 1984. *Nama/Namibia: Diary and Letters of Nama Chief Hendrik Witbooi, 1884–1894.* Boston: Boston University African Studies Centre.

Guillemard, I. 2020. Equating language, genes and subsistence? The appearance of herding in southern Africa. *Azania* 55: 97–120.

Gürich, G. 1891. Deutsch Südwest-Afrika: Reisebilder und Skizzen aus den Jahren 1888 und 1889 mit einer Originale Routenkarte. *Mitteilungen der Geographische Geschichte* 1: 1–216.

Gustafsson, K. 2005. The trade in slaves in Ovamboland, ca 1850–1910. *African Economic History* 33: 31–68.

Haacke, W.H.G. & Eiseb, E. 2002. *A Khoekhoegowab dictionary.* Windhoek: Gamsberg Macmillan.

Hahn, C.H. *Tagebücher 1837–1860 Diaries: A missionary in Nama- and Damaraland.* ed. Lau, B. in *Archeia* 1–5, Archives Services Division of the Department of National Education, Windhoek, Namibia, 1984/1985.

Hampson, J., Challis, W., Blundell, G. & De Rosner, C. 2002. The rock art of Bongani Mountain Lodge and its environs, Mpumalanga Province, South Africa: An introduction to problems of southern African rock-art regions. *South African Archaeological Bulletin* 57: 15–30.

Hangara, N., Kavari, J.U. & Tutjavi, E. 2020. *Ozongombe mOmbazu ya Kaoko: Cattle Culture of the Kaoko Ovaherero.* Windhoek: University of Namibia Press.

Hardung, C. 2014. God, the warlord and the way of the ancestors: On the intertwinement of Christianity and ancestry in Hendrik Witbooi's politico-religious mission of the 1880s (Southwest Africa). *Civilizations* 63: 81–98.

Härke, H. ed. 2000. *Archaeology, ideology and society: The German experience.* Gesellschaften und Staaten im Epochenwandel 7, Frankfurt am Main: Peter Lang.

Harlan, J. 1993. The tropical African cereals. In Shaw, T., Sinclair, P., Andah, B. & Okpoko, A. eds *The Archaeology of Africa: Food, Metals and Towns.* London: Routledge, pp. 53–60.

Harris, A.C., Tally, L., Muelken, P., Banal, A., Schmidt, C.E., Cao, Q. & LeSage, M.G. 2015. Effects of nicotine and minor tobacco alkaloids on intracranial-self-stimulation in rats. *Drug and Alcohol Dependence* 153: 330–4.

Hartmann, W., Silvester, J. & Hayes, P. 1999. *The Colonizing Camera: Photographs in the making of Namibian history.* Cape Town: University of Cape Town Press.

Hay, R.L. 1976. *Geology of the Olduvai Gorge.* Berkeley: University of California Press.

Henrichsen, D. 1997. *Herrschaft und Alltag in Zentralnamibia: das Herero- und Damaraland im 19 Jahrhundert.* Unpublished doctoral dissertation, University of Hamburg, Hamburg.

Henschel, J. 2004. *!Nara: Fruit for the development of the !Khuiseb Topnaar.* Windhoek: Namibia Scientific Society.

Henschel, J., Burke, A. & Seely, M. 2005. Temporal and spatial variability of grass productivity in the central Namib Desert. *African Study Monographs* Suppl. 30: 43–56.

Henshilwood, C.S., d'Errico, F., Yates, R., Jacobs, Z., Tribolo, C., Duller, G., Mercier, N., Sealy, J., Valladas, H., Watts, I. & Wintle, A. 2002. Emergence of modern human behaviour: Middle Stone Age engravings from South Africa. *Science* 295: 1278–80.

Heywood, A. & Maasdorp, E. 1989. *The Hendrik Witbooi Papers.* Windhoek: National Archives of Namibia, *Archeia* 13.

Hillier, B. & Hanson, J. 1984. *The Social Logic of Space.* Cambridge: Cambridge University Press.

Hitchcock, R.K., Crowell, A.L., Brooks, A.S., Yellen, J.E., Ebert, J.I. & Osborn, A.J. 2019. The ethnoarchaeology of ambush hunting: A case study of ǂGi Pan, Western Ngamiland, Botswana. *African Archaeological Review* 36: 119–44.

Hodgson, F.D.I. 1972. *The geology of the Brandberg Aba-Huab area, South West Africa.* Unpublished DSc thesis, University of the Orange Free State, Bloemfontein.

Hoeck, H.N. 1982. Population dynamics, dispersal and genetic isolation in two species of hyrax (*Heterohyrax brucei* and *Procavia johnstoni*) on habitat islands in the Serengeti. *Zeitschrift für Tierpsychologie* 59: 177–210.

Holling, C.S. 1973. Resilience and stability of ecological systems. *Annual review of ecology and systematics* 4 (1):1–23.

Hollmann, J. 2001. 'Big pictures': Insights into southern African San rock paintings of ostriches. *The South African Archaeological Bulletin* 56: 62–75.

Hollmann, J. ed. 2004. *Customs and beliefs of the /Xam Bushmen.* Johannesburg: Witwatersrand University Press.

Hollmann, J. 2007. ǀKaggen's code: Paintings of moths in southern African hunter-gatherer rock art. *Southern African Humanities* 19: 83–101.

Holmgren, K., Lee-Thorp, J.A., Cooper, G.J., Lundblad, K., Partridge, T.C., Scott, L., Sithaldeen, R., Talma, A.S., & Tyson, P.D. 2003. Persistent millennial-scale climatic variability over the past 25 thousand years in southern Africa. *Quaternary Science Reviews* 22: 2311–26.

Horsburgh, K. & Rhines, A. 2010. Genetic characterization of an archaeological sheep assemblage from South Africa's Western Cape. *Journal of Archaeological Science* 37: 2906–10.

Huffman, T.N. 1996. Archaeological evidence for climatic change during the last 2000 years in southern Africa. *Quaternary International* 33: 55–60.

Huffman, T.N. 2006. Bantu migrations in southern Africa. In Soodyall, H. ed. *The Prehistory of Africa: Tracing the lineage of modern man.* Johannesburg: Jonathan Ball, pp. 97–108.

Huffman, T.N. 2010. Intensive El Niño and the Iron Age of southeastern Africa. *Journal of Archaeological Science* 37(10): 2572–86.

Hull, I.V. 2005. *Absolute Destruction: Military Culture and the Practices of War in Imperial Germany.* Ithaca: Cornell University Press.

Huntley, B. 1985. The Kuiseb environment. In Huntley, B. ed. *The Kuiseb environment: The development of a monitoring baseline.* S.A. National Scientific Programmes Report 106: 7–20.

Ikeya, K. 1993. Goat raising among the San in the central Kalahari. *African Study Monographs* 14: 39–52.

Illius, A.W. & O'Connor, T.G. 1999. On the relevance of non-equilibrium concepts to arid and semi-arid grazing systems. *Ecological Applications* 9: 798–813.

Ingman, M., Kasessmann, H., Pääbo, S. & Gyllensten, U. 2000. Mitochondrial genome variation and the origins of modern humans. *Nature* 408: 708–13.

Ingold, T. 1980. *Hunters, pastoralists and ranchers: Reindeer economies and their transformations.* Cambridge: Cambridge University Press.

Jacobs, Z., Roberts, R.G., Galbraith, R.F., Deacon, H.J., Grün, R., Mackay, A., Mitchell, P., Vogelsang, R. & Wadley, L. 2008. Ages for the Middle Stone Age of southern Africa: Implications for human behaviour and dispersal. *Science* 322: 733–35.

Jacobson, L. 1977. A pottery cache from the Bethanie District, South West Africa. *Cimbebasia* 2 (10).

James, S.R. 1989. Hominid use of fire in the lower and middle Pleistocene: A review of the evidence. *Current Anthropology* 30: 1–26.

Jerardino, A. 1996. *Changing social landscapes of the Western Cape coast of southern Africa over the last 4500 years.* Unpublished PhD thesis, University of Cape Town, Cape Town.

Jerardino, A., Klein, R.G., Navarro, R., Orton, J. & Horwitz, L. 2013. Settlement and subsistence patterns since the terminal Pleistocene in the Elands Bay and Lamberts Bay areas. In Jerardino, A., Malan, A. & Braun, D. eds *The Archaeology of the West Coast of South Africa.* Cambridge Monographs in African Archaeology 84: 85–108.

Jerardino, A. & Navarro, R. 2018. Large-scale hunter-gatherer exploitation of marine resources in South Africa, Part 1: 'Kreefbaai C' Megamidden, Lamberts Bay area. *South African Archaeological Bulletin* 73: 93–107.

Jerardino, A. & Swanepoel, N. 1999. Painted slabs from excavations at Steenbokfontein Cave: Implications for past and future research. *Current Anthropology* 40: 542–8.

Johnson, M. 2010. *Archaeological theory: An introduction*. New York: John Wiley & Sons.

Jolly, P. 1996. Symbiotic interactions between Black farmers and southeastern San: Implications for southern African rock art studies, ethnographic analogy and hunter-gatherer cultural identity. *Cultural Anthropology* 37: 277–306.

Jolly, P. 2006. Dancing with two sticks: Investigating the origin of a southern African rite. *South African Archaeological Bulletin* 61 (184): 172–80.

Jones, P.R. 1994. Results of experimental work in relation to the stone tool industries of Olduvai Gorge. In Leakey, M.D. & Roe, D.A. eds *Olduvai Gorge: Excavations in Beds III, IV and the Masek Beds 1968–1971*. Cambridge: Cambridge University Press, pp. 254–98.

Jorde, L., Watkins, W., Bamshad, M., Dixon, M., Ricker, C., Seilstad, M. & Baxter, M. 2000. The distribution of human genetic diversity: A comparison of mitochondrial, autosomal and Y-chromosome data. *American Journal of Human Genetics* 66: 979–88.

Joubert, E. & Mostert, P.K.N. 1975. Distribution patterns and status of some mammals in South West Africa. *Madoqua* 9 (1): 5–44.

Journal of British Resident Magistrate, Walvis Bay. 1885–1897. Cape Archives Depot 1/WLB 6/1.

Jouzel, J., Masson-Delmotte, V., Cattani, O., Dreyfus, G., Hoffmann, G., Minster, B., Nouet, J., Barnola, J., Chapellaz, J., Fischer, H., Gallet, J., Johnsen, S., Leuenberger, M., Loulergue, L., Leuthi, D., Oerter, H., Parenin, E., Raisbech, G., Raynaud, D., Schilt, A., Schwander, J., Selmo, E., Souchez, R., Spahni, R., Stauffer, B., Steffensen, J., Stenni, B., Stocker, T., Tison, J., Werner, M. & Wolff, E. 2007. Orbital and millennial climate variability over the past 800,000 years. *Science* 317: 793–6.

Jull, A.J.T., Burr, G.S. & Hodgins, G.W.L. 2013. Radiocarbon dating, reservoir effects, and calibration. *Quaternary International* 299: 64–71.

Katjivena, U.E.K. 2020. *Mama Penee: Transcending the Genocide*. Windhoek: University of Namibia Press.

Katz, R. 1982. *Boiling energy: Community healing among Kalahari !Kung*. Cambridge: Harvard University Press.

Kavari, J.U. 2001. The social organization, religion and cosmos of the Ovaherero. *Journal of Religion and Theology in Namibia* 3 (1): 116–60.

Kelly, H.E. 1993. *Scottish sponge-printed pottery traditional patterns, their manufacturers and history.* Glasgow: The Lemonside Press.

Kelly, R.L. 1983. Hunter-gatherer mobility strategies. *Journal of anthropological research* 39: 277–306.

Kettis, E. & Enflo, L. 1996. *Copper production experiment: An archaeological study in Namibia.* Stockholm: Minor Field Study, Department of Archaeology, University of Stockholm.

Kienetz, A. 1977. The key role of the Oorlam migrations in the early Europeanization of South-West Africa (Namibia). *International Journal of African Historical Studies* 4: 553–72.

Kinahan, J. 1980. Eighteenth century coppersmiths in central Namibia: Comments on some sources and syntheses. *Namibiana* 2: 17–22.

Kinahan, J. 1984a. On the relative homogeneity of a short Holocene sequence of stone tool assemblages from the central Namib Desert. *South African Journal of Science* 80: 273–5.

Kinahan, J. 1984b. The archaeological structure of pastoral production in the central Namib Desert. In Hall, M. & Smith, A.B. eds *Prehistoric pastoralism in southern Africa.* South African Archaeological Society Goodwin Series 5: 69–82.

Kinahan, J. 1986. Settlement patterns and regional exchange: Evidence from recent Iron Age sites on the Kavango River, north-eastern Namibia. *Cimbebasia* (B) 3 (4): 109–16.

Kinahan, J. 1990. Four thousand years at the Spitzkoppe: Changes in settlement and landuse on the edge of the Namib Desert. *Cimbebasia* 12: 1–14.

Kinahan, J. 1993. The rise and fall of nomadic pastoralism in the central Namib Desert. In Shaw, T., Sinclair, P., Andah, B. & Okpoko, A. eds *The archaeology of Africa: Food, Metals and Towns.* London: Routledge, pp. 372–85.

Kinahan, J. 1994. A new archaeological perspective on nomadic pastoralist expansion in south-western Africa. *Azania* 24: 211–26. https://doi.org/10.1080/00672709409511677

Kinahan, J. 1995a. Theory, practice and criticism in the history of Namibian archaeology. In Ucko, P. ed. *World perspective on archaeological theory: Diversity in theory and practice.* London: Routledge, pp. 76–95.

Kinahan, J. 1995b. Weisse Riese – Schwarze Zwerge? Empirismus und ethnische Deutung in der Archäeologie Namibias. *Archäeologische Informationen* 18/1: 7–18.

Kinahan, J. 1996a. Alternative views on the acquisition of livestock by hunter-gatherers in southern Africa: A rejoinder to Smith, Yates and Jacobson. *South African Archaeological Bulletin* 51: 106–8.

Kinahan, J. 1996b. The Archaeology of Social Rank among Eighteenth Century Nomadic Pastoralists in Southern Namibia. *African Archaeological Review* 13 (4): 225–45. DOI: 10.2307/25130603

Kinahan, J. 1999. Towards an archaeology of mimesis and rain-making in Namibian rock art. In Ucko, P.J. & Layton, R. eds *The Archaeology and Anthropology of Landscape.* London: Routledge, pp. 336–57.

Kinahan, J. 2000a. Traumland Südwest: Two moments in the history of German archaeological inquiry in Namibia. In Härke, H. ed. *Archaeology, Ideology and Society: The German Experience.* Gesellschaften und staten im epochenwandel 7. Peter Lang: Frankfurt am Main, pp. 353–74.

Kinahan, J. 2000b. Dâures, the burning mountain – issues of research and conservation in the Brandberg of Namibia. *Cimbebasia* 9: 1–16.

Kinahan, J. 2000c. Fifteenth century agropastoral responses to a disequilibrial ecosystem in south-eastern Botswana. In Barker, G. & Gilbertson, D. eds *The Archaeology of Drylands: Living at the margins.* London: Routledge, pp. 233–51.

Kinahan, J. 2001a. *Pastoral nomads of the Namib Desert: The people history forgot.* 2nd edn Windhoek: Namibia Archaeological Trust.

Kinahan, J. 2001b. The presence of the past: Archaeology, environment and land rights on the lower Cunene. *Cimbebasia* 17: 23–39.

Kinahan, J. 2005. The late Holocene human ecology of the Namib Desert. In Smith, M. & Hesse, P. eds *23 Degrees South: Archaeology and environmental history of the Southern Deserts.* Canberra: National Museum of Australia, pp. 120–31.

Kinahan, J. 2010a. The rock art of ǀUi-ǁaes (Twyfelfontein), Namibia's first World Heritage Site. *Adoranten* 2010: 39–51.

Kinahan, J. 2010b. *Reconnaissance investigation of a late Pleistocene archaeological site on EPL3345, Erongo Region.* Windhoek: QRS Report 89.

Kinahan, J. 2011. From the Beginning: The Archaeological Evidence. In Wallace, M. & Kinahan, J. *A history of Namibia: From the Beginning to 1990*. London: Hurst & Co., pp. 15–44.

Kinahan, J. 2013a. The use of skeletal and complementary evidence to estimate human stature and identify the presence of women in the recent archaeological record of the Namib Desert. *South African Archaeological Bulletin* 68: 72–8. DOI: 10.2307/23631485

Kinahan, J. 2013b. The acquisition of ceramics by hunter-gatherers on the middle Zambezi in the first and second millennium AD. *Journal of African Archaeology* 11: 197–209. DOI: 10.2307/43135609

Kinahan, J. 2014a. Cattle paths and the choreography of late pre-colonial contact and trade on the Namib Desert coast. *South African Archaeological Bulletin* 69: 96–102. DOI: 10.2307/24332735

Kinahan, J. 2014b. *Recovery and analysis of human remains at Husab Mine, Site QRS 105/117*. Report commissioned by Swakop Uranium (Pty) Ltd.

Kinahan, J. 2015. Archaeological survey and assessment of EPL 4167, vicinity of Cape Cross, Erongo Region. Windhoek: QRS Report 216.

Kinahan, J. 2016a. Human responses to climatic variation in the Namib Desert during the last one thousand years. *African Archaeological Review* 33 (2): 183–203. DOI: 10.2307/43916785

Kinahan, J. 2016b. Archaeological evidence of domestic sheep in the Namib Desert during the first millennium AD. *Journal of African Archaeology* 14 (1): 7–17. DOI: 10.2307/44296866

Kinahan, J. 2017a. The Solitary Shaman: Itinerant healers and ritual seclusion in the Namib Desert during the second millennium AD. *Cambridge Archaeological Journal* 27 (3): 553–69. DOI: 10.1017/S0959774317000348

Kinahan, J. 2017b. The Dancing Kudu: Women's initiation in the Namib Desert during the second millennium AD. *Antiquity* 91: 1043–57. DOI: 10.15184/aqy.2017.48

Kinahan, J. 2018a. A ritual assemblage from the third millennium BC in the Namib Desert and its implications for the archaeology and rock art of shamanic performance. *Azania* 53: 40–62. https://doi.org/10.1080/0067270X.2018.1423757

Kinahan, J. 2018b. Holocene human adaptation in the Namib Desert: A model based on the concept of Holling's loop. *Journal of Arid Environments* 157: 124–36.

Kinahan, J. 2019. The Origins and Spread of Pastoralism in Southern Africa. *Oxford Research Encyclopedia, African History* (oxfordre.com/africanhistory). Oxford University Press.

Kinahan, J. & Kinahan, J.H.A. 1984. Holocene subsistence and settlement on the Namib coast: The example of the Ugab River Mouth. *Cimbebasia* B 4 (6): 59–72.

Kinahan, J. & Kinahan, J.H.A. 2003. Excavation of a late Holocene cave deposit in the southern Namib Desert, Namibia. *Cimbebasia* 18: 1–10.

Kinahan, J. & Kinahan, J.H.A. 2006. Preliminary report on the late Holocene archaeology of the Awasib-Gorrasis Basin complex in the southern Namib Desert. *Studies in the African Past* 5: 1–14.

Kinahan, J. & Kinahan, J.H.A. 2009. *Archaeological investigation of a Late Pleistocene chert quarry and workshop site QRS 72/48*. Windhoek: QRS Report 72.

Kinahan, J. & Kinahan, J.H.A. 2016. Post-Pleistocene archaeology and geomorphological processes on the Namib Desert coast of southwestern Africa. *Journal of Island and Coastal Archaeology* 12 (1): 65–77. https://doi.org/10.1080/15564894.2016.1216477

Kinahan, J., Pallett, J., Vogel, J., Ward, J. & Lindeque, M. 1991. The occurrence and dating of elephant tracks in the silt deposits of the lower !Khuiseb River, Namibia. *Cimbebasia* 13: 37–44.

Kinahan, J. & Vogel, J.C. 1982. Recent copper-working sites in the !Khuiseb drainage, Namibia. *South African Archaeological Bulletin* 37: 44–5. DOI: 10.2307/3888579

Kinahan, J.H.A. 1988a. The etymology and historical use of the term Cimbebasia. *Cimbebasia* 10: 5–8.

Kinahan, J.H.A. 1988b. *The Pillar in the Mist: A History of the Dias Padrão at Lüderitz*. Windhoek: National Monuments Council.

Kinahan, J.H.A. 1990. The impenetrable shield: HMS *Nautilus* and the Namib coast in the late eighteenth century. *Cimbebasia* 12: 23–62.

Kinahan, J.H.A. 1991. The historical archaeology of nineteenth century fisheries at Sandwich Harbour on the Namib coast. *Cimbebasia* 13: 1–27.

Kinahan, J.H.A. 1992. *By Command of their Lordships: The exploration of the Namibian coast by the Royal Navy, 1795 –1895*. Windhoek: Namibia Archaeological Trust.

Kinahan, J.H.A. 2000. *Cattle for Beads: The archaeology of historical contact and trade on the Namib coast*. Uppsala University: Studies in African Archaeology 17.

Kinahan, J.H.A. 2004. *Where the ancestors speak: A Himba experience*. Windhoek: Namibia Archaeological Trust.

Kinahan, J.H.A. & Kinahan, J. 2009. 'A thousand fine vessels are ploughing the main...' Archaeological traces of the nineteenth century 'Guano Rage' on the south-western coast of Africa. *Australasian Historical Archaeology* 27: 43–54.

Kinahan, J.H.A. & Kinahan, J. 2021. Constructed emptiness: The Namib Desert as terra nullius. In Goetcheus, C. & Brown, S. eds *Routledge Handbook on Cultural Landscapes*. London: Routledge.

King, R. & McGranaghan, M. 2018. The Archaeology and Materiality of Mission in Southern Africa: Introduction. *Journal of Southern African Studies* 44 (4): 629–39.

Kirst, G.J., Schneider, R.R., Müller, P.J., von Storch, I. & Wefer, G. 1999. Late Quaternary Temperature Variability in the Benguela Current System Derived from Alkenones. *Quaternary Research* 52: 92–103.

Klein, R.G. 2000. The Earlier Stone Age of Southern Africa. *South African Archaeological Bulletin* 55: 107–22.

Klein, R.G., Avery, G., Cruz-Uribe, K., Halkett, D., Hart, T., Milo, R.G. & Volman, T.P. 1999. Duinefontein 2: An Acheulean site in the western Cape Province of South Africa. *Journal of Human Evolution* 37: 153–90.

Köhler, O. 1959. *A Study of Omaruru District, South West Africa*. Pretoria: Government Printer.

Kooitjie, S. 1997. *Historic Overview of the ǂAonîn (Topnaar), Khoi-Khoi*. Unpublished manuscript. Walvis Bay.

Kose, E. 2009. New light on iron-working groups along the middle Kavango in northern Namibia. *South African Archaeological Bulletin* 64: 130–47.

Köβler, R. 2019. Diversity in the post-colonial state: The case of the return of looted heirlooms from Germany to Namibia in 2019. *Nuovi Autoritarismi e Democrazie: Diritto, Istituzioni, Società* 1 (2): 109–24.

Kraak, M. 2003. The space-time cube revisited from a geovisualization perspective. Proceedings of the 21st International Cartographic Conference, Durban, South Africa.

Kramer, P.A. 2012. *The history, form and context of the 19th century corbelled buildings of the Great Karoo.* Unpublished MA thesis, University of Cape Town, Cape Town.

Kriegskarte von Deutsch-Südwestafrika (1910). Berlin: Dietrich Riemer. 3rd Reprint edition 1987. Windhoek: National Archives of Namibia.

Kroukamp, M. 2004. *Meat Quality Characteristics of the Springbok (Antidorcas marsupialis).* Unpublished M.Sc. thesis. Stellenbosch: University of Stellenbosch, Stellenbosch.

Krüger, G. & Henrichsen, D. 1996. "We Have Been Captives Long Enough, We Want To Be Free": Land, Uniforms, and Politics in the History of Herero during the Interwar Period. In Hayes, P., Wallace, M. & Sylvester, J. eds *Trees Never Meet: But People Do.* Windhoek: Longman Namibia.

Laland, K.N. & O'Brien, M.J. 2011. Cultural niche construction: An introduction. *Biological Theory* 6(3): 191–202.

Lambacher, N., Gerdau-Redonic, K., Bonthorne, E. & Valle de Tarrazaga Montero, F.J. 2016. Evaluating three methods to estimate the number of individuals from a commingled context. *Journal of Archaeological Science: Reports* 10: 674–83.

Lancaster, N. 1981. Palaeoenvironmental implications of fixed dune systems in southern Africa. *Palaeogeography, Palaeoclimatology, Palaeoecology* 33: 327–46.

Lancaster, N. 1984. Aridity in southern Africa: Age, origins and expression in landforms and sediments. In Vogel, J.C. ed. *Late Cainozoic palaeoclimates of the Southern Hemisphere.* Rotterdam: Balkema, pp. 433–44.

Lancaster, N. 1995. *Geomorphology of Desert Dunes.* London: Routledge.

Lancaster, N. 1996. Desert environments. In Adams, W.M., Goudie, A.S. & Orme, A.R. eds *The Physical Geography of Africa.* Oxford University Press, pp. 211–37.

Lane, P., Reid, A. & Segobye, A. eds 2000. *Ditswa mmung: The archaeology of Botswana.* The Botswana Society: Pula Press.

L'Ange, G. 1991. *Urgent Imperial Service: South African forces in German South West Africa 1914–1915.* Rivonia: Ashanti.

Larsen, G. & Chilingar, G.V. eds 1983. *Developments in Sedimentology.* Amsterdam: Elsevier.

Lau, B. 1987. *Namibia in Jonker Afrikaner's time.* Windhoek: National Archives of Namibia, *Archeia* 8.

Lau, B. 1989. Uncertain certainties: The Herero – German war of 1904. *Mibagus* 2: 4–8.

Lee, R.B. 1972. The intensification of social life among the !Kung Bushman. In Spooner, B. ed. *Population growth: Anthropological implications.* Cambridge M.I.T Press, pp. 343–50.

Lee, R.B. 1979. *The !Kung San: Men, women and work in a foraging society.* Cambridge: Cambridge University Press.

Lee-Thorp, J.A., Holmgren, K., Lauritzen, S.-E., Linge, H., Moberg, A., Partridge, T.C., Stevenson, C. & Tyson, P.D. 2001. Rapid climatic shifts in the southern African interior throughout the mid to late Holocene. *Geophysical Research Letters* 28 (23): 4507–10.

Lefébure, C. 1979. Introduction: The specificity of nomadic pastoral societies. In *Pastoral production and society, L'Equipe ecologie et anthropologie des sociétiés pastorals.* Cambridge: Cambridge University Press, pp. 1–14.

Legassick, M. 1989. The northern frontier to c. 1840: The rise and decline of the Griqua people. In Elphick, R. & Giliomee, H. eds *The Shaping of South African Society 1652–1840.* Cape Town: Maskew Miller Longman, pp. 358–420.

Le Meillour, L. 2017. *Beware the antelopes: Apports de la paléoprotéomique aux stratégies de subsistance en Afrique australe au Later Stone Age.* Unpublished MA dissertation, Muséum National d'Histoire Naturelle, Paris.

Lenssen-Erz, T. 1998. Introduction. In Pager, H. *The Rock Paintings of the Upper Brandberg, Part 4: Umuab and Karoab Gorges.* Köln, Heinrich Barth Institut.

Lenssen-Erz, T. 2004. The landscape setting of rock-painting sites in the Brandberg (Namibia): Infrastructure, *Gestaltung*, use and meaning. In Chippendale, C. & Nash, G. eds *Pictures in place: The figured landscapes of rock-art.* Cambridge, Cambridge University Press, pp. 131–50.

Lenssen-Erz, T. & Vogelsang, R. 2005. Populating no-man's-land – rock art in northern Namibia. In Blundell, G. ed. *Further approaches* to *southern African rock art*. South African Archaeological Society Goodwin Series 9: 54–62.

Le Quellec, J-L. 2016. *The White Lady and Atlantis: Ophir and Great Zimbabwe*. Oxford: Archaeopress.

Leutwein, T. 1906. *Elf Jahre Gouverneur in Deutsch-Südwestafrika*. Berlin: Ernst Siegfried Mittler und Sohn.

Levinson, O. 1973. *Adolph Jentsch*. Human and Rousseau.

Lévi-Strauss, C. 1966. *The Savage Mind*. London: Weidenfeld and Nicholson.

Lewis-Williams, J.D. 1981. *Believing and seeing: Symbolic meanings in southern San rock paintings*. London: Academic Press.

Lewis-Williams, J.D. 1982. The Economic and Social Context of Southern San rock art. *Current Anthropology* 23 (4): 429–49.

Lewis-Williams, J.D. 1983. *The Rock Art of Southern Africa*. Cambridge: Cambridge University Press.

Lewis-Williams, J.D. 1984. Ideological continuities in prehistoric southern Africa: The evidence of rock art. In Schrire, C. ed. *Past and present in hunter-gatherer studies*. Orlando: Academic Press, pp. 225–52.

Lewis-Williams, J.D. 1995. Modelling the production and consumption of rock art. *South African Archaeological Bulletin* 50: 143–54.

Lewis-Williams, J.D. 2000. *Stories that float from afar: Ancestral folklore of the San of southern Africa*. Cape Town: David Philip.

Lewis-Williams, J.D. 2003. Putting the record straight: Rock art and shamanism. *Antiquity* 77: 165–70.

Lewis-Williams, J.D. & Dowson, T.A. 1988. The signs for all times: Entoptic phenomena in upper Palaeolithic cave art. *Current Anthropology* 29: 201–45.

Lewis-Williams, J.D. & Dowson, T.A. 1989. *Images of power: Understanding Bushman rock art*. Johannesburg: Southern.

Lewis-Williams, J.D. & Dowson, T.A. 1990. Reply to Bednarik. *Current Anthropology* 31 (1): 80–3.

Lewis-Williams, J.D. & Pearce, D.G. 2004. Southern African San rock painting as social intervention: A study of rain-control images. *African Archaeological Review* 21: 199–228.

Lewis-Williams, J.D. & Pearce, D. 2012. The southern San and the trance dance: A pivotal debate in the interpretation of San rock paintings. *Antiquity* 86: 696–706.

Lewis-Williams, J.D. & Pearce, D. 2015. San rock art: Evidence and argument. *Antiquity* 89: 732–9.

Li, S., Schlebusch, C. & Jakobsson, M. 2014. Genetic variation reveals large-scale population expansion and migration during the expansion of Bantu-speaking peoples. *Proceedings of the Royal Society B: Biological Sciences* 281 (1793). https://doi.org/10.1098/rspb.2014.1448

Lieberman, D.E., Bramble, D.M., Raichlen, D.A. & Shea, J.J. 2009. Brains, brawn, and the evolution of human endurance running capabilities. In Grine, F.E., Fleagle, J.G. & Leakey, R.E. eds *The First Humans: Origin and Early Evolution of the Genus Homo*. Springer Science & Business Media, pp. 77–92.

Lilienthal, A. 1997. *Art in Namibia*. Windhoek: National Art Gallery of Namibia.

Lindholm, K.-J. 2006. *Wells of Experience: A pastoral land-use history of Omaheke, Namibia*. Uppsala University: Studies in Global Archaeology 9.

Lombard, M. 2005a. The Howiesonspoort of South Africa: What we know, what we think we know, what we need to know. *Southern African Humanities* 17: 33–55.

Lombard, M. 2005b. Evidence of hunting and hafting during the Middle Stone Age at Sibudu Cave, KwaZulu-Natal, South Africa: A multianalytical approach. *Journal of Human Evolution* 48: 279–300.

Lombard, M. 2011. Quartz-tipped arrows older than 60ka: Further use-trace evidence from Sibudu, KwaZulu-Natal, South Africa. *Journal of Archaeological Science* 38: 1918–30.

Lombard, M. & Badenhorst, S. 2019. A Case for Springbok Hunting with Kite-Like Structures in the Northwest Nama Karoo Bioregion of South Africa. *African Archaeological Review* 36: 383–96.

Lombard, M. & Haidle, M. 2012. Thinking a Bow-and-arrow Set: Cognitive Implications of Middle Stone Age Bow and Stone-tipped Arrow Technology. *Cambridge Archaeological Journal* 22: 237–64.

Lombard, M. & Högberg, A. 2018. The Still Bay points of Apollo 11 Rock Shelter, Namibia: An inter-regional perspective. *Azania* 53: 312–340.

Lombard, M. & Parsons, I. 2015. Milk not meat: The role of milk amongst the Khoe peoples of southern Africa. *Journal of African Archaeology* 13: 149–66.

Louw, G.N. & Seely, M.K. 1982. *Ecology of Desert Organisms*. London: Longman.

Lovejoy, C.O. 1985. Dental wear in the Libben population: Its functional pattern and role in the determination of adult skeletal age at death. *American Journal of Physical Anthropology* 68 (1): 47–56.

Lundy, J.K. & Feldesman, M.R. 1987. Revised equations for estimating living stature from the long bones of the South African Negro. *South African Journal of Science* 83: 54–5.

MacGregor, G. & Goldbeck, M. 2014. *The First World War in Namibia*. Windhoek: Gondwana.

Macholdt, E., Lede, V., Barbieri, C., Mpoloka, S.W., Chen, H., Slatkin, M., Pakendorf, B. & Stoneking, M. 2014. Tracing pastoralist migrations to southern Africa with lactase persistence alleles. *Current Biology* 24: 875–79.

MacNeil, R. 2001. Time after time: Temporal frontiers and boundaries in colonial images of the Australian landscape. In Russel, L. ed. *Colonial frontiers: Indigenous–European encounters in settler societies*. Manchester: Manchester University Press, pp. 48–9.

Madella, M., Alexandre, A. & Ball, T. 2005. International Code for Phytolith Nomenclature 1.0. *Annals of Botany* 96: 253–60.

Maggs, T. 1984. The Great Galleon São João: Remains from a mid-sixteenth century wreck on the Natal South Coast. *Annals of the Natal Museum* 26:173–86.

Magurran, A.E. 1988. *Ecological Diversity and its Measurement*. London: Croom Helm.

Malan, J. 1995. *Peoples of Namibia*. Wingate Park: Rhino Publishers.

Manica, A., Amos, W., Balloux, F. & Hanihara, T. 2007. The effect of ancient population bottlenecks on human phenotypic variation. *Nature* 448: 346–8.

Marker, M.E. 1982. Aspects of Namib geomorphology: A doline karst. *Palaeoecology of Africa* 15: 187–99.

Marsh, A.C. 1986. Ant species richness along a climatic gradient in the Namib Desert. *Journal of Arid Environments* 11: 235–41.

Marsh, A.C. 1987. The foraging ecology of two Namib Desert harvester ant species. *African Zoology* 22: 130–6.

Marshall, L. 1999. *Nyae Nyae !Kung: Beliefs and rites*. Cambridge (MA): Peabody Museum of Archaeology and Ethnology, Harvard University.

Matmon, A., Enzel, Y., Vainer, S., Grodek, T., Mushkin, A. & ASTER Team. 2018. The near steady state landscape of western Namibia. *Geomorphology* 313: 72–87.

Mazel, A.D. 1987. The archaeological past from the changing present: Towards a critical assessment of South African Later Stone Age studies from the early 1960's to the early 1980's. In Parkington, J.E. & Hall, M. eds *Papers in the Prehistory of the Western Cape, South Africa*. Oxford: British Archaeological Reports, pp. 504–29.

Mazel, A.D. 1989. People making history: The last ten thousand years of hunter-gatherer communities in the Thukela Basin. *Natal Museum Journal of Humanities* 1: 1–168.

Mazel, A.D. 2003. Dating rock paintings in the uKhahlamba-Drakensberg and the Biggarsberg, KwaZulu-Natal, South Africa. *Southern African Humanities* 15: 59–73.

Mazel, A.D. 2009. Images in time: Advances in the dating of Maloti-Drakensberg rock art since the 1970s. In Mitchell, P.J. & Smith, B.W. eds *The eland's people: New perspectives in the rock art of the Maloti-Drakensberg Bushmen. Essays in memory of Patricia Vinnicombe*. Johannesburg: Witwatersrand University Press, pp. 81–97.

Mazel, A.D. & Watchman A.L. 1997. Accelerator radiocarbon dating of Natal Drakensberg paintings: Results and implications. *Antiquity* 71: 445–9.

McBrearty, S. 2003. Patterns of technological change at the origins of *Homo sapiens*. *Before Farming* [print version] 3 (9): 22–6.

McCall, G.S. 2007. Add shamans and stir? A critical review of the shamanism model of forager rock art production. *Journal of Anthropological Archaeology* 26: 224–33.

McCall, G.S. & Thomas, J.T. 2012. Still Bay and Howiesons Poort foraging strategies: Recent research and models of culture change. *African Archaeological Review* 29: 7–50.

McGinnies, W.G. 1979. Description and structure of arid ecosystems: General description of desert areas. In Goodall, D.W., Perry, R.A. & Howes, K.M.W. eds *Arid Land Ecosystems: Structure, Functioning and Management*. Cambridge: Cambridge University Press.

McGranaghan, M. 2015. 'Hunters with sheep': The ǀXam Bushmen of South Africa between pastoralism and foraging. *Africa* 85: 521–45.

McNabb, J., Binyon, F., Hazelwood, L., Machin, A., Mithen, S., Petraglia, M.D., Rolland, N., White, M., Wynn, T. & McNabb, J. 2004. The large cutting tools from the South African Acheulean and the question of social traditions. *Current Anthropology* 45: 653–77.

Meaker, M. 1984. Adolph Jentsch – Prayers in paint. *Gallery Magazine.*

Meehan, B. 1982. *Shell Bed to Shell Midden.* Canberra: Australian Institute for Aboriginal Studies.

Meigs, P. 1953. World distribution of arid and semi-arid homoclimates. *Reviews of Research on Arid Zone Hydrology* 1: 203–10.

Meillassoux, C. 1981. *Maidens, meal and money: Capitalism and the domestic economy.* Cambridge: Cambridge University Press.

Mendelsohn, J., Jarvis, A., Roberts, C. & Robertson, T. eds 2002. *Atlas of Namibia: A portrait of the Land and its People.* Cape Town: David Philip.

Merxmuller, H. & Büttler, K.P. 1975. Nicotiana in der Afrikanischen Namib – ein pflanzengeographisches Rätsel. *Mitteilungen der Botanischen Staatsammlung München* 12: 91–104.

Messem, W. 1855. The Exploration of Western Africa. *Nautical Magazine,* April 1855: 210–15.

Metin, G. & Ilkyaz, A. 2008. Use of otolith length and weight in age determination of Poor Cod (*Trisopterus minutus* Linn., 1758). *Turkish Journal of Zoology* 32: 293–7.

Miller, J.M. & Sawchuk, E.A. 2019. Ostrich eggshell bead diameter in the Holocene: Regional variation with the spread of herding in eastern and southern Africa. *PLoS One*: 14 (11): e0225143.

Miller, D.E. & Kinahan, J. 1992. The metallurgical analysis of copper beads and ore from archaeological sites in central Namibia. *Communications of the Geological Survey of Namibia* 8: 67–79.

Miller, McG. R. 2000. Geology of the Brandberg massif, Namibia and its environs. In Kirk-Spriggs, A. & Marais, E. eds *Dâures – biodiversity of the Brandberg Massif, Namibia.* Cimbebasia Memoir 9: 17–38.

Misihairabgwi, J. & Cheikhyoussef, A. 2017. Traditional fermented foods and beverages of Namibia. *Journal of Ethnic Foods* 4: 145–53.

Mitchell, P. 1990. A palaeoecological model for archaeological site distribution in southern Africa during the Upper Peniglacial and

Late Glacial. In Gamble, C. & Soffer, O. eds *The World at 18000 BP: Vol. 2, Low Latitudes*. London: Unwin Hyman, pp. 189–205.

Mitchell, P. 1996. Prehistoric exchange and interaction in south-eastern southern Africa: Marine shells and ostrich eggshell. *African Archaeological Review* 13: 35–76.

Mitchell, P. 2002. *The archaeology of southern Africa*. Cambridge: Cambridge University Press.

Mitchell, P. 2003. Anyone for Hxaro? Thoughts on the theory and practice of exchange in southern African Later Stone Age archaeology. In Haour, A. & Hobart, J.H. eds *Researching Africa's Past: New Contributions from British Archaeologists*. London: Oxford School of Archaeology, pp. 35–43.

Mitchell, P. 2010. Genetics and southern African prehistory. *Journal of Archaeological Science* 88: 73–92.

Mitchell, P. 2014. The canine connection II: Dogs and southern African herders. *Southern African Humanities* 26: 1–19.

Mitchell, P. 2017. I rode through the desert: Equestrian adaptations of indigenous peoples in southern hemisphere arid zones. *International Journal of Historical Archaeology* 21: 321–45.

Mitchell, P., Plug, I., Bailey, G. & Woodborne, S. 2008. Bringing the Kalahari debate to the mountains: Late first millennium AD hunter-gatherer/farmer interaction in highland Lesotho. *Before Farming* 2008 (2), article 4, 1–22.

Mohanty, S.P., Babu, S.S. & Nair, N.S. 2001. The use of arm-span as a predictor of height: A study of South Indian women. *Journal of Orthopaedic Surgery* 9: 19–23.

Moisel, L. 1982. Wanderungen in Brandbergmassiv, mit einem Nachtrag zur Pflanzenliste des Brandberges. *Dinteria* 16: 21–26.

Moritz, E. 1915. Die ältesten Reiseberichte über Deutsch-Südwestafrika. *Mitteilungen aus den Deutschen Schutzgebieten* 1915: 28–31.

Moritz, E. 1916. Die ältesten Reiseberichte über Deutsch-Südwestafrika. Die Berichte der Rheinischen Mission bis zum Jahre 1846. *Mitteilungen aus den Deutschen Schutzgebieten mit benutzung amtlicher quellen herausgeben von Dr H. Marquardsen* 29 (4). Berlin: Ernst Siegfried Mittler & Sohn.

Mossolow, N. 1993. *Otjikango or Gross Barmen: The history of the first Rhenish Herero mission station in South West Africa, 1844–1904*. Windhoek: John Meinert.

Mossop, E.E. ed. 1935. *The Journal of Hendrik Jacob Wikar (1779)*. Cape Town: Van Riebeeck Society.

Morse, S.A., Bennett, M.R., Liutkus-Pierce, C., Thackeray, F., McClymont, J., Savage, R. & Crompton, R.H. 2013. Holocene footprints in Namibia: The influence of substrate on footprint variability. *American Journal of Physical Anthropology* 151 (2): 265–79.

Mounier, A. & Lahr, M.M. 2019. Deciphering African late middle Pleistocene hominin diversity and the origin of our species. *Nature Communications* 10 (1): 1–13.

Muigai, A.W. & Hanotte, O. 2013. The origin of African sheep: Archaeological and genetic perspectives. *African Archaeological Review* 30 (1): 39–50.

Müller, M.A.N. 1984. *Grasses of South West Africa/Namibia*. Windhoek: Directorate of Agriculture and Forestry.

Munsell Soil Color Charts. 1992. Revised edition. New York: Kollmorgan Instruments Corporation.

Muschalek, M. 2020. *Violence as usual: Policing and the colonial state in German South West Africa*. Windhoek: University of Namibia Press.

Musonda, F. 1987. The significance of pottery in Zambian Later Stone Age contexts. *African Archaeological Review* 5: 147–58.

Ndobochani, N.M. 2020. The Kwena of Botswana and the cattle post institution. *Azania: Archaeological Research in Africa* 55: 258–89.

Nel, P.S. & Opperman, D.P.J. 1985. Vegetation types of the gravel plains. In Huntley, B.J. ed. *The Kuiseb Environment: The Development of a Monitoring Baseline*. Pretoria: South African National Scientific Programmes Report No. 106: 118–25.

Nic Eoin, L. 2016. Geophytes, grasses and grindstones: Replanting ideas of gathering in southern Africa's Middle and Later Stone Ages. *South African Archaeological Bulletin* 71: 36–45.

Nicholson, S.E. 2000. The nature of rainfall variability over Africa on timescales of decades to millennia. *Global and Planetary Change* 26: 137–58.

Nicholson, S.E. & Entekhabi, D. 1986. The quasi-periodic behaviour of rainfall variability in Africa and its relationship to the Southern Oscillation. *Archives for Meteorology, Geophysics, and Bioclimatology*, Series A, 34: 311–48.

Nicoll, K. 2010. Geomorphic development and Middle Stone Age archaeology of the Lower Cunene River, Namibia–Angola Border. *Quaternary Science Review* 29: 1419–31.

Nienaber, G.S. & Raper, P.E. 1980. *Toponymica Hottentotica*. Johannesburg: GAU.

Noddle, B. 1974. Ages of epiphiseal closure in feral and domestic goats and ages of dental eruption. *Journal of Archaeological Science* 1: 195–204.

Nordenstam, B. 1974. The flora of the Brandberg. *Dinteria* 11: 3–67.

Noy-Meir, I. 1973. Desert ecosystems: Environment and producers. *Annual Review of Ecological Systematics* 4: 25–51.

Ohde, T. & Mohrholz, V. 2011. Interannual variability of sulphur plumes off the Namibian coast. *International Journal of Remote Sensing* 32 (24): 9327–42.

Olley, J.M., Roberts, R.G., Yoshida, H. & Bowler, J.M. 2006. Single-grain optical dating of grave-infill associated with human burials at Lake Mungo, Australia. *Quaternary Science Reviews* 25 (19–20): 2469–74.

Olmstead, R.G., Bohs, L., Migid, H.A., Santiago-Valentin, E., Garcia, V.F. & Collier, S.M. 2008. A molecular phylogeny of the Solanacae. *Taxon* 57 (4): 1159–81.

Olszewski, J. 2000. Brandberg climatic considerations. In Kirk-Spriggs, A. & Marais, E. eds *Dâures – biodiversity of the Brandberg Massif, Namibia*. National Museum of Namibia: Cimbebasia Memoir 9: 39–48.

Olusoga, D. & Erichsen, C. 2010. *The Kaiser's Holocaust: Germany's forgotten genocide and the colonial roots of Nazism*. London: Faber & Faber.

O'Reilly, T.L. 1918. *Union of South Africa. Report On the Natives of South-west Africa and Their Treatment by Germany. Prepared in the Administrator's Office, Windhuk, South-west Africa, January 1918*. London: His Majesty's Stationery Office, pp. 1–224.

Orton, J. 2012. *Late Holocene archaeology in Namaqualand, South Africa: Hunter-gatherers and herders in a semi-arid environment*. Unpublished D. Phil. Thesis, University of Oxford, Oxford.

Orton, J., Mitchell, P., Klein, R., Steele, T. & Horsburgh, K.A. 2013. An early date for cattle from Namaqualand, South Africa: Implications for the origins of herding in southern Africa. *Antiquity* 87: 108–20.

Ossendorf, G. 2017. Two Holocene Later Stone Age stratigraphies from the Sesfontein area, north-western Namibia. *Azania* 52: 233–66.

Ouzman, S. 2001. Seeing is deceiving: Rock art and the non-visual. *World Archaeology* 33: 237– 56.

Owen, W.F.W. 1833. *Narrative of Voyages to Explore the Shores of Africa, Arabia and Madagascar Performed in H.M. Ships Leven and Barracouta under the Direction of Captain W.F.W. Owen, R.N.* London: Richard Bentley.

Owen-Smith, N. 1987. Pleistocene extinctions: The pivotal role of megaherbivores. *Palaeobiology* 13: 351–62.

Owen-Smith, N. 1992. *Megaherbivores: The influence of very large body size on ecology.* Cambridge: Cambridge University Press.

Pager, H. 1980. *Felsbildforschungen am Brandberg in Namibia.* Beitrage, Allgemeine und Vergleichende Archeologie, Deutsches Archeologisches Institut, Bonn 2: 351–357.

Pager, H. 1989. *The Rock Paintings of the Upper Brandberg, Part 1: Amis Gorge.* Köln: Heinrich Barth Institut.

Pager, H. 1993. *The Rock Paintings of the Upper Brandberg, Part 2: Hungorob Gorge.* Köln: Heinrich Barth Institut.

Pager, H. 1995. *The Rock Paintings of the Upper Brandberg, Part 3: Southern Gorge 2.* Köln: Heinrich Barth Institut.

Pager, H. 1998. *The Rock Paintings of the Upper Brandberg, Part 4: Umuab and Karoab Gorges.* Köln: Heinrich Barth Institut.

Pager, H. 2000. *The Rock Paintings of the Upper Brandberg, Part 5: Naib Gorge (A) and the Northwest.* Köln: Heinrich Barth Institut.

Pager, H. 2006. *The Rock Paintings of the Upper Brandberg, Part 6 (Vol. 1): Naib, Circus and Dom Gorges.* Köln: Heinrich Barth Institut.

Parkington, J. 1972. Seasonal mobility in the Late Stone Age. *African Studies* 31: 223–43.

Parkington, J. 1980. Time and place: Some observations on spatial and temporal patterning in the Later Stone Age sequence in southern Africa. *South African Archaeological Bulletin* 35: 75–83.

Parkington, J. 2001. Presidential address: Mobility, seasonality and southern African hunter-gatherers. *South Africa Archaeological Bulletin* 56: 1–7.

Parkington, J. 2006. The archaeology of Late Pleistocene encephalization in the Cape, southern Africa. In Soodyall, H. ed. *The prehistory* of Africa: Tracing the lineage of modern man. Johannesburg: Jonathan Ball, pp. 64–75.

Parkington, J. & Hall, M. 1987. Patterning in recent radiocarbon dates from southern Africa as a reflection of prehistoric settlement and interaction. *Journal of African History* 28: 1–25.

Parsons, I. 2015. Is Niche Construction Theory Relevant to the Proposed Adoption of Domesticates by Hunter-Gatherers in Southern Africa? *African Archaeological Review* 32 (1): 35–47.

Parsons, I. & Lombard, M. 2017. The power of women in dairying communities of eastern and southern Africa. *Azania* 52: 33–48.

Penn, N. 2005. *The Forgotten Frontier: Colonist and Khoisan on the Cape's northern frontier in the 18th century.* Athens: Ohio University Press.

Phillipson, D. 2005. *African archaeology.* 3rd edition. Cambridge: Cambridge University Press.

Phillipson, L. 1978. *The Stone Age Archaeology of the Upper Zambezi Valley.* British Institute in Eastern Africa, Memoir 7.

Pickett, S.T.A., Kolasa, J., Armesto, J. & Collins, S.L. 1989. The ecological concept of disturbance and its expression at various hierarchical levels. *Oikos* 54:129–36.

Pickford, M. & Senut, B. 1999. *Geology and Palaeobiology of the Namib Desert, Southwestern Africa.* Windhoek: Geological Survey of Namibia, Memoir 18.

Piperno, D. 2006. *Phytoliths: A comprehensive guide for archaeologists and palaeoecologists.* Lanham: Alta Mira.

Pleurdeau, D., Imalwa, E., Detroit, F., Lesur, J., Veldman, A., Bahain, J.-J. & Marais, E. 2012. Of sheep and men: Earliest direct evidence of caprine domestication in southern Africa at Leopard Cave (Erongo, Namibia). *PLoS ONE* 7 (7): e40340.

Popper, K. 1980. *The Logic of Scientific Discovery.* London: Hutchinson.

Price, T.D., Burton, J.H. & Bentley, R.A. 2002. The characterization of biologically available strontium isotope ratios for the study of prehistoric migration. *Archaeometry* 44 (1): 117–35.

Prins, F.E. 1990. Southern Bushmen descendants in the Transkei: Rock art and rain-making. *South African Journal of Ethnology* 13: 110–16.

Quinlan, A.R. 2000. The ventriloquist's dummy: A critical review of shamanism and rock art in far western North America. *Journal of California and Great Basin Anthropology* 22: 92–108.

Rashid, A. 1986. *Mapping zinc fertility of soils using indicator plants and soil analyses.* Unpublished PhD thesis, University of Hawaii, Mānoa, Honolulu.

Reid, A. 2004. Access to Cattle Resources in a Tswana Capital. In *African Historical Archaeologies.* London: Kluwer Academic/Plenum Publishers, pp. 301–324.

Reitz, D. 1994. *The Trilogy of Denys Reitz.* Johannesburg: Wolfe Publishing.

Remarks onboard His Majesty's Sloop Star on a cruise along the western coast of Africa. 1795–6. Original manuscript, Hydrographic Department, Ministry of Defence, Taunton.

Republic of Namibia. 2012. *Namib Sand Sea World Heritage Nomination. Nomination dossier for UNESCO for inscription into the World Heritage List.* Windhoek: Namibia National Committee for World Heritage.

Republic of Namibia. 2013. *National Policy on Community Based Natural Resource Management.* Windhoek: Ministry of Environment and Tourism.

Richter, J. 1984. Messum I: A Later Stone Age pattern of mobility in the Namib Desert. *Cimbebasia* (B) 4(1): 1–12.

Richter, J. 1991. *Studien zur Urgeschichte Namibias – Holozäne Stratigraphien im Umkreis des Brandberges.* Africa Praehistorica 3, Köln.

Richter, J. 2002. The Giraffe People: Namibia's Prehistoric Artists. In Lenssen-Erz, T. & Tegtmeier, U. eds *Tides of the Desert: Contributions to the archaeology and environmental history of Africa in honour of Rudolf Kuper.* Köln, Heinrich Barth Institut, pp. 523–34.

Richter, J. 2005. Archaeology along the Kavango River, Namibia. *Southern African Field Archaeology* 11/12: 78–104.

Ridsdale, B. 1883. *Scenes and Adventures in Great Namaqualand.* London.

Rifkin, R. 2011. Assessing the efficacy of red ochre as a prehistoric hide tanning ingredient. *Journal of African Archaeology* 9 (2): 131–58.

Rifkin, R., Dayet, L., Queffelec, A., Summers, B., Lategan, M. & d'Errico, F. 2015. Evaluating the photoprotective effects of ochre on human skin by in vivo SPF assessment: Implications for human evolution, adaptation and dispersal. *PLoS One* 10 (9): e0136090.

Rifkin, R., Henshilwood, C. & Haaland, M. 2015. Pleistocene figurative *Art Mobilier* from Apollo 11 Cave, Karas Region, Southern Namibia. *South African Archaeological Bulletin* 70: 113–23.

Robertshaw, P.T. 1990. ed. *A history of African Archaeology*. London: James Currey.

Robbins, L. 1986. Estimating height and weight from size of footprints. *Journal of Forensic Sciences* 31(1): 143–52.

Robbins, L., Murphy, M.L., Brook, G.A., Ivester, A.H., Campbell, A.C., Klein, R.G., Milo, R.G., Stewart, K.M., Downey, W.S. & Stevens, N.J. 2000. Archaeology, palaeoenvironment, and chronology of the Tsodilo Hills White Paintings Rock Shelter, north-west Kalahari Desert, Botswana. *Journal of Archaeological Science* 27: 1085–113.

Robbins, L., Campbell, A., Murphy, M., Brook, G., Srivastava, P. & Badenhorst, S. 2005. The advent of herding in southern Africa: Early AMS dates on domestic livestock from the Kalahari Desert. *Current Anthropology* 46: 671–7.

Roche, H., Brugal, J.-P., Delagnes, A., Feibel, C., Harmand, S., Kibunjia, M., Prat, S. & Texier, P.-J. 2003. Les sites archéologiques Plio-Pléistocènes de la Formation de Nachukui (Ouest Turkana, Kenya): Bilan préliminaire 1996–2000. *Comptes Rendus Palévol* 2(8): 663–73.

Rohrbach, P. 1907. *Deutsche Kolonialwirtschaft*. Schöneberg: Berlin.

Ross, R. 2012. Khoesan and immigrants: The emergence of colonial society in the Cape, 1500– 1800. In Hamilton, C., Mbenga, B.K. & Ross, R. eds *The Cambridge History of South Africa: From Early times to 1885*. Cambridge: Cambridge University Press, pp. 168–210.

Rossouw, L. 2010. *A forensic anthropological investigation of skeletal remains recovered from a 1000 year old archaeological site in north-western Namibia*. Unpublished MSc (Applied Anatomy) thesis, University of Cape Town, Cape Town.

Rudner, J. 1968. Strandloper pottery from South and South West Africa. *Annals of the South African Museum* 49 (2): 441–663.

Russell, T. 2020. The role of the Cape's unique climatic boundaries in sustaining specialised pastoralists in southern Africa during the

last 2000 years. *Azania: Archaeological Research in Africa* 55: 242–57.
Russell, T. & Lander, F. 2015. 'The bees are our sheep': The role of honey and fat in the transition to livestock keeping during the last two thousand years in southernmost Africa. *Azania* 50: 318–342.
Sadr, K. 1998. The First Herders at the Cape of Good Hope. *African Archaeological Review* 15: 101–32.
Sadr, K. 2008a. An ageless view of first millennium AD southern African ceramics. *Journal of African Archaeology* 6 (1): 103–29.
Sadr, K. 2008b. Invisible Herders? The Archaeology of Khoekhoe Pastoralists. *Southern African Humanities* 20 (1): 179–203.
Sadr, K. 2013. A short history of early herding in southern Africa. In Bollig, M., Schnegg, M. & Wotzka, H.P. eds *Pastoralism in Africa: Past, present and future.* New York and Oxford: Berghahn Books, pp. 171–97.
Sadr, K. & Fauvelle-Aymar, F-X. eds 2008. Khoekhoe and the origins of herding in southern Africa. *Southern African Humanities* 20 (1): 1–248.
Sadr, K. & Sampson, G. 2011. Through thick and thin: Early pottery in southern Africa. *Journal of African Archaeology* 4 (2): 235–52.
Sadr, K. & Smith, A.B. 1991. On ceramic variation in the south-western Cape, South Africa. *South African Archaeological Bulletin* 46: 107–14.
Sampson, G. 2001. An Acheulian settlement pattern in the Upper Karoo region of South Africa. In Milliken, S. & Cook, J. eds *A very remote period indeed: Papers on the Palaeolithic presented to Derek Roe.* Oxford: Oxbow, pp. 28–36.
Sandelowsky, B. 1977. Mirabib – an archaeological study in the Namib. *Madoqua* 10(4): 221–83.
Sandelowsky, B. 1979. Kapako and Vungu Vungu: Iron Age sites on the Kavango River. *South African Archaeological Society Goodwin Series* 3: 52–61.
Sandelowsky, B., Van Rooyen, J. & Vogel, J.C. 1979. Early evidence for herders in the Namib. *South African Archaeological Bulletin* 34: 50–51.
Sander, H. & Becker, T. 2002. Klimatologie des Kaokolandes. In Bollig, M., Brunotte, E. & Becker, T. eds *Interdisziplinäre Perspektiven*

zu Kultur- und Landschaftswandel im Ariden und Semiariden Nordwest Namibia. Köln: Geographisches Institut, pp. 57–68.

Sarkin, J. 2011. *Germany's Genocide of the Herero: Kaiser Wilhelm II, His Generals, His Settlers, His soldiers*. Cape Town: University of Cape Town Press.

Saunders, N. & Faulkner, N. 2010. Fire on the desert: Conflict archaeology and the Great Arab Revolt in Jordan, 1916–18. *Antiquity* 324: 514–27.

Scerri, E.M.L., Thomas, M.G., Manica, A., Gunz, P., Stock, J.T., Stringer, C., Grove, M., Groucutt, H.W., Timmermann, A., Rightmire, P., d'Errico, F., Tryon, C.A., Drake, N.A., Brooks, A.S., Dennell, R.W., Durbin, R., Henn, B.M., Lee-Thorp, J., deMenocal, P., Petraglia, M.D., Thompson, J.C., Scally, A. & Chikhi, L. 2018. Did our species evolve in Subdivided Populations across Africa, and Why Does it Matter? *Trends in Ecology and Evolution* 2399 (2018).

Scherz, E.R. 1970. *Felsbilder in Südwest-Afrika: Teil I*. Köln: Böhlau Verlag.

Schlebusch, C.M., Malmström, H., Günther, T., Sjödin, P., Coutinho, A., Edlund, H., Munters, A.R., Vicente, M., Steyn, M., Soodyall, H. & Lombard, M. 2017. Southern African ancient genomes estimate modern human divergence to 350,000 to 260,000 years ago. *Science* 358 (6363): 652–5.

Schlebusch, C., Prins, F., Lombard, M., Jakobsson, M. & Soodyall, H. 2016. The disappearing San of south-eastern Africa and their genetic affinities. *Human Genetics* 135: 1365–73.

Schlebusch, C.M. & Jakobsson, M. 2018. Tales of human migration, admixture, and selection in Africa. *Annual review of genomics and human genetics* 19: 405–28.

Schmidt, I., Ossendorf, G., Hensel, E., Bubenzer, O., Eichhorn, B., Gessert, L., Gwasira, G., Henselowsky, F., Imalwa, E., Kehl, M., Rethemeyer, J., Röpke, A., Sealy, J., Stengel, I. & Tusenius, M. 2016. New investigations at the Middle Stone Age site of Pockenbank Rockshelter, Namibia. *Antiquity* 90: 1–6.

Schmidt, S. 1975. Einige Bemerkungen zum 'Loch'-spiel (mankala) in SWA. *Journal of the South West Africa Scientific Society* 29: 67–77.

Schmidt, S. 1979. The rain bull of the South African Bushmen. *African Studies* 38: 201–24.

Schneider, G. 2004. *The roadside geology of Namibia*. Sammlung Geologischer Führer, Berlin: Gebr. Borntraeger.

Schneider, H.P. 2012. The history of veterinary medicine in Namibia. *Journal of the South African Veterinary Association* 83: 1.

Schweitzer, F. 1974. Archaeological evidence for sheep at the Cape. *South African Archaeological Bulletin* 29: 75–82.

Scott, L., Cooremans, B., de Wet, J.S. & Vogel, J.C. 1991. Holocene environmental changes in Namibia inferred from pollen analysis of swamp and lake deposits. *The Holocene* 1 (1): 8–13.

Sealy, J.C. 1989. *Reconstruction of Later Stone Age diets in the southwestern Cape, South Africa: Evaluation and application of five isotopic and trace element techniques*. Unpublished PhD thesis, University of Cape Town, Cape Town.

Sealy, J.C. & Pfeiffer, S. 2000. Diet, body size, and landscape use among Holocene people in the southern Cape, South Africa. *Current Anthropology* 41 (4): 642–54.

Sealy, J.C. & Van der Merwe, N.J. 1986. Isotope assessment and the seasonal mobility hypothesis in the southwestern Cape of South Africa. *Current Anthropology* 27: 135–50.

Sealy, J.C., van der Merwe, N.J., Sillen, S., Kruger, F.J. & Krueger, H.W. 1991. $^{87}Sr/^{86}Sr$ as a dietary indicator in modern and archaeological bone. *Journal of Archaeological Science* 18: 399–416.

Seely, M. 1978. Grassland productivity: The desert end of the curve. *South African Journal of Science* 74: 295–7.

Seely, M. & Louw, G. 1980. First approximation of the effects of rainfall on the ecology and energetics of a Namib Desert dune ecosystem. *Journal of Arid Environments* 3: 25–54.

Seymour, C. & Milton, S. 2003. *A collation and overview of research information on* Acacia erioloba *(camelthorn) and identification of relevant research gaps to inform protection of the species*. Contract No. 2003/089. Pretoria: Department of Water Affairs and Forestry.

Shackley, M.L. 1980. An Acheulean site with *Elephas recki* fauna from Namib IV, South West Africa/Namibia. *Nature* 284: 340–1.

Shackley, M.L. 1985. *Palaeolithic archaeology of the central Namib Desert: A preliminary survey of chronology, typology and site location*. Cimbebasia Memoir 6.

Shannon, L.V., Boyd, L.J., Brundrit, G.B. & Taunton-Clark, J. 1986. On the existence of an El Niño-type phenomenon in the Benguela System. *Journal of Marine Research* 44 (3): 495–520.

Shi, N., Dupont, L.M., Beug, H.-J. & Schneider, R. 2000. Correlation between vegetation in southwestern Africa and oceanic upwelling in the past 21 000 years. *Quaternary Research* 54: 72–80.

Shigwedha, V.A. 2018. The return of Herero and Nama bones from Germany: The victims' struggle for recognition and recurring genocide memories in Namibia. In Dreyfus, A.M. & Anstett, É. eds *Human remains in society: Curation and exhibition in the aftermath of genocide and mass violence.* Manchester: Manchester University Press, pp. 197–219.

Sievers, C. 1984. Test excavations at Rosh Pinah Shelter, southern Namibia. *Cimbebasia* (B) 4 (3): 29–40.

Silver, I.A. 1969. The aging of domestic animals. In Brothwell, D. & Higgs, E.S. eds *Science in Archaeology: A survey of progress and research.* London: Thames & Hudson.

Silvester, J. & Gewald, J.-B. 2003. *Words Cannot Be Found. German Colonial Rule in Namibia: An Annotated Reprint of the 1918 Blue Book.* Leiden: Brill.

Simon, D. 1983. The evolution of Windhoek. In Saunders, C. ed. *Perspectives on Namibia: Past and present.* University of Cape Town, Centre for African Studies Occasional Papers 4: 83–108.

Sinclair, P.J., Pikirayi, I., Pwiti, G. & Soper, R. 1993. Urban trajectories on the Zimbabwean plateau. In Shaw, T., Sinclair, P.J., Andah, B. and Okpoko, A. eds *The archaeology of Africa: Food, Metals and Towns.* London: Routledge, pp. 705–31.

Skotnes, P. 1996. The thin black line: Diversity and transformation in the Bleek and Lloyd Collection and the paintings of the southern San. In Deacon, J. & Dowson, T.A. eds *Voices from the Past: /Xam Bushmen and the Bleek and Lloyd Collection.* Johannesburg: Witwatersrand University Press, pp. 234–44.

Sletten, H.R., Railsback, L.B., Liang, F., Brook, G., Marais, E., Hardt, B.F., Cheng, H. & Edwards, L.R. 2013. A petrographic and geochemical record of climate change over the last 4600 years from a northern Namibia stalagmite, with evidence of abruptly wetter climate at the beginning of southern Africa's Iron Age. *Palaeogeography, Palaeoclimatology, Palaeoecology* 376: 149–62.

Smith, A.B. 1990. The origins and demise of the Khoikhoi: The debate. *South African Historical Journal* 23: 3–14.

Smith, A.B. 1999. On becoming herders: Khoikhoi and San ethnicity in southern Africa. *African Studies* 49: 50–73.

Smith, A.B. & Jacobson, L. 1995. Excavations at Geduld and the appearance of early domestic stock in Namibia. *South African Archaeological Bulletin* 50: 3–14.

Smith, B.W. & Blundell, G. 2004. Dangerous ground: A critique of landscape in rock art studies. In Chippendale, C. & Nash, G. eds *Figured Landscapes of Rock Art*. Cambridge: Cambridge University Press, pp. 239–62.

Smith, B.W. & Ouzman, S. 2004. Taking stock: Identifying Khoekhoen herder rock art in southern Africa. *Current Anthropology* 45: 499–526.

Smith, M. 2013. *The Archaeology of Australia's Deserts*. Cambridge: Cambridge University Press.

Smith, M. & Hesse, P. 2005. Capricorn's deserts. In Smith, M. & Hesse, P. eds *23° South: Archaeology and Environmental History of the Southern Deserts*. Canberra: National Museum of Australia, pp. 1–12.

Smith, W.D. 1980. Frederich Ratzel and the Origins of Lebensraum. *German Studies Review* 3: 51–68.

Smithers, R.H.N. 1986. *Land mammals of southern Africa: A field guide*. Johannesburg, Macmillan.

Solomon, A. 1998. Ethnography and method in southern African rock art research. In Chippendale, C. & Taçon, P. eds *The Archaeology of Rock Art*. Cambridge: Cambridge University Press, pp. 268–84.

Solomon, A. 2013. The death of trance: Recent perspectives on San ethnographies and rock art. *Antiquity* 87: 1208–13.

Soodyall, H. ed. 2006. *The Prehistory of Africa: Tracing the lineage of modern man*. Johannesburg: Jonathan Ball.

Soressi, M. & Dibble, H. eds 2003. *Multiple Approaches to the Study of Bifacial Technologies*. Museum of Archaeology and Anthropology: University of Pennsylvania.

Speich, R. 2010. *Sie bauten, doch sie bleiben nicht: Zur steinkreisarchitektur der einstigen Wanderhirten in der Namib*. Göttingen: Klaus Hess.

Spellman, G. 2000. The dynamic climatology of drylands. In Barker, G. & Gilbertson, D. eds *The archaeology of drylands: Living at the margins*. London: Routledge, pp. 19–44.

Steenkamp, C.J., Vogel, J.C., Fuls, A., van Rooyen, N. & van Rooyen, M.W. 2008. Age determination of *Acacia erioloba* trees in the Kalahari. *Journal of Arid Environments* 4: 302–13.

Stengel, H.W. 1964. The rivers of the Namib and their discharge into the Atlantic. Part 1 Kuiseb and Swakop. *Scientific Papers of the Namib Desert Research Station* 22.

Stephens, J., Killick, D., Wilmsen, E., Denbow, J. & Miller, D. 2020. Lead isotopes link copper artefacts from northwest Botswana to the Copperbelt of Katanga Province, Congo. *Journal of Archaeological Science* 117, article 105124.

Stewart, B.A., Zhao, Y., Mitchell, P.J., Dewar, G., Gleason, J.D. & Blum, J.D. 2020. Ostrich eggshell bead strontium isotopes reveal persistent macroscale social networking across late Quaternary southern Africa. *Proceedings of the National Academy of Sciences* 117: 6453–62.

Steyn, R. 2018. *Louis Botha: a Man Apart*. Johannesburg: Jonathan Ball.

Stone, D. 2001. White men with low moral standards? German anthropology and the Herero genocide. *Patterns of Prejudice* 35: 33–45.

Stoneking, M. & Krause, J. 2011. Learning about human population history from ancient and modern genomes. *Nature Reviews Genetics* 12: 603–14.

Straus, L.G. 1992. L'Abbé Henri Breuil: Archaeologist. *Bulletin of the History of Archaeology* 2 (1): 5–9.

Straus, L.G. n.d. The Abbé Henri Breuil: Pope of Paleolithic Prehistory, Snead-Wertheim Lecture in Anthropology and History, University of New Mexico, Albuquerque, New Mexico.

Stringer, C. 2006. The origins of modern humans 1984–2004. In Soodyall, H. ed. *The Prehistory of Africa: Tracing the lineage of modern man*. Johannesburg: Jonathan Ball, pp. 10–20.

Stuut, J.B.W. 2001. *Late Quaternary Southwestern African terrestrial-climate signals in the marine record of Walvis Ridge, SE Atlantic Ocean*. Unpublished PhD thesis, Utrecht University, Utrecht.

Sullivan, S. 1998. *People, plants and practice in drylands: Socio-political and ecological dimensions of resource-use by Damara farmers in north-west Namibia*. Unpublished PhD dissertation, University College London, London.

Sullivan, S. 1999. Folk and formal, local and national – Damara knowledge and community conservation in southern Kunene, Namibia. *Cimbebasia* 15: 1–28.

Sullivan, S. 2009. Green capitalism, and the cultural poverty of constructing nature as service-provider. *Radical Anthropology* 3: 18–27.

Sullivan, S. 2013. Banking nature? The spectacular financialisation of environmental conservation. *Antipode* 45: 198–217.

Suzman, J. 2017. *Affluence without abundance: The disappearing world of the Bushmen*. New York: Bloomsbury.

Swenson, G.W.P. 1972. *Pictorial History of the Rifle*. New York: Bonanza Books.

Sydow, W. 1967. *The pre-European pottery of South West Africa*. Cimbebasia Memoir 1.

Symon, D. 2005. Native tobaccos (Solanaceae: *Nicotiana* spp.) in Australia and their use by Aboriginal peoples. *The Beagle* 21: 1–10.

Taleb, N.N. 2007. *The Black Swan: The impact of the highly improbable*. New York: Random House.

Taussig, M. 1993. *Mimesis and Alterity: A particular history of the senses*. London: Routledge.

Thackeray, J.F. 1979. An analysis of faunal remains from archaeological sites in southern South West Africa (Namibia). *South African Archaeological Bulletin* 34: 18–33.

Thomas, D.S.G. & Shaw, P. 1991. *The Kalahari Environment*. Cambridge: Cambridge University Press.

Thomas, E. 1988. *The Harmless People*. Cape Town: David Phillip.

Tindall, B.A. 1959. *The Journal of Joseph Tindall Missionary in South West Africa 1839–55*. Cape Town: Van Riebeeck Society.

Tobin, B.F. 1999. *Picturing Imperial Power: Colonial subjects in eighteenth century British painting*. London: Duke University Press.

Toth, N. 1985. The Oldowan reassessed: A close look at early stone artefacts. *Journal of Archaeological Science* 12: 101–20.

Townshend, P. 1976. The SWA game of ǁhūs (das Lochspiel) in the wider context of African mankala. *Journal of the South West Africa Scientific Society* 31: 85–98.

Townshend, P. 1979. African Mankala in Anthropological Perspective. *Azania* 14: 109–38.

Trench, R. 1986. *Arabian Travellers.* London: Macmillan.

Trigger, B.G. 1989. *A history of archaeological thought.* Cambridge: Cambridge University Press.

Tunbridge, J.E. & Ashworth, G.J. 1996. *Dissonant Heritage: The Management of the Past as a Resource in Conflict.* London: John Wiley & Sons.

Tyson, P.D. 1986. *Climatic change and variability in southern Africa.* Oxford: Oxford University Press.

Tyson, P.D., Karlén, W., Holmgren, K. & Heiss, G.A. 2000. The Little Ice Age and medieval warming in South Africa. *South African Journal of Science* 96: 121–6.

Van den Eynden, V., Vernemmen, P. & Van Damme, P. 1992. *The Ethnobotany of the Topnaar.* Commission of the European Community, University of Ghent.

Van der Walt, J. & Lombard, M. 2018. Kite-like structures in the Nama Karoo of South Africa. *Antiquity* 92: 1–6.

Van der Waterin, F.M. & Dunai, T.J. 2001. Late Neogene passive margin denudation history – cosmogenic isotope measurements from the central Namib Desert. *Global and Planetary Change* 30: 271–307.

Van Oudtshoorn, F. 1999. *Guide to the Grasses of Southern Africa.* Pretoria: Briza.

Van Reenen, J.F. 1986. Tooth mutilating and extraction practices amongst the peoples of South West Africa (Namibia). In Singer, R. & Lundy J.K. eds *Variation, culture and evolution in African populations: Papers in honour of Dr Hertha de Villiers.* Johannesburg: Witwatersrand University Press, pp. 159–69.

Van Warmelo, N.J. 1951. *Notes on the Kaokoveld (South West Africa) and its People.* Pretoria: Department of Native Affairs, Ethnological Publications 26.

Vandermeer, J.H. & Goldberg, D.E. 2013. *Population ecology: First principles.* Princeton: Princeton University Press.

Vedder, H. 1966. *South West Africa in Early Times.* London: Frank Cass & Co.

Vercruijsse, E. 1984. *The penetration of capitalism: A west African case study.* London: Zed.

Vigne, R. 1991. James Archbell's 'Beschrijving der Walvischbaai en omliggende plaatsen aan de westkust van Afrika' in 1823: An English translation with introduction and notes. *Cimbebasia* 13: 29–36.

Vogel, J.C. 1989. Evidence of past climatic change in the Namib Desert. *Palaeogeography, Palaeoclimatology, Palaeoecology* 70: 355–66.

Vogel, J.C. 2003. The age of dead trees at Sossus and Tsondab Vleis, Namibia. *Cimbebasia* 18: 247–51.

Vogel, J.C. & Visser, E. 1981. Pretoria radiocarbon dates II. *Radiocarbon* 23 (1): 43–80.

Vogelsang, R. 1998. *Middle Stone Age Fundstellen in Südwest-Namibia.* Köln: Africa Praehistorica 11, Heinrich Barth Institut.

Vogelsang, R. & Eichhorn, B. 2011. *Under the mopane tree: Holocene settlement in northern Namibia.* Köln: Afrika Praehistorica 24.

Vogelsang, R., Eichhorn, B. & Richter, J. 2002. Holocene human occupation and vegetation history in northern Namibia. *Die Erde* 133: 113–32.

Vogelsang, R., Richter, J., Jacobs, Z., Eichhorn, B., Linseele, V. & Roberts, R.G. 2010. New excavations of Middle Stone Age deposits at Apollo 11 Rockshelter, Namibia: Stratigraphy, archaeology, chronology and past environments. *Journal of African Archaeology* 8 (2): 185–218.

Vogt, A. 2004. *National Monuments in Namibia: An inventory of proclaimed national monuments in the Republic of Namibia.* Windhoek: Macmillan.

Volman, T.P. 1984. Early prehistory of southern Africa. In Klein, R.G. ed. *Southern African Prehistory and Palaeoenvironments.* Rotterdam: Balkema, pp. 169–220.

Von Estorff, L. 1979. *Wanderungen und Kämpfe in Südwestafrika, Ostafrika und Südafrika: 1894–1910.* Windhoek: J. Meinert.

Wadley, L. 1979. Big Elephant Shelter and its role in the Holocene prehistory of central South West Africa. *Cimbebasia* (B) 3: 1–76.

Wadley, L. 1984. On the move: A look at prehistoric food scheduling in central Namibia. *Cimbebasia* (B) 4 (4): 41–50.

Wadley, L. 1987. *Later Stone Age hunters and gatherers of the southern Transvaal: Social and ecological interpretation* (Vol. 25). British Archaeological Reports.

Wadley, L. 1992. Reply to Barham: Aggregation and dispersal phase sites in the Later Stone Age. *The South African Archaeological Bulletin* 47: 52–5.

Wadley, L. 2005. Putting ochre to the test: Replication studies of adhesives that may have been used for hafting tools in the Middle Stone Age. *Journal of Human Evolution* 49: 587–601.

Wadley, L. 2014. Gender in the Prehistory of Sub-Saharan Africa. In Boler, D. ed. *A Companion to Gender Prehistory*. Oxford: Wiley, pp. 313–32.

Wadley, L. 2015. Those marvellous millennia: The Middle Stone Age of southern Africa. *Azania* 50 (2): 155–226.

Wadley, L. & Binneman, J. 1995. Arrowheads or penknives? A microwear analysis of mid-Holocene stone segments from Jubilee Shelter, Transvaal. *South African Journal of Science* 91: 153–5.

Wadley, L., Luong, S., Sievers, C. & Prinsloo, L. 2019. Underground transfer of carbonized organic residues to lithics during preliminary fire experiments: Implications for archaeology. *Heritage Science* 7: 59.

Walker, N.J. 1995. *Late Pleistocene and Holocene hunter-gatherers of the Matopos*. Studies in African Archaeology 10. Uppsala: Societas Archaeologica Upsaliensis.

Wallace, M. & Kinahan, J. 2011. *A history of Namibia: From the beginning to 1990*. London: Hurst & Co.

Walrath, D.E., Turner, P. & Bruzek, J. 2004. Reliability test of the visual assessment of cranial traits for sex determination. *American Journal of Physical Anthropology* 125: 132–7.

Ward, J.D. 1987. *The Cenozoic succession of the Kuiseb valley, Central Namib Desert*. Windhoek, Geological Survey of Namibia, Memoir 9.

Ward, J.D., Seely, M.K. & Lancaster, N. 1983. On the antiquity of the Namib. *South African Journal of Science* 79: 175–83.

Ward, J.D. & von Brunn, V. 1985. Sand dynamics along the lower Kuiseb. In Huntley, B.J. ed. *The Kuiseb Environment: The Development of a Monitoring Baseline*. Pretoria: South African National Scientific Programmes Report 106: 7–20.

Webley, L. 1992a. *The History and Archaeology of Pastoralist and Hunter-Gatherer Settlement in the North-western Cape*. Unpublished PhD dissertation, University of Cape Town, Cape Town.

Webley, L. 1992b. Early evidence for sheep from Spoeg River Cave, Namaqualand. *Southern African Field Archaeology* 1: 3–13.

Webley, L. 2007. Archaeological evidence for pastoralist land-use and settlement in Namaqualand over the last 2,000 years. *Journal of Arid Environments* 70: 629–40.

Weeks, S.J., Currie, B., Bakun, A. & Peard, K.R. 2004. Hydrogen sulphide eruptions in the Atlantic Ocean off southern Africa: Implications of a new view based on SeaWiFS satellite imagery. *Deep Sea Research Part I: Oceanographic Research Papers* 51 (2): 153–72.

Wendt, W.E. 1972. Preliminary report on an archaeological research programme in South West Africa. *Cimbebasia* (B) 2: 1–61.

Wendt, W.E. 1974. Art mobilier aus der Apollo 11-Grotte in Südwest-Afrika. *Acta Praehistorica et Archaeologica* 5/6 (5): 1–42.

Wendt, W.E. 1975. Die ältesten datieren Kunstwerke Afrikas. *Bild der Wissenschaft* 10: 44–50.

Wendt, W.E. 1976. 'Art mobilier' from the Apollo 11 Cave, South West Africa: Africa's oldest dated works of art. *South African Archaeological Bulletin* 31 (121/122): 5–11.

Wendt, W.E. 1988. The End of a Legend Part 1: The legend, the archaeological evidence, the dating. *South African Archaeological Bulletin* 43: 79–82.

Werner, W. 1980. *An exploratory investigation into the mode of production of the Herero in pre-colonial Namibia to ca. 1870.* Unpublished B. Soc. Sci. (Hons) thesis, University of Cape Town, Cape Town.

Wessels, M. 2010. *Bushman letters: Interpreting /Xam narrative.* Johannesburg: Witwatersrand University Press.

West, S., Jansen, J.H.F. & Stuut, J.-B. 2004. Surface water conditions in the Northern Benguela Region (SE Atlantic) during the last 450 ky reconstructed from assemblages of planktonic foraminifera. *Marine Micropaleontology* 51: 321–44.

Widlok, T. 2001. Relational Properties: Understanding Ownership in the Namib Desert and Beyond. *Zeitschrift für Ethnologie* 126: 237–68.

Wiessner, P. 1982. Risk, reciprocity and social influences on !Kung San economics. In: Leacock, E. & Lee, R. eds *Politics and history in band societies.* Cambridge: Cambridge University Press, pp. 61–84.

Wiessner, P. 2009. Parent–offspring conflict in marriage: Implications for social evolution and material culture among the Ju/'Hoansi

Bushmen. In Shennan, S. ed. *Pattern and Process in Cultural Evolution*. Berkeley: University of California Press, pp. 251–63.

Wilke, S. 2006. Romantic images of Africa: Paradigms of German Colonial Paintings. *German Studies Review* 29: 285–98.

Willcox, A.R. 1978. So-called 'infibulation' in African rock art: A group research project. *African Studies* 37: 203–26.

Williams, A.N. 2012. The use of summed radiocarbon probability distributions in archaeology: A review of methods. *Journal of Archaeological Science* 39: 578–89.

Williamson, B.S. 1997. Down the microscope and beyond: Microscopy and molecular studies of stone tool residues and bone samples from Rose Cottage Cave. *South African Journal of Science* 93: 458–64.

Wilmsen, E. 1989. *Land filled with flies: A political economy of the Kalahari*. Chicago: University of Chicago Press.

Wilson, M.L. & Lundy, J.K. 1994. Estimated living statures of dated Khoisan skeletons from the south-western coastal region of South Africa. *South African Archaeological Bulletin* 49: 2–8.

Wilson, T.B. & Witkowski, E.T.F. 1998. Water requirements for germination and early seedling establishment in four African savannah woody plant species. *Journal of Arid Environments* 38: 541–50.

Wings, O. 2004. *Identification, distribution, and function of gastroliths in dinosaurs and extant birds with emphasis on ostriches* (Struthio camelus). Unpublished PhD dissertation, Universitäts-und Landesbibliothek Bonn, Bonn.

Winterhalder, B. 2001. The behavioural ecology of hunter-gatherers. In Panter-Brick, C., Layton, R.H. & Rowley-Conwy, P. eds *Hunter-gatherers: An interdisciplinary perspective*. Cambridge: Cambridge University Press, pp.12–38.

Witelson, D.M. 2019. *A painted ridge: Rock art and performance in the Maclear District, Eastern Cape Province, South Africa*. Cambridge Monographs in African Archaeology 98.

Wobst, M.H. 1990. Afterword: Minitime and megaspace in the Palaeolithic at 18K and otherwise. In Gamble, C. & Soffer, O. eds *The world at 18,000 BP*. Vol 2 *Low latitudes*. London: Unwin Hyman, pp. 322–34.

Wolf, E.R. 1982. *Europe and the People without History*. Berkeley: University of California Press.

Wolfram, S. 2000. *Vorschprung durch Technik* or "Kosinna Syndrome"? In Härke, H. ed. *Archaeology, Ideology and Society: The German experience*. Gesellschaften und Statten im Epochenwandel 7: 180–201. Frankfurt am Main: Peter Lang.

Woodborne, S. 2004. *A water stress history of an* Acacia erioloba *(kameeldoring) tree from the Koichab*. Unpublished report. Pretoria: Environmentek.

Wrangham, R. 2017. Control of Fire in the Paleolithic: Evaluating the Cooking Hypothesis. *Current Anthropology* 58: 303–13.

Wright, D.K. 2017. Accuracy vs. Precision: Understanding potential errors from radiocarbon dating on African landscapes. *African Archaeological Review*. https://doi.org/10.1007/s10437-017-9257-z

Wurz, S. 2002. Variability in the Middle Stone Age lithic sequence, 115,000 to 60,000 years ago at Klasies River. *Journal of Archaeological Science* 29: 1001–15.

Wynn, T. 1993. Two developments in the mind of early *Homo*. *Journal of Anthropological Archaeology* 12: 299–322.

Yates, R., Golson, J. & Hall, M. 1985. Trance performance: The rock art of Boontjieskloof and Sevilla. *The South African Archaeological Bulletin* 40: 70–80.

Yates, R., Parkington, J. & Manhire, T. 1990. *Pictures from the past: A history of the interpretation of rock paintings and engravings of southern Africa*. Pietermaritzburg: Centaur Publications.

Zeder, M. & Lapham, H. 2010. Assessing the reliability of criteria used to identify postcranial bones in sheep, Ovis, and goats, Capra. *Journal of Archaeological Science* 37: 2887–905.

Zollmann, J. 2010. Slavery and the colonial state in German South West Africa 1880s to 1918. *Journal of Namibian Studies* 7: 85–118.

Zollmann, J. 2020. Becoming a good farmer – Becoming a good farm worker: On colonial education policies in Germany and German South-West Africa, circa 1890–1918. In Matasci, D., Jeronimo, M. & Dores, H. eds 2020. *Education and Development in Colonial and Postcolonial Africa*. Global Histories of Education, Cham: Palgrave Macmillan, pp. 109–142.

INDEX

|Khomas 207, 288, 302, 374, 394
|Ui-||aes xvi, 118, 119, 120, 122, 195, 197, 198, 199, 200, 201, 203, 206, 207, 208, 209, 210, 211, 212, 213, 289, 290, 371, 437
|Xam 190
||Khauxa!nas 353, 356, 357, 358, 359, 360, 361, 362, 363, 364, 365, 430, 437
ǂAonîn 322, 329, 331, 332, 345, 348, 442
ǂGorogos 378
ǂKhîsa-||gubus 253, 255, 322, 324, 325, 331, 332, 333, 334, 335, 337, 342, 344, 345, 347, 437
ǂNūkhoen xvi, 285, 288
!Khuiseb 44, 49, 50, 55, 88, 90, 179, 182, 183, 184, 207, 249, 253, 255, 302, 310, 312, 317, 319, 321, 322, 323, 325, 331, 332, 333, 335, 336, 337, 342, 343, 344, 345, 347, 348, 349, 370, 371, 372, 442
!Khuisenin 345, 434
!Nabas 353
!nara 99, 100, 104, 217, 218, 219, 220, 244, 249, 255, 256, 324, 325, 328, 330, 334, 336, 377, 378, 381, 435
!Nau-aib 293, 305
α phase 32, 84, 126, 129, 193, 213, 217, 349, 352, 365, 372
Ω phase 32, 83, 126, 129, 213, 311, 312, 349, 382, 386

Aawambo 285
Abbé Henri Breuil 9
Acheulean 48, 56, 57, 58, 60
adaptive cycle ix, 33, 34, 35, 37, 40, 83, 130, 213, 217, 218, 311, 317, 348, 382, 429, 430, 431, 433, 435, 436, 441
Afrikaner clan 352, 362, 382
aggregation 83, 109, 120, 121, 125, 129, 153, 155, 186, 255, 288, 290, 293, 294, 296, 299, 301, 309, 363, 364, 365
Aha Hills 46
ambush 54, 60, 63, 77, 223, 224, 225, 227, 228
Angola 5, 8, 43, 61, 92, 93, 106, 273, 337, 353, 434
Angola-Benguela Front 92

Angola Current 90, 92, 93, 106
Anichab 89, 90
Apollo 11 64, 73, 74, 75, 76, 79, 109, 437
Arechademab 228
Aruab 252
Arusis 252
Atlantic 1, 3, 5, 43, 44, 49, 55, 85, 100, 105, 106, 108, 128, 151, 290, 321
Austerlitz Rock Shelter 106
Australia 26
Australopithecus 15
Awa-gamteb 49
Awasib Gorrasis 181

Bantu 2, 23, 24, 218
Barby 252
Bay Road 353, 370, 380, 381, 383, 414, 415
Benguela Current 4, 44, 61, 89, 91, 92, 93
Benguela marine ecosystem 106
Benguela Southern Oscillation 85
Big Elephant Shelter 144, 146
Bogenfels Pan 89
Botswana 7
botulism 275, 278
bow and arrow 63, 144, 161
Brandberg 5, 132
British 132, 344, 376, 378, 383, 387, 410, 411, 412, 413, 416, 420, 421, 442
burials 94, 285, 298, 324, 333, 344, 359

camelthorn 107, 178, 179, 180, 181, 182, 183, 184, 185, 187, 188, 191, 222, 338
Cape 2, 61, 64, 90, 91, 115, 152, 164, 165, 166, 176, 220, 245, 262, 264, 307, 310, 315, 334, 351, 352, 353, 354, 356, 370, 376, 377, 382, 441
Cape Cross 90, 91, 307
Cape hunting dog 164, 165, 166
cattle 156, 200, 208, 259, 260, 262, 264, 265, 266, 267, 269, 270, 271, 272, 273, 274, 275, 276, 277, 278, 280, 281, 288, 298, 299, 310, 315,

322, 325, 330, 334, 337, 338, 340, 341, 342, 343, 351, 353, 356, 367, 369, 370, 376, 378, 380, 381, 383, 388, 393, 405, 438, 440
chert 66, 67, 68, 69, 72, 98, 100, 103
Chobe 5
Chowagas 6
Christian 380, 402, 403
Christianity 351, 397
Chuos Mountains 242
client herders 214, 279, 345, 347, 348
climate 1, 4, 20, 21, 42, 86, 96, 178, 179, 184, 281, 432, 448, 452
climatic instability 62, 78, 79, 84, 433
collapse or release Ω phase 317, 352
colonial ix, x, xvi, 2, 3, 14, 15, 24, 26, 37, 132, 210, 264, 265, 315, 349, 351, 353, 359, 361, 362, 363, 365, 366, 373, 380, 382, 383, 386, 387, 388, 389, 392, 394, 395, 396, 398, 399, 403, 406, 407, 410, 421, 422, 424, 425, 430, 432, 440, 448
communal hunting 206, 216, 217, 224, 226, 227, 229, 233, 432, 438
competition 79, 143, 254, 257, 264, 311, 346, 347, 434
concentration camps 403, 404, 407, 410
Congo Air Boundary xix, 4, 86
consumer and resource 83, 85, 177, 178, 219, 432
copper 7, 100, 208, 210, 252, 264, 279, 283, 302, 303, 311, 336, 344, 370, 371, 372, 373, 374, 375, 376, 434
cosmetic ochre 245, 252, 265, 306, 307
cowrie 139, 151, 336, 345
Cradle of Mankind 16
Cuvelai 5
Cypraea annulus 302, 336, 345

Dancing Kudu 201, 202, 203, 205, 210, 236, 241
dancing rattles 160, 161, 162, 167, 168, 169, 171
Dâures xvi, 5, 43, 105, 117, 128, 129, 130, 131, 132, 133, 134, 135, 136, 143, 151, 153, 154, 156, 158, 160, 161, 171, 173, 177, 185, 190, 191, 193, 200, 209, 210, 212, 213, 220, 249, 288, 291, 292, 298, 307, 346, 437
density dependent 28, 29, 83, 85, 291, 432
density independent 28, 83, 85, 224, 233, 291, 432
domestic livestock 14, 22, 30, 126, 215, 256, 257, 310
Drakensberg 115
dune sea 43, 100, 223, 224, 376

ecotone 42, 79, 84, 105, 107, 121, 177, 437
elephant 2, 52, 55, 102, 118, 183, 187, 188, 189, 191, 192, 193, 283, 338, 340
Elizabeth Bay 106, 108, 316, 317, 346
El Niño Southern Oscillation 4
engravings 63, 110, 118, 119, 124, 197, 200, 201, 206, 207, 210, 241
ESA xix, 18, 19
escarpment 3, 5, 7, 40, 44, 82, 83, 84, 101, 102, 104, 105, 106, 108, 109, 110, 111, 115, 121, 125, 177, 223, 233, 249, 255, 265, 281, 309, 344, 383
Etemba 14 Rock Shelter 106
Etosha palaeolake 52
Etosha Pan 7, 47
European 4, 15, 23, 24, 35, 220, 262, 304, 307, 309, 312, 314, 317, 318, 321, 324, 336, 343, 344, 348, 351, 352, 353, 359, 366, 367, 369, 371, 372, 373, 376, 377, 378, 382, 386, 424, 425, 440
exchange 23, 36, 100, 128, 130, 151, 152, 153, 172, 187, 214, 229, 252, 254, 256, 301, 302, 303, 304, 311, 315, 317, 336, 346, 354, 372, 430, 432
expansion r phase 218, 257, 263, 311, 317, 348, 352, 382, 386

Fackelträger Rock Shelter 106
Falls Rock Shelter 131, 132, 136, 137, 138, 139, 140, 141, 142, 143, 144, 145, 146, 148, 149, 150, 151, 152, 154, 155, 160, 161, 163, 166, 167, 168, 171, 187, 192, 194, 205, 210, 249, 252, 253, 301, 303, 304, 305, 306, 307, 437
fire 48, 52, 77, 113, 271, 274, 328, 419, 420
food storage 28, 246
footprints 119, 343, 344
forced labour 378, 398
fortification 360

Ganab 232
gastroliths 99, 100
genocide ix, 390, 396, 397, 403, 421, 437
German 3, 10, 24, 132, 365, 378, 380, 381, 383, 384, 386, 387, 388, 389, 390, 392, 393, 396, 397, 398, 399, 401, 405, 406, 407, 409, 410,

411, 412, 413, 414, 415, 418, 419, 420, 421, 422, 423, 425, 430, 434
giraffe 2, 112, 118, 206, 340
glass trade beads 317, 336, 337, 338, 373, 378
Goanikontes 414
Gorrasis-Awasib basin 96
Gorrasis Rock Shelter 97, 98, 100, 101, 104, 106, 107, 437
grass seed 205, 217, 218, 219, 230, 233, 235, 244, 249, 254, 256, 290, 305, 308, 328, 346
grazing 40, 133, 143, 263, 266, 267, 275, 277, 279, 281, 291, 293, 296, 298, 299, 301, 309, 311, 333, 334, 351, 356, 367, 386, 393, 397, 410, 416, 452
guano 94, 376, 377

Habis 253, 255
Hamakari 389
harvester ants 230, 231, 234
heirloom 30, 279
Hendrik Witbooi 382, 383
hiatus 95, 97, 100, 104, 182, 222
hierarchical 353, 362, 382
Holling loop 32, 429
Holocene 14, 18, 19, 20, 21, 22, 35, 36, 40, 41, 73, 74, 75, 76, 81, 82, 83, 84, 85, 86, 87, 88, 89, 91, 92, 93, 94, 95, 96, 97, 99, 101, 102, 104, 106, 107, 108, 109, 110, 120, 121, 125, 127, 128, 129, 130, 131, 133, 135, 138, 143, 151, 153, 169, 171, 176, 177, 178, 185, 188, 190, 197, 200, 208, 209, 210, 215, 216, 222, 224, 227, 229, 233, 243, 291, 311, 317, 321, 322, 346, 432, 436, 438
hominin 15, 39, 40, 61, 62, 77, 78, 443
Homo erectus 16, 48, 55, 62
Homo helmei 62
Homo sapiens 19
Hornkranz 383
Hottentot Bay. *See* Anichab
household 271, 279, 281, 288, 294, 353, 360, 361, 363, 365
Howiesonspoort Industry 73
Huab 288, 289, 290, 291, 298, 310
Hungorob Ravine 118, 132, 135ff, 190, 288, 291, 299, 335
hunter-gatherer ix, xvi, 9, 14, 15, 22, 23, 24, 35, 36, 37, 40, 59, 78, 79, 81, 83, 85, 96, 101, 109, 110, 112, 114, 120, 121, 124, 125, 127,

128, 129, 130, 131, 135, 151, 152, 153, 160, 172, 173, 174, 175, 176, 177, 178, 190, 193, 200, 207, 209, 210, 213, 214, 216, 217, 218, 223, 229, 244, 263, 272, 290, 304, 310, 311, 346, 372, 430, 433, 436, 437, 438, 442
hunting blinds 97, 223, 224, 225, 226, 227, 228, 438
Hurinin 345, 347, 378, 434
Husab 225, 227, 228, 414, 416, 417, 418, 419
hut circles 288, 293
hydrolysis 97, 138
hyrax 64, 77, 84, 88, 104, 131, 132, 133, 134, 143, 144, 146, 152, 154, 431

Ichabo Island 376
Indian Ocean 23
Indigenous xv, 9, 15, 35, 36, 222, 317, 343, 352, 365, 373, 382, 394, 410
initiation ix, 36, 114, 124, 129, 176, 200, 201, 202, 203, 205, 206, 207, 208, 209, 210, 213, 216, 217, 227, 229, 241, 243, 256, 272, 290, 311, 371, 403, 433
inselbergen 5, 130, 135, 153, 185, 220
Inter Tropical Convergence Zone 4
ivory 23, 187, 283, 362, 370, 376, 378

Jakalswater 414, 419, 420
Jonker Afrikaner 353, 363, 366, 370, 381, 382, 430
Jurassic era 197

Kalahari 7, 9, 23, 25, 42, 44, 46, 77, 128, 172, 173, 181, 210, 212, 213, 262, 276, 388, 389, 390
Kaoko 2
Karibib 414, 420
Kavango 5, 42, 46
Khaeros 338, 339, 342, 347
Khan River 181
Khoe 23, 249, 262, 351, 352, 353, 354, 356, 365, 382
Khoekhoegowab xvi, 132, 206, 208, 299, 302, 308
Khommabes Carbonate Member 49

Khorixa-ams 281, 282, 283, 284, 285, 286, 287, 288, 289, 291, 312, 346, 403, 437
klipspringer 77, 99, 103, 134, 143, 148
Koichab 290
K phase 32, 83, 126, 129, 130, 213, 257, 263, 311, 317, 346, 348, 382, 386
Kubub Rock Shelter 102, 103
kudu 112, 194, 197, 199, 201, 202, 205, 240, 241, 242, 432
Kunene x, 2, 5, 25, 43, 47, 49, 52, 53, 54, 55, 77, 264, 278, 279, 336
Kwando 5

Langer Heinrich 418, 419
Langewandt 91
Last Glacial Maximum xix, 20, 21, 35, 39, 40, 41, 43, 76, 77, 79, 84, 102, 188, 436
Last Interglacial 21, 42, 63, 78
Later Stone Age 16, 19, 21, 22
League of Nations 421
lebensraum 386, 393, 410, 424
Lesotho 43
LGM xix, 20, 21
lion 120
Little Ice Age 178, 179, 182, 186, 388, 436
livestock enclosures 276, 277, 288, 296, 298, 309, 396
Lothar von Trotha 389
Louis Botha 412
LSA xix, 22
Lüderitzbucht 404

Maack Shelter 161, 162
mankala 206, 207, 208, 210, 272, 311, 371
Marine Isotope Stages 20
Matchless Mine 370, 371, 372, 373, 375, 376
Medieval Warm Epoch 178, 179, 182, 185, 188, 222, 254, 281, 312, 436
Mediterranean 9
Messum 1 Rock Shelter 105
Middle Stone Age 19
mid-Holocene Optimum 84, 92, 101, 105

milk 190, 267, 274, 275, 276, 279, 284, 310, 334
Miocene 16
Mirabib 88, 90, 155, 183, 325
missionaries 351, 353, 366, 367, 377, 397, 404
Mode 1 19, 47, 48, 49, 51, 52, 54, 55, 59, 72, 77, 78
Mode 2 19, 48, 49, 52, 56, 57, 58, 59, 60, 62, 67, 68, 72, 77
Mode 3 19, 56, 62, 63, 64, 66, 68, 73, 77, 78
Mode 4 19, 64, 72, 73
Mode 5 19, 74, 84, 98, 103, 139, 142
Moth cocoons 167, 168
Moçâmedes 8
MSA xix, 19

Nama 3, 380, 410, 412, 421, 437
Nama Karoo 3
Namib Desert Archaeological Survey x, 25, 94
Namibia xiii, xvi, 2, 3, 5, 7, 8, 9, 10, 13, 24, 46, 47, 64, 76, 88, 104, 115, 148, 155, 182, 184, 207, 218, 220, 264, 265, 266, 267, 268, 276, 278, 280, 302, 328, 336, 351, 353, 359, 360, 367, 371, 382, 384, 386, 388, 393, 394, 397, 398, 399, 405, 417, 420, 421, 425, 426, 427, 429, 431, 442, 443
Namib IV 51, 52, 54, 59
Namib Sand Sea World Heritage Site 442
Nazi 422, 423
networks ix, 23, 29, 30, 36, 40, 100, 121, 128, 130, 131, 151, 152, 153, 155, 171, 172, 187, 214, 229, 252, 255, 301, 303, 304, 311, 344, 345, 430, 432
Nicotiana africana 220, 308, 433, 435
nomadic x, xiii, xvi, 29, 35, 36, 134, 158, 223, 264, 265, 314, 356

occultation 170, 172, 173, 175, 193, 194, 201, 205, 208, 210
Okahandja 367, 389
Okandombo 264, 266, 268, 274, 278, 279, 307
Okavango 7
Omaheke 389, 396
Omaruru 292
Omungunda Rock Shelter 106
Omuramba Eiseb 389, 390, 391, 392, 393

Orange x, 5, 7, 8, 25, 43, 44, 49, 54, 55, 106, 156, 185, 190, 245, 262, 263, 314, 318, 351, 352, 354, 356, 366, 382, 411
Orlam 348, 351, 352, 353, 356, 357, 359, 362, 365, 366, 373, 382, 386, 388, 434, 437
Orumbo 252
Oruwanje 77, 155
oryx 104, 118, 223, 225, 227, 228, 229, 274
ostrich 75, 94, 99, 100, 118, 119, 120, 143, 151, 152, 154, 155, 164, 167, 172, 187, 206, 229, 241, 304, 338
ostrich eggshell beads 75, 143, 151, 152, 154, 155, 172, 187, 304
Oswater gravels 49
Otavipithecus namibiensis 16
Otjiherero 266, 267, 272, 398
Otjikango Otjinene 366, 367, 368, 369, 370
Otjikoto 88, 90
Otjinene 389, 390, 391, 393, 396, 397, 410
Otjohorongo 191, 192, 193, 195, 196, 197, 198, 201, 210, 212, 213, 225, 290, 437
Otjomuise 357
Otjovasandu 268
Out of Africa 1 16
Out of Africa 2 20
Ovaherero xvi, 191, 284, 290, 332, 353, 357, 366, 367, 369, 380, 381, 382, 383, 386, 387, 388, 389, 390, 391, 393, 394, 395, 396, 397, 398, 401, 402, 403, 404, 408, 410, 412, 413, 421, 424, 426, 430, 434, 437
Ovahimba 264, 265, 266, 267, 268, 269, 270, 271, 272, 273, 274, 275, 276, 277, 279, 280, 281, 284, 288, 293, 294, 306, 308, 309, 311, 330, 332, 335, 336, 347, 395, 431
Ovatjimba 279, 347
Ovizorumbuku Rock Shelter 106
ox wagon 362, 370, 380, 381
Ozombu Zo Vindimba 389, 393

paintings 75, 76, 118, 124, 136, 160, 161, 171, 190, 193, 197, 198, 305
panarchy 35, 311, 317, 386, 430, 452
Panner Gorge 66–72
Parotomys brantsii 184

pastoralism 14, 23, 36, 129, 172, 173, 206, 208, 210, 214, 219, 252, 254, 259, 262, 263, 264, 275, 277, 279, 288, 291, 310, 311, 312, 332, 334, 348, 349, 386, 397, 432, 433, 436, 438, 440
pastoralists ix, x, 15, 24, 124, 134, 158, 174, 190, 191, 249, 262, 265, 270, 276, 277, 279, 281, 288, 290, 291, 292, 298, 308, 309, 312, 314, 317, 330, 331, 332, 333, 343, 344, 345, 348, 351, 352, 353, 357, 382
permeability analysis 363
Pforte 415
Phoenician 9
Pleistocene 1, 16, 18, 19, 20, 21, 35, 36, 39, 40, 41, 42, 43, 46, 47, 49, 50, 53, 54, 55, 56, 60, 61, 62, 63, 65, 67, 72, 73, 75, 77, 78, 79, 81, 89, 97, 102, 105, 109, 185, 432
Pliocene 21, 52, 53, 72
Pockenbank Rock Shelter 105
pollen 84, 86, 88, 90
Portuguese 314, 336, 417
pottery ix, 22, 30, 126, 137, 141, 143, 148, 150, 151, 153, 155, 158, 172, 173, 202, 205, 214, 218, 219, 220, 235, 241, 243, 244, 245, 246, 247, 248, 249, 252, 253, 254, 255, 256, 257, 259, 262, 263, 276, 288, 290, 305, 308, 310, 324, 325, 346, 377, 378, 437
pre-colonial xiii, xv, 3, 15, 23, 36, 37, 103, 128, 220, 290, 336, 359, 363, 364, 365, 373, 375, 396, 398, 432
primary resource sites 28, 29, 83, 109, 121, 185, 186, 200, 291, 432
projectile 84, 99, 103, 106

quartz xviii, 58, 73, 98, 100, 103, 139, 227, 423
Quaternary 47

radiocarbon xvii, xviii, xix, 25, 33, 89, 93, 94, 95, 96, 100, 101, 102, 103, 107, 108, 134, 138, 140, 148, 178, 179, 181, 182, 184, 185, 191, 246, 283, 301, 338, 339, 371, 372
railway 381, 398, 399, 401, 403, 405, 411, 414, 420
rainfall 4, 5, 7, 20, 23, 26, 27, 43, 64, 77, 79, 82, 84, 85, 86, 88, 89, 91, 92, 96, 100, 101, 106, 107, 109, 110, 130, 133, 135, 176, 178, 179, 180, 182, 183, 184, 185, 186, 187, 188, 193, 222, 228, 230, 231, 234, 254, 264, 267, 276, 279, 280, 281, 288, 290, 291, 292, 359, 441

rain-making 124, 176, 188, 190, 193, 209, 290, 437
Rainman Shelter 192, 193, 194, 195, 196, 201, 225
refugium 36, 79, 130, 131, 133, 141, 145, 146, 153, 160, 171, 173, 187, 213, 291, 301, 346, 431, 437
re-orientation α phase 354, 382
resilience ix, 27, 31, 32, 33, 37, 107, 127, 130, 208, 365, 434, 440, 441, 443
Reutersbrunn 91
Riet 381, 414, 418, 419
Rift Valley 15
Rinderpest (Paramyxovirus) epidemic 381, 388, 398
risk 29, 130, 277, 279, 313, 372, 434, 440
ritual 7, 22, 29, 77, 82, 83, 85, 109, 110, 112, 113, 114, 115, 117, 121, 124, 125, 128, 129, 131, 136, 143, 151, 158, 160, 161, 164, 165, 166, 167, 168, 169, 170, 171, 172, 173, 174, 175, 190, 192, 193, 194, 200, 201, 202, 205, 209, 210, 212, 213, 215, 216, 217, 222, 228, 244, 271, 290, 314, 430, 433
rock art ix, 9, 14, 22, 29, 42, 75, 76, 82, 85, 92, 107, 109, 110, 111, 112, 113, 114, 115, 118, 120, 121, 124, 125, 128, 129, 130, 131, 135, 136, 137, 158, 160, 161, 168, 169, 170, 171, 172, 173, 175, 188, 189, 190, 193, 194, 195, 197, 200, 201, 205, 207, 209, 210, 213, 216, 241, 262, 272, 290, 310, 314, 372, 432, 448
rock hare 134, 143
rock shelter 41, 42, 77, 81, 94, 98, 100, 101, 102, 110, 155, 167, 193, 223, 225, 233, 235, 246, 248, 305
Rosh Pinah Rock Shelter 104
r phase 32, 40, 83, 84

Samuel Maharero 380, 389
San xvi, 167, 190
Sandwich Harbour 377, 378, 379
sea level 20, 317
Sebra 56, 58, 59, 60
secondary resource sites 28, 29, 83, 178, 185, 186, 432
seed harvesting 219, 230, 231, 232, 233, 236, 241, 242, 243, 255
Serra Cafema 52, 53, 54
shamanic 14, 22, 36, 42, 76, 109, 112, 115, 124, 128, 129, 130, 131, 158, 161, 164, 168, 170, 173, 175, 188, 190, 193, 195, 201, 205, 209, 210, 213, 216, 290, 310, 372
shamanism 36, 114, 124, 126, 130, 209, 213, 436

Shark Island 404
sheep 132, 138, 148, 150, 151, 153, 155, 156, 158, 159, 172, 173, 191, 209, 252, 257, 259, 263, 277, 298, 304, 325, 330, 331, 332, 334, 335, 342, 369
shell middens 94, 106, 108, 317, 320, 346
slag 373, 374, 375, 376
slavery 398, 430
Snake Rock 131, 136, 137, 138, 139, 140, 143, 144, 148, 149, 150, 158, 159, 160, 170, 190, 210
Sossus Tsondab 181
South African 13, 15, 217, 329, 387, 411, 412, 415, 419, 421, 422, 426
South America 26
spears 62, 63, 77, 225, 329, 335
specular haematite 252, 253, 254
Speleothem 88
Sperrgebiet, or Forbidden Zone 426
Spitzkoppe 90, 260
St Helena 376
stock loans 277
stock post 309
stone tool 18, 19, 20, 22, 40, 41, 48, 62, 81, 84, 143
strontium 151, 152, 153, 155, 171, 172, 187, 249, 255, 256, 305, 347
Succulent Karoo 3, 84, 104
summer rainfall 4, 92, 106, 185
supernatural 83, 110, 112, 113, 120, 124, 125, 175, 244
Swakopmund 381, 398, 399, 403, 405, 406, 407, 408, 409, 410, 411, 412, 423, 431
Swakop River 367, 381, 414, 415, 418, 419

Tanzania 420
terra nullius 2, 424
Tertiary 7, 49
Theodor Leutwein 388, 394
Third Reich 421
Tinkas 228
trance 113, 114, 115, 116, 119, 120, 136, 137, 169, 210, 212
transhumant 296, 298, 299, 308, 397
Treaty of Versailles 421
Tsauchab River 88, 90
Tsaun 27

Tsisab Ravine 161, 162
Tsodilo Hills 46, 77
Tsondab sandstones 49

Ugab River 255, 298, 318, 319, 320, 321, 322, 346
Uhabis 8
UNESCO World Heritage List 426
Uniab River 263

Walvis Bay 312, 315, 322, 324, 329, 330, 333, 336, 339, 341, 342, 343, 344, 347, 348, 353, 370, 373, 377, 378, 381, 382, 383, 410, 430, 442
wells 266, 279, 288, 387, 388, 390, 391, 392, 393, 410, 438
Welwitsch Siding 399, 400, 401, 402, 403, 404, 410
Whaling 376
'White Lady' 161, 162, 169, 170, 446
wilderness 270, 425, 442
wild tobacco. *See Nicotiana africa*
Windhoek 3, 76, 88, 90, 356, 357, 366, 398, 424
winter rainfall 86, 104, 106, 185
World War I 387, 411, 420, 421
World War II 10, 423

Zambezi 5
Zambia 5, 371
Zimbabwe 115

Printed in the United States
by Baker & Taylor Publisher Services